ANSELM OF BEC *and* ROBERT OF MEULAN

ANSELM OF BEC *and* ROBERT OF MEULAN

The Innocence of the Dove and the Wisdom of the Serpent

SALLY N. VAUGHN

UNIVERSITY OF CALIFORNIA PRESS
BERKELEY   LOS ANGELES   LONDON

University of California Press
Berkeley and Los Angeles, California

University of California Press, Ltd.
London, England

Library of Congress Cataloging-in-Publication Data

Vaughn, Sally N.
  Anselm of Bec and Robert of Meulan.

  Includes index.
  1. Great Britain — History — Norman period, 1066 – 1154 —
Biography.   2. Anselm, Saint, Archbishop of Canterbury,
1033 – 1109.   3. Beaumont, Robert de, comte de Meulan,
ca. 1046 – 1118.   4. England — Biography.   I. Title.
DA198.9.V38   1987   942.02'092'2 [B]   86-891
ISBN 0-520-05674-4 (alk. paper)

Printed in the United States of America
1 2 3 4 5 6 7 8 9

To Loyd

Thus we may say of peace what we have said of
Eternal Life — that it is our highest good; . . .
Peace between a mortal man and his Maker consists in ordered obedience, guided by faith, under
God's eternal law; peace between man and man
consists in regulated fellowship. . . . Peace, in its
final sense, is the calm that comes of order. Order
is an arrangement of like and unlike things
whereby each of them is disposed in its proper
place.

St. Augustine
City of God 19.11, 13

Behold, I send you out as sheep among wolves;
be therefore as wise as serpents and as innocent
as doves.

Matthew 10:16

Contents

Illustrations

Maps

Figures

Preface

Two of the most archetypical images of the Middle Ages are that of the saint and that of the heroic knight-courtier — the sacred and the secular. This book examines two great men of the Anglo-Norman world, St. Anselm and Robert count of Meulan, who exemplified these images. I intend to demonstrate the complexity and sophistication of their behavior, their interconnectedness, and, in some respects, their similarities. Anselm served as prior and abbot of Bec in Normandy for some thirty years, then moved on to become the second Norman archbishop of Canterbury in England, where he was immediately plunged into disputes with the Norman kings that lasted almost until the end of his life. Robert of Meulan's life spans nearly this identical period of time. As a member of the pre-Conquest baronage in Normandy, he was one of the few who we can be certain fought in the Battle of Hastings itself. He went on to become an important figure at the courts of King William I and Duke Robert Curthose, and finally the chief adviser to Kings William Rufus and Henry I.

Anselm and Robert met early in their lives in Normandy and clashed for the first time at Bec in about 1088, where each sought to protect what he saw as "traditional" rights to the abbey's direction and control. This episode prefigured their roles in England, where they found themselves repeatedly opposed on the issues of the rights of *regnum* and *sacerdotium*. As Anselm formulated the official policy of the English church, so Robert formulated the official policy of the English state in those disputes, which formed a continuous struggle from the moment

Anselm became archbishop in 1093 until the settlement of the Investiture Contest in 1107. Throughout this struggle Robert of Meulan was Anselm's major adversary.

But although Anselm and Robert of Meulan are connected primarily through their lifelong adversarial relationship, in the end they reached the same concord and peace that each had sought separately for the Anglo-Norman realm. Though each had a different vision of "right order" for the Christian kingdom, these were reconciled in a compromise that achieved the goals of both men.

St. Anselm and Count Robert of Meulan have now occupied my mind, my time, my office, my library, and at times my kitchen table for more than a decade. I have endeavored here to compile for students, colleagues, and other readers the substance of their lives, intertwined as they were in the political arenas of Normandy, England, Rome, and the principalities of northern continental Europe. I welcome the opportunity that this book affords to develop and modify many ideas previously offered in preliminary articles and in my first book. More importantly, I have presented these ideas here as an integrated whole, as a complex of related events that will have a larger meaning in such an expanded format.

Both Anselm and Robert enjoyed great renown in their lifetimes, but while Anselm is now revered as a saintly theologian and an example of the heights that Christian love can reach, Robert has faded into the mists of our cultural memory for all but the most specialized scholars. I hope here to broaden our perspective of the forms that Anselm's sanctity could take, and to restore the luster to Robert of Meulan's remarkable achievements. The focus of the book is on political events, actions, and theories. While I have not dwelt on Anselm's theology, my portrayal of his personality reflects the profundity of his theological works and the sweetness of his soul. Nevertheless, it is his politics with which I have been primarily concerned here, although not to the exclusion of philosophical and monastic influences upon his thinking.

The journey through the artifacts of Anselm's and Robert's lives has been a long, time-consuming, and at times frustrating one; sometimes the sources would yield the pieces of the puzzle only with great reluctance. In particular, Anselm's theology first seemed quite divorced from his daily, practical activities, until "lightning struck" in the form of a chance comment by a student looking at Anselm's philosophy for the first time. I saw then the relationship that I had been leaning toward.

The mosaic I have created from the bits and pieces of evidence gives me great pleasure in its form and color; I now present it for your inspection.

No study of this magnitude could have been produced without the contributions of many friends and colleagues, and the loving cooperation of my family. Professor C. Warren Hollister has inspired, encouraged, and sometimes prodded me through three drafts, not counting the original doctoral dissertation with which this story began. Indeed the first seeds for this work were planted in my first seminar paper, on Robert of Meulan, for Professor Hollister. I am most fortunate to have benefited from his own expert articles, his suggestions, and perhaps especially, from the many conversations that provided opportunities to launch ideas (often torpedoed) and defend them. Similarly, many other colleagues have provided encouragement and suggestions, from my days in Santa Barbara to the present. The late Dr. Denis Bethell made me more sensitive to religious issues in many long conversations, while Dr. David Bates's work, and later conversations with him, sharpened my analysis and use of the sources. Professors Edward J. Kealey, Bernard Bachrach, Marcia Colish, Marc Meyer, and Robert Patterson provided at some times pertinent questions or observations, at others sorely needed encouragement to continue in the process of my investigations. Many years ago, Mrs. Kathy Drake patiently worked through the literature of the monks of Bec and some of Anselm's letters with me, so that I could go on to translate them all. More recently, Professor Loyd S. Swenson, Jr., aided me in the tedious task of proofreading several drafts; Professor R. H. C. Davis and Professor Christopher Holdsworth read through the manuscript and provided valuable comments and criticisms; and University of California Press editors Rose Vekony and Jonas Weisel rendered artful assistance in smoothing and refining the manuscript and overseeing its production. I am grateful to them all for their helpful suggestions.

The excellent translations of Marjorie Chibnall, R. W. Southern, Geoffrey Bosanquet, Charles Johnson, and Peter Fisher, of Orderic, Eadmer, Hugh the Chantor, and the *Vita Herluini,* respectively, have been most helpful, and in many cases (although not all) I have been guided by their wisdom. I owe many thanks to all these friends and colleagues, but absolve them of any responsibility for the final product; my errors are my own, whether in mechanics or in judgment.

I also owe particular thanks to many persons who have been of special help — indeed invaluable aid — in acquiring research materials:

the librarians at the University of California at Santa Barbara, the University of Houston, the University of London, the Institute for Historical Research in London, the British Library, Cambridge University, Lambeth Palace, the Bodleian Library, and the Bibliothèque Nationale.

My oldest sons, Jerry and David, spent their formative years sandwiched between my graduate studies and the research and writing of the original dissertation. My youngest son, John, likewise endured the patterning of his life around the completion of this manuscript. I hope they will consider the results worth their sacrifices.

Abbreviations

AEp.

Sancti Anselmi Cantuariensis archiepiscopi opera omnia (letters), ed. F. S. Schmitt (6 vols., Stuttgart-Bad Canstatt, 1963–68). Cited by epistle number.

AN

Annales de Normandie

ANS

Anglo-Norman Studies: Proceedings of the Battle Conference (6 vols., Woodbridge, Suffolk, 1979–84).

ASC

Anglo-Saxon Chronicle, many editions. Cited by year.

Augustine,
City of God

St. Augustine, *De Civitate Dei,* ed. Bernard Dombart and Alphonse Kalb (4th ed., reprinted Tournhout, 1955). Cited by book and chapter.

Barlow,
English Church

Frank Barlow, *The English Church, 1066–1154* (London, 1979).

Barlow, *Rufus*

Frank Barlow, *William Rufus* (Berkeley, 1983).

Bates,
Normandy

David Bates, *Normandy Before 1066* (London, 1982).

Bede   *Historiam Ecclesiasticam gentis Anglorum,*
                        ed. Charles Plummer (Oxford, 1896). Cited
                        by book and chapter.

BIHR   *Bulletin of the Institute of Historical Re-
                        search*

Brett,   Martin Brett, *The English Church Under
English Church*   Henry I* (Oxford, 1975).

Canterbury   *Canterbury Professions,* ed. Michael Richter
Professions   (Torquay, Devon, 1973).

CB   *Chronicon Beccensis,* in *PL* 150, cols. 639–
                        90. Cited by column number.

CDF   *Calendar of Documents Preserved in France,*
                        vol. 1, ed. J. H. Round (London, 1899). Cited
                        by document number.

Complete Peerage   *The Complete Peerage of England, Scotland,
                        and Ireland,* ed. G. E. C. (12 volumes, Lon-
                        don, 1919–59). Cited by volume and page.

David,   C. W. David, *Robert Curthose, Duke of Nor-
Robert Curthose*   mandy* (Cambridge, Mass., 1920).

DB   Domesday Book (2 vols., Record Commis-
                        sion, London 1783).

DLB   *De libertate Beccensis monasterii,* in *Annales
                        Ordinis Sancti Benedicti,* vol. 5, ed. J. Mabil-
                        lon (Paris, 1745), pp. 601–5.

Douglas, *WC*   David Douglas, *William the Conqueror* (Lon-
                        don, 1964).

DuBoulay   F. R. N. DuBoulay, *The Lordship of Canter-
                        bury* (New York, 1966).

EHD   *English Historical Documents,* vol. 2, ed.
                        D. C. Douglas and D. Greenway (2d ed., Lon-
                        don, 1981).

EHR   *English Historical Review*

Fauroux	Marie Fauroux, ed., *Recueil des actes des ducs de Normandie (911–1066)* (Mem. Soc. Ant. Norm. 36, Caen, 1961). Cited by document number.
Florence	Florence of Worcester, *Chronicon ex chronicis*, ed. B. Thorpe (2 vols., London, 1848–49). Cited by volume and page number.
Freeman, *Rufus*	E. A. Freeman, *The Reign of William Rufus* (2 vols., London, 1882).
Gibson, *Lanfranc*	Margaret Gibson, *Lanfranc of Bec* (Oxford, 1978).
GP	William of Malmesbury, *De gestis pontificum Anglorum*, ed. N. E. S. A. Hamilton (RS, London, 1870).
GR	William of Malmsbury, *De gestis regum Anglorum*, ed. W. Stubbs (2 vols., RS, London, 1887–89).
Gregory the Great, *Pastoral Care*	Gregory I, *Liber Regulae Pastoralis*, PL 77, pp. 13–128. Cited by book and chapter.
HA	Henry of Huntingdon, *Historia Anglorum*, ed. Thomas Arnold (RS, London, 1879).
Haskins, *Norman Institutions*	Charles Homer Haskins, *Norman Institutions* (Cambridge, Mass., 1918).
HCY	Hugh the Chantor, *History of the Church of York*, ed. Charles Johnson (London, 1961).
HN	Eadmer, *Historia novorum in Anglia*, ed. M. Rule (RS, London, 1884).
Jaffé-Wattenbach	*Regesta Pontificum Romanorum*, ed. P. Jaffé, 2d ed. revised W. Wattenbach, S. Lowenfeld, F. Kaltenbrunner, P. Ewald (Leipzig, 1881–88).
JEH	*Journal of Ecclesiastical History*
JMH	*Journal of Medieval History*

Knowles, *Heads*	*The Heads of Religious Houses in England and Wales, 940–1216*, eds. David Knowles, C. N. L. Brooke, and Vera Lonson (Cambridge, England, 1972).
Knowles, *Monastic Order*	David Knowles, *The Monastic Order in England* (2d ed., Cambridge, 1963).
LEp.	*The Letters of Lanfranc,* eds. Helen Clover and Margaret Gibson (Oxford, 1979). Cited by epistle number.
MacDonald, *Lanfranc*	A. J. MacDonald, *Lanfranc: A Study of His Life and Writing* (Oxford, 1944).
Mem. Soc. Ant. Norm.	Mémoires de la Société des Antiquaires de Normandie
MGH	*Monumenta Germaniae Historica*
OV	Orderic Vitalis, *The Ecclesiastical History of Orderic Vitalis*, ed. Marjorie Chibnall (6 vols., Oxford, 1969–80).
PL	*Patrologia cursus completus, series Latina,* ed. J.-P. Migne (221 volumes, Paris, 1844–64). Cited by volume and column, and occasionally by epistle number.
Porée, *Bec*	A. A. Porée, *Histoire de l'abbaye du Bec* (2 vols., Evreux, 1901).
Regesta	*Regesta Regum Anglo-Normannorum*, vol. 1, ed. H. W. C. Davis (Oxford, 1913); vol. 2, eds. C. Johnson and H. A. Cronne (Oxford, 1956). Cited by volume and document number.
RHS	Royal Historical Society
Robert of Torigni	Robert of Torigni, *Chronicle*, in *Chronicles in the Reigns of Stephen, Henry II, and Richard I*, ed. Richard Howlett (vol. 4, RS, London, 1889).
RS	Rolls Series

Sanders, *Baronies*	I. J. Sanders, *English Baronies: A Study of Their Origin and Descent, 1086 – 1327* (Oxford, 1960).
SB	*Spiciligium Beccensis* (vol. 1, Paris, 1959).
Southern, *Anselm*	R. W. Southern, *St. Anselm and His Biographer* (Cambridge, England, 1963).
TRHS	*Transactions of the Royal Historical Society*
VA	Eadmer, *Vita Anselmi* in *The Life of St. Anselm*, ed. R. W. Southern (London, 1972).
VB	*Vita Bosonis*, in *PL* 150, cols. 723 – 32. Cited by column number.
VCH	*Victoria History of the Counties of England*
VG	*Vita Gundulfi*, ed. Rodney Thompson (Toronto, 1977).
VH	*Vita Herluini*, in J. Armitage Robinson, *Gilbert Crispin, Abbot of Westminster* (Cambridge, England, 1911), pp. 87 – 110.
VL	*Vita Lanfranci*, in *PL* 150, cols. 29 – 58. Cited by column number.
VW	*Vita Willelmi*, in *PL* 150, cols. 713 – 24. Cited by column number.
WP	William of Poitiers, *Histoire de Guillaume le Conquerant*, ed. Raymonde Foreville (Paris, 1952).

One

Prologue:
St. Anselm, Robert of Meulan,
and the Historical Sources

In the heart of Normandy, in a wooded vale near a stream flowing into the River Risle, lies the abbey of Bec. Nearby, on the Risle itself, the ruins of an old Norman castle overlook the small town of Brionne. Around the year 1088, when St. Anselm had been abbot of Bec for some ten years, the new lord of Brionne Count Robert of Meulan approached the abbey with his men and suggested that Anselm and his monks place themselves under Robert's protection in return for generous gifts. Anselm held him at bay with soft words, meanwhile sending a delegation of monks to Robert Curthose duke of Normandy to obtain a pledge of protection against the implied threat of his powerful magnate. Robert of Meulan continued to tempt Anselm to relinquish the abbey's independence with soothing phrases and promises of rich donations of lands. Anselm pursued his appeal to the duke without the count's knowledge, until he had assured the abbey's freedom from Robert's domination. When Robert of Meulan at length attended the duke's court, he found to his surprise that Curthose had become convinced that Robert was trying to steal his abbey.[1] The duke was so incensed that he seized Brionne and, perhaps for this reason as well as others, threw Robert of Meulan into prison. Robert

1. *DLB*, 601–2.

languished there until his father managed to free him by promising Curthose he would control his son's behavior in the future.[2]

Such was the first encounter between two great contemporaries — St. Anselm (1033 – 1109), abbot of Bec and later archbishop of Canterbury, and Robert (1046 – 1118), count of Meulan in France, lord of Beaumont in Normandy, and later earl of Leicester. They were to meet often in the next twenty years, for both subsequently became great men at the courts of the Anglo-Norman kings. Their careers were not only parallel but intertwined: Anselm represented the pinnacle of the Anglo-Norman spiritual world, devoted to God's service and to his own responsibilities as abbot and, later, archbishop. Robert of Meulan was one of the most ambitious and successful of the secular magnates of the Anglo-Norman aristocracy and perhaps the most influential baron at the courts of Kings William Rufus (1087 – 1100) and Henry I (1100 – 1135). The controversy at Bec circa 1088 prefigures the great church-state disputes in the reigns of these two English kings. As at Bec, so also in the wider world of Norman England, Robert of Meulan and Anselm represented the two poles of dissension, *regnum* and *sacerdotium*. But the issues involved far more than a mere power struggle; both participants represented broader visions of a proper world order. In the twenty years during which their rivalry was played out, there emerged in the Anglo-Norman world a new conception of the English church, the English kingdom, and even political conduct. And in some measure the interaction between Anselm and Robert of Meulan shaped these new conceptions, hastening the transition from the simpler, more straightforward early medieval approach to political problems to the more sophisticated, more complex, and subtler methods of the twelfth century.

Although historians have considered St. Anselm and Robert of Meulan separately, their interaction has never been examined. Emile Houth's short article on Robert of Meulan portrays him as an interesting but rather pedestrian baron. Houth concentrates primarily on enumerating the Beaumont charters and considers Robert mostly in his French and Norman sphere. While acknowledging that Robert played an eminent role in England, Houth makes no effort to place

---

2. OV 4:204 – 6. Orderic contends that Robert was imprisoned because of a quarrel over the castles of Brionne and Ivry; but as we shall see in Chapter 4, passim, where the incident is fully treated, the controversy at Bec may have caused the imprisonment.

him in the context of English and Norman historical developments.[3] Otherwise, Robert of Meulan and his family, the Beaumonts, have been treated tangentially in numerous larger modern works, but no definitive study of the Beaumonts or Robert of Meulan has yet appeared, although at this time Dr. David Crouch has in press a study of Robert of Meulan's twin sons.

Books and articles pertaining to St. Anselm and his works, on the other hand, number in the hundreds.[4] Anselm has long been celebrated as one of the most original philosophers and foremost saints of the Middle Ages. Most authors, however, intrigued by Anselm's philosophy and piety, have ignored his political career or minimized its importance. Even A. A. Porée, in his great study of the abbey of Bec, passes quickly over the politics surrounding Anselm's administration of the abbey. Although he details most of the evidence for political activities at Bec, he concentrates his attention quite understandably on Bec's great spiritual achievements.[5]

Norman Cantor's study of the English Investiture Controversy does focus on St. Anselm's political career, but only as archbishop of Canterbury, not as prior or abbot of Bec. Cantor views Archbishop Anselm as a competent politician of strong Gregorian inclinations, who acted in the Investiture Contest as an agent of Pope Urban II. According to this perspective, Anselm became disillusioned when Paschal II succeeded Urban, and retreated somewhat from his earlier Gregorian position. For Cantor the Investiture Contest was the first of the great world revolutions, and he takes for granted that Anselm recognized its overriding significance and applied all his intelligence and energy to it.[6] In actuality, however, Anselm's vision was not so all-encompassing, and as a result of this misinterpretation, as well as other factors, Cantor's views have been superseded by those of Sir Richard Southern.

Southern sees Anselm as a theologian and spiritual adviser caught in an unfamiliar milieu in his role as archbishop of Canterbury, a role

3. Emile Houth, "Robert Prud'homme, comte de Meulan et de Leicester (8 Avril 1081–5 Juin 1118)," *Bulletin philologique et historique (jusqu'à 1610) du comité des travaux historiques et scientifiques*, vol. 1963, pt. 2 (1966), pp. 801–29.

4. See Jasper Hopkins, *A Companion to the Study of St. Anselm* (Minneapolis, 1972), for a complete bibliography to 1972.

5. Porée, *Bec.*

6. Norman Cantor, *Church, Kingship, and Lay Investiture in England, 1089–1107* (Princeton, 1958).

that he neither sought nor enjoyed, in a political environment that he never fully comprehended. As a monk, Anselm had withdrawn from the secular world to devote himself to a life of simplicity, prayer, and obedience. As archbishop, his strict obedience to the pope and his unwillingness to compromise betrayed an inability to function effectively in the arena of practical politics, where one must often settle for small gains when larger goals are unattainable. Principled and unbending, Anselm proved a disappointment to the Canterbury monks and an embarrassment to the royal court.[7]

This portrait of Anselm, sketched with consummate skill by one of the most sensitive and astute historians of the present generation, is now generally accepted.[8] But there are grounds — some of which are suggested by Southern himself — for doubting that Anselm was quite so politically naive. Southern gives full credit to Anselm for advancing the cause of the Canterbury primacy far beyond the point at which his predecessor Lanfranc had left it. Indeed, as Southern aptly observes, it was under Anselm that the primacy reached its height. And with respect to Henry I relinquishing the right to invest his prelates, Southern remarks that in the end a state of affairs had been created that might otherwise have taken generations to achieve.[9] In the English Investiture Controversy, as in the struggle for the Canterbury primacy, Anselm's triumphs were notable, and it seems reasonable to suppose that they were, at least to some degree, of his own making. With this possibility in mind, let us now briefly survey the sources on Anselm's career.

Southern's description of Anselm finds support in the Anglo-Norman narrative sources, most of which dwell on his sanctity and erudition. In the *Vita Anselmi*, the monk Eadmer of Canterbury, Anselm's constant companion during his career as archbishop and his major biographer, stresses Anselm's holiness and all but ignores his political activities.[10] William of Malmesbury calls Anselm the Light of England[11]: "No one was ever more tenacious of justice, no one at

7. Southern, *Anselm*, pp. 122–93.
8. Brett, *English Church*, p. 71; Barlow, *English Church*, pp. 69–70,. 287–92, 297–302; and Barlow, *Rufus*, pp. 300–309. Barlow portrays Anselm as a churchman "with considerable experience of the Norman feudal scene" who "understood worldly affairs perfectly well" (*English Church*, p. 287), but Anselm's "theoretical arguments, often rather divorced from the political scene, could be exasperating to grosser beings," and "he could be alarmingly innocent" (*Rufus*, p. 308).
9. Southern, *Anselm*, pp. 122–93.
10. *VA*, passim.
11. *GR* 2:376.

that time was such an anxious teacher; he was the father of his country, the *speculum* of the world."[12] Henry of Huntingdon calls Anselm "a holy and venerable man,"[13] "the philosopher of Christ."[14] To Orderic Vitalis, Anselm was "a profoundly learned scholar,"[15] the fame of whose learning "was spread all over the Latin world."[16] He "shone like a lantern in the temple of God."[17] Similarly, Anselm is remembered in the Bec sources — the *Lives* of abbots Herluin, William, and Boso, the *Vita Lanfranci,* and *De Libertate Beccensis* — as the ideal abbot.[18] In all these sources Anselm's sanctity, teaching, and philosophical brilliance overshadow his political actions.

One source on St. Anselm widely used by his biographers, medieval and modern, is his massive correspondence, of which nearly five hundred letters remain. Some criticisms of the holy philosopher do emerge in the correspondence. When Anselm became archbishop of Canterbury, the monks of Bec complained that he had deserted them and had broken his vows of obedience to them in order to assume the higher office. Some accused him of greed, cupidity, and ambition.[19] Later, when he was in exile in 1103–6, the monks of Canterbury complained that he was allowing the king to plunder the church of Canterbury and was failing to protect it by his presence, while the bishops of England wrote that his absence was allowing the churches of England to fall into ruin.[20] These last criticisms are consistent with Southern's portrait of the unbending, impractical prelate; Anselm himself responded that principle prevented him from acting as his detractors wished, that God's higher authority compelled him to take the office of archbishop and later to go into exile. Anselm, in fact, failed to convince all his detractors of the purity of his motives in accepting the archbishopric of Canterbury in 1093 or of his wisdom in choosing exile and leaving Canterbury leaderless in 1103. In subsequent chapters, however, I will argue that Anselm accepted the archbishopric for reasons altogether consistent with the highest contemporary standards of Christian conduct and that his exile of 1103–6 was an essential precondition for the English Investiture settlement. These conclusions emerge from a careful correlation of the correspondence with

12. *GR* 2:370.   13. *HA* 216 and 314.   14. *HA* 237.
15. OV 2:12.   16. OV 2:294–96.   17. OV 4:306.
18. See S. Vaughn, *The Abbey of Bec and the Anglo-Norman State* (Bury St. Edmunds, 1981), for translations.
19. AEp. 148, 150, 153, 155, 156, 159, 160, 163, 165, 166, and 176.
20. AEp. 310, 326, 327, 336, 363, 365, 386, and 391.

Eadmer's second book, the *Historia Novorum in Anglia*,[21] which tells the story of Anselm's political trials and tribulations.

The chief purpose of the *Historia Novorum* was to outline the events surrounding the struggle to secure the Canterbury primacy over all Britain and the resulting conflicts with the archbishops of York. The Investiture Contest is treated in some detail, but only as one aspect of what Eadmer views as his central theme — the effort to advance the rights and liberties of Canterbury. In the *Historia Novorum,* just as in the *Vita Anselmi,* Eadmer portrays Anselm as the holy philosopher that he was. Yet the *Historia Novorum* also discloses, sometimes rather obliquely, the skill with which Anselm handled political crises and thus reveals a greater depth to the man than does Eadmer's hagiographical effort. It also leaves no doubt that Anselm's major adversary in his disputes with William Rufus and Henry I, as in his earlier defense of the liberties of Bec, was Robert count of Meulan, chief adviser to both kings and the guiding intelligence behind their policies toward the church.

Robert of Meulan appears briefly but spectacularly in the chronicles of his age. Contemporary writers praise him as the architect of a rich and influential family estate; a statesman of the first order, with singular powers and abilities; and the chief adviser to Kings William Rufus and Henry I. Born into a Norman baronial family about 1046 – 48, around the time that Duke William the Bastard assured his rule in Normandy with his victory at Val-ès-Dunes, Robert had risen to great power by the time of his death in 1118, midway through the reign of King Henry I. Robert joined William II's court in 1092 – 93 and, unlike many of his baronial contemporaries in the turbulent arena of Anglo-Norman politics, remained firmly loyal to the monarchy. But like Anselm, Robert has been variously judged by modern historians. E. A. Freeman remarked of Robert, "On the whole his character stands fair."[22] Sir Richard Southern portrays him very differently as "a loyal and malevolent force in Henry's councils" who "used his commanding position to enrich himself without scruple."[23]

Contemporary assessments of Robert of Meulan emphasize his formidable political abilities. Uniform in their judgments of Robert's influence, power, and position, all acknowledge his talent as a states-

21. *HN.*
22. Freeman, *Rufus,* 1:186.
23. R. W. Southern, *Medieval Humanism and Other Studies* (Oxford, 1970), p. 212.

man, his loyalty to the king, and his power in government. The sources agree that Robert intelligently and competently aided Henry I in both formulating and realizing policy, while one writer attributes to Robert a certain influence on the social mores of the day as a style setter and popularizer of new customs — that is, eating and dressing with less ostentation and more moderation.[24] It is significant that these habits were much desired and encouraged by the church.

Robert's intelligence and wisdom reach almost legendary proportions in the accounts of William of Malmesbury and Henry of Huntingdon. He also receives ample recognition in the comments of Orderic Vitalis and Eadmer. Malmesbury describes Robert as shrewd and subtle, gradually rising to fame until he attained its pinnacle during the reign of Henry I as the "Oracle of God."[25] Henry of Huntingdon adds that Robert was "the wisest man in secular affairs of all men from here to Jerusalem, and counsellor of King Henry. He was famous for his knowledge, persuasive in his eloquence, astute in his shrewdness, wise in his foresight, ingeniously crafty, insurmountable in his prudence, profound in his counsel, great in his wisdom."[26] Both William of Malmesbury and Orderic Vitalis call Robert the chief adviser to William Rufus and Henry I,[27] while Eadmer describes him as "the person by whose advice the king in all matters of policy determined his course of action."[28]

Robert's political influence and power were directed toward both domestic and foreign affairs. "In law," Malmesbury writes, "he was the supporter of justice; in war, the insurer of victory, urging his lord to enforce the rigor of the statutes, following existing ones, proposing new ones."[29] Henry of Huntingdon attributes to Robert the power of promoting peace or provoking war between the kings of France and England,[30] suggesting that Robert played a role of either mediator or a power behind the throne. But William of Malmesbury calls him "the persuader of peace, the dissuader of strife, capable of very speedily bringing about whatever he desired from the powers of his eloquence,"[31] implying that Robert played the role of diplomat rather than warrior, possibly serving Henry as a liaison with the French court. Malmesbury's description suggests that Robert contributed significantly to one of the major goals of Henry's reign — that of keeping

24. *GR* 2:483.   25. *GR* 2:483.   26. *HA* 306.
27. *GR* 2:438; OV 5:248.   28. *HN* 170.
29. *GR* 2:483.   30. *HA* 306.   31. *GR* 2:483.

the peace. A man of superior intelligence and keen analytical abilities, Robert bent these talents toward the practical management of the king's affairs—exhibiting a quality that the chroniclers call "prudence," which they praise very highly as a vehicle for practical achievement and wise management. Despite the negative connotations to us of his reputed craftiness, shrewdness, and cunning, contemporary observers clearly admired these qualities, which connote intelligence, wit, cleverness, psychological insight, and effectiveness, as well as the deceit and dissembling that modern interpreters are prone to place on them. Robert was thus admired as an advocate of government by law rather than by force, based on the authority of the king, and, in foreign affairs, as one who worked toward settling international differences by diplomacy rather than by war. But above all, Robert was a committed royalist: "Free himself from treachery toward the king, he was the avenger of it in others."[32]

Not all accounts of Robert's career are so enthusiastic. Eadmer views Robert rather consistently as a villain and identifies him as the person responsible "for the evils perpetrated in England [upon the church] while Anselm [was] in exile, and for the delay in his return."[33] Orderic Vitalis states that on at least one occasion, during Rufus's reign, Robert was motivated by jealousy and self-interest rather than by a desire to serve the king: "This wily old man was the chief among the king's counselors and justices and therefore feared to admit an equal or superior into the royal council chamber."[34] Orderic follows this statement by attributing to Robert a speech advising Rufus of the dangers of admitting into his inner councils Elias of Maine, from whom Rufus had just seized the county and title of Maine.[35]

Robert's motives were also denigrated by Henry of Huntingdon in his letter to Walter, "De contemptu mundi"—a somber epistle from which few important Anglo-Normans emerge unscathed. Robert is here accused of obtaining some of his extensive lands by force or fraud. Henry cites Robert's refusal to restore these lands to their rightful owners at the request of the priests and archbishop who attended him on his deathbed as evidence of his disturbed mind in the last years of his life. Robert's degeneration from "man's highest wisdom . . . not only to sheer folly but to blind insanity" is said to have resulted from the loss of his young wife, carried off by an unnamed earl.

32. *GR* 2:483.   33. *HN* 171.
34. OV 5:248.   35. OV 5:248.

Robert replied to the ecclesiastics that he had acquired the lands for his sons and intended them to have their inheritance.[36] Robert thus fell from the heights of earthly power and achievement into a grievous sin jeopardizing his immortal soul.

The biases of Robert's detractors may explain their negative judgments. Henry of Huntingdon wrote his "De contemptu mundi" to illustrate the vanity of earthly achievements by recounting the falls in fortune of great men. In making his point, he may occasionally have overrated their greatness and exaggerated their falls. Robert's greatness, however, is substantiated by others. His downfall is his death from grief at the age of seventy-two; his forceful refusal to renounce his acquisitions, the accumulations of a lifetime, was perhaps derangement only in the eyes of a cleric writing on earthly vanities. Eadmer's contention that Robert was responsible for evils in England reflects the writer's own position as Archbishop Anselm's associate in the church-state disputes under Kings William Rufus and Henry I. And Orderic's comment on Robert's advice to exclude Elias of Maine from the royal circle suggests a blend of self-interest and good counsel: Robert's practical desire to protect his own position at court and his shrewd suspicion that the king's interests would not be served by the counsels of a dispossessed former enemy. Orderic's reconstruction of the event implies a certain ambiguity toward Robert, seen on the one hand as an opponent of Rufus's chivalrous instincts and on the other as a wise political adviser. The tone of the passage is doubtless influenced, too, by Orderic's fondness for Count Elias.

During the reign of Henry I, Robert of Meulan's power reached its zenith. His influence was universally acknowledged, his wisdom legendary, and his loyalty unwavering. Such was the man with whom Anselm had to contend. They met first at Bec in 1087–93. They were adversaries again between 1093 and 1100 when Anselm was archbishop of Canterbury under William Rufus and Robert of Meulan was the king's chief adviser. Finally they confronted one another once more between 1100 and 1107, under Henry I, when the Investiture Contest pitted Henry's shrewd political counselor against the saintly archbishop. In this latter case Anselm pressed the reform Gregorian principles on Henry I, and Robert contrived the royal resistance to them.

36. *HA* 306–7.

Robert of Meulan thus constituted the link between the ecclesiastical policies of two successive kings of very different character and personality. In his conflicts with William Rufus, as in those with Henry I, Anselm had to deal with the astute intelligence of Count Robert — an intelligence that guided the actions of both monarchs. As compared to Anselm, whose life was chronicled by his two contemporary biographies and voluminous correspondence, Robert of Meulan must necessarily play a far less vivid role in this book. But although Robert had neither a collection of letters nor a biographer to bring him out of the shadows, the contemporary evidence makes it clear beyond all doubt that his prominence in Anglo-Norman politics was fully equal to Anselm's. This dual biography will therefore deal with two men of radically different historical visibility but parallel political importance, whose lives were tightly intertwined. In 1097, when Anselm's conflict with Rufus reached its climax and propelled the archbishop into exile, the king and Count Robert spoke with one voice. When Paschal II, at Anselm's instigation, excommunicated Henry I's advisers in 1105, only Count Robert was singled out by name. And in the closing days of Anselm's life, when he was struggling desperately for royal support against the Church of York, he appealed by letter to Robert of Meulan.

That Anselm more than held his own against this formidable figure, backed now by the strength of the Anglo-Norman monarchy, suggests that the archbishop himself possessed a good measure of practical and political wisdom. And this conclusion can be corroborated from a careful reading of the sources. In the hagiographical *Vita Anselmi*, Eadmer praises Anselm as being such a shrewd judge of character that he could easily reveal to people the secrets of their hearts.[37] Anselm used this psychological insight in the training of his students, flattering them and weaning their spirits from wantonness with what Eadmer calls "a certain holy guile."[38] This *sancta calliditas* — holy guile or cunning — Anselm recommended to an abbot under him in training young boys through kindness rather than physical violence,[39] and indeed he used it himself when he became prior of Bec. Some of the monks, resentful of Anselm's advancement, rebelled and formed factions against him. But, in Eadmer's words, he "repaid their slanders

37. *VA* 13.
38. *VA* 16.
39. *VA* 37–39.

with the offices of brotherly love, preferring to overcome evil with good." Eadmer says that in this way the monks were turned from their evil path "by Anselm's guile" — *quo dolo Anselmi.*[40]

Thus Anselm used psychological insight to analyze and overcome his opponents and was well aware of the value of kindness, friendliness, loving overtures, and his own good example in influencing their behavior and leading them to his point of view. "To overcome evil with good" is, of course, to follow the Christian ethic, and it is not to be imagined that Anselm's sanctity was a facade. But in describing such behavior as "holy guile," Eadmer is making clear that Anselm was no simple saint. He knew how, by a conscious application of his love and good cheer, he could influence the opinions of others and direct the outcome of events.

Sir Richard Southern shows Anselm seized from the quiet life of philosopher and teacher at Bec and plunged into a political maelstrom at Canterbury for which he was prepared neither by experience nor by inclination.[41] But as abbot of a wealthy and influential Norman monastery, Anselm had regularly dealt with an abundance of secular matters. The abbey held numerous lands, the claims to which sometimes had to be defended in court. These lands had to be secured by written documents, which were gaining more and more in importance in the Anglo-Norman legal system. There were rents and provisions to be collected for the sustenance of the monks, and there were taxes and tolls to be paid. A politically adroit abbot could gain exemptions from certain of these obligations. In short, the financial and legal complexities of a great monastic institution demanded an abbot of administrative skill and practical intelligence.

Eadmer makes clear that Anselm possessed these qualities in full measure, that he functioned with remarkable effectiveness in the world of high politics at Bec. No one could hope to defraud Bec while Anselm was there. While Anselm's adversaries

were diligently investigating together by what cleverness and cunning they could fortify their own case so that it would be upheld, and fraudulently lie in ambush for his case . . . he would discourse on the gospels or sometimes go to sleep. And when sometimes it happened that frauds had been prepared by subtle machinations, upon hearing them he would immediately detect and

---

40. *VA* 15–16.
41. Southern, *Anselm,* p. 122. Southern does not discuss Anselm's administrative activities as prior and abbot of Bec.

disentangle them, not like a man who had just been sleeping, but like one who had been penetratingly vigilant and in touch with the matters at hand.[42]

Eadmer thus characterizes Anselm as a clever protector, skilled in the courts, lulling his opponents into overconfidence by seeming to doze.

These incidents embedded in the *Vita Anselmi* make it apparent that Anselm had another side to his character than that of the other-worldly saint, the characterization uppermost in Eadmer's mind as he wrote the biography. Eadmer was quite aware that to ignore Anselm's political talents altogether would have been to portray him as an ineffective prelate — and this Eadmer had no wish to do. Anselm's biographer once again stresses his skill at court in the Council of Rockingham in 1095. The bishop of Durham reported to the king that he and his fellow bishops could find no answer to invalidate Anselm's reasoning, "especially when all his reasoning rests upon the will of God." Thus having defeated his adversaries at legal argument, he must be crushed by force. When the barons tried their luck, they found that Anselm "just goes to sleep and then, when these arguments of ours [which they had spent all day preparing] are brought out in his presence, straightaway with one breath of his lips he destroys them as if they were cobwebs."[43]

Anselm himself was aware of the effectiveness of "holy guile." In 1093 he outlined for his successor at Bec a blueprint for action along the lines suggested by Eadmer's passages:

Remember indeed for what reason I was always careful to acquire friends for the church of Bec, and by this example you should hasten to acquire faithful friends from every side, striving after the good work of hospitality, extending kindness to all, and when this is not feasible, reaching out to please with affable words. Nor believe yourself ever to have enough friends, but gather all to you in friendship, whether rich or poor; so that this can both bring profit for the utility of your church and increase the safety of those you love.[44]

Anselm thus makes it clear that he was consciously endeavoring to acquire friends for Bec. He explains both his methods and his motives. Although by nature a warm, loving man, he also understood that friends could be useful to his abbey as benefactors and guardians. Fully conscious of how his actions and words could influence the outcome of events, he admonished the new abbot to follow his good example. His advice is a characteristic blend of sanctity and practical

42. *VA* 45–46.   43. *HN* 63–64.   44. AEp. 165.

wisdom: kindness   ~~~ at once natural to Anselm,
pleasing to God, a
    Similarly, in a   )f
Beauvais, a forn   1e
practical value c   m
the charge that   :u-
pidity and avar   nce
and his true in   iry,
he explains, th   iple
for his people   l by
anyone. 45

    Anselm wa   t call
psychology a   : was
aware of hov   affect
their reactiol   ealing
with people   it in a
letter he wi   shown
only agains   vith the
one offend   the offended on   ke at."46
One migh   ek" in a
new way.   and presumably   : he gave
to Prior I

And it is   of kindness
as in the   ife . . . lest
the imm   l growth by
the consolation __   d by austere
hardness. Therefore I beg of your ____   m in govern-
ment becomes you, and it is needful for the aforesaid brother, that overlooking all his past perversity, you would nourish the infancy of his good intentions with the milk of perceptible kindness, lest perchance (which I expect not) he might, not from weakness but from malice, fall back into his former wickedness.47

Anselm seems to have been quite aware that he possessed certain practical gifts. Reflecting on his decision to abandon Bec for Canterbury, he states: "I presumed I would defend myself through my own fortitude and cleverness; but God was stronger and more clever, and

45. AEp. 160.   46. AEp. 9.   47. AEp. 67.

therefore my presumption was nothing."[48] Thus he regarded himself
as possessing *ingenium,* which was overcome only by God's far greater
ingenium. Passages such as this suggest that Anselm normally felt
himself in control of events around him and confident in his dealings
with others. He was not the sort to be blown about by forces beyond
his control, except perhaps by the will of God, which seized him, as he
thought, for the archbishopric. Once he was convinced that God's will
had placed him there, he maneuvered expertly, through correspondence and negotiation, to secure his position and enhance the power
of his episcopal office.

These thoughts and actions were not without precedent in the
medieval world. As is well known, Anselm derived much of his
theology from St. Augustine,[49] and it is therefore not surprising that
Augustine, too, was deeply interested in the psychology of human
behavior. In his *Confessions* Augustine closely examines how his own
life was shaped and molded by his experiences, attributing them to
God's direction in his life — a divine discipline.[50] He also developed a
theory of behavioral psychology, which has been seen as closely akin
to that of the modern B. F. Skinner — a theory of environmental determinism from the habits people develop.[51] Skinner, of course, would
call them conditioned responses. As Eadmer describes Anselm's training of his students, he outlines how the abbot had modified Augustine's thinking. Where Augustine recommends harsh discipline [such
as God gave him as a child], Anselm substitutes loving conditioning. Anselm scolded "a certain abbot" for beating his small charges:
" 'You never give over beating them? And what are they like when
they grow up?' 'Stupid brutes,' he said." Anselm responded by comparing the rearing of young people to the art of a goldsmith, who
molds his leaf into a beautiful shape by pressing and tapping it gently,
and even more gently raising it with careful pressure and giving it
shape. " 'So, if you want your boys to be adorned with good habits,
you too, besides the pressure of blows, must apply the encouragement
and help of fatherly sympathy and gentleness.' "[52]

48. AEp. 156, lines 132–34: "Praesumebam de fortitudine et ingenio meo ad me
defendendum; sed fortior et ingeniosior me deus fuit, et ideo praesumptio mea nihil fuit."
49. Hopkins, *Study of St. Anselm,* pp. 16–17.
50. St. Augustine, *Confessions, PL* 32, cols. 659–868.
51. St. Augustine, *City of God,* 5.2. See also Peter Brown, *Augustine of Hippo*
(Berkeley and Los Angeles, 1967).
52. VA 37–39.

wisdom: kindness and generosity were at once natural to Anselm, pleasing to God, and profitable to Bec.

Similarly, in a more or less contemporary letter to Bishop Fulk of Beauvais, a former student of Bec, Anselm is acutely aware of the practical value of a good public reputation. Defending himself from the charge that he accepted the Canterbury archbishopric out of cupidity and avarice, he stresses that he must publicize his innocence and his true intention of following the will of God. It is necessary, he explains, that the head of the English church set a good example for his people, and therefore he should not be thought wicked by anyone.[45]

Anselm was quite concerned with the uses of what we might call psychology and its effects on those he sought to influence. He was aware of how his basic attitude and approach to people could affect their reactions to him. He apparently conceived this method of dealing with people quite early in his life, for he expresses this thought in a letter he wrote when still a young man: "But since anger is shown only against an adversary, if the guilty one associates himself with the one offended, by agreement with his opinion, the impulse of the offended one must subside, since he can find no enemy to strike at."[46] One might almost say that he would "turn the other cheek" in a new way. His own methods of dealing with his subordinates, and presumably with his enemies also, are reflected in the advice he gave to Prior Henry of Canterbury, his former student at Bec:

And it is known to your prudence that there is never so great need of kindness as in the early, incomplete conversion from a bad to a good life . . . lest the immature virtues that may be nourished and brought to full growth by the consolation of kindness should be checked or quite crushed by austere hardness. Therefore I beg of your beloved holiness, since wisdom in government becomes you, and it is needful for the aforesaid brother, that overlooking all his past perversity, you would nourish the infancy of his good intentions with the milk of perceptible kindness, lest perchance (which I expect not) he might, not from weakness but from malice, fall back into his former wickedness.[47]

Anselm seems to have been quite aware that he possessed certain practical gifts. Reflecting on his decision to abandon Bec for Canterbury, he states: "I presumed I would defend myself through my own fortitude and cleverness; but God was stronger and more clever, and

45. AEp. 160.   46. AEp. 9.   47. AEp. 67.

therefore my presumption was nothing."[48] Thus he regarded himself as possessing *ingenium,* which was overcome only by God's far greater *ingenium.* Passages such as this suggest that Anselm normally felt himself in control of events around him and confident in his dealings with others. He was not the sort to be blown about by forces beyond his control, except perhaps by the will of God, which seized him, as he thought, for the archbishopric. Once he was convinced that God's will had placed him there, he maneuvered expertly, through correspondence and negotiation, to secure his position and enhance the power of his episcopal office.

These thoughts and actions were not without precedent in the medieval world. As is well known, Anselm derived much of his theology from St. Augustine,[49] and it is therefore not surprising that Augustine, too, was deeply interested in the psychology of human behavior. In his *Confessions* Augustine closely examines how his own life was shaped and molded by his experiences, attributing them to God's direction in his life — a divine discipline.[50] He also developed a theory of behavioral psychology, which has been seen as closely akin to that of the modern B. F. Skinner — a theory of environmental determinism from the habits people develop.[51] Skinner, of course, would call them conditioned responses. As Eadmer describes Anselm's training of his students, he outlines how the abbot had modified Augustine's thinking. Where Augustine recommends harsh discipline [such as God gave him as a child], Anselm substitutes loving conditioning. Anselm scolded "a certain abbot" for beating his small charges: " 'You never give over beating them? And what are they like when they grow up?' 'Stupid brutes,' he said." Anselm responded by comparing the rearing of young people to the art of a goldsmith, who molds his leaf into a beautiful shape by pressing and tapping it gently, and even more gently raising it with careful pressure and giving it shape. " 'So, if you want your boys to be adorned with good habits, you too, besides the pressure of blows, must apply the encouragement and help of fatherly sympathy and gentleness.' "[52]

---

48. AEp. 156, lines 132–34: "Praesumebam de fortitudine et ingenio meo ad me defendendum; sed fortior et ingeniosior me deus fuit, et ideo praesumptio mea nihil fuit."
49. Hopkins, *Study of St. Anselm,* pp. 16–17.
50. St. Augustine, *Confessions, PL* 32, cols. 659–868.
51. St. Augustine, *City of God,* 5.2. See also Peter Brown, *Augustine of Hippo* (Berkeley and Los Angeles, 1967).
52. *VA* 37–39.

Anselm's psychology is described elsewhere with even greater clarity:

> There was a certain monk . . . Osbern by name, in years little more than a boy. . . . his good qualities were much disfigured by his really difficult character. . . . [Anselm] began with a certain holy guile to flatter the boy with kindly blandishments; he bore indulgently his boyish pranks, and — so far as was possible without detriment to the Rule — he allowed him many things to delight his youth and to tame his unbridled spirit. The youth rejoiced in these favors, and gradually his spirit was weaned from its wildness. He began to love Anselm, to listen to his advice, and to refashion his way of life. . . . [Anselm] nursed and cherished him, and by his exhortation and instruction he encouraged him in every way to improve. Then slowly he withdrew the concessions made to his youth and strove to draw him on to a mature and upright way of life.

Only when Anselm was absolutely sure that the youth was firmly set in good and proper ways did he proceed to use physical punishment to improve his character and behavior.[53]

This modification of St. Augustine's theories of psychology was also not without precedent. Gregory the Great, in his *Pastoral Care*, discusses at some length the ways in which a conscientious pastor should adapt his words to the capacities of his audiences, demanding more of the virtuous than of the weak until all are led into godly lives.[54] Anselm had surely read Gregory's *Pastoral Care*, since it enjoyed a wide circulation throughout Europe. In England, the cult of St. Gregory was especially strong; and it may be significant that Eadmer, Anselm's student, in describing Anselm's behavior, paraphrases Gregory's advice: he describes Anselm as showing himself "cheerful and approachable to everyone, conforming himself, so far as he could without sin, to their various habits. . . . 'to those who were without law' he made himself 'as without law . . . that he might gain them that were without law.' . . . For he adapted his words to every class of men, so that his hearers declared that nothing could have been spoken more appropriate to their station. He spoke to monks, to clerks, and to laymen ordering his words to the way of life of each."[55]

53. *VA* 16 – 17.
54. Gregory the Great, *Pastoral Care*, 3, Prologue; 2.9, 10.
55. *VA* 54 – 55; cf. *The Earliest Life of Gregory the Great*, ed. Bertram Colgrave (Lawrence, 1968), pp. 45 – 48, for Gregory's popularity in England. See also F. Holmes Dudden, *Gregory the Great: His Place in History and Thought*, 2 vols. (London, 1905), 2:239, and Jeffrey Richards, *Consul of God: The Life and Times of Gregory the Great* (London, 1980), p. 264.

At whatever date Anselm encountered Bede's history of the English church, he would have found these theories of teaching translated into political action by Pope Gregory himself. Gregory advised another St. Augustine, that of Canterbury, to relax the strict laws of the church for the barbarous English: "For in these days the church corrects some things strictly, and allows others out of lenience; others again she deliberately glosses over and tolerates, and by so doing often succeeds in checking an evil of which she disapproves."[56] And in this spirit Gregory ordered Augustine of Canterbury through Abbot Mellitus not to destroy the pagan temples of the people, but to cleanse them with holy water, destroy the idols, set up Christian altars, and deposit Christian relics in them. He is to substitute devout feasts on holy days for their pagan sacrifices.

They are no longer to sacrifice beasts to the Devil, but they may kill them for food to the praise of God and give thanks . . . for the plenty they enjoy. If the people are allowed some worldly pleasures in this way, they will more readily come to desire the joys of the spirit. For it is certainly impossible to eradicate all errors from obstinate minds at one stroke, and whoever wishes to climb a mountaintop climbs gradually step by step, and not in one leap. It was in this way that the Lord revealed Himself to the Israelite people.[57]

St. Augustine of Hippo implies this sort of toleration of pagan practices, which can later be adapted to Christian practices, in the fifth book of the *City of God*. Here he discusses "by what virtues the ancient Romans merited that the true God, although they did not worship him, should enlarge their empire." He concludes that the ancient Romans must have been virtuous for God to reward them. Certain good men deserved their positions of power and prominence because they gained them by "the true way" — the way of virtue — rather than by deceit and fraud; they ruled for the "public good" rather than for their own gains; and the praise and glory that was their chief end or goal was in itself a kind of virtue. Although in the Christian view a vice, this praise became a virtue relative to other vices, because it restrained them from more serious crimes. He then goes on to explain that the Christian must go a step further up the ladder of virtue, rejecting public praise for God's praise alone.[58] Although neither cites them, both Gregory the Great and Anselm seem to draw on these views in formulating theories of human behavior.

56. Bede 1.27.5
57. Bede 1.30.
58. St. Augustine, *City of God*, 5.12–13; 5.14.

It seems clear that Anselm consciously applied these psychological theories in his care of the Bec monks, and it is not surprising that he transferred these skills to other areas of Christian life, as did Gregory the Great. We have noted Anselm's practical advice to his successor at Bec on the importance of winning friends. As Pierre Michaud-Quantin has shown, psychological terminology and concepts appear also in Anselm's theology — in his concepts of the mind, the senses, and the conscience, as opposed to the intellect.[59]

Applying these concepts to practical matters, Anselm abandoned none of his saintliness. A simple holy man could live as innocently as a child and thus escape the blame of his contemporaries. But Anselm was also possessed of a penetrating intellect, and he applied it to the service of God, always with the motive of creating God's "right order" in the world. With models such as St. Augustine of Hippo, St. Gregory the Great, and St. Augustine of Canterbury, who also lived active (as opposed to contemplative) lives in God's service, Anselm followed a time-worn and venerated path. In doing so, he exercised the cardinal virtue of prudence. Ever since Plato's time, prudence has been regarded as the first of the four cardinal virtues. St. Augustine of Hippo lists them as prudence, temperance, courage, and justice. He describes all four as only the same love of God in different aspects or exercises. Prudence is commonly defined as practical common sense. St. Augustine implies that it gets things done. "Prudence shall provide . . . ; justice shall distribute . . . ; temperance shall moderate. . . ."[60] Anselm would have been keenly aware of the virtue of prudence, and equally aware of Christ's instruction to his followers to be not only "as innocent as doves," but also "as wise as serpents."[61] It is significant that William the Conqueror respected both Lanfranc and Anselm for their prudence.[62]

The evidence presented here reveals a man conscious of the effects of his actions on others, capable of influencing those around him by understanding their motives, so that God's will might be accomplished. His skill at arguing at court is clear from Eadmer's writings, and his own insight into the workings of human events shows through in his own letters. The great philosopher, exhibiting prudence, applied his intellect and "holy guile" to the practicalities of daily life. Robert of

59. Abbé Pierre Michaud-Quantin, "Notes sur le vocabulaire psychologique de St. Anselme," SB 23 – 31.
60. St. Augustine, City of God, 5.20. He does not go on to describe courage.
61. Matthew 10:16.   62. HN 23.

Meulan himself, when his men returned from Bec empty-handed in the Bec-Brionne incident, is said to have been "astonished" at Anselm's "prudence" in the arguments he had presented against Robert's claims on the abbey.[63]

The portrait of St. Anselm that emerges from this discussion reveals some important parallels to the virtues attributed to Robert of Meulan by his contemporaries. Both were considered the wisest of men, renowned for their great knowledge and their devotion to law and justice. Both were praised for their eloquence and powers of persuasion. Both were noted for their diplomatic abilities in settling controversies at courts of various kinds. Both were credited with guile or cleverness, in association with prudence or practical common sense. And both were seen to possess the outstanding virtue applicable to the role each played—Anselm's holiness and love of God, Robert of Meulan's loyalty and fidelity to his king. Thus each was a person of the highest rectitude with respect to the role expected of him.

But notwithstanding these parallels, the differences between the two men sharply divided them, and indeed made them adversaries. Anselm, the epitome of the perfect cleric, possessed a vision of "right order" for the world that was centered on God and church, whereas Robert of Meulan's vision of "right order" was centered on divinely sanctioned kingship responsible for ruling over the church. As at Bec around 1088, so also in the courts of William Rufus and Henry I, the interests of *regnum* and *sacerdotium* clashed in the persons of these two men, a conflict culminating in the great English Investiture Controversy in the reign of Henry I. Robert of Meulan was cast in the role of defender of traditional royal rights, arguing from custom. He was pitted against a learned holy man who was committed to a set of values that centered on the customs and rights of the church. In the two chapters that follow, the early careers of these two Norman neighbors and adversaries will be examined in more detail—first Anselm through the years at Bec, then Robert up to the time of his luckless effort to bring the abbey under his authority.

63. *DLB* 601.

Two

St. Anselm and Bec: Novice, Monk, Prior, and Abbot, 1033–1092

When Anselm became a monk of Bec in 1060, the abbey was already a quarter-century old. In order to comprehend the customs and traditions he encountered there, we must examine in some detail the circumstances of its creation and early development.

Bec was founded by a converted knight, Herluin, in 1034–37. Herluin had spent his young manhood in the retinue of Count Gilbert of Brionne, grandson of Duke Richard I of Normandy.[1] According to Gilbert Crispin, Herluin's early-twelfth-century biographer, he acquired an enviable reputation for honesty, courage, and loyalty, when, at the age of thirty-seven, he turned toward God. Abandoning his knighthood, he "broke the rope by which he was held under the service of an earthly lord. Renouncing his embassy totally, he went away from the court." After returning briefly to obtain a formal "release" from his service to the court and "power and authority" over his patrimonial estates,[2] Herluin gathered a few followers and began building an abbey at Bonneville not far from the Beaumont lands in central Normandy. At the age of forty he taught himself to read and studied grammar and the scriptures.[3] Visiting neighboring

1. *VH* 87.   2. *VH* 90.
3. *VH* 91; *CB* 641.

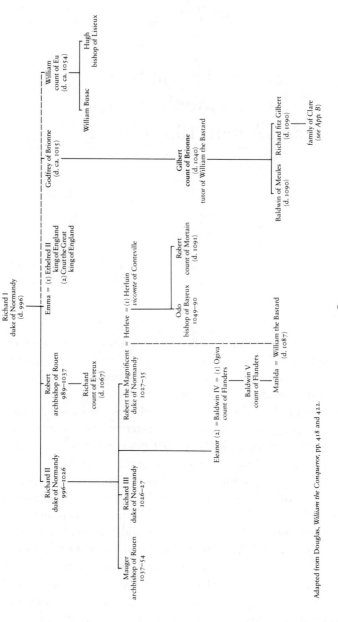

I.

The Brionne Connection to the Norman Dukes

Adapted from Douglas, *William the Conqueror*, pp. 418 and 422.

monasteries to see how monks lived, he was very discouraged to find
the inhabitants of the Norman abbeys to be violent, worldly, undeco-
rous, and unkind—thoroughly "depraved."[4] Discouraged, Herluin
returned to his own small abbey, built on his paternal lands. The
church was consecrated by Herbert bishop of Lisieux, who also conferred upon Herluin the habit of a monk in 1037. Two of Herluin's
own men received the habit at the same time. Then, having been
consecrated as a priest by the same bishop, he was appointed abbot of
the brothers.[5]

Soon, having been divinely warned by a vision—and since the
chapel at Bonneville was disease-ridden and lacked water—he transferred his house to another part of his patrimony. The new location
was Bec, which stood by a flowing stream, in the valley of Brionne.
"This place is in the woodland of Brionne, within a deep valley
hemmed in on this side and that by forested hills, providing every due
convenience for people's use; because of its dense trees and refreshing
stream, it was a favorite haunt for wild animals. There were only three
houses there belonging to three mills, and very little ground that was
habitable."[6] Herluin held only a third part of two of the mills, but,
according to Gilbert Crispin, "With firm hope in God Herluin began
to devote himself to the business, and God very plainly began to
collaborate. For his partners in property and the adjacent neighbors
either by sale or by free gifts gave up all their portions to him, and
within a short period he gained possession of the whole surrounding
wood of Brionne."[7]

A ducal confirmation of 24 February 1041 casts further light on the
founding of Bec. It records an earlier act (1034–35) wherein Herluin,
with the consent of his brothers and of Gilbert count of Brionne,
Robert duke of Normandy, Robert archbishop of Rouen, and others,
grants to his monastery the lands he had inherited from his mother's
dowry: a third of the lands of Bonneville, le Petit-Quevilly, Surcy, and

---

4. *VH* 91–92. Christopher Harper-Bill, in his "Herluin, Abbot of Bec and his
Biographer," in *Religious Motivation: Biographical and Sociological Problems for the
Church Historian*, ed. Derek Baker (Oxford, 1978), pp. 18–19, suggests the possibility
that Herluin's near illiteracy contributed to the chilly reception he encountered at neighboring monasteries patterned on Cluny.
5. *VH* 93. *CB* 639, 641. See also OV 2:13.
6. *VH* 94, 95. *CB* 641.
7. *VH* 96.

MAP I.
Normandy under William the Conqueror: Brionne and Bec

Cernay, and their appurtenances. The 1040 confirmation records further gifts to Bec by Gilbert of Brionne, his successor Guy of Burgundy,
Robert son of Humphrey (probably Robert of Meulan's paternal
uncle), and Duke William himself, who granted the tithe of his revenues from Brionne and the customs and dues of Servaville. The confirmation is attested by such notable figures as Duke William and his
son Robert Curthose, Archbishop Mauger, Nigel *vicomte* of the Cotentin, Ralph Taison, Count William Busac, and his brother Hugh bishop
of Lisieux — who must have added his *signum* after his episcopal consecration in 1049.[8]

Despite these marks of favor from high places, Bec was impoverished during its early years. It stood in sharp contrast to the richly

8. Fauroux, no. 98 and p. 31.

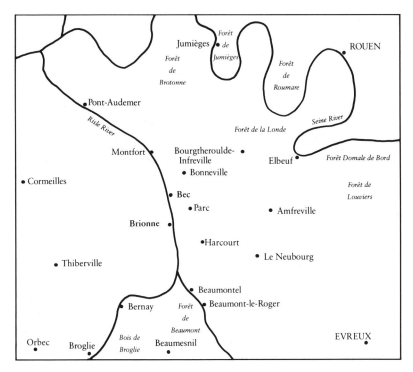

MAP 2.
Brionne and Bec: Enlarged View

endowed ducal and aristocratic foundations that typified Norman monasticism at the time. Herluin and his monks constructed a modest church at Bec, and near it they built a cloister of wooden columns, a wooden dormitory, and workshops. When the dormitory collapsed, Herluin rebuilt it of stone. Lanfranc of Pavia arrived at Bec about 1042 to find Herluin building an oven with his own hands.[9] Only later, when the fame of Lanfranc's school was spreading, did Bec's prosperity commence.

The community at Bec always looked back to its foundation by Herluin, and these circumstances became the first principles of the Bec tradition of autonomy. The author of *De Libertate Beccensis,* written after 1136, stressed that Herluin swore no profession of obedience to the archbishop of Rouen, in whose diocese Bec lay, because the see was vacant just then. Nor did Herluin profess obedience to the bishop

9. *VH* 94–96; *VL* 31.

of Lisieux who had ordained him, because it was not the custom for an abbot to profess to a bishop of another diocese.[10] The writer's emphasis on abbatial professions reflects a concern more characteristic of the 1130s than of the 1030s; Norman bishops seem to have been pressing for written professions from abbots only in the years following the Norman Conquest.[11] Nevertheless, when in later years archbishops of Rouen demanded written professions from abbots of Bec as the quid pro quo for consecration, the Bec monks evidently found it useful in defending their autonomy to point out that no abbot of Bec, from the founding abbot onward, had ever rendered such a profession.

The author of *De Libertate Beccensis* also stressed the fact that Herluin "never did homage to anyone for the possessions of his church."[12] As we have seen, Herluin was formally released from the lordship of Count Gilbert of Brionne on entering religious life. Duke Robert I gave his consent to Herluin's donation of some of his own inherited lands to his new abbey in 1034. But shortly afterwards the duke departed on a pilgrimage to the Holy Land from which he never returned. There is little evidence bearing on the question of Norman prelates rendering homage to lay lords before the Norman Conquest, and the attention given to the issue in *De Libertate Beccensis* may again be anachronistic. On the other hand, Eadmer speaks of the Conqueror's introduction of episcopal and abbatial homage into England as though it were one of "the usages and laws which he and his fathers before him were accustomed to have in Normandy."[13] English abbots, most of them from Normandy, are not reported to have grumbled when they rendered homage to William I at Salisbury in 1086,[14] nor is there any hint, in the relatively abundant sources of post-Conquest Normandy, of any abbot refusing homage on the grounds that it was uncustomary,[15] except at Bec. When Robert of Bellême demanded homage from Ralph d'Escures abbot of Séez circa

10. Vaughn, *Abbey of Bec*, p. 27.
11. OV 5:260–62.
12. Vaughn, *Abbey of Bec*, p. 134.
13. HN 9. Cf. p. 1. For these and other references bearing on the issue of clerical homage, I am indebted to Cassandra Potts, who reviewed the question in a valuable paper delivered at the Second Haskins Conference, Houston, November 1983: "The Homage of Prelates in Eleventh Century Normandy."
14. Florence, 2:19; ASC, A.D. 1086.
15. It was precisely on these grounds that abbots of St-Evroul, for example, refused to profess obedience to the bishop of Lisieux.

1103, Ralph refused not because abbatial homage was unsanctioned by Norman custom, but because it had been prohibited by Urban II.[16]

Pope Urban first banned clerical homage at the Council of Clermont in 1095, and the historical context of this prohibition suggests strongly that Urban's purpose was to extend the battlefront of Gregorian reform against a deeply rooted custom rather than to ban a pernicious novelty. In a letter of 1109 to Paschal II, Ivo of Chartres responded to the prohibition by pointing out that the homage of prelates to lay princes had been a custom of the realm of France since time immemorial.[17] And when, in 1124, Boso abbot elect of Bec refused homage to Henry I, again on the grounds of Urban II's prohibition at the Council of Clermont (which Boso had attended), John bishop of Lisieux is reported to have objected that the bishops and abbots of Normandy rendered homage to the duke "according to the ancient custom of the land."[18] John bishop of Lisieux (1107–41), the chief official in Henry I's regime in Normandy and former archdeacon of Séez, ought to have been just as capable as Boso of remembering back into the eleventh century, when his ecclesiastical career had commenced, but the fact that he could view the homage of prelates as an ancient custom of the land (or that a Bec writer could attribute such a view to him) cannot be taken to imply that the custom was necessarily in existence as early as Herluin's consecration in 1034 — at a time when the Norman political structure of fiefs and hierarchical bonds of allegiance was just beginning to take form.[19]

16. *GP* 127.

17. *PL* 158, col. 196.

18. *VB* 728. Vaughn, *Abbey of Bec*, p. 129; cf. *DLB* 141. The paucity of references to prelates doing homage in eleventh-century Norman sources could, of course, mean either that the custom did not exist or that it was so common as to be unworthy of notice unless in some newsworthy context. For example, it is mentioned only in passing at Salisbury in 1086, where the noteworthy occurrence was the rendering of homage and fealty to the king not only by tenants-in-chief but by undertenants as well. Other examples include instances following the papal ban at Clermont, when the homage was refused — by Archbishop Anselm in 1100, Abbot Ralph d'Escures about 1103, and Abbot Boso in 1124. Similarly, Orderic's notices of investiture at St-Evroul (2:16–18, 74, 144–46; 4:254 and n. 5) occur because he was at pains to distinguish between temporalities and spiritualities; these notices do not necessarily imply the absence of homage, which was not at issue and therefore not of interest to Orderic. As in the case of Anselm's elevation to Canterbury, the ceremonies of investiture and homage could be separated by a considerable span of time: *HN* 35, 41.

19. Lucien Musset, "Origines et nature du pouvoir ducal en Normandie jusqu'au milieu du XIᵉ siècle," *Les Principautés au Moyen Age: Communications du Congrès de Bordeaux en 1973* (Bordeaux, 1979), p. 59; cf. Bates, *Normandy*, pp. 122–28 and n. 142; Emily Zack Tabuteau, "Definitions of Feudal Military Obligations in Eleventh-

The Norman evidence is extremely fragmentary before about 1050, and it can sometimes be as hazardous to deny as to affirm the existence in the middle eleventh century of customs and practices subsequently regarded as "ancient." But whether remarkable or unremarkable, Herluin's avoidance of homage became a significant component of the Bec tradition. When Bec monks of the Anglo-Norman period insisted on freedom from homage to lay lords, and from obedience to the archbishop of Rouen, they could look to Herluin as their model.

Herluin set other precedents that became Bec traditions. Bec was founded in abject poverty. The abbot and the monks were required to work with their own hands in the fields and in the construction of monastic buildings. The early abbey of Bec had a Cistercian-like quality of the veneration of manual labor long before the founding of Cîteaux. It also had a zeal for learning even before the arrival of Lanfranc. The illiterate Herluin had spent his evening hours teaching himself to read.[20]

Because the monks lived on the edge of starvation, Abbot Herluin was compelled to devote most of his time to gathering money and goods for their sustenance, and to defending their rights to their meager possessions: "Herluin was skilled in dissolving controversies to do with secular cases, prudent in those things that related to the world outside; in building and in procuring all their necessities, he could not have been cleverer or more effective without sacrificing his religious scruples."[21] Thus, proper and efficient administration and involvement in business and litigation were part of Herluin's style of rule — a style that was later imitated and came to be regarded as one of the founding principles of Bec. Prudence, cleverness, and effectiveness were three of his foremost virtues. He was a good steward — a protector of his abbey and his charges: "With what justice, with what serenity he ruled those under him! Well-versed in the law of his fatherland, he was a protector for his men against wicked judges. And if any difference arose amongst them, he settled it immediately with great fairness. Wherever or to whomever he spoke, his words were listened to for their worth was preeminent."[22] As well as laboring in the fields and in

---

Century Normandy," *On the Laws and Customs of England: Essays in Honor of Samuel E. Thorne*, ed. M. S. Arnold, T. A. Green, S. A. Scully, and S. D. White (Chapel Hill, 1981), pp. 18–59.

20. *VH* 91–93.
21. *VH* 96; cf. 95; see also *VL* 32.
22. Ibid.

the building, Bec's founder also labored in the law courts to preserve and enhance the material well-being of his abbey.

It was in this condition and with these precedents that Lanfranc of Pavia found the abbey of Bec about 1042. Lanfranc built on these traditions and proved another model for Anselm to follow when the young man entered his school at Bec, decided to become a monk there, and at length became prior and abbot.

Lanfranc was an Italian layman well educated in the secular arts of learning, especially in law and administration, according to Orderic and later Bec sources.[23] Most historians would agree that Lanfranc had some legal knowledge: "his father was a lawman," Southern writes, "and the young Lanfranc, who was to have succeeded to this position, must have been brought up from an early age to be familiar with the Lombard law."[24] His legal cast of mind governed his approach to theology as well. As Margaret Gibson writes, "his fundamental skill, as always, was presenting material to make a case."[25] But many have been skeptical of Orderic's enthusiastic portrait of the young Lanfranc showing "so much wisdom in interpreting judgements that lawyers, judges, and civic officials gladly supported his opinion."[26] Margaret Gibson has rightly argued that the kind of law Lanfranc is reported to have practiced in Italy — deriving from a systematic academic study of Lombard or Roman legal texts — did not exist at that time, but came into being only a half century later.[27] Nevertheless, Marjorie Morgan Chibnall has suggested that the virtually identical passages in Orderic and the *Vita Lanfranci* praising Lanfranc's legal skill may both have been taken from the lost concluding

23. OV 2:248–49. Orderic wrote around 1124. The author of the *Vita Lanfranci* wrote around 1136 (*VL* 29, 39; cf. Vaughn, *Abbey of Bec*, pp. 10–11, 57–59, and 63–64). The anonymous *Miracles of St. Nicholas* was written about 1140 (Gibson, *Lanfranc*, p. 199). Robert of Torigni, a Bec monk writing in the 1150s, and the *Chronicon Beccensis*, begun about 1150, repeat the story with Robert's addition that Lanfranc was a colleague of Irnerius of Bologna.

24. R. W. Southern, "Lanfranc of Bec and Berengar of Tours," *Studies in Medieval History Presented to F. M. Powicke*, ed. R. W. Hunt, W. A. Pantin, and R. W. Southern (Oxford, 1948), p. 29. On the issue of Lanfranc's knowledge of law, see ibid., 27–32; J. H. Wigmore in *Law Quarterly Journal* 58 (1942): 61–81; Frank Barlow, "A View of Archbishop Lanfranc," *JEH* 16 (1965): 163–67, reprinted in Frank Barlow, *The Norman Conquest and Beyond* (London, 1983), pp. 223–37; the latter edition will be cited hereafter; and Gibson, *Lanfranc*, pp. 4–11.

25. Gibson, *Lanfranc*, p. 85.

26. OV 2:248–49.

27. MacDonald, *Lanfranc*, pp. 4–9, gives the Italian sources in detail. Gibson, *Lanfranc*, pp. 4–11.

section of William of Poitiers's *Gesta Guillelmi*. If the account is not only earlier than Orderic, but as early as the 1070s, Chibnall remarks, "the story of the brilliant young lawyer at Pavia may well be a legend, but it seems at least to be a legend that was current in Lanfranc's lifetime."[28] And whatever the degree of his mastery of Lombard law, Lanfranc revealed himself during his years at Bec as conscious of and active in the law of the duchy.

When Lanfranc decided to enter religious life, he investigated all the abbeys of Normandy and finally chose Bec.[29] Marjorie Chibnall's important study of ecclesiastical patronage at the time of the Norman Conquest demonstrates the degree to which Norman aristocratic families exercised control over their monasteries and used these foundations to extend their own influence.[30] Her examples include the Bellême foundations and the patronage of the Giroie-Grandmesnil family over St-Evroul. Monastic foundations were regarded as a means of extending family control over new territory, and were kept under family control by means of patronage and endowments. It is significant that Bec alone of all the Norman abbeys was not under this sort of lay control. Poverty stricken and destitute even of literacy (for Crispin fails to tell us that Herluin ever succeeded in his quest to read and write, and never mentions it again), Bec had only its autonomy to recommend it.

Bec's autonomy extended beyond lay jurisdiction. The community was entirely separate from the network of spiritual influence that was spreading swiftly across Normandy, binding the major ducal and aristocratic houses into a single movement of monastic observance based ultimately on Cluny. Cluniac reform came to Normandy by way of St-Bénigne, Dijon, when, at Duke Richard II's invitation, William of Volpiano, a former monk of Cluny and abbot of St-Bénigne, became abbot of the great ducal foundation of Fécamp in 1001. Under William of Volpiano (1001–28) and his disciple John of Fécamp (1028–79), the abbey of Fécamp became the nexus of a reform network that extended across the duchy.[31] Abbot William himself undertook the reform of Bernay (1025–27), and close associates of his took in hand the reform of St-Ouen, Jumièges, Mont-St-Michel, and St-Wandrille.

28. OV 2:248–49, n. 3; cf. n. 2.
29. *GP* 38.
30. Marjorie Chibnall, "Ecclesiastical Patronage and the Growth of Feudal Estates at the Time of the Norman Conquest," *AN* (1958): 101–18.
31. Douglas, *WC*, pp. 108–18; Knowles, *Monastic Order*, pp. 84–88, 701.

These reformed houses, in turn, provided abbots and monks for the new aristocratic foundations. Fécamp itself sent the first abbot to the Tosny abbey of Conches (ca. 1035) and would later do the same service for the Montgomery abbey of Troarn (1050–59). St-Evroul's first abbot came from Jumièges (1050), while from St-Ouen came the first five abbots of Holy Trinity, Rouen (1030 ff.), and the first abbots of Cerisy-la-Forêt (ca. 1030), La Croix-St-Leuffroi (1035), St-Victor-en-Caux (1055), and Beaumont-en-Auge (1060–66). Holy Trinity, Rouen, extended the network by sending abbots to the count of Eu's new abbeys at St-Pierre-sur-Dive (1046) and Le Tréport (1059), and William fitz Osbern's foundation at Cormeilles (ca. 1060). The list can be extended: St-Amand, Rouen; Montvilliers; and Lire similarly passed under the influence of the Fécamp movement, which itself was all but eclipsing an earlier wave of monastic reform begun in 960 by Mainard of St. Peter's, Ghent, which had reconstituted religious life at St-Wandrille and Mont-St-Michel and, through them, St-Vigor, Bayeux; Préaux; and Grestain. In time, as we have seen, both St-Wandrille and Mont-St-Michel passed under the influence of the Fécamp movement.

These houses, which constitute almost the entirety of the pre-Conquest Norman religious establishments, were all founded, reformed, colonized, or provided with abbots by Fécamp or its direct or indirect affiliates. Their members, although administratively independent for the most part, have the aspect of a single, interacting religious confraternity extending across the duchy, bound together by personal ties and shared Cluniac ideals. Herluin of Bec had visited some of these houses and had been disappointed in the quality of their spiritual life. At Bec he strove to create a distinctly different kind of religious community, independent of the established and swiftly growing Norman monastic constellation with its ducal or aristocratic affiliations, its community of personnel, and — in his judgment — its inadequate religious observance. Religious life at Bec was to be simpler, more austere, and less ceremonious than that of the Cluniac tradition. The monks of Bec — of whom thirty-four had joined the community before Lanfranc's arrival[32] — were converts from secular life, not monks from an established house shaped by the Fécamp reform. Herluin had sought no seasoned abbot from elsewhere; he undertook the task himself,

32. Porée, *Bec* 1:629.

having learned little from his visits to neighboring abbeys except that Bec must be set on a fresh course. In later years when Bec established a monastic network of its own, overshadowing Fécamp's and in part absorbing it, there was little apparent hostility between the Bec movement and the older one. Norman and Anglo-Norman religious life was, to a degree, inspired by the purity of the Bec observance and the good order that characterized both its internal life and its relations with the world. And conversely, as Bec grew wealthy and famous and its own austerity ebbed, it drew closer to the other abbeys of the Anglo-Norman world. The founding of Bec, however, constituted a quiet reproach to the state of contemporary Norman monasticism.

Bec was neither wealthy nor famous when Lanfranc arrived. But as a perceptive observer, he might well have glimpsed its potential. Unlike Cluny and the houses under its inspiration, Bec was free from time-consuming hours of ritual. It had no entrenched hierarchy of monastic officials and no specific requirements for novices. It had not been colonized by seasoned monks from an older house. It had no prior and no schoolmaster. And Bec alone in Normandy was free of the control of a ducal or aristocratic patron, lay or ecclesiastical. To Lanfranc, familiar with Lombard law and, more recently, with the condition of Norman monasticism, Bec's circumstances, although economically precarious, may well have seemed singularly promising.[33] Its unparalleled autonomy, if preserved and nourished, could become the foundation of a new reform.

Orderic reports that on Lanfranc's arrival at Bec "he enriched it by his wisdom and painstaking administration, raising it to a condition of perfect order, ruling it with a discipline that was both strict and merciful."[34] The *Vita Herluini*, followed by the *Vita Lanfranci*, tells much the same story but in greater detail. Lanfranc's entry into the Bec community was followed by three years of study and self-abnegation, "cultivating the newly plowed field of his heart with continual reading of scripture."[35] The analogy of Herluin's cultivation of actual fields to Lanfranc's cultivation of sacred texts suggests a broadening of the concept of physical labor to include learning. But while Lanfranc

33. At Bec, the monks strove to implement a certain "right order" within the world in which they lived. *DLB* 601; cf. AEp. 165, 198, and below, Chapter 2, after n. 272 to end.

34. OV 2:250; similar wording in *VL* 41 suggests an earlier common source; see OV 2:xvii–xxi.

35. *VH* 96–97; *VL* 32.

was studying scripture and humbly following the routine of a simple monk, he was growing inwardly disturbed at what he came to regard as the excessive laxity of the Bec religious life. He resolved to flee the community and live as a hermit but was dissuaded by Herluin, who subsequently elevated him above his more senior fellow monks to become the abbey's first prior.[36] Thereafter Lanfranc is reported to have taken full charge of Bec's internal affairs, molding its liturgical practices and rules of monastic conduct to his own strict ideals.[37] Herluin attended to the abbey's external affairs — its secular legal cases, its buildings, and its material necessities. "Each was a model for the flock, one of the active life, the other of the contemplative."[38] The austerity of the Bec liturgy[39] and the stringent regularity of the Bec religious life, which in subsequent years would influence a growing number of monasteries in Normandy and England, was thus implanted by Herluin but reshaped and systematized by Lanfranc into what Orderic could describe as a condition of perfect order and a discipline that was both strict and merciful.[40]

But the Bec tradition alleging that Herluin continued to direct the external affairs of his house cannot be accepted without reservations. The *Vita Lanfranci*,[41] in a passage intended to demonstrate Lanfranc's humility, discloses in passing that the prior was sent out to "preserve and restore" an estate given to Bec by a lay benefactor, leaving the impression that Lanfranc engaged routinely in such activities. Whatever the truth behind Gilbert Crispin's statement that Duke William took Lanfranc "as his counselor in administering the business of the whole province,"[42] it suggests that the monks of Bec regarded their prior as a person with the skill and experience to assume such a role. Although Herluin retained ultimate authority on the matter of buildings at Bec, he seems to have undertaken few if any initiatives until Lanfranc "began to take Abbot Herluin to task over the construction of a larger monastery and outbuildings" on a more suitable site. Herluin resisted this advice "now that his life was in decline,"[43] until prodded by the divine sign of a collapsing presbytery.

36. From a letter of the former Bec monk William abbot of Cormeilles to Abbot William of Bec: Gibson, *Lanfranc*, pp. 198 – 99; echoed in *VL* 33 – 34.

37. Gibson, *Lanfranc*, p. 27.   38. *VH* 96.

39. Arnold Klukas, "The Architectural Implications of the Decreta Lanfranci," *ANS* 6 (1984): 136 – 71; cf. *VA* 9.

40. Cf. Harper-Bill, "Herluin," pp. 20 – 21.

41. *VL* 33.   42. *VH* 97.   43. *VH* 98.

In 1060, "strongly trusting the help of his counselor, Lanfranc, all of whose work brought success to him," Herluin "began a new monastery and outbuildings in a much healthier place."[44] When the project was at last completed in 1077, Lanfranc was given full credit for its inception: as archbishop of Canterbury, he journeyed to Bec to consecrate "the church which he began."[45] Orderic thus seems fully justified in crediting Lanfranc with enriching Bec not only by his wisdom but by his "painstaking administration" as well.

But it was Lanfranc's wisdom that made Bec famous and influential. The school that he established may possibly have been limited at first to the instruction of child oblates and perhaps other children of the region.[46] But Gilbert Crispin reports that "in a short time the man's outstanding reputation proclaimed Bec and Abbot Herluin throughout the world. Clerics came running, the sons of dukes, the most renowned masters of Latin learning."[47] Lanfranc's pupils included so many future prelates that Marjorie Chibnall could refer to Bec under Lanfranc and Anselm as "a seminary of bishops and abbots."[48] Pope Nicholas II sent several young protégés from Italy to study under Lanfranc,[49] and Williram abbot of Ebersberg, writing about 1060, spoke of crowds of German youths descending on Bec to attend Lanfranc's classes on scripture.[50] Similarly, Orderic states that Lanfranc's fame spread across Europe "until many flocked from France, Gascony, Brittany, and Flanders to sit at his feet."[51] Among his students were the future archbishop of Canterbury, St. Anselm; the future archbishop of York, Thomas I; and a number of future bishops including Gundulf bishop of Rochester, the respected scholar Guitmund bishop of Aversa, and, in all probability, the great canonist Ivo bishop of Chartres.[52]

The fact that Ivo's attendance at Bec is first mentioned only in the 1150s in the chronicle of Robert of Torigni has roused scholarly suspicions, but although Robert is a late source, he spent much of his career at Bec, and his testimony is both unequivocal and plausible. It is consistent with general statements such as those just quoted, to which can be added Hugh the Chantor of York's rather grudging admission that Lanfranc "had been the master of nearly everyone in France . . .

44. VH 99.   45. VH 106.   46. Gibson, *Lanfranc*, p. 34.   47. VH 97.
48. Marjorie Morgan, *The English Lands of the Abbey of Bec* (Oxford, 1946), p. 10.
49. PL 143, cols. 1349–50.
50. Gibson, *Lanfranc*, pp. 35, 204.   51. OV 2:250.
52. HCY 2. OV 2:271, n. 4; Robert of Torigni, 4:100.

who had then any considerable reputation as a man of letters."[53]
If Ivo's status as a student of Lanfranc cannot be taken as certain, it
is at least very likely.

Lanfranc has traditionally been credited with another famous student, Anselm of Baggio — the future Pope Alexander II. Although
recent scholarly studies have all but rejected that tradition, the issue is
of sufficient importance to warrant further investigation. Tilmann
Schmidt in his magisterial study of Alexander II devotes fifteen closely
reasoned pages to showing that Alexander probably did not study
under Lanfranc, and his conclusion has since been enshrined in the
Dictionary of the Middle Ages.[54] Schmidt thinks it suspicious that no
reference to a master-student relationship occurs in the correspondence between Lanfranc and Alexander, but no such reference occurs
in Lanfranc's archiepiscopal correspondence with others known to
have been his students: Archbishop Thomas I of York, Gundulf,
William Bonne-Ame, and St. Anselm.[55] The first positive testimony
that Alexander studied under Lanfranc is straightforward and relatively early: Eadmer reports that Lanfranc, while visiting Rome in 1070,
was greeted by Pope Alexander with the words, "We have shown
you the honor that we know is due you, not as archbishop, but as the
magister to whose learning we are indebted for the knowledge we
possess."[56] Recounting the same meeting in his *Gesta Pontificum*,
William of Malmesbury blurs the picture by having Alexander honor
Lanfranc not for his archiepiscopacy but for his mastery of letters
("magisterio litterarum"), and the *Vita Lanfranci*, which states blunt-
ly that Alexander studied under Lanfranc at Bec, has been dismissed
as a late and unreliable source.[57] The issue thus turns on Malmesbury's statement, which could mean either that Alexander studied

53. HCY 2; cf. Gibson, *Lanfranc,* pp. 36–37, 198; Gibson offers some valuable
observations regarding Lanfranc and Bec's connections with Beauvais, where Ivo spent
his early years.

54. Tilmann Schmidt, *Alexander II (1061–1073) und die Römische Reformgruppe
seiner Zeit* (Stuttgart, 1977), pp. 10–25; Robert Somerville, "Alexander II, Pope,"
Dictionary of the Middle Ages, ed. Joseph Strayer, 1 (New York, 1982), p. 146. Frank
Barlow expresses similar doubts: "Lanfranc," p. 230 and n. 4. Most of the evidence is
summarized and carefully evaluated in Gibson, *Lanfranc,* p. 197, where the issue is left
unresolved.

55. LEp. 12, 23, 26 (Thomas), 61 (William), 53 (Gundulf), and 18 (Anselm).

56. HN 11: "Honorem . . . exhibuimus, non quem archiepiscopatui tuo, sed quem
magistro cujus studio sumus in illis quae scimus imuti, debuimus."

57. GR 65: "Professus, hanc venerationem non se illius archiepiscopatui, sed magisterio litterarum deferre"; VL 49, quoting Alexander II: "Non ideo assurrexi ei

under Lanfranc or, more literally, that Lanfranc was simply a famous *magister*. A previously overlooked passage in William of Malmesbury's *Vita Wulfstani*, by clarifying the ambiguous statement in his *Gesta Pontificum*, resolves the issue conclusively: in addressing the Canterbury-York dispute, Alexander is described as being "reluctant to offend Lanfranc who in former days had been his master."[58]

The assurance that Anselm of Baggio studied under Lanfranc provides decisive evidence that the school of Bec had become an international center of learning much earlier than the date suggested by Margaret Gibson, Lanfranc's most recent biographer. Gibson proposes that the school of Bec was originally an ordinary cloister school for child oblates and remained so until about 1059 or 1060 when, on the evidence of the *Vita Lanfranci*, it opened its doors to external adult students as a means of funding a major building program from student fees.[59] But as has been observed, the *Vita Lanfranci* is a late source, valuable in reflecting Bec traditions yet not altogether reliable. If, as its author reports, Lanfranc began taking external students only in about 1060, and then left in 1063 to become abbot of Caen, one would have to conclude that the reputation of his school at Bec has been much exaggerated. But the idea of a school attaining international fame during a life span of only three or four years is both inherently implausible and inconsistent with the evidence relating to Anselm of Baggio's career. His studies at Bec necessarily antedated his election to the bishopric of Lucca in 1056, and he cannot have moved into that office directly from Bec. In 1055 he had been ordained a priest at Milan, where he may have been involved in the patarine movement,[60] and it seems most unlikely that he would have journeyed to Bec in the early 1050s or late 1040s unless the school had already earned international distinction. That it had done so is suggested by a remark of Lanfranc's former student, Guitmund bishop of Aversa, that Berengar of Tours

---

quia archiepiscopus Cantuariae est; sed quia Becci ad scholam ejus fui, et ad pedes ejus cum aliis auditor consedi."

58. *Vita Wulfstani*, ed. Reginald R. Darlington (Royal Historical Society, London, 1928), pp. 24–25: "Tum papa qui Lanfranchum ut pote magistrum suum quondam grauaretur offendere." No contemporary sources apart from those discussed here provide any hint as to where Anselm of Baggio obtained his education.

59. *VL* 38: "Lanfrancus quoque licentia abbatis sui iterum scholam tenuit, et ea quae a scholasticis accipiebat abbati conferebat, abbas operariis dabat"; Gibson, *Lanfranc*, pp. 34–35.

60. Schmidt, *Alexander II*, pp. 30–37; Cinzio Violante, *La Pataria Milanese e la riforma ecclesiastica*, 1 (Rome, 1955), pp. 147–73.

proclaimed his novel and controversial Eucharistic doctrine about 1047–48 in order to gain attention and win back students who were by then flocking to Bec to study under Lanfranc.[61]

The evidence thus fully supports Gilbert Crispin's observation that scholars began flocking to Lanfranc "a short time" after his entry into the Bec community,[62] and suggests that Lanfranc may well have offered advanced instruction there for some eighteen years. Moreover, the current view that the school ceased to be important after Lanfranc's departure in 1063 is inconsistent with the narrative sources. On the straightforward testimony of Eadmer and Orderic, the school continued to flourish for the next thirty years under Anselm, who attracted learned clerks "from every nation,"[63] and filled Bec "with learned and pious monks" who became "devoted to the study of letters."[64]

Bec's growing fame as a center of learning was accompanied by a flood of pious gifts, including important benefactions from the duke. Sometime between 1050 and 1066 William granted Bec all the churches of Auge, which had been in his demesne.[65] Between 1041 and 1066 he gave Bec all *consuetudines de sanguine et teloneo* that he had held in the region and permission to establish a town at Bec.[66] In a charter of 1047–66, perhaps issued at Brionne in 1050, William granted to Bec the portion of the forest of Brionne previously held by Guy of Burgundy, with the assent of William fitz Osbern, who had custody of it.[67] In a possibly concurrent act, Duke William, at Brionne *ante cameram suam,* confirmed William fitz Osbern's gift to Bec of the land and forest that a certain Yves *clericus* had held of him.[68] The duke also gave formal consent to Roger of Beaumont's gift to Bec of the tithe of the forest of Brionne (1041–66),[69] and to William fitz Geré's grant of the land of La Roussière (1049–50) in exchange for lands and

---

61. Guitmund, *De corporis et sanguinis Christi veritate in Eucharistia, PL* 149, col. 1428: "Sed postquam a D. Lanfranco in dialectica de re satis parva turpiter est confusus, cumque per ipsum D. Lanfrancum virum aeque doctissimum liberales artes Deus recalescere, atque optime reviviscere fecisset, desertum se iste a discipulis dolens, ad eructanda impudenter divinarum Scripturarum sacramenta, ubi ille adhuc adolescens et aliis eatenus detentus studiis nondum adeo intenderat, sese convertit."

62. *VH* 97.   63. *VA* 40.

64. OV 2:294, 296. Orderic alludes to "external" students — clerks and laymen — who "came to sit at the feet of the renowned philosopher," but the weight of the evidence indicates that Anselm preferred that his students become monks of Bec. See below, Chapter 2 at nn. 250–52.

65. Fauroux, no. 179.   66. Ibid., no. 178.   67. Ibid., no. 189.
68. Ibid., no. 181.   69. Ibid., p. 33, no. 16 and n. 74.

a church in Ouche, previously held by Bec, on which the Gerés and Grandmesnils established their abbey of St-Evroul.[70]

Lanfranc's final years as prior witnessed the initial steps in the development of a network of religious houses colonized by Bec monks and inspired by the Bec liturgy and rule — a network that was to expand notably during Anselm's years as prior and abbot. The abbey of Lessay in the Cotentin, which remains an architectural monument to the simplicity and austerity of the Bec religious life, was founded about 1060 and colonized by Bec monks, one of whom, Roger, became Lessay's first abbot — the first of many Bec monks who would become abbots of other houses in the years and generations to come.[71] And in 1063, the year that Lanfranc left Bec for Caen, Duke William gave Bec a church in a suburb of Rouen, which became the Bec priory of Notre Dame du Pré or Bonne Nouvelle.[72]

During these same years Lanfranc brought Bec from its former obscurity into the limelight of Norman and international politics by developing strong personal relationships with Duke William and the reform papacy. The details of these relationships are not always clear, however, and recent historians have questioned the statement in the *Vita Herluini* (expanded in the *Vita Lanfranci*) that the duke chose Prior Lanfranc "as his counselor in administrating the business of the whole province."[73] For example, when discussing Lanfranc's elevation in 1063 to the abbacy of the great new ducal foundation at Caen, Margaret Gibson finds it something of a surprise "that the prior of Bec, who had not put his name to a single surviving charter, should at a stroke be transformed into the unique figure in Norman politics."[74] But although it is wise to be cautious of the enthusiastic claims of the Bec biographers, the interpretation of witness lists requires similar caution. Pre-Conquest Norman charter evidence is extremely fragmentary, and surviving ducal *acta* are rarely attested by priors of religious houses. Indeed, few are attested by abbots. The most celebrated abbot of mid-eleventh-century Normandy, John of Fécamp — recently described as "the doyen of the Norman church"[75] — attested only four of William the Conqueror's surviving charters during the entire forty-

70. Ibid., p. 32, no. 8 and n. 66; OV 2:16.
71. *La Normandie bénédictine au temps de Guillaume le Conquerant* (Lille, 1967), pp. 289–92, 298.
72. CB 645.   73. VH 97; VL 34.
74. Gibson, *Lanfranc*, p. 98.
75. Bates, *Normandy*, p. 203.

four years from William's accession in 1035 to John's death in 1079,[76] and only one of these four can be dated securely to the eighteen years during which Lanfranc was prior of Bec.[77] Another important Norman abbot, Ansfrey of Préaux (1040–72), attests no surviving pre-Conquest ducal charter, and Durand abbot of Troarn (1059–88) attests only once before the Conquest.[78] Even more remarkably, Lanfranc himself as abbot of Caen (1063–70) attests no surviving ducal or royal charters. Since other evidence makes it clear that all these abbots were active in the ecclesiastical affairs of the duchy,[79] one must conclude that attestation statistics cannot be used to gauge the influence of monastic officials on Norman governance or to modify the testimony of narrative sources.

Thus, to determine Lanfranc's influence in pre-Conquest Normandy, we have to depend on the narrative sources, which provide generalizations but few details. Only Orderic Vitalis affords us occasional glimpses of Lanfranc's activities in the ecclesiastical affairs of the duchy. In 1056 Lanfranc visited Orderic's abbey of St-Evroul in the company of the recently installed Archbishop Maurilius of Rouen, Ansfrey abbot of Préaux, and other prelates. They came as ducal representatives to judge the case of Thierry, abbot of St-Evroul, whose reforming policies had provoked his prior and monks to the point of revolt.[80] Archbishop Maurilius (1055–67), a native of Reims and former monk of Fécamp, had suffered a similar uprising when, during his brief tenure as abbot of Santa Maria, Florence, he had ruled his monks so strictly that they expelled him. Not surprisingly, he and Lanfranc and their fellow judges ruled in Abbot Thierry's favor.

It was during Maurilius's pontificate that Norman ecclesiastical reform achieved full momentum,[81] and he appears to have worked with Lanfranc in a spirit of common purpose and mutual admiration. Clearly, Maurilius held the religious life of Bec in the highest regard, for two of his most gifted and devout young protégés — Gundulf, future bishop of Rochester, and William, future archbishop of Rouen — became Lanfranc's disciples at Bec and Caen,[82] and in 1060 Maurilius encouraged Anselm to join the Bec community.[83]

76. Fauroux, nos. 107, 134, 166, and 231; *Regesta* 1, no. 4 = Fauroux, no. 231.
77. Fauroux, no. 107.   78. Ibid., no. 222.
79. Gibson, *Lanfranc*, p. 98; Bates, *Normandy*, p. 203; OV 4:90.
80. OV 2:66.   81. Douglas, *WC* 121–22.
82. *VG* 25–29; cf. Southern, *St. Anselm*, p. 29.
83. *VA* 11.

Lanfranc appears as a ducal counselor in another succession crisis at St-Evroul, this time without Maurilius. Orderic reports that in 1060 Duke William named Osbern prior of Cormeilles as the new abbot of St-Evroul "on the advice of Ansfrey abbot of Préaux and Lanfranc prior of Bec and other ecclesiastics" (unnamed).[84] The appointment angered and divided the monks of St-Evroul, whose former abbot, Robert of Grandmesnil, had been banished from Normandy by the duke. Mainer, claustral prior of St-Evroul, seems to have offended all sides by journeying to Bec and discussing with Lanfranc the possibility of substituting another abbot.[85] Although nothing resulted from the discussion, it may well be significant that Mainer, in his effort to change abbots, should have sought out Lanfranc. The fact that Lanfranc's recorded activities in the duke's service focused on St-Evroul plainly results from the accident that Orderic's history was by far the most comprehensive narrative of the age.

Although the evidence for Lanfranc's specific activities in the governance of Normandy is fragmentary and skewed, these rare glimpses are consistent with the more general testimony of the narrative sources. William of Poitiers, a contemporary writing about 1077, reports in his florid prose that during the years before Lanfranc's advancement to Caen, Duke William admitted him into his most intimate familiarity, venerating Lanfranc "as a father, respecting him as a master, loving him as he would love a brother or a son."[86] Prior Mainer's visit to Bec may well be a reflection of William of Poitiers's statement that the duke conferred on Lanfranc authority over the ecclesiastical orders of all Normandy, putting him, as it were, on a watchtower to oversee the duchy.[87] Only later in William of Poitiers's account did the duke appoint Lanfranc abbot of St-Etienne, Caen.[88]

The testimony of William of Poitiers thus lends considerable weight to Gilbert Crispin's statement (followed by the *Vita Lanfranci*) that the duke took Lanfranc "as his counselor in administering the business of the whole province."[89] The Bec writers go so far as to imply that Lanfranc's role as ducal counselor had begun by the late 1040s. They report a falling out between the two, caused by false accusations against Lanfranc that embittered the duke so deeply that he banished Lanfranc from Normandy and had the Bec village of Le

84. OV 2:90–92.   85. OV 2:96.
86. WP 126 = VL 41.   87. WP 126 = VL 41.
88. WP 126.   89. VH 97; VL 34.

Parc burned to the ground. The matter was happily resolved when Lanfranc, leaving Bec for exile and leading a lame horse, chanced to encounter the duke and won him over with a joke: "If you want me to be able to carry out your command, get me a better horse." William then permitted Lanfranc to clear himself of the charges against him, and Lanfranc did so with his accustomed skill. He and Duke William renewed their affection with embraces and kisses, and "it was promised that everything the duke had recently ordered to be ravaged should be restored with great addition."[90]

The story must surely be correct in essence. Frank Barlow rightly describes it as "an embarrassment" to Lanfranc's admirers, and they would scarcely have invented it.[91] Indeed, Gilbert Crispin is so embarrassed that he chooses not to tell his readers what offense Lanfranc was accused of committing. No trivial accusation can have so roused the ducal fury. The later *Vita Lanfranci* supplies an answer by reporting the tradition that Lanfranc was alleged to have opposed Duke William's marriage with Matilda of Flanders on the grounds of consanguinity.[92] Barlow accepts the *Vita Lanfranci* account because it "makes sense."[93] Margaret Gibson proposes that the quarrel occurred around 1047–50 in connection with the duke's war with Guy of Burgundy and his three-year siege of Guy's castle of Brionne.[94] Gibson's hypothesis is not necessarily at odds with Barlow's: Duke William's siege of Brionne was concurrent with his Flemish marriage negotiations, and both were efforts to restore his authority in Normandy and strengthen his position relative to neighboring princes.[95] To Duke William, the defeat of Guy of Burgundy and the Flemish marriage were related initiatives in what has been called his "war for survival";[96] from the ducal perspective, opposition by a Norman prelate to his projected marriage could be seen as an act of treason. Whatever the details, the rift between William and Lanfranc, and their subsequent reconciliation, very probably occurred toward the close of the 1040s, and William's wrath would most likely have been aroused by rumors of Lanfranc's opposition to the marriage plan.[97]

90. *VH* 98; *VL* 35.
91. Barlow, "Lanfranc," p. 231.   92. *VL* 35.
93. Barlow, "Lanfranc," p. 231.   94. Gibson, *Lanfranc*, p. 31.
95. Douglas, *WC*, pp. 55 ff., 76–80; cf. p. 117, n. 83.
96. Ibid., pp. 53–80.
97. The grounds for the charge of consanguinity between William and Matilda are by no means clear; Douglas, *WC*, pp. 76–77, discusses the several possibilities.

Lanfranc has traditionally been credited with providing intellectual leadership to the papacy in its opposition to the heterodox Eucharistic doctrine advanced by Berengar of Tours,[98] while at the same time negotiating a papal dispensation for Duke William's marriage in return for William's and Matilda's pledge to found the two Caen abbeys. But David Bates has persuasively argued that the story of Lanfranc negotiating the marriage dispensation at Pope Nicholas II's Roman synod of spring 1059 depends entirely on the late testimony of the *Vita Lanfranci*.[99] And Margaret Gibson has pointed out that Lanfranc's major contribution to the Berengar controversy, his treatise *De corpore et sanguine Domini* of circa 1061–63, was preceded by a spate of treatises against Berengar written by churchmen of Normandy and elsewhere in the 1050s during the heat of the dispute. Since Berengar's teachings received formal condemnation at the Roman synod of 1059, the subsequent appearance of Lanfranc's treatise seems anticlimactic. Moreover, Bates and Gibson both call attention to a letter in which Pope Nicholas II (1059–61) expresses regret that Lanfranc had been prevented by his studies from visiting him in Rome,[100] clearly implying that Lanfranc did not attend the Roman synod of 1059.[101]

Bec's corporate memory of Lanfranc's activities thus seems to have become blurred by the time of the *Vita Lanfranci*. Bates suggests that its author was misled by his slovenly reading of Lanfranc's *De corpore,* which describes the 1059 synod, with its 113 bishops unanimously condemning Berengar, but does not attest explicitly to Lanfranc's own presence.[102] Writing in the mid-1120s, Orderic Vitalis seems to make a similar error when he refers to Lanfranc defeating Berengar in public debate in Rome,[103] for only in 1059 were Berengar and Lanfranc alleged to have been in Rome at the same time.[104] Orderic and the *Vita Lanfranci* author could have drawn the same unwarranted

98. MacDonald, *Lanfranc,* pp. 37–39, 41–55; on the Eucharistic controversy, see Southern, "Lanfranc," pp. 27–48; and Gibson, *Lanfranc,* pp. 63–97.

99. VL 35–36, followed by CB 644–45; Bates, *Normandy,* pp. 199–202.

100. PL 143, cols. 1349–50; Gibson, *Lanfranc,* p. 69, n. 4; Bates, *Normandy,* pp. 200–201.

101. Nicholas was enthroned on 24 January 1059; the synod opened on 13 April; Nicholas died on 27 July 1061.

102. Bates, *Normandy,* p. 200; cf. Lanfranc, *De corpore et Sanguine Domini, PL* 150, col. 409.

103. OV 2:252.

104. They are unlikely to have met at Rome on some other, unrecorded occasion, because such a meeting would surely have been mentioned by Lanfranc or Berengar in the tendentious treatises that they hurled at one another: Lanfranc, *De corpore,* passim;

inference form Lanfranc's *De corpore*.[105] Alternatively, both may have been misled by material in the lost sections of William of Poitiers's *Gesta Guillelmi*. We know that Orderic drew heavily from the *Gesta*. Marjorie Chibnall has called attention to passages in Orderic on Lanfranc's early career that are nearly identical to passages in the later *Vita Lanfranci*. These passages reflect a style uncharacteristic of Orderic but suspiciously similar to William of Poitiers.[106] Chibnall suggests that such passages constitute independent adaptations by Orderic and the Bec writer from lost portions of the *Gesta Guillelmi*, and her hypothesis is corroborated by two neighboring sections of Chapter 13 of the *Vita Lanfranci*. The first is a transcription, with minor variations, of a passage in William of Poitiers's *Gesta*;[107] the second closely parallels a passage in Orderic, which itself was probably drawn from a lost portion of the *Gesta*.[108] In short, the author of the *Vita Lanfranci* had at hand a complete version of the *Gesta Guillelmi*, portions of which have since perished. In parts of the *Vita Lanfranci*, as in Book 4 of Orderic, one is faced with the problem of distinguishing between materials drawn from a lost portion of William of Poitiers's nearly contemporary account and materials drawn from later sources or oral tradition.[109] This problem is often insoluble. But one might reasonably suppose that Orderic or the *Vita Lanfranci* author — or William of Poitiers — is likelier to have erred on the date or place of a council than to have been misled on his fundamental points — that Lanfranc played an important part in the Berengar controversy (Orderic) and that he helped obtain a papal dispensation for Duke William's marriage (*Vita Lanfranci*).[110]

On the issue of the marriage, David Bates has proposed a drastic reinterpretation of events that is almost surely correct. We know from independent and reliable evidence that the duke's marriage plan was formally condemned at a great papal council at Reims presided over by Leo IX in October 1049.[111] Bates is rightly suspicious of the notion

Berengar, *De Sacra Coena adversus Lanfrancum*, ed. W. H. Beekenkamp (The Hague, 1941).

105. OV 2:252, n. 1.   106. OV 2:xvii–xxi, 248–50.
107. VL 41 = WP 126.   108. VL 41 = OV 2:250.
109. Cf. Chibnall, in OV 2:xviii.

110. Lanfranc and Berengar themselves sometimes get confused as to what occurred at what council: MacDonald, *Lanfranc*, pp. 47–48.

111. Anselm of St-Remi provides an eyewitness report: "Interdixit et Balduino cometi Flandrensi ne filiam suam Wilhelmo Nortmanno nuptui daret, et ei ne eam acciperet": PL 142, col. 1431. No reason is provided, but other marriage cases before the council involved either desertion or incest.

that the dispute then dragged on for ten years until the Roman synod of 1059. No source except the *Vita Lanfranci* mentions any papal sanctions against Normandy in response to the marriage, which probably took place in 1050 or 1051.[112] In 1054 Duke William sought and obtained papal license to depose Archbishop Mauger of Rouen,[113] and there is nothing to indicate that ducal-papal relations were other than friendly throughout the 1050s. Bates concludes that the matter of the "incestuous" marriage was resolved fairly swiftly, probably in the course of the year 1050.[114]

But although the *Vita Lanfranci* writer errs on the matter of chronology, he is very likely correct in placing Lanfranc at the center of the negotiations. The concurrent controversy over Berengar allows us to plot Lanfranc's itinerary in 1049–50 with unusual precision. He was probably present at the Reims council of early October 1049, where the projected marriage was prohibited.[115] Afterward, he either remained in Pope Leo's entourage or had rejoined it by 14 November when it had reached Remiremont in the Vosges.[116] He remained at the pope's side for the next ten months, attending the Roman synod of spring 1050, where Berengar was condemned in absentia, and continuing to follow the papal court, at Leo IX's request, until the Council of Vercelli in September 1050.[117] At Vercelli Leo had hoped that Lanfranc would defend the orthodox position against Berengar in open debate, but Berengar once again failed to appear. The evidence strongly suggests that Lanfranc left the papal court immediately after Vercelli to attend a ducal council at Brionne in October 1050. There he reported the papal condemnation of Berengar's doctrines to the duke and the council and probably debated with Berengar, who had come to Brionne at Duke William's invitation.[118] It was at approximately this time (1050–51) that Duke William and Matilda of Flanders were wed, without any apparent papal objection despite the prohibition of October 1049.

112. Douglas, *WC*, p. 392; Bates, *Normandy*, p. 201.
113. OV 4:84–86.
114. Bates, *Normandy*, p. 201.
115. Lanfranc, *De corpore*, PL 150, col. 413; and below, Chapter 2 at nn. 119–24.
116. LEp. 14: see Gibson, *Lanfranc*, p. 67, for the chronology; MacDonald, pp. 45–47, n. 7, for an analysis of the sources and the problems in interpreting them.
117. Jaffé-Wattenbach, 1, no. 4226.
118. Gibson, *Lanfranc*, p. 67; Bates, *Normandy*, p. 201; MacDonald, *Lanfranc*, pp. 45–46, n. 7, and sources cited therein.

Other Norman ecclesiastics may have participated in the marriage negotiations with Leo IX,[119] but none was so suitably placed to mediate as Lanfranc. His close association with Duke William seems to have been well established by the closing months of 1049. We know from Lanfranc's own words that his months in the papal entourage won him Leo IX's high regard.[120] A decade later Pope Nicholas II could laud Lanfranc for his valuable counsels to previous popes, while urging him to continue keeping watch on Duke William, who "so we have heard, has found pleasure in your advice."[121] That Lanfranc and Leo left the marriage prohibition undiscussed during their months together immediately following its enactment remains a possibility, but a rather unlikely one. Although the tradition reported in the *Vita Lanfranci* that Lanfranc negotiated the papal dispensation for Duke William is not corroborated explicitly by earlier sources, the circumstantial evidence is very strong.

Scholars have been similarly skeptical of the report in the *Vita Lanfranci* that William and Matilda promised to found the Caen abbeys as a quid pro quo for the dispensation,[122] but this statement, too, is probably correct. It is corroborated by earlier twelfth-century writers — by Orderic Vitalis writing before April 1109 and, as a common belief, by William of Malmesbury.[123] It is not surprising that sources of the Conqueror's time are silent on the matter. That the abbeys owed their establishment to a political bargain with the papacy rather than to disinterested ducal generosity would have been an embarrassment to the monks and nuns of Caen as well as to the Conqueror's panegyrists. William of Jumièges and William of Poitiers both provide detailed accounts of the marriage, but since both maintain a discreet and total silence on the matter of the papal prohibition,[124] they can hardly be expected to discuss the terms of its subsequent

---

119. *PL* 143, cols. 797–800: letter of John abbot of Fécamp to Leo IX (1049–54) reporting his activities as a papal legate and alluding in passing to the warm friendship between the Normans and the papacy — further corroborating Bates's revised chronology.

120. *De corpore, PL* 150, col. 413; cf. Gibson, *Lanfranc*, p. 67.

121. *PL* 143, cols. 1349–50: the same letter that expresses regret that Lanfranc cannot visit Rome.

122. *VL* 37; Bates, *Normandy*, pp. 200–201; Gibson, *Lanfranc*, pp. 109–10.

123. Orderic Vitalis, "Interpolations," in William of Jumièges's *Gesta Normannorum Ducum*, ed. Jean Marx (Rouen, 1914), pp. xxv–xxvi, 181–82; *GR* 2:327: "Ferunt quidam . . ."; for these and later sources, see Gibson, *Lanfranc*, p. 110 and n. 2.

124. *Gesta Normannorum Ducum*, pp. 127–28; WP 48–50.

repeal. The papacy itself may well have hesitated to advertise the arrangement: penances were normally assessed for past sins, with a promise of future amendment. If the Conqueror's marriage was incestuous, it should have been annulled; if not, it should never have been prohibited. Here, as before, we are confronted with an event about which contemporary evidence neither exists nor could reasonably be expected to exist, but which is both plausible and straightforwardly asserted by later writers — in this case by a very reputable historian writing in the first decade of the twelfth century who provides the first narrative account of Norman history since William of Jumièges and William of Poitiers. Under the circumstances one must deal in probabilities rather than certainties. The probability is that Lanfranc, serving in some sense as a ducal agent during his prolonged attendance at the papal court in 1049–50, was primarily responsible for persuading Leo IX to quash the prohibition of Duke William's marriage in return for William's promise to found the two great abbeys. Lanfranc would thus have emerged from the negotiations as a friend and invaluable servant of both duke and pope.

It is as a friend and servant of the papacy that Lanfranc's role in the Berengar controversy should be viewed. Lanfranc was a former student of Berengar's.[125] Shortly before the October 1049 synod at Reims, Berengar had written a somewhat tart but not unfriendly letter to Lanfranc requesting that he reconsider his disapproval of Berengar's teaching on the Eucharist, asking for Lanfranc's support and urging a face-to-face discussion.[126] Lanfranc later informed Berengar that the messenger bearing the letter, "finding that I had left Normandy," gave it to some priests, and that a priest of Reims brought it to Rome.[127] It was read aloud at the 1050 synod, where Lanfranc publicly cleared himself of any taint of heresy that might have been surmised from his association with Berengar: "I rose; what I felt, I said; what I said, I proved; and what I proved was pleasing to everyone and displeasing to none."[128] The council condemned Berengar's teachings, as we have seen, and Leo IX ordered Berengar to defend himself in person at a coming council at Vercelli (September 1050) while asking Lanfranc to remain with the curia until then, presumably to serve as a spokesman for the papal position. "Certain-

---

125. Guitmund of Aversa, *De corporis*, in *PL* 149, col. 1428.
126. *PL* 150, col. 63; Gibson, *Lanfranc*, p. 66.
127. *De corpore*, *PL* 150, col. 413.   128. Ibid.

ly," Orderic later reports, "his spiritual eloquence cut down Berengar of Tours in synods at Rome and Vercelli."[129]

Nevertheless, as Margaret Gibson has shown, the papacy itself tended to vacillate on the issue during the 1050s. Berengar continued to enjoy the support of a number of churchmen, and "even Rome was anxious rather than hostile: at the council of Tours in 1054 the legate Hildebrand accepted — as an interim solution — a very simple compromise formula proposed by Berengar himself."[130] In the meantime, although he had served the papacy with his spiritual eloquence in the synods of 1050, Lanfranc seems to have hedged his bets by committing none of his Eucharistic views to writing. While the papacy wavered, Lanfranc left it to others to write fiery treatises against Berengar. At length, at Nicholas II's Easter synod of 1059, Berengar publicly recanted. His teachings were formally condemned in his presence, he threw his books into a fire that he himself had lit, and he swore to accept a doctrinal formula, drawn up by Cardinal Humbert, that asserted in unambiguous terms Christ's true presence in the Eucharist.[131] Afterward, returning to France, Berengar repudiated his oath as having been sworn under duress and returned to his former view.[132] Only then did Lanfranc turn to writing his treatise against Berengar.

At the time that Lanfranc wrote his *De corpore et sanguine Domini*, circa 1060 – 63, the papacy had committed itself unequivocally, and Lanfranc's own student, Alexander II, occupied the papal throne. Lanfranc wrote less as an earnest dialectician defending his deep convictions against Berengar's errors than as a lawyer making a case for his client, the Roman church. The treatise opens not with an attempt to refute Berengar's views by logical analysis but with the argument that they had been examined and condemned by a series of church councils, culminating in Nicholas II's council of 1059 with its 113 bishops.[133] Such was the foundation on which Lanfranc built, and he declined to do so until the foundation was complete. He remained, as before, a defender of the papacy, "most useful in Roman and apostolic service."[134]

129. OV 2:250.   130. Gibson, *Lanfranc*, p. 69.
131. *De corpore*, PL 150, cols. 409 – 12.
132. Ibid., col. 412.   133. Ibid., cols. 407 – 9.
134. Nicholas II to Lanfranc: *PL* 143, col. 1349: "quem in Romanis et apostolicis servitiis satis opportunum." Cf. LEp. 1 (p. 32: Lanfranc to Alexander II): "ut taceam multa alia in quibus uobis uestrisque antecessoribus pro rerum ac temporum qualitate nonnunquam seruiui."

By 1063, then, when Lanfranc left Bec for Caen, he had long been a major ducal adviser and was the friend and former schoolmaster of Pope Alexander II. No source names the intermediary who persuaded Alexander to grant the papal banner that Duke William carried on the field of Hastings, and one can only observe that Lanfranc was better placed than anyone else to conduct such negotiations. Whatever the case, when William conquered England, a devoted former student of his chief ecclesiastical adviser occupied the papal throne.

Lanfranc accepted his promotion to Caen with great reluctance and protestations of unworthiness. But although he was in no sense an ecclesiastical careerist seeking wealth and power, he cannot have helped but realize that his advancement to the headship of the great new ducal abbey provided a tremendous opportunity to spread the ideals of the Bec religious life, which he himself had shaped and to which he was deeply devoted. St-Etienne, Caen, with its princely endowment, was the new family monastery of the dukes of Normandy, replacing Fécamp. It would serve the duke by providing "a supply of literate men and written documents, a means of control over a complex of estates, a source of ready cash, a community to pray for the duke and finally an impressive mausoleum."[135] And its monks would be, as Abbot Herluin proudly described them, sons of his sons.[136]

From his advancement to Caen to his departure for Canterbury, and despite the continuing absence of his name on William's witness lists, Lanfranc was unquestionably the dominating influence in the Norman church. On the death of Archbishop Maurilius in 1067, the church of Rouen chose Lanfranc to succeed him, "King William with his magnates and the populace at large gladly consenting." Refusing the archbishopric on the grounds of unworthiness, Lanfranc arranged the election of the reformer John bishop of Avranches. Then, in his lawyerlike way, Lanfranc went to Rome to obtain Alexander II's license for John's consecration "to ensure that the translation would be canonical" and returned with the license and the pallium.[137] The Rouen succession of 1067 marks the sole occasion in Lanfranc's career when his refusal of a higher office met with success. Perhaps it would be rash to connect this success with events of the previous year, which promised an early end to Archbishop Stigand's tenure at Canterbury, but Marjorie Chibnall raised the possibility.[138]

135. Gibson, *Lanfranc*, pp. 99–100.
136. *VH* 103.   137. OV 2:200.   138. OV 2:200, n. 1.

Only three years before Lanfranc's advancement from prior to abbot, Anselm of Aosta entered the Bec community. His Anglo-Norman contemporaries regarded him as an Italian, like Lanfranc, but he actually came from a crossroads of medieval Europe. Eadmer reports that his birthplace was Aosta, on the border of Burgundy and Lombardy.[139] He was born about 1033 of a Lombard father, Gundulf, and Ermenberga, an Aostan native. Aosta is in Savoy, a French-speaking province that was originally Gallo-Roman and later became Burgundian.[140] Dom F. G. Fruatz has suggested that Anselm may have descended from the counts of Savoy, and he was surely related to the ruling family in Aosta.[141] His father Gundulf, in the tradition of his class, was devoted to the secular life, careless of his goods and lavish in his munificence, "so that he was regarded not only as generous and good hearted, but even as prodigal and spendthrift." Ermenberga, on the other hand, was prudent, careful, thrifty, and conscientious. Anselm followed her example.[142]

He was taught letters and in a short time progressed far in his studies. Before he had reached fifteen, he had decided to become a monk, but a neighboring abbot refused to admit him, fearing to offend Anselm's father,[143] who thus must have been quite influential in the region. Gundulf apparently began to exert more influence on his life, for Anselm turned from his religious resolve, gave up his studies, and assumed worldly ways. But when his mother died, Anselm's father persecuted him and made his life unbearable. Resolving to leave, he gave up his patrimony and crossed the Alps at Mont Cenis.[144] After spending three years in France, he went to Normandy, attracted by the reputation of Lanfranc at Bec. Dom Laporte believes that Anselm arrived at Bec in 1059,[145] but he may have arrived somewhat earlier. He spent quite some time as a secular student of Lanfranc at Bec before he became a monk in 1060, and he also contemplated assuming the habit for some time before he received it.[146]

The spiritual influence of Cluny had deeply penetrated Anselm's native province,[147] and Anselm considered the option of becoming a

139. VA 3.
140. Bernard Secret, "St. Anselme, Bourguignon d'Aoste," SB 1:561–70.
141. F. G. Fruatz, "Saint Anselme et la Vallée d'Aoste," Revista Storica Benedettina, anno 4, fasc. 15 (1909), pp. 67–89.
142. VA 3–4.   143. VA 5–6.   144. VA 6–7.
145. Dom Jean Laporte, "St. Anselme et l'ordre monastique," SB 1:456.
146. VA 8–12. See also AEp. 156.
147. Secret, "Anselme," p. 563.

Cluniac. As an ambitious young man in his mid-twenties, "not yet tamed" as he later observed, he feared that if he remained at Bec he would be quite overshadowed by Lanfranc and would be insignificant in comparison. Equally, though, he reflected that the severity of the Cluniac life would render fruitless all the time he had spent in study.[148] He also considered the possibility of returning to Aosta and receiving his patrimony, for his father had since died. He even thought of becoming a hermit. He turned for advice to Lanfranc, who declined to offer an opinion but suggested that they both go to Archbishop Maurilius to seek his judgment. Maurilius recommended the monastic profession, Anselm "heard and approved," and, at the age of twenty-seven, he became a monk of Bec.[149]

As it turned out, Anselm was overshadowed at Bec for only three years. On Lanfranc's departure for Caen in 1063, the thirty-year-old Anselm succeeded his master as Bec's prior, schoolmaster, and intellectual luminary. If Anselm was aware of this possibility when he entered the community in 1060, Eadmer does not mention it in his *Vita Anselmi*, nor can one expect him to have done so. But by 1060 the establishment of St-Etienne would have been well under way, and the identity of its future abbot would have been a source of curiosity among the Norman clergy. Perceptive observers can hardly have overlooked the oddity that the prelate whom Duke William had set on a "watchtower" to govern the Norman church, and whom Nicholas II addressed in about 1060 as the duke's associate and adviser, was as yet a mere prior.[150] The duke may well have planned to make Lanfranc abbot of Caen ever since the project's inception, and Lanfranc himself might reasonably be expected to have foreseen the possibility. As for Anselm, he had resisted entering Bec for fear not only of having his ambitions frustrated by Lanfranc's commanding presence but also of being rendered fruitless. "Let me therefore carry out my plan," Anselm had reflected, "at a place where I can both display my knowledge and be of service to others."[151] Anselm quickly detected and repudiated his vainglorious desire to display his knowledge, but neither then nor thereafter did he turn aside from the Christian goal of being of service to others. The redundance of having two of the foremost minds in Christendom housed in a single abbey would have remained an impediment to

148. *VA* 9.
149. *VA* 10–11.
150. *WP* 126; *PL* 143, cols. 1349–50.　　　151. *VA* 9.

Anselm's entering Bec. But if Lanfranc possessed information that would quiet this doubt, it would have been quite out of character for the humble prior to discuss the situation openly. It could more tactfully have been explained to the young Anselm by the chief prelate of the Norman church, Maurilius, archbishop of Rouen.

Alternatively, the traditional view, based on a straightforward reading of the *Vita Anselmi*, remains a possibility. Perhaps Maurilius, Lanfranc, and Anselm were all unaware in 1060 that in 1063 William would promote his beloved friend and counselor to the abbacy of Caen. Whatever the case, events worked out so that of Anselm's forty-nine years as a churchman, he spent only three as a simple monk.[152] Despite the envy and grumblings of some of his more senior brethren, who seem not to have had a voice in the matter,[153] Anselm was designated Lanfranc's successor as prior of Bec under Abbot Herluin, who was now nearing seventy. Prompted perhaps by the grumblings, Anselm journeyed once more to Rouen and begged Archbishop Maurilius to relieve him of the burdens of his office.[154] Maurilius not only ordered him to continue as prior (which cannot have surprised him) but also told him that he would soon be promoted to a higher office and must not decline it. Maurilius must surely have had in mind the office then occupied by the elderly Herluin.

Eadmer relates that Anselm managed to win over the unhappy monks by responding to their hatred and scandalous gossip with love: "To those who hated peace, he showed himself peaceful," preferring to overcome evil with good.[155] This was the new prior's first political success, and it is significant for the further development of political methodologies and human relations at Bec. Anselm seems to have reinterpreted Lanfranc's prudent and persuasive ways with colleagues and opponents, transforming them into a doctrine of Christian love on

152. AEp. 156: Anselm to the monks of Bec, summer 1093: "Sic enim vixi iam per triginta tres annos in habitu monachico, tribus scilicet sine praelatione, quindecim in prioratu, totidem in abbatia annis."
153. *VA* 15; Anselm was the sixty-eighth monk to have entered the Bec community: Porée, *Bec* 1:629.
154. Cf. AEp. 425: Anselm warns Arnulf abbot of Troarn against resigning his abbacy through willfulness and disobedience; one can vacate an abbacy only by episcopal license, and, even then, only for a very substantial cause such as illness. It is unclear why Anselm petitioned Maurilius instead of his own abbot. Lanfranc himself, while seeking firmer backing in the Canterbury-York dispute, urged Pope Alexander II to relieve him of the archbishopric of Canterbury: LEp. 1; cf. LEpp. 4, 5, and 6. Lanfranc was sufficiently familiar with episcopal customs and practices to have predicted Alexander II's response.
155. *VA* 15–17.

a very practical level. He literally loved his enemies until they submitted to his rule, and there is no doubt that his love was sincere. Yet, as we have seen, Eadmer describes this behavior as a kind of "holy guile," suggesting that Anselm acted purposefully to shape behavior and consciously used love to achieve certain desirable ends. And from this point forward, Anselm's love seems to dominate the Bec reform movement as he applied it with great logical insight to the educational, administrative, legal, and practical business affairs of his abbey.[156]

We have already seen how Anselm, drawing from the wisdom of St. Augustine and Gregory the Great, used his love and psychological understanding to win the devotion and shape the character of the young Bec monk Osbern — how he flattered Osbern with promises and bore his boyish pranks indulgently until in time, withdrawing these concessions little by little, Anselm refashioned the young man into a model monk.[157] Anselm used a similar system of training — a delicate balance of love and discipline — as he guided other young men in the school of Bec. The "prudent pilots and spiritual charioteers" whom Orderic mentions emerging from Bec were thus molded and shaped into the kind of men that Anselm viewed as his ideal. Eadmer expressly states that Anselm gave more attention to the training of young men than of older ones, explaining that Anselm likened the time of youth to a piece of wax of the right consistency for the impress to be clear and whole. If one teaches such a man of the right age, one can shape him as one wishes.[158] These carefully trained men, stamped with Anselm's image, were to play a major role in his abbatiate and archiepiscopate. They constituted a network of reformers who with few exceptions remained close to him and heeded his counsel. Men from Bec continued to work together after they had left for higher positions, and those who remained at Bec considered themselves bound to Anselm even after he became archbishop.[159]

---

156. See above, Chapter 1 at nn. 44–48.
157. VA 16–17; above, Chapter 1 at nn. 44 and 46.
158. VA 20–21.
159. Laporte, "St. Anselme," p. 470. The abbot owed obedience to the monks collectively, and the monks of Bec owed virtually permanent obedience to their superiors at Bec, even if either or both left the abbey. AEp. 57 attests Anselm's continued obedience to Lanfranc. AEpp. 64 and 6 show that Anselm continued to hold obedience over his former students. AEp. 156 to the monks of Bec: "But I will never give up the power of binding and loosing, and of advising you, which I had over you, so long as the abbot who shall succeed me, and you who will be under him, shall yield it to me." In AEp. 302, Anselm attests that a monk can profess several times, and must be formally freed from such obedience. In 1106 (AEp. 378), Anselm as archbishop still used monks of Bec as his

Anselm seems to have trained his monks not only in Christian piety, but, at least by example, in administration as well. As Eadmer says, "besides being occupied in [scholarly work], he was harassed by the varied business of many people which drove away at times his peace of mind."[160] And Anselm himself is quoted as saying, "I am harassed by secular business, which I hate."[161] Here, as on other occasions, Anselm is expressing an attitude that is at once heartfelt and deeply rooted in the Christian tradition. Eadmer returns repeatedly to Anselm's aversion to administrative matters as a means of associating him with the topos of the saint who despises worldly affairs yet handles them skillfully when God calls upon him to do so. Thus, Gregory VII complained bitterly and repeatedly of the political and administrative burdens that oppressed him.[162] As archbishop, Lanfranc grieved that the many troubles and vexations that he daily endured were starving his spirit.[163] St. Bernard of Clairvaux would later write to Pope Eugenius III, "Let me begin with the pressure of business. If you hate it, I sympathize with you. If you don't, I mourn

---

trusted messengers. AEp. 196 to Richard, a monk of Bec, written after Anselm became archbishop: "Yield . . . if you wish to obey me, if you wish to please me, if you wish to retain my love for you, and therefore do not wish to vex me and the abbot you are under." Girard archbishop of York was not required to swear obedience to Anselm as archbishop of Canterbury because he had already sworn obedience to Anselm when Girard was bishop of Hereford: Anselm considered the obedience still binding (HN 186–87).

DLB shows that Bec monks continued to function as members of the community even after accepting positions as abbots, and that the Bec monks sought to keep themselves under Anselm's authority after he became archbishop, and placed their election of a new abbot under his jurisdiction. The Bec monk Roger, now abbot of Lessay, returned to Bec at Anselm's order to supervise the election (pp. 602, 604). Cf. VL 41: Lanfranc agreed to being translated from the abbacy of Caen to the archbishopric of Canterbury only after having been ordered to do so by Herluin, "whom it was Lanfranc's custom to obey as he would obey Christ." Similar language in OV 2:252 suggests a common source, probably, again, a lost section of William of Poitiers. When Herluin visited Lanfranc in England shortly after 1070, "the supreme pontiff and apostolic vicar . . . Lanfranc, subordinated himself to the man once his abbot, Herluin, just as if the archbishop were any other monk" (VH 102; VL 43). When Lanfranc returned to Bec for the dedication of the completed abbey church, "he conducted himself amongst the brothers with the greatest possible humility" and "sat in the cloister with the brothers, just like any one of them" (VH 105; VL 44–45). "In the church he did not wish the bishop's chair to be made ready for him, but took the prior's seat, saying that he still held this rank since he had not yet put aside his priorate" (seven years after he had departed the abbey, and while Anselm was prior: VL 45).

160. VA 21.
161. VA 70.
162. For example, Gregory VII, Epistolae Vagantes, ed. H. E. J. Cowdrey (Oxford Medieval Texts, 1972), pp. 2–5 (A.D. 1073).
163. LEp. 1, p. 32.

all the more, because the unconscious patient is in the greater danger."[164] As Karl Leyser has said, "The temptations and dangers of administrative tasks were and remained important moralistic commonplaces."[165] Enjoying secular business was only a step away from enjoying worldly vanities; the saint-prelate, although responsible for meeting his administrative responsibilities, should at the same time, in the *de contemptu mundi* tradition, have contempt of this fleeting life.[166]

Accordingly, Eadmer chose to pass over Anselm's conduct of the business of the abbey "in silence," stating merely that he wrote numerous letters, not only for his own abbey's business but also to the many people who sought his advice about their own affairs.[167] Most of these letters are now lost, possibly because Anselm felt that they need not or should not be preserved.[168] Nevertheless, as Herluin grew older and feebler, "it fell to Anselm as prior to do whatever was necessary," and he was "often obliged to leave the monastery on all kinds of business."[169]

On 26 August 1078, Herluin died and Anselm was at once unanimously elected abbot, as Maurilius had predicted. After a display of reluctance to accept the honor[170] — again, both a topos and an expression of strong personal inclination — he set about to fulfill the duties that being abbot of Bec required.[171] The first and most urgent such duty was to preserve the liberties of Bec. The duke-king William the Conqueror did not oppose the election, but according to *De Libertate Beccensis,* he postponed granting his permission and presentation of the abbacy until he should arrive at Brionne, which he planned to visit soon. Arriving there, he is reported to have sent three of his magnates to the church — Roger of Montgomery, William of Breteuil, and Roger of Beaumont — to find out and report back whether the monks agreed

164. Quoted in R. W. Southern, *Western Society and the Church in the Middle Ages* (Harmondsworth, Middlesex, 1970), p. 111.
165. Karl Leyser, "Ottonian Government," *EHR* 96 (1981): 723.
166. See *HA* 306; Nancy Partner, *Serious Entertainments: The Writing of History in the Twelfth Century* (Chicago, 1977), p. 28–48.
167. *VA* 32.
168. See above, Chapter 1 at nn. 19–21; Southern, *St. Anselm*, p. 67 and n. 1.
169. *VA* p. 40 and n. 1: Herluin was about sixty-nine when Anselm became prior, and died at the age of eighty-four.
170. See S. Vaughn, "St. Anselm, Reluctant Archbishop?" *Albion* 6 (1974): 240–250.
171. *VA* 44 and n. 1.

unanimously in the election of their new abbot.[172] The mission
obviously reflected a degree of doubt on the duke's part with respect
to Anselm's succession.

The *De Libertate Beccensis* account goes on to say that William's
magnates returned to him with the assurance that Anselm's election
was indeed unanimous.[173] Thereupon, at William's command, the
magnates went back to Bec and escorted Anselm and some of his
monks to the ducal court. We are left to assume that Duke William
was still at Brionne, but the *De Libertate* does not say so explicitly.
Anselm met the duke, whether at Brionne or elsewhere, and William
invested him with the pastoral staff, "as was the custom in that
province," but "did not require any homage from him." Afterward,
"since the church of Rouen was then without a pastor," Gilbert
bishop of Evreux consecrated Anselm abbot in the church of Bec on
22 February 1079 "without any mention of a profession." To make
explicit the distinction between lay investiture for the properties of the
abbey and episcopal consecration to the holy office itself, Anselm
refused to carry the pastoral staff until the moment of his consecration
by Gilbert of Evreux.[174]

The issue of the abbot's homage and profession, on which *De
Libertate Beccensis* dwells, would have been of far more urgent
concern at Anselm's election in 1078 than at Herluin's installation
back in the 1030s. Most likely, the duke was receiving homages from
his prelates,[175] and the Norman bishops were by now beginning to
demand professions of obedience from the abbots in their dioceses and
refusing to consecrate nonprofessing abbots.[176] Fifteen years later
Anselm would intervene personally in support of his successor's
refusal to profess to the archbishop of Rouen.[177] But in the months
following Herluin's death in August 1078, Archbishop John of Rouen
was in no position to demand professions or consecrate abbots. He
had been stricken with paralysis in July 1077, and from then until his
death on 9 September 1079, he was unable to meet the responsibilities

172. *DLB* 601.
173. Ibid.; cf. *VA* 44, confirming the unanimity of the monks but saying nothing
about the duke.
174. *DLB* 601.
175. On clerical homage, see above, Chapter 2 at nn. 12–19.
176. *OV* 5:260–62. The issue is first reported in connection with Gilbert bishop of
Lisieux (1077–1101) and Serlo abbot of St-Evroul (1089–91), who succeeded Abbot
Mainer (1066–89).
177. *VW* 718; cf. *DLB* 603 and *AEp.* 165.

of his office.[178] The closing months of 1078 would thus have found
the monks of Bec relieved to be able to install a new abbot without
trouble from Rouen, but anxious to seize the opportunity before
John's death and replacement. The duke's delay must have heightened
their anxiety.

During these same months William the Conqueror was deeply involved in wars and rebellions.[179] His eldest son, Robert Curthose, was
in arms against him, and he was also engaged in hostilities against
Rotrou count of Perche and a group of rebellious lords at Rémalard.
The narrative sources report that toward the end of 1078 King Philip I
of France, who had allied himself with Robert Curthose, installed the
young rebel and his followers in the French castle of Gerberoi, near
Beauvais, where more knights from Normandy and France joined
their garrison. The Conqueror may indeed have tarried briefly at
Brionne as *De Libertate* asserts, but shortly after Christmas 1078 he
moved into France and laid siege to Gerberoi. Some three weeks
thereafter, Curthose and his men sallied out of the castle and assailed
the besiegers, wounding both the Conqueror and his son William
Rufus, and putting the royal force to flight.[180]

The circumstances of King William's defeat at Gerberoi are in fact
much more complex than the narrative sources suggest. Their implication that Curthose enjoyed Philip I's backing at the time of his victory
is confuted by the evidence of an unquestionably authentic charter of
January 1079, issued by Philip I on behalf of the church of St-Quentin,
Beauvais.[181] The charter was issued "circa" Gerberoi during the
siege, and its list of signators is headed by "Philippus rex Francorum" and "Willelmus rex Anglorum." The other signators are
members of the French royal household and entourage, including
Philip I's brother Hugh, count of Vermandois and the Vexin,[182] along
with representatives of the clergy of Beauvais and, most surprisingly,
Anselm "abbot of Bec." As Douglas observes, the charter poses "a
great difficulty."[183] The words "Actum publice in obsidione predicto-

178. Douglas, *WC*, p. 329; OV 3:12 and n. 2; 18.
179. Douglas, *WC*, pp. 238–39.
180. Ibid., p. 239, from OV 3:108–110; *ASC*, A.D. 1079; *GR* 2:317.
181. *Recueil des actes de Philippe Ier, roi de France (1059–1108)*, ed. M. Prou
(Paris, 1908), no. xciv.
182. Father of Isabel of Vermandois, who would marry Robert count of Meulan:
below, Chapter 5, at nn. 231–38.
183. Douglas, *WC*, p. 239, n. 6.

rum regum, videlicet Philippi regis Francorum et Guillelmi Anglorum regis, circa Gerborredum" demonstrate that Philip I and William I were "in association outside the walls of Gerberoi" in January 1079,[184] leaving us to conclude that Philip had somehow been lured from Curthose's side to William's and was actually participating in the siege of the castle that he had earlier placed at Curthose's disposal. Philip's defection helps explain the fact that Curthose's victory gained him little or nothing. Deprived of his royal backer, he capitulated to his father during the months following the siege, in an agreement designed by Norman baronial mediators whose efforts were directed toward persuading William, not Curthose, to make peace.[185]

Anselm's *signum* as abbot of Bec makes it clear that the Conqueror had invested him during or just preceding the siege of Gerberoi. If nothing else, Anselm's presence suggests the urgency of obtaining the ducal presentation and investiture while Rouen remained without a functioning archbishop. The siege of Gerberoi would otherwise seem an odd place for a noted theologian to turn up at the height of his career. The fact that King William and Abbot Anselm are the only two Anglo-Norman signators on an otherwise typical French royal witness list raises the possibility that the two men were acting in some special relationship with respect to Philip and his court. We know nothing of the negotiations that resulted in Philip's change of sides, but the possibility cannot be dismissed that Anselm, with his considerable international prestige, was involved in the process. The reconciling of warring princes was a task often undertaken by holy men. The Bec monk Gundulf, as bishop of Rochester, mediated between William II and his magnates at the siege of Rochester castle in 1088, and again, in 1101, Gundulf "did everything possible to unite the king [Henry I] and his enemies in the bonds of peace."[186] In 1106, St. Vitalis of Savigny sought vainly to mediate between King Henry I and Duke Robert Curthose on the field of Tinchebrai,[187] and in 1120 the holy and widely respected Thurstan archbishop of York was instrumental in arranging a peace between Henry I and Louis VI.[188] Anselm seems to have enjoyed the respect and admiration of both royal courts. Orderic

184. Ibid.; Prou, *Recueil*, p. 242, n. 1, for the date.
185. OV 2:357–60; 3:97–113 and p. 108, n. 1.
186. *VG* 51, 59.   187. OV 6:86.
188. C. W. Hollister, "War and Diplomacy in the Anglo-Norman World," *ANS* 5 (1984): 74–76, where it is also shown that Suger abbot of St-Denis served on several occasions as a peacemaker between the French and English monarchs: pp. 87–88.

quotes William I on his deathbed as naming Anselm and Lanfranc among the four Norman churchmen who were his "constant companions" and whose good counsels he was always happy to follow.[189] And among those present at the consecration of the new church of Bec on 23 October 1077—less than fifteen months before the siege of Gerberoi—were "the most celebrated *consules* of the kingdom of France."[190]

The reason for William's earlier delay in presenting Bec to Anselm remains unexplained in the sources. It may well have been the very reason that Henry I would later have as he delayed presenting the abbatiate to Boso, abbot-elect of Bec—the question of homage.[191] Anselm did eventually obtain William's license, without doing homage and in time to avoid the Rouen profession issue. But in achieving this end he was evidently obliged to travel to the battlefield of Gerberoi and accompany the Conqueror into the encampment of Philip I. Whether William invested Anselm without requiring homage out of appreciation for Anselm's diplomacy remains both a mystery and an intriguing possibility.

By way of postscript, when Archbishop John of Rouen succumbed in September 1079, half a year after Anselm's consecration, the Conqueror chose as John's successor William Bonne-Ame (1079–1110), a protégé of Lanfranc's who had entered monastic life at Caen, had been sent to Bec for a time,[192] and had become the second abbot of Caen on Lanfranc's advancement to Canterbury in 1070. The Conqueror's confidence and gratitude toward Lanfranc and Anselm is perhaps nowhere more clearly demonstrated than by his elevation, during the 1070s, of two sons of Bec to the foremost sees of England and Normandy.

Anselm's success in becoming established in his abbatiate without giving homage to the duke or professing to the archbishop was long

---

189. OV 4:90.

190. *VH* 106; cf. AEp. 341: Philip I, ca. 1104, offered the exiled Anselm deepest condolences and refuge in his court. Eadmer speaks of Anselm during the Conqueror's reign as "known, loved, and welcomed throughout Normandy and France for the merit of his excellent holiness": *HN* 23. It was also sometime in 1077 that Philip I granted to Bec the Bec dependency of Notre-Dame de Poissy: Porée, *Bec* 1:241–42. M. Prou, *Recueil*, no. xc, prints the charter, pp. 232–34. The many witnesses include Hugh of Meulan, who gives the church of Meulan, and Paganos, *vicomes de Mellento*. It is a general confirmation, apparently of many French donations to Bec, possibly issued during or shortly after the dedication of the church of Bec.

191. *VB* 727–29.   192. *VL* 38.

remembered at Bec. It was seen as a crucial contribution to the Bec tradition of autonomy, stretching back to Herluin's time, and it became a model for Anselm's successors. To the author of *De Libertate Beccensis* it was one of the precedents that undergirded the liberties of Bec:

I think it worth the effort to put into writing, for those who are here now and for those who will come after us, the status and privilege with which the church of Bec has stood from its beginning. For it seems reprehensible if, through our neglecting to transcribe those events of former times, any sort of disturbance should at some time befall this church. Knowledge of the past can often be very valuable.[193]

Anselm himself was acutely aware of the function of precedents in the Anglo-Norman world. Running all through his correspondence is the concept that a precedent once established is unbreakable law.[194]

Anselm's consecration as abbot of Bec by no means brought an end to his writing, teaching, and meditations. But even as prior during Herluin's declining years, he had been obliged to assume increasing responsibility for the abbey's affairs. Now, as abbot, his responsibility was absolute and his distractions many. Norman monasteries of the later eleventh century participated fully in the political life of their neighborhoods, of the duchy, and later of the Anglo-Norman *regnum*. Abbots visited the court of the duke, and later the king, for a variety of practical purposes: to receive grants of land and income from the Norman magnates; to have existing grants confirmed and thus secure their rights; to defend their lands, incomes, and exemptions against rival claims in lawsuits; to advise and consent to synods and councils sponsored by the archbishop or the duke or both; and to advise the duke on matters of political importance. As a great Norman lord and holder of many benefices, the abbot was obliged to hold his own local court, to dispense local justice, and to provide for the temporal well-being of his monks and the inhabitants of his estates. While the purpose of the abbeys was primarily spiritual, their security and economic well-being depended on the proper administration of lands, churches, tithes, taxes and tolls, manors, mills, woods, and crops. The leader of a wealthy and famous monastery, such as Bec became under Lanfranc and Anselm, could scarcely avoid his duty to oversee these temporal

193. *DLB* 601.
194. AEpp. 176, 210, 251, 264, 293, 311, 319.

matters and secure the abbey's rights at the ducal or royal court. He was the steward of the possessions granted by magnates directly, but by God ultimately, whose will governs the course of events. The abbot's responsibility was to serve God by striving for the prosperity, well-being, and visual splendor of God's special communities of servants on earth — the abbeys. Indeed Gregory the Great in his *Pastoral Care* singles out as the most common error of the pastor the neglect of the physical necessities of his flock. He points out that minds will not accept good and worthy correction while stomachs are in want.[195] St. Augustine remarks that high office is necessary for government, and that a prelate ought to "look out for" those placed under him.[196]

Thus, having avoided the menaces that threatened his pathway to consecration, Anselm now turned to the task of administering his abbey in the style favored by the Bec traditions. As a result of his efforts as prior and abbot, Bec acquired extensive new lands and revenues and notable jurisdictional privileges. Anselm was diligent in securing grants and revenues for his abbey, whether great or small. Immediately on becoming abbot, he wrote to Lanfranc thanking him for sending twenty pounds. He was in urgent need of money, for he had had to make special purchases of beans and oats. He had also purchased costly lands and had incurred other expenses as well. In the same letter he shows how he took diligent care to preserve his abbey's property. John archbishop of Rouen had previously granted to the abbey a certain estate from the gift of William fitz Osbern.

But when the king inquired whether he himself had confirmed the gift, we could find absolutely no one who could remember. Therefore if you remember anything about the grant of the king, or when the same William granted you his holding in the area of Brionne, or when he gave anything to our monastery, or when the aforesaid archbishop gave his gift in Pont-Anthou: in whatever way it seems to you that you can help, notify us and the king; and inform us if the same archbishop gave it to us before he gave it to the diocese of Avranches, to which he gave it after twelve years had passed; and tell us if you know how our abbey's demesne acquired the tithes which Fulbert, clerk of Liveth held, which the lord abbot Herluin held of Hugh, bishop of Lisieux; because we are forced to sue about these things in the presence of the king on the Sunday after the feast of St. Andrew.[197]

As a good abbot and steward of his abbey's possessions, Anselm was thus maintaining those grants that his predecessor had received.

195. Gregory the Great, *Pastoral Care*, 2.8.
196. St. Augustine, *City of God*, 19.19.
197. AEp. 89.

Clearly he was preparing his case in the manner described by Eadmer, conscientiously securing the rights of his abbey.

Anselm's Bec was not poor, yet it was in constant need of money. Shortly after the letter just quoted, Anselm again wrote to Lanfranc apologizing that he had been compelled to spend the gold that Lanfranc had sent to be shaped into a chalice, and promising that a gold chalice would be made in the future.[198] Bec was also receiving financial aid from Anselm's devoted friend, Gundulf bishop of Rochester, for during his abbatiate Anselm wrote to thank the bishop for his largess to the abbey.[199] Anselm received further aid from his friends in England; after his return from a visit to Bec's English holdings he sent Dom Baldwin to England to be aided by Lanfranc "for our necessities."[200] He took care that money due the abbey was actually paid: in a letter to his friend Ida countess of Boulogne, he informed her that he had been unable to persuade the king to return her abbey to her, and added that she was to send him Dom Richard's money through the letter-bearer.[201]

Anselm was remarkably successful in increasing the lands and jurisdiction of the abbey through the reign of William the Conqueror (d. 1087) and the early years of his son, Robert Curthose (1087–1106), who granted Bec patronage over three churches in nearby Brionne.[202] Laporte suggests that Anselm and Gerbert the Teuton, abbot of St-Wandrille, may have cooperated in the transfer of Us priory, formerly held by St-Wandrille, to Bec, observing that "St-Wandrille thus submitted freely to the influence of the abbot of Bec."[203] Sometime between 1070 and 1077 the Conqueror regranted to Bec the right to build a town around the abbey.[204] A town was an important asset because Bec would have received the tolls and taxes associated with the town market, and certain rents as well. Moreover, a town would have added to Anselm's administrative responsibilities, for there would have been local law courts to oversee, building to supervise,

---

198. AEp. 90.   199. AEp. 107.

200. AEp. 124. Dom Laporte has misinterpreted this letter, thinking that it is a request to Anselm's Lombard friends for money (Laporte, "St. Anselme," p. 461).

201. AEp. 131. See Schmitt's notes for dating—probably after Anselm's second journey to England in the time of William I. The addressee is Ida of Ardennes, second wife of Eustace II count of Boulogne who fought at Hastings. Her abbey was probably St-Vaast near Boulogne, where Ida was buried.

202. Ferdinand Lot, *Etudes critiques sur l'Abbaye de St-Wandrille* (Paris, 1912), p. 91.

203. Laporte, "St. Anselme," p. 464.

204. Porée, *Bec* 1:144. Porée believes the date to be 1077.

and grants to be made. Anselm delegated some of these administrative tasks to his monks but took personal charge of all "important business of the church."[205]

Anselm made several trips to England as abbot, and while in the kingdom, he kept close watch over the Bec interests in Normandy. On what was probably the first such visit, he received news of the death of Hugh count of Meulan (d. 15 October, possibly 1080), who had resigned his countship to become a monk of Bec.[206] He wrote to assure his monks that he was endeavoring to see that Bec obtained the properties that Hugh had granted to the abbey. "I have not yet secured the end that I sought. Consequently, if anyone should reseise what you seised, do nothing further. But hold the movable goods which you now possess." At the same time, he was endeavoring to secure the abbey's newly acquired English lands, explaining to his monks that the king was reluctant "to confirm our charter of the things which we possess in England except in the presence of the donors, who were not all present at the Easter court."[207]

Anselm worked strenuously at the courts of the English king and the Norman duke to secure his abbey's rights. But like Lanfranc before him, he was also in communication with the reform papacy. In 1090 he persuaded Urban II (1088–99) to overlook alleged irregularities in the ordination of Fulk, a former monk of Bec, as bishop of Beauvais, on the condition that Anselm aid and counsel him. When a papal legate journeying to England to collect Peter's Pence had died while visiting Anselm at Bec, Urban asked that the legate's goods and Peter's Pence be sent to him.[208] Anselm was also in touch with Ivo bishop of Chartres, the noted canonist and former Bec student.[209] Through these and many other contacts, Anselm spread his influence into France and the papal court as well as across Normandy and England.

But Anselm's major concern was Normandy. As well as handling the business of Bec, he frequented the court of the duke-king. Thus on 7 January 1080, Anselm served on a panel of six judges at the court of William I at Caen, in a suit tried between the abbots of Lonlay and St-Florent of Saumur.[210] On 14 July 1080, again at Caen, Anselm

---

205. *VA* 45.

206. See Chapter 3 at nn. 59–63, and n. 62, for further discussion of this letter, which was written shortly after Easter 1081 or, just possibly, 1082.

207. *AEp.* 118. See also Porée, *Bec* 1:166, 171.

208. *AEp.* 125.   209. *AEp.* 181.   210. *Regesta* 1, no. 120.

witnessed a charter of William I to the abbey of Lessay, along with
Archbishop William Bonne-Ame, Archbishop Lanfranc, the future
King Henry I, Roger of Beaumont and his sons Robert and Henry —
the future *comites* of Meulan and Warwick — and other distinguished
persons.[211] And in an interesting case of 5 September 1082 Anselm
was one of a number of witnesses to the resolution of a dispute between two of his close associates, Gerbert abbot of St-Wandrille and
William archbishop of Rouen. St-Wandrille won its right to be free of
all jurisdictional claims from bishops and archdeacons in respect of
four neighboring churches. Among Anselm's fellow witnesses were
his friends Hugh earl of Chester and William Crispin, along with a
number of royal advisers including Roger of Beaumont and his sons
Robert of Meulan and Henry.[212] This agreement presages a later jurisdictional dispute between Archbishop William and Anselm himself.

During his final years at Bec, Anselm continued to involve himself
in the business of the world. In 1091, acting as Lanfranc had earlier
done, he supported with his presence and approval the election of
Roger du Sap as abbot of St-Evroul, in the company of Serlo bishop
of Séez, Ralph abbot of Séez (the future archbishop of Canterbury),
Arnulf abbot of Troarn, and others unnamed.[213]

Perhaps the most significant of Abbot Anselm's administrative
achievements was the resolution of his differences with Archbishop
William Bonne-Ame. Although Anselm received consecration without
rendering obedience to the archbishop of Rouen, he nevertheless had
to contend with the authority customarily exercised by the archbishop
over the abbeys in his diocese. The issue apparently lay dormant, or
perhaps was the subject of unrecorded negotiations, for more than ten
years. It was resolved at last in 1091 or 1092 on terms recorded in
a charter issued by William Bonne-Ame. The charter indicates that
Anselm had been raising *querelas et calumnias* (complaints at law)
against the archbishop both in the churches controlled by Bec and in
other parishes, and had also declined to recognize some of William
Bonne-Ame's archiepiscopal rights. The charter itself is virtually a
treaty reconciling the two prelates. William conceded to Anselm and
Bec freedom from all episcopal exactions; jurisdiction over the ordination of clerics and public penalties in its lands, and the fees for such

211. Ibid., no. 125. Roger abbot of Lessay (ca. 1060–1106) was also a former monk
of Bec. See below, Chapter 2 at n. 257.
212. Ibid., no. 146a.   213. OV 5:265.

jurisdiction; jurisdiction over pleas of the sword, and the fees for such jurisdiction (a right previously granted by William the Conqueror); and jurisdiction over freemen who held no property in their parish. In return, Anselm agreed to demonstrate honor and service toward the archbishop by attending masses at Rouen on great feast days (living at the archbishop's expense); saying the mass at Rouen if the archbishop was unable to be present; ceasing his complaints at law; and conceding to the archbishop all episcopal customs in whatever lands the church had acquired outside of Bec (apparently excluding Bec itself).[214]

Other abbeys had received similar jurisdictional privileges from Norman bishops: Mont-St-Michel in 1061, Troarn in 1068, and Bec's "sister house" of St-Etienne, Caen, in 1077.[215] Moreover, in 1090 – 94, the abbey of Fécamp was also pressing its claim to freedom from Bonne-Ame's jurisdiction. Fécamp succeeded in winning the support of Pope Urban II, who went so far as to deprive William Bonne-Ame of his pallium; in this case, Duke Robert Curthose sided with his archbishop.[216] Similarly, in 1068, Alexander II had granted St-Etienne, Caen, the special protection of the papacy, exempting it from the control of the bishop of Bayeux except with regard to cases involving moral offenses.[217] Bec was thus not alone in its efforts to obtain episcopal concessions of jurisdictional rights, but Bec and Caen were in the front ranks of the movement, and their privileges were exceptionally broad. Ironically, the rights that Anselm wrung from Archbishop William Bonne-Ame in the early 1090s were not unlike those that William Bonne-Ame himself, as abbot of Caen, had received from Odo bishop of Bayeux in 1077.[218]

The charter recording Bec liberties in regard to Rouen is witnessed by Robert of Meulan along with all the great lords of the area surrounding Bec, as well as by Duke Robert and most of the great ecclesiastics of Normandy, indicating that it may have been drawn up at the council of Rouen in June 1091. Anselm thus gained significant concessions from the archbishop with few and relatively insignificant

214. *Gallia Christiana*, 11, *Instrumenta*, p. 17.
215. J. F. Lemarignier, *Etude sur les privilèges d'exemption et de juridiction ecclésiastique des abbayes normandes depuis les origines jusqu'en 1140* (Paris, 1937), pp. 172, 173, 176; cf. pp. 294–96 for the text of the Caen charter of 1077.
216. G. H. Williams, *The Norman Anonymous of 1100 A.D.* (Cambridge, Mass., 1951), pp. 11–12.
217. MacDonald, *Lanfranc*, p. 57.
218. Lemarignier, *Etude*, p. 174.

concessions on his own part, possibly in the context of a great public convocation. The archbishop granted Anselm important economic and jurisdictional rights, in return for which Anselm agreed merely to engage in formalities that enhanced the archiepiscopal prestige. We have no information about the negotiations behind this agreement, but its significance is apparent. Anselm had confirmed important liberties for his abbey at little expense. Nowhere is his profession of obedience mentioned, and the abbey remained free of episcopal control at the cost of a few moments of nominal public deference. Anselm's political skills are clearly reflected in this charter.

Marjorie Chibnall has shown that Anselm worked with similar skill and effectiveness in acquiring English lands for his abbey.[219] Eadmer reports that "in the very year of his consecration" [1079] Anselm set out for England to visit the lands that Bec already possessed there, but there is reason to believe that Eadmer erred and that Anselm's first visit actually occurred in the period between summer 1080 and summer 1081.[220] As Southern observed, "a visit to supervise the administration of the scattered possessions in England and to take homage and oaths of fealty would be a normal action for a new abbot."[221] Anselm was conscientiously doing his duty to safeguard Bec's interests in the kingdom. After first conferring with Lanfranc, he went through England, visiting the lands of Bec and "transacting the business for which he had come," advancing the interests of his monastic community. He also visited other monastic houses and the courts of certain noblemen,[222] and Lanfranc took him to the court of King William to negotiate his business with the ruler. William is said to have greeted him in great friendship: listening to his advice, the king gave to Bec and other churches "lands, tithes, and other rents useful to the service of God."[223] In a letter probably of spring 1081 to the

219. Marjorie Chibnall, "The Relations of St. Anselm with the English Dependencies of the Abbey of Bec, 1079–1093," in *SB* 1:521–30.
220. *VA* 48. Anselm's first known attestation after his consecration (on 23 February 1079) was at Caen on 7 January 1080 (*Regesta* 1, no. 120), which would leave adequate time for an intervening visit to England. But Eadmer speaks of a meeting between Anselm and William I in the course of Anselm's first visit to England, and there is no evidence that the Conqueror was in England at any time during 1079, or the first half of 1080. Anselm also attested at Caen on 31 May (probably: *Regesta* 2, p. 394) and 14 July 1080, but could have visited England thereafter. This later date is further suggested by a letter of Anselm (AEp. 118), which seems to have been written during his first visit to England and is best dated 1081, after Easter (4 April): See Chapter 3, n. 62.
221. *VA* 48 and n. 2.
222. *VA* 54.   223. *VA* 56; *HN* 23.

monks of Bec, Anselm wrote that William I had assured him that he would grant a general confirmation of Bec lands in England at his Pentecost court (23 May 1081). If this was indeed the case, the date of William I's confirmation charter, discussed by H. E. Salter after the publication of *Regesta* I, can be narrowed from Salter's date range of 1081–87.[224] The charter confirms gifts of lands, churches, and tithes in Wiltshire, London, Middlesex, Essex, Devon, Oxfordshire, Gloucestershire, Berkshire, Buckinghamshire, and Surrey, from such notable patrons as Queen Matilda, Hugh of Gournay, Henry of Ferrers, Ernulf of Hesdin, Milo Crispin, Baldwin of Exeter son of Gilbert of Brionne, and Baldwin's brother Richard fitz Gilbert of Clare.

This was only the first of Anselm's visits to England during his abbatiate. Marjorie Chibnall, connecting the confirmation charter just mentioned to the Domesday Survey, and therefore favoring a date of Pentecost 1086 for its issuance, suggests that Anselm made a total of three visits to England — the first in 1080 or 1081, the second running from Lent until after Pentecost 1086, and the third beginning in autumn 1092 and culminating in Anselm's election to the see of Canterbury on 6 March 1093.[225] Eadmer, on the other hand, implies that Anselm made frequent visits to England during the fourteen years of his abbatiate: "from this time [his first departure from England] England was familiar to him, and was visited by him as business of various kinds required."[226] Whatever the case, Chibnall's observation that Anselm's visits resulted in a large accumulation of grants to Bec is

224. AEp. 118; H. E. Salter, "Two Deeds about the Abbey of Bec," *EHR* 40 (1925): 73–76. Salter's date is established by William of St-Calais's consecration as bishop of Durham (3 January 1081) and the Conqueror's last departure from England (before summer 1087). The fact that three of Milo Crispin's Oxfordshire manors were held in subtenancy by Hugh fitz Milo in the charter but by a certain "Willelmus" in the Domesday Book, and the further fact that "Hugh fitz Milo" was alive about 1115, suggested to Salter that the charter was probably issued in 1087, after the Domesday survey. The Domesday evidence is, as he recognizes, suggestive but inconclusive, and he calls attention to the difficulty that Queen Matilda (d. 3 November 1083) is referred to as *uxor mea* without a preceding *quondam*. A further difficulty is that certain benefactions not mentioned in the charter appear to antedate the Domesday survey — for example, Ralph of Tosny's gift of East Wretham, Norfolk (Marjorie Morgan, *The English Lands of the Abbey of Bec*, p. 148). That the charter antedates the queen's death in 1083 is strongly suggested by the fact that it records one of the two manors that she gave to Bec (Brixton Deverill, Wilts.) but not the other (Quarley, Hants.: ibid., p. 149); note, however, that at the time of the Domesday survey "the gift had not yet become effective"; Quarley is listed under *terra regis: DB* 1, fol. 39.
225. Chibnall, "Relations of St. Anselm"; cf., by the same author, "Some Aspects of the Norman Plantation in England," in *La Normandie Bénédictine*, p. 405.
226. *VA* 57.

surely correct and seems to be substantiated by the documents and Eadmer's account. Chibnall remarks that few of the gifts in William's charters can be dated before 1080.[227] These include Walter Giffard's gift of the manor of Blakenham (Suffolk) in 1075, which is the only precisely dated pre-1080 grant in Chibnall's appendix to *The English Lands of the Abbey of Bec*,[228] although many other grants are dated "tempus William I." The confirmation charter of circa 1081 must surely have included grants resulting from Anselm's visit in 1080–81, as well as previously held lands and tithes. In his account of Anselm's first visit, Eadmer states that Anselm visited the courts of a number of noblemen and was always "received with joy and cared for with all the gracious offices of charity."[229] And further, "There was no earl or countess in England, or any other important person, who did not consider that he had lost a chance of gaining merit with God, if he happened not to have shown any kindness to Abbot Anselm of Bec at that time." King William himself "unbent and became amiable with Anselm. . . . Laden with gifts, which are known to enhance the honor and serve the needs of his church to the present day, he set out to return to Normandy."[230]

The nature of the gifts recorded in the confirmation charter bears out this statement. The men of Milo Crispin, for example, seem to have reacted to Anselm almost as if they had undergone a mass conversion, giving numerous generous benefactions. Richard fitz Gilbert's gifts are so numerous (as are those of Hugh fitz Milo) that they seem unlikely to have all been given at the same time. Likewise, the men of Girold gave in such numbers (five of his men are listed) that they seem to corroborate Eadmer's account of the great love with which Anselm was received by men in all stations of life.[231] (See Appendix A.) Oddly, the one grant that we can definitely date before the confirmation charter was issued — Walter Giffard's manor of Blakenham (Suffolk) — is missing from the charter. Queen Matilda's grant of Quarley (Hants.), certainly made before her death in 1083, also does not appear. And there are a number of discrepancies between Domesday listings and the Bec confirmation charter (see Appendix A). But Sally Harvey has made a convincing case for the compilation of Domesday over an extended period of time and has shown that in some cases

227. Chibnall, "Relations of St. Anselm," pp. 521–22.
228. See Appendix A.   229. VA 54.
230. VA 56–57.   231. Ibid.

Domesday was based on earlier existing surveys.[232] Thus it is quite possible that grants made to Bec in 1081–82 or before might not have been included in the Domesday listings.

As he administered these lands in England and those he possessed in Normandy and France, Anselm seems to have organized the collection of tithes and produce so well that the monks of Bec never suffered shortages. As Eadmer observed, "The monks' food was so organized that they lacked nothing that their necessity required, although very often they . . . feared the next day might find them utterly destitute." But their "almost nothing [was] never so little that they suffered want." When the monks feared shortages, and the cellarers, chamberlains, and sacrists appealed to Anselm, he told them that God would provide. "In a miraculous way events would turn out to justify [his confidence]. You would see soon after . . . quite without exception before anyone suffered real want, either ships from England laden with every provision for their use would come to land nearby, or some rich man seeking fraternal association with the monastery would arrive with a large sum of money."[233]

With the acquisition of lands came the foundation of Bec cells and colonies in England, created largely through the influence of friends whom Anselm had won for the abbey in Normandy. His most conspicuous lay friends were the descendants of Gilbert of Brionne, the count who had released Herluin from his service. Gilbert's son Richard, first lord of Clare, brought the initial colony of Bec monks to England at St. Neots about 1081–82, which thereafter was a daughter house of Bec. In 1090, Richard's son and heir, Gilbert fitz Richard, chose to replace the canons of the college of St. John the Baptist at Clare with Bec monks, and the priory, which was moved to Stoke-by-Clare in 1124, became a dependency of Bec. Between 1090 and 1096, Count Gilbert's grandson William son of Baldwin granted Cowick on the outskirts of Exeter to Bec, and a colony of Bec monks was established there sometime between the date of the grant and the 1140s.[234] (See Appendix B for Clare genealogy.) Finally, in 1092 or 1093, Hugh earl of

232. Sally Harvey, "Domesday Book and its Predecessors," *EHR* 86 (1971): 753–73.

233. *VA* 47–48. The miraculous appearance of food may be another saintly topos: cf. St. Bernard, *Vita Prima, PL* 77, cols. 241–42; and Gregory the Great, *Dialogues,* Book 2, chaps. 21 and 29, in *PL* 66, cols. 125–204.

234. Chibnall, "Relations of St. Anselm," pp. 522–23; 526–28; David Knowles and R. N. Hadcock, *Medieval Religious Houses, England and Wales,* 2d ed. (London, 1971), p. 63; cf. Sanders, *Baronies,* p. 69, and Morgan, *English Lands,* p. 11.

Chester, who as we shall see was influential in Anselm's election as archbishop, refounded St. Werburgh's, Chester, with Bec monks under a Bec abbot. Although not constitutionally a Bec dependency, St. Werburgh's was clearly a part of Bec's friendship network.

Bec benefited from the generosity not only of Baldwin and Gilbert of Clare, Hugh of Gournay, and the other magnates whose gifts were confirmed by the Conqueror's charter, but also, in later years, of Robert count of Meulan, who granted a manor in Berkshire to Beaumont-le-Roger, a Bec dependency (with a portion of the tithe reserved for Bec), and another in Dorset directly to Bec. In addition, he confirmed two gifts of his men, a third gift by Roger de Mandeville, and the chapel of a Wiltshire manor given by Geoffrey of Brionne. Bec received a manor in Suffolk from the Clare in-law Walter Giffard, Queen Matilda gave an additional manor, Hugh of Grandmesnil donated two manors in Anselm's time or shortly thereafter, and the abbey also received manors from Ernulf de Hesdin's wife Emmalina, Ralph of Tosny (1085–86), and Hugh of Chester (before 1100).[235] Such were the grants of the friends of Bec in England in the time of St. Anselm. Through these friends the abbey was much enriched, and Anselm took great pains to secure the gifts for posterity. As Marjorie Chibnall concludes, "Eadmer's insistence that Anselm spared no effort to secure the rights of Bec in England seems amply borne out. He made sure nothing was lost through lack of a proper title. There was little litigation over the abbey's claims in the early twelfth century."[236]

The monastic cells of Bec founded in England were paralleled by priories in Normandy and France — and by less formal ties, which gave Anselm a degree of influence over other Norman abbeys. As we have seen, Anselm seems to have had some influence at St-Wandrille, and Bec had a relationship of confraternity with the monks of St-Etienne, Caen — "sons of her sons." During Anselm's years as prior and abbot, Bec acquired the French and Norman priories of St-Pierre de Canchy in Amiens (given in 1076), Conflans (given in 1081 by Ivo II count of Beaumont-sur-Oise), St-Martin de la Garenne (given ca. 1081 or earlier by Hilduin vicomte de Mantes), St-Pierre de Pontoise (given ca. 1082), St.-Hilaire de Tillères (before 1077, given by Gilbert Crispin), and perhaps St-Pierre de Longueville (no date — given by Hugh of Gournay).[237]

235. Morgan, *English Lands,* pp. 139–49.
236. Chibnall, "Relations of St. Anselm," p. 529.
237. Porée, *Bec* 1:384–444.

But the influence of Bec cannot be measured simply by listing its dependent priories. Bec never intended to follow the model of Cluny — to rule a vast congregation of daughter houses. Rather, Bec became a school of reform, which instilled into its sons its own distinctive principles of austerity, order, worship, piety, and mutual affection. These principles then spread far and wide as monks of Bec — products of Anselm's school — departed to colonize and rule other houses as "prudent pilots and spiritual charioteers."[238]

During Anselm's years as prior and abbot, as under Lanfranc, the school of Bec remained a celebrated international center of learning. Even as an ordinary monk studying under Lanfranc's guidance, Anselm was already "teaching carefully to others the things that they required."[239] Lanfranc had built the foundations of a library at Bec, devoting himself to correcting defective texts,[240] and his collection of works on theology and the liberal arts was "magnificently increased by Anselm."[241] Some evidence indicates, however, that Anselm was less enthusiastic than Lanfranc about providing instruction to external students, preferring to teach his own monks, or to enlist his secular pupils into the Bec community.[242] Alexander II sent his kinsmen and friends to study under Lanfranc at Caen rather than Anselm at Bec,[243] and Pope Urban II would later chide Anselm for presuming to raise a clerk of the Roman church to the priesthood and to enroll him as a monk of Bec.[244] Similarly, Boso, who was to become Bec's fourth abbot, had originally sought out Anselm to find answers to many perplexing theological problems. Anselm resolved his problems, and Boso, captivated by his love and admiration for Anselm, quickly became a monk of Bec.[245] These and similar instances suggest that the students who went to Anselm for formal instruction tended to become Bec monks.

238. OV 2:296.
239. VA 8.
240. Robert of Torigni, 1:74; Porée, Bec 1:91 and n. 3; for an early list of works in the Bec library, see MacDonald, Lanfranc, pp. 29–30.
241. OV 2:296. AEpp. 42, 43, 60, 64: Anselm to Maurice, former monk of Bec now with Lanfranc at Canterbury, requesting copies of several books including a work of Virgil.
242. Southern, St. Anselm, p. 31 and n. 1.
243. LEp. 1, p. 32; Gibson, Lanfranc, p. 103.
244. John, later abbot of Telese and cardinal-bishop of Tusculum; VA 106 and n. 1; AEp. 125.
245. VA 60–61; VB 723–25.

This change in direction reflected Bec's changed circumstances. When Lanfranc had begun accepting "external" students, Bec was small and impoverished. Few among his crowds of students actually professed at Bec; most would have thought twice about the prospect of taking lifetime vows at a small, ramshackle abbey. By the time of Lanfranc's departure in 1063, however, Bec's intellectual reputation was firmly established, its spacious new buildings were rising, its numbers were growing swiftly, and it was beginning to send out monks to rule other houses. Lanfranc's external school, although internationally admired, could also be regarded as subversive to monastic solitude and single-minded devotion to the life of the religious community. In Lanfranc's time the monks of Bec were probably outnumbered by his nonprofessing students, who were a source of wealth and fame for Bec but also, necessarily, a distraction. Strict monastic reformers had begun to frown upon external schools of Lanfranc's kind.[246] By 1063 Anselm was in a position to bring the school of Bec into closer alignment with reform ideals without diminishing its quality.

The school of Bec flourished under Anselm, the fame of whose learning "spread all over the Latin world."[247] "From every nation," Eadmer states, "there arose and came to him many noblemen, learned clerks, and active knights offering themselves and their goods to God's service in the monastery," so that Bec grew "inwardly in holiness, outwardly in manifold possessions."[248] According to Orderic, writing in the mid-1120s, Anselm did not reject secular students altogether: "Clerks and laymen came to sit at the feet of the renowned philosopher."[249] But Orderic puts greater emphasis on Anselm's teaching within the confines of his own monastic community, stating that he filled Bec "with learned and pious monks," who became "so devoted to the study of letters, so eager to solve theological problems, that almost all of them seem to be philosophers."[250]

A list of Bec monks, ranked in order of their entry into the community, tends to corroborate the testimony of Eadmer and Orderic. Only 34 monks had entered Bec at the time of Lanfranc's arrival in about

246. *VA* 8, n. 2, citing Emile Lesne, *Les écoles de la fin du VIIIe siècle à la fin du XIIe, Histoire de la propriété ecclésiastique en France*, vol. 5 (Lille, 1940), pp. 433–41.

247. OV 2:296. For a different view, see Gibson, *Lanfranc*, pp. 35–38, who holds that the school was of no importance after the departure of Lanfranc.

248. *VA* 40.

249. OV 2:294.

250. Ibid., 294, 296.

1042; 33 others had professed before Anselm became a monk in 1060; during the next eighteen years, between Anselm's profession and his nomination as abbot, 69 monks entered Bec; and Anselm's fourteen years as abbot (1079–93) witnessed no less than 160 new professions.[251] Expressed in other terms, professions averaged 1.8 a year in the period between Lanfranc's and Anselm's entry into Bec (ca. 1042–60), rising to 3.8 a year during Anselm's years as monk and prior (1060–78), and soaring to 11.4 a year during his abbacy (1079–93). As a consequence of this shift from external to internal instruction, Anselm's students who left Bec for careers elsewhere remained bound to him not only by ties of respect and friendship, such as those linking Alexander II to Lanfranc, but by the further and much stronger bonds of monastic obedience and brotherhood.[252]

The spread of Bec's influence across the Anglo-Norman world and beyond caught the imagination of contemporary writers. As Christopher Harper-Bill has observed, Gilbert Crispin's *Vita Herluini* steadily widens in scope from a life of Herluin to an account of Lanfranc's contributions to Bec, and, finally, to a celebration of Bec's impact on the ecclesiastical life of its age.[253] Gilbert Crispin speaks of a vision by which Herluin was warned of Lanfranc's impending promotion from Caen to Canterbury: "It seemed that in an orchard he had an apple tree whose branches were extensive and whose fruit was abundant, a delicious type of apple with a wonderful taste. King William begged for this tree, wishing to transfer it to his own garden. . . . The abbot was reluctant . . . but . . . the king overruled him and carried the tree away." Yet the roots remained, and from them twigs sprouted and swiftly grew into tall trees.[254]

According to Gilbert, the dream was fulfilled as follows: "The abbot's orchard was the church of Bec, whose greatest tree, the teacher Lanfranc, sustained not only Bec but all other churches throughout the land by his example and instruction. . . . How great was his fruit afterward in England, the renewed state of church organization over the length and breadth of the land testified." The order of monks,

---

251. Porée, *Bec* 1, App., pp. 629–31: the professions are not dated; they are divided by changes of abbots, not of priors, making it impossible to determine exactly the number of professions up to the time that Anselm became prior in 1063.

252. See n. 159; the list of monks who professed during Anselm's years at Bec includes three future bishops and ten future abbots: Porée, *Bec* 1, App., 629–31.

253. Harper-Bill, "Herluin," p. 23.

254. *VH* 100.

dissolute and corrupt, was transformed "with the discipline of the best-approved monasteries. The churchmen were restrained under canonical rule. The people . . . were educated toward the right pattern of believing and living."[255] The author concludes the dream imagery with the following: "From the roots which remained of that large tree . . . , the abbot afterward saw certain sprouting twigs grow into tall trees. That is, many undertook a great increase of good works through Lanfranc's instruction. . . . Herluin saw the sons of his church established as fathers of other churches. . . . The number reached into the hundreds . . . and spread to the farthest nations."[256]

During Anselm's final years as abbot, Bec's influence was swiftly eclipsing that of the old Fécamp network. The Bec reforms had become firmly planted at St-Etienne, Caen, and at Christ Church, Canterbury — both of which were linked to Bec by relationships of confraternity. Gundulf bishop of Rochester, Fulk bishop of Beauvais, Gilbert Crispin abbot of Westminster, Roger abbot of Lessay, Richard abbot of Chester, and William abbot of Cormeilles were all former Bec monks. Others included Henry prior of Canterbury (who became abbot of Battle in 1096), John abbot of Telese (who became cardinal bishop of Tusculum about 1100 and remained in touch with Anselm), Durand abbot of Ivry, and Lanfranc who served briefly and badly as abbot of St-Wandrille (1089 – 91). Further, Roger abbot of Mont-St-Michel (1085 – 1105) was a former monk of Caen, as was the controversial Thurstan abbot of Glastonbury (ca. 1077/8 – 96), Paul abbot of St. Albans (1077 – 93), and of course William archbishop of Rouen. Another monk of Caen, William of Rots, ruled Fécamp itself (1079 – 1107).[257]

These prelates and others from Bec and Caen shared similar ideals and a sense of common purpose. Circumstances might put them at odds with one another, as when Anselm and William Bonne-Ame pitted the liberties of Bec against the prerogatives of Rouen. But apart from such rare exceptions, they functioned almost as a team, linked by ties of loving friendship, exchanging letters and helping one another in a variety of ways.[258] The ties of love and obedience that bound the

255. *VH* 100.
256. *VH* 103.
257. This list could be extended: see Porée, *Bec* 1:103.
258. See, for example, LEp. 61, Lanfranc to William Bonne-Ame, abbot of Caen (1070): William has urgently requested Lanfranc's advice as to who should be appointed prior of Caen to replace Gundulf, whom Lanfranc had summoned to join him at

monks of Bec to each other and to their abbots continued to bind those who had left Bec for prelacies elsewhere. Thus Gilbert Crispin, followed by Orderic, explains that Lanfranc unwillingly left his abbacy at Caen to become archbishop at the command of Abbot Herluin of Bec, "whom Lanfranc obeyed just as if he were God."[259] And Anselm himself, at the beginning of his archiepiscopate, would send Roger abbot of Lessay to Bec to supervise his former brethren in their election of a new abbot.[260]

What exactly were the ideals shared by this new network of reformers, and to what degree were they exclusive to Bec? Their exclusiveness must not be exaggerated: Bec's emphasis on obedience, austerity, and an ordered religious life was, to a point, common to all Benedictine monasticism and, in particular, to the reformed monasticism of William of Volpiano and his disciples. The distinction between Fécamp reform and Bec reform was much narrower than the distinction between Norman reformed monasticism and late Anglo-Saxon practices. When Archbishop Lanfranc wrote his "Monastic Constitutions" for the guidance of Christ Church, Canterbury, and other English houses, he drew not only from Bec but also from Cluny, in particular from the customs recently drawn up by the Cluniac monk Bernard in 1067.[261] And when the former Caen monk Thurstan abbot of Glastonbury provoked his monks to rebellion in 1083 by insisting that they adopt continental practices, the last straw was his order that they use a chant composed at Fécamp.[262]

Nevertheless, the Bec reform ideology remained a distinctive blend of Herluin's austerity, Lanfranc's fondness for law and system, and Anselm's logic and love. The austerity of the Bec religious life, although necessarily modified at the great ducal abbey of Caen and the archiepiscopal see of Canterbury, has nonetheless left traces in the architectural arrangements of English monasteries and monastic cathedrals under the direct or indirect influence of Bec. As Arnold Klukas has recently observed, Lanfranc introduced into England "an atti-

---

Canterbury. Lanfranc suggests Ernost, a monk of Bec, if Abbot Herluin consents. Lanfranc further instructs William to "act according to the advice you receive personally from the lord abbot Herluin and from Dom Anselm."

259. *VH* 100; OV 2:252; *VL* 41.

260. See below, Chapter 4, at nn. 138–39.

261. *The Monastic Constitutions of Lanfranc,* ed. David Knowles (Nelson Medieval Texts, London, 1951), pp. xi–xiii.

262. Florence 2:16–17 (A.D. 1083).

tude towards observance which he had learned at Bec, an attitude that favored austerity in customs and simplicity in language," along with a more than ordinary scholarly interest in original sources and logical arguments, and a rejection of poetic allusions and dramatic figures of speech.[263]

Although all monasteries were concerned with their liberties and privileges, Bec alone in the Anglo-Norman world produced a series of treatises demonstrating the development and preservation of its liberties through the efforts of its early abbots. Lanfranc and Anselm both appear to have grasped the significance of Bec's uniquely autonomous origins, and both, in turn, as successive archbishops of Canterbury, would press for Canterbury's primatial rights to a degree unmatched by their predecessors. Anselm, who had managed to obtain consecration as abbot without professing to Rouen, and who had later negotiated a charter safeguarding his abbey's liberties against the pressures of Archbishop William Bonne-Ame, would spend his dying months struggling with all his power to force a written profession from the archbishop-elect of York.

There was, however, a far more attractive side to the Bec tradition than the defense of liberties and assertion of prerogatives. Christopher Harper-Bill, echoing Jean Leclercq, has rightly stressed Bec's contribution to a new doctrine of the monastic life "in which the positive value of charity replaced penitential mortification for the sins of the world as the prime purpose of the life of a monk."[264] Bec's insistence on due order, in both the life of the cloister and the community's relationship with the larger world, was accompanied by a shining spirituality akin to that of the twelfth-century Cistercians. Anselm had advised his successor at Bec, William of Beaumont, to use kindness, affable words, and hospitality to win friends, whether rich or poor, for the utility of Bec and the safety of his loved ones.[265] Anselm had himself won friends far and wide, and their gifts enriched his abbey enormously. But although he was quite aware of the connections between friends, gifts, and good stewardship, Anselm clearly believed that friendship was an expression of the Christian life, and he lavished

263. Klukas, "The Architectural Implications of the Decreta Lanfranci," ANS 6 (1984), 137–71.
264. Harper-Bill, "Herluin," p. 24; cf. LeClerq in SB 1:477–88.
265. AEp. 165. See below, Chapter 4, at nn. 161-62; and above, Chapter 1 at nn. 43–44.

it on rich and poor alike. His advice to Abbot William mirrored Christ's own words: "And so I tell you this: use money, tainted as it is, to win you friends, and thus make sure that when it fails you, they will welcome you into the tents of eternity."[266] Under Anselm, Bec's hospitality became as famous as its school. "The doors of Bec are always open to any traveler," Orderic wrote, "and their bread is never denied to anyone who asks for it in the name of Christ."[267] Eadmer describes Abbot Anselm as sparing neither himself nor his goods in the entertainment of guests: "And if at times there was not quite enough food to refresh their bodies as he would have wished, his goodwill and cheerful countenance among his guests richly supplied what was lacking."[268]

To Anselm, then, friendship and hospitality could bring material benefits, yet they were, above all else, acts of love. Jesus had taught that God is love and that love can transform the world. Anselm applied this dictum in a very practical way, training his monks with loving guidance, acquiring friends for the abbey so that all the monks' material needs would be met, and loving his opponents until they came to see his point of view. While Lanfranc set Bec on its path toward legal and administrative excellence, Anselm's two great contributions to the Bec reform movement were the practical applications of love and reason to bring about "right order." He loved and was beloved by all, from the duke-king William the Conqueror to the lowliest son of Bec. His friends numbered in the hundreds, and the combination of Anselm's great love for all of God's children and their love for Anselm resulted in the tremendous growth of Bec in both prestige and material assets during the thirty years in which Anselm was prior and abbot.

Eadmer reports Anselm's words in a typical encounter with his friends, which embodies both his magnanimous love and his reasoned exposition:

For he who has love . . . has something for which God rewards him; but this is by no means true of the man who is merely the recipient of love. For what thanks does God owe me if you or someone else loves me? If then it is better to have something for which God rewards a man, than to have something for which he does not; and if he rewards a man for the love which he shows, and

266. Luke 16:9.
267. OV 2:296.
268. VA 46–47.

not for that which he receives; then it is proved that he who shows love to another has something greater than the man to whom it is shown. . . . Therefore if we consider these things in their true light, we shall see how much more we should rejoice if we love others, than if we are loved by them.[269]

Anselm's love seemed limitless. It could include such notorious characters as Hugh "the wolf" earl of Chester, Arnulf of Montgomery earl of Pembroke, and the Conqueror's son William Rufus, the only person ever reported to have hated Anselm in his maturity. But Anselm directed his most lavish expressions of affection toward his fellow monks. For example, he addressed Gilbert Crispin, whom Lanfranc had summoned from Bec to Canterbury, as "brother, friend, beloved lover," and continued: "Sweet to me are the gifts of your sweetness, sweetest friend, but they cannot possibly console my desolate heart for its want of your love. . . . The anguish of my heart when thinking of this bears witness, and so too do the tears dimming my eyes and moistening my face and the fingers that write this."[270]

This letter, typical of many, exemplifies the emotionally charged affection that bound Anselm to his monks and friends. Expressions of this sort have misled some historians into the unlikely supposition that Anselm was a repressed homosexual.[271] The ardor of his language — which became a model for subsequent Cistercian expressions of spiritual friendship — can more accurately be viewed as a reflection of his heartfelt devotion to his comrades in God's service, lamenting their absence and rejoicing in their presence.[272] It attests to the emotional intensity that fused the sons of Bec into a potent force for reform in the Anglo-Norman world.

Bearing all these characteristics in mind, can Anselm's Bec truly be regarded as a new order? In time Bec and its daughter houses had achieved sufficient cohesion that, by the thirteenth century, their monks were describing themselves as belonging to an *ordo Beccensis*.[273] The abbots of Bec had by then imposed upon their community and its dependent priories a common ritual, special statutes, and a

269. Ibid., pp. 48–49.   270. AEp. 84.
271. For example, John Boswell, *Christianity, Social Tolerance, and Homosexuality* (Chicago, 1980), pp. 218–19.
272. See Southern, *Anselm*, pp. 72–76; Brian P. McGuire, "Love, Friendship, and Sex in the Eleventh Century: The Experience of Anselm," *Studia Theologica* 28 (1974): 11–52.
273. Morgan, *English Lands*, p. 15.

distinctive white habit. Some of these developments may reflect Cistercian influence, but there is much to indicate that even in Lanfranc's and Anselm's time the monks of Bec, and those who had left it to rule other churches, regarded themselves as a distinctive brotherhood. Anselm himself urged the monks of Bec to "always so join one to the other that on all sides the inviolate order of the monastery can be preserved rightly."[274] Anselm composed statutes, now lost, to be read annually in the chapter house of the Bec priory of Stoke-by-Clare, and these may well have embodied customs described later by the Bec monks as common to the whole order, approved by the blessed fathers Herluin, Lanfranc, Anselm, and others.[275] Some evidence suggests that the monks of Bec had adopted the white habit as early as the mid-twelfth century, and a later tradition ascribes this change to Abbot Anselm.[276]

Whatever the case, one must always bear in mind the distinction between, on the one hand, the Bec "congregation" of mother house and dependent priories and, on the other hand, the network of friendship and informal affiliation, which was far more important in Anselm's time, binding Bec with Caen, Canterbury, and the numerous abbeys and bishoprics ruled by former monks of those houses. The bishopric of Rochester, for example, can hardly be regarded as a Bec daughter house in the constitutional sense, nor can St-Etienne, Caen, but both were united with Bec by ties of intimate friendship and fraternity. Between 1075 and 1108 two monks of Bec and comrades of Anselm — Arnost and Gundulf — served in turn as bishops of Rochester, and it came naturally to Anselm to request Gundulf's protection of Bec's new priories in England: "I commend to your fatherly love . . . our brothers and yours whom we are sending to England, that in their every need they can be supported by your aid and guided by your counsel, and that their lives may be carefully examined by you and judiciously praised or corrected."[277] And Lanfranc, as abbot of Caen and archbishop of Canterbury, remained to the end a son of Bec — revering Herluin as if he were God and Anselm as "a friend and

274. AEp. 165.
275. Morgan, *English Lands*, p. 13 and n. 2; Chibnall, "Relations of St. Anselm," p. 527.
276. Porée, *Bec* 1:505 – 7: Porée doubts the tradition on the grounds that Orderic contrasts the white habit of the Cistercians with the black habit of the traditional Benedictines, including, presumably, the monks of Bec; but Orderic's contrast is not as clear as Porée suggests: OV 4:310 – 12, 324 – 26.
277. AEp. 91.

brother with whom he was of one mind."[278] This sense of a brother-hood of reformers driven by a single vision of the religious life is nowhere more clearly demonstrated than on the occasion when William Bonne-Ame, the future abbot of Caen and archbishop of Rouen, first entered religious life under Abbot Lanfranc at St-Etienne. Lanfranc immediately sent William to study for a time under Anselm at Bec "so that he could learn more about the order there," because the abbey of Caen, being newly established, "could not as yet teach others perfectly."[279]

These texts make it clear that Lanfranc and Anselm and their colleagues were conscious of an *ordo Beccensis,* based not on any constitutional authority exercised by Bec over houses ruled by its former monks, nor on a distinctive habit or written rule, but on the devotion of the sons of Bec, linked by deep mutual affection, to a mode of religious life developed and perfected at Bec and then disseminated across the Anglo-Norman world and beyond.

278. *VA* 51; *VH* 100, 102, 105.
279. *VL* 38: "Iste Willelmus cum habitum religionis Cadomi suscepisset, missus est Beccum, ut ordinem ibi addisceret, quia novella plantatio ipsius loci nondum poterat alios perfecte instruere."

Three

Robert of Meulan
and the Beaumonts:
Son, Heir, Knight, and Baron,
1046–1092

While St. Anselm was deeply involved in administering his abbey, training his students, and writing theological tracts, the man who was to be his adversary for the rest of Anselm's life was building the foundations for his own political career. Robert of Meulan, son of the lord of Beaumont, appears infrequently in the chronicles during his early years, but documentary evidence shows that he was active at the ducal court at the side of his father, Roger of Beaumont. And when Robert became a magnate in his own right by inheriting the county of Meulan in France, he began to play an increasingly important role in the French and Norman worlds.

The counts of Meulan have been of interest to French historians because of the proximity of the county to Paris, and their role in the French monarchy's struggle to control the French Vexin, defend it against the Normans, and extend royal authority into the *Vexin Normand*. In the time of King Philip I of France (1060–1108) the counts of Meulan were vitally important vassals in the Vexin border wars between the French and the Normans. Traditionally the counts had found it in their interest to support the French monarchy, but their allegiance shifted when Count Hugh II died in 1080, leaving no direct heirs. The county passed through Hugh's sister Adeline, who had married the Norman magnate Roger of Beaumont, to her eldest son. Robert of Beaumont thus became count of Meulan.

Emile Houth, Robert of Meulan's only modern biographer, approaches him from the French perspective. In a series of articles on the early counts of Meulan, Houth performs an important service in calendaring their documents, but he devotes little attention to Norman history as separate from French history, and he overlooks major English sources. His collection of charter evidence from the French and Norman archives is thorough and valuable, but he does not place Robert of Meulan in the larger context of Anglo-Norman politics.[1] As adviser to Kings William Rufus and Henry I, Robert's political influence was immense, and his career can properly be understood only in terms of the growth and development of the Anglo-Norman state and the politics that furthered that growth.

Robert of Meulan's family origins go several generations back into Norman history. Son of a rising aristocratic family, the Beaumonts, he was said to have been connected to the Norman ducal house through his grandfather, Humphrey de Vieilles. The aura of legend surrounding Humphrey's ancestors is difficult to dispel. His father is alleged to have been a certain Thorald lord of Pont-Audemer, the son of a sister of Gunnor, wife of Duke Richard I of Normandy (942–66).[2] Whatever the accuracy of the early genealogy, the Beaumont family acquired its ancestral lands through the efforts of Robert's father, Roger of Beaumont, who set the family on its road to wealth and fame.

Humphrey's generation participated in a social, political, and economic reordering of Normandy in which a new lineage-based aristocracy emerged and enriched itself at the expense of the church.[3] In

1. Emile Houth, "Robert Prud'homme," pp. 801–29.

2. Robert of Torigni, "Interpolations" in *Gesta Normannorum Ducum*, p. 324. The author of the *Complete Peerage* account of the Leicester earldom finds Robert of Torigni's pedigrees questionable, and cites a charter to St. Pierre's of Préaux (*Gallia Christiana*, 11, *Instrumenta*, cols. 201–2) in which Roger mentions his mother's brother Turchitill, from whom he inherited Pont-Audemer. Turchitill, according to the *Complete Peerage*, was either a brother of Thorold or his son, brother of Humphrey (7:521; 523, n. b). David C. Douglas agrees with G. H. White that family connections to the Duchess Gunnor contributed in some degree to the rise of many of the great Norman houses in the latter years of her son's reign (*WC*, p. 89), but Bates (*Normandy*, p. 112) argues that nearly all the genealogies prior to 1040 or 1050 are mythical. He attributes this seeming loss of memory to the social and political metamorphosis occurring among the Norman aristocracy at this time.

3. Douglas, *WC*, pp. 86, 90.

addition to his lands at Pont-Audemer, Humphrey acquired, between 1025 and 1035, the lands of Vieilles, Beaumont, and Beaumontel. All these were previously held by the abbey of Bernay, which had received them about 1017 from the wife of Richard II (996–1026), the countess Judith, who had held them as dower lands.[4] Among the witnesses of Judith's subsequent charter of 1025 confirming her gifts to Bernay is someone named Humfredus, who may well be Humphrey de Vieilles.[5] As Le Prévost points out, the chronicle of Robert of Torigni mentions a Raoul or Ralph de Beaumont as prior or guardian of the abbey of Bernay, and as a relative of Humphrey (*consanguineo suo*). Ralph de Beaumont may have been both Humphrey's connection to the acquired lands and the instrument of their acquisition, which Le Prévost dates before 1035.[6] It is by no means clear whether the toponym "de Vieilles" was adopted by Humphrey himself or attributed to him anachronistically by later writers.[7] Whatever the case, he was so named because Vieilles, which probably included the forests of Barc and Ouche, was more important than Pont-Audemer.[8] A supporter and frequent companion of both Richard II and Robert I (1027–35),[9] Humphrey married a certain Aubrée, whom Robert of Torigni later identifies as Aubrée de la Haie, heiress of the forest of Brotonne.[10] Humphrey and Aubrée had three sons — Roger, Robert, and William — and a daughter, Dunelme.[11]

Duke Robert's death in 1035 and the succession of his son William the Bastard at the age of seven initiated a period of anarchy, during which the aristocracy seized the opportunity to increase their power and wealth. It was at just this time that the abbey of Bec was founded.

---

4. Fauroux, no. 11. See Bates, *Normandy,* p. 193.

5. Fauroux, no. 35. Auguste le Prévost, *Mémoires et Notes de M. Auguste le Prévost pour servir à l'histoire du Département de l'Eure,* vol. 1 (Evreux, 1862), pp. 200–202; Douglas, *WC,* p. 90.

6. Le Prévost, *Eure* 1:202. Roger "of Beaumont" made a gift to Préaux during the reign of Robert I (Fauroux, no. 88, A.D. 1034–35), thus placing the acquisition of the Beaumont lands before 1035. Roger must have been very young in 1035 since he died sixty years later in 1094.

7. Bates, *Normandy,* p. 113.

8. Le Prévost, *Eure* 1:202.

9. Fauroux, p. 30 and nos. 29, 32, 35(?), 55, 85, 88; cf. 89.

10. Le Prévost, *Eure* 1:201.

11. *Complete Peerage* 7:522, n. a, with references. Roger was the heir; Robert received lands in the Cotentin from the duke and was styled *dapifer* (Fauroux, no. 149 and index); William is listed with his two brothers in an early source (*Gallia Christiana,* 11, *Instrumenta,* col. 201a) but is otherwise obscure. Dunelme's daughter entered religious life at St-Léger de Préaux (*Neustria Pia,* p. 523). See also le Prévost, *Eure* 1:203.

One of Humphrey's neighbors, Roger de Montgomery, seized vast estates from the abbey of Bernay and wrested Troarn and Almenèches from Fécamp. Another neighboring magnate, Roger of Tosny (or Conches), accompanied by his two sons and by Robert I of Grandmesnil, ravaged the lands of Humphrey de Vieilles himself. Humphrey responded by sending his son Roger against the Tosnys and Grandmesnils. In a fierce, prolonged conflict, Roger of Beaumont and his men slew Roger of Tosny and his sons, mortally wounded Robert of Grandmesnil, and thereby secured the Beaumont family lands.[12]

Roger's inheritance passed to him during or shortly after the wars of William's minority (1035–47), which saw the deaths of his brother Robert and both his parents, Humphrey de Vieilles circa 1044–54 and Aubrée circa 1045.[13] Humphrey had founded two monasteries at Préaux, St-Pierre, for men (ca. 1034–35) and St.-Léger for women (ca. 1050),[14] and Roger continued to support them lavishly, while also granting lands to the abbey of St-Wandrille. He built a strong castle at Beaumont-le-Roger, on the hill above Vieilles, which thereafter superseded Vieilles as the family *caput,* and he involved himself in the administration of local justice.[15]

Roger of Beaumont rendered notable service to Duke William, attending his court and advising him as he reestablished the ducal powers after the anarchy of his minority.[16] Orderic reports that Roger "stood by Duke William against all, always faithful . . . in all his views and foresights most like Sulla," suggesting optimistically that Roger had the qualities of the celebrated Roman senator and general.[17] Roger's constant attendance at court[18] and his close association with the duke before 1066 led William to appoint him as head

12. OV 2:40. Orderic Vitalis, "Interpolations," in *Gesta Normannorum Ducum,* p. 158; *Complete Peerage,* loc. cit.
13. *Complete Peerage,* loc. cit.; OV 2:13, and n. 3; Fauroux, no. 149.
14. Fauroux, p. 30 and nos. 88 and 89; *Gallia Christiana,* 11, *Instrumenta,* col. 199; OV 2:12 and 13, n. 3. Chibnall, following Fauroux's conclusion that Humphrey probably died "vers 1050" (no. 149), suggests that St-Léger was founded "probably before 1050."
15. Le Prévost, *Eure* 1:203; Douglas, *WC,* pp. 113, 151–52. In *CDF,* no. 320, there appears a case in which Roger mediates between the abbey of Préaux and a knight who wishes to reclaim his gift to the abbey.
16. Douglas, *WC,* pp. 143–44; OV 2:140; WP 148.
17. Orderic Vitalis, "Interpolations," in *Gesta Normannorum Ducum,* pp. 158–59.
18. Douglas, *WC,* p. 87, n. 1. *Complete Peerage* 7:522. Fauroux, nos. 141, 156, 197, 213, 228, 229, and p. 62, notes, where Roger occurs as the fifth most frequent attestor of Duke William's preconquest acts, behind Roger of Montgomery, William fitz Osbern, Ralph Taisson, and Robert count of Mortain.

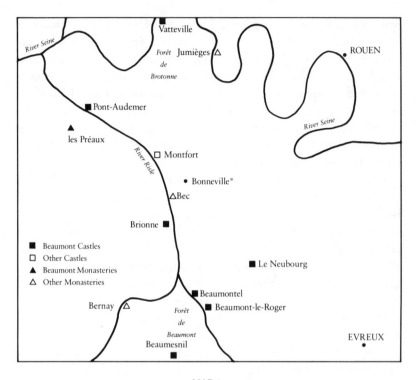

MAP 3.
The Beaumont Castles, Forests, and Monasteries in Normandy
*Original site of the abbey of Bec

of a council of regents to advise Duchess Matilda in overseeing domestic affairs during the duke's venture in England in 1066. William of Poitiers reports that none of the neighboring lords dared make any incursions into Normandy during William's absence.[19] Besides his service to Matilda, Roger contributed sixty ships[20] and his son Robert of Beaumont to the English endeavor.[21]

In about 1045 or 1046, Roger had married Adeline, sister of Count Hugh of Meulan.[22] David Bates reports that Adeline and Hugh's

19. WP 260.
20. "Brevis Relatio," in *Scriptores Rerum Gestarum Willelmi Conquestoris,* ed. J. A. Giles (London, 1845), p. 22. The list of men who contributed ships is, however, late and perhaps garbled; it is plausible on the whole, but might well contain inaccuracies. See OV 2:144, n. 1.
21. WP 192.
22. Le Prévost, *Eure* 1:203. Orderic reports the marriage of Adeline's sister Duda to William of Moulins-la-Marche, a French lord. Of her two sons, Simon and Hugh, the

father Waleran had been a boyhood friend of Roger of Beaumont. Although it is not clear how or why this association occurred, Waleran had been in contact with the Norman ducal line, witnessing ducal charters in the last years of Richard's reign. Nevertheless, he remained a vassal of the French King Henry I, Dreux count of the Vexin, and Odo II count of Blois-Chartres. Although Waleran is known to have fought against Duke William's father Robert, he later joined a rebellion against King Henry I in the Ile-de-France, was expelled from his estates, and, it appears from charter attestations, took refuge with the Beaumonts. These events occurred between 1041 and 1045,[23] and shortly after this time the marriage must have occurred. Given Waleran's precarious circumstances, the marriage was no doubt more advantageous to him than to his new son-in-law. Robert of Beaumont was born about 1046 – 48,[24] and his brother Henry and sister Aubrée soon after.[25] Robert was thus the oldest son of a rapidly rising Norman aristocratic family, which had acquired and preserved impressive estates in the heart of Normandy through the resourcefulness of Robert's grandfather and the abilities of his father.

Robert's father provided for him an example of loyalty and service to the duke, and skill in the administration of a wealthy lordship. Roger of Beaumont introduced his son to the ducal court when Robert was only a child. A "Robert son of Roger," probably Robert of Beaumont, attested a notice of gifts to Marmoutier in autumn 1055, which was also attested by Duke William, Archbishop Maurilius, and other notables of the ducal entourage. In about 1050 – 60 Robert — together with his father Roger, Duke William, and the duke's sons and half brothers — attested a grant by the duke's stepfather, Herluin of Conteville, associated with the founding of Grestain Abbey.[26] Thus Roger was initiating young Robert into the role of a great Norman

latter lived until at least 1119, when he was fighting against France on the side of Henry I. OV 3:132 – 33 and n. 3.

23. See Bates, *Normandy*, pp. 66, 71, 74; Fauroux, nos. 104, 105, 107.

24. *Complete Peerage* 7:523 suggests about 1046: this date may be too early, since William of Poitiers (p. 192) describes him at the Battle of Hastings as newly knighted (*tiro*) and engaging in combat for the first time in his life.

25. *Complete Peerage* 7:523, n. e, gives convincing evidence of Aubrée's existence and her office as abbess of St-Léger de Préaux.

26. Houth, "Robert Prud'homme," p. 801; Charles Bréard, *L'abbaye de Notre-Dame de Grestain* (Rouen, 1904), p. 199; Fauroux, p. 30 and no. 137 (cf. index, p. 534, where "Robert son of Roger" is identified as Robert of Beaumont; it is unlikely to have been Roger of Montgomery's son, Robert of Bellême, who was unborn or an infant in

magnate at an early age, introducing him to the duties that would be required of him in the future. In 1066 Roger sent his son, now in his late teens or perhaps just twenty, to represent the Beaumont family in the army that the duke was assembling for the conquest of England.

The Norman political arena was a scene of conflict and strife, where a baron's loyalty depended in considerable measure on his self-interest. But in the years just preceding and following the Norman Conquest, the aristocracy's self-interest could best be served by loyalty and service to the duke, for their own enrichment and his. Thus the young Robert turned toward the ducal service, which seemed his heritage as the eldest son of a great Norman family and as the son of one of the duke's first counselors, Roger of Beaumont. Since Roger lived throughout the remainder of William's reign and into the reigns of King William Rufus and Duke Robert Curthose, Robert of Beaumont enjoyed the advice and support of his father for perhaps another quarter century or more.

At Hastings, young Robert of Beaumont, newly knighted,[27] commanded a battalion on the Norman army's right flank, which he led in an audacious charge that terrified the English.[28] He may have fought on with William's army in the campaigns of 1068–69 in the west and north of England. Although he is not mentioned in the sources, his Domesday holdings in Northamptonshire, Leicestershire, and, especially, Warwickshire[29] suggest his participation in William's northward march in 1068 from Westminster through Warwick into Yorkshire. As William met the uprisings of the English, he fortified and garrisoned strategic places and rewarded his vassals with confiscated lands. Robert's brother Henry probably crossed to England with the

---

1055: ibid., no. 219; *Complete Peerage* 7:689 and n. g; cf. Fauroux, no. 213, a ducal confirmation for Jumièges of 1055–66, where the attestation of "Rogerus Belmontis" is followed by that of "Rotbertus filius ejus." Fauroux's date of 1050 for the founding of Grestain Abbey (p. 30) is almost certainly too early. It is based on unsupported statements in *Neustria Pia* (p. 528), *Gallia Christiana* (11, col. 843: "post annum 1050"), and Bréard, *Grestain,* pp. 16, 20, and 24. For a criticism of Bréard's date, see le Marquis Louis de Saint-Pierre, "L'abbaye de Grestain et ses fondateurs," in *La Normandie Bénédictine au temps de Guillaume le Conquérant* (Facultés Catholiques de Lille, 1967), pp. 265; 273, n. 14.

27. WP 192, followed by OV 2:174–75. Both sources use *tiro,* which Foreville translates as "jeune" and Chibnall as "newly knighted."

28. WP 193.

29. Levi Fox, "The Honor and Earldom of Leicester: Origin and Descent, 1066–1399," *EHR* 54 (1939): 386–87.

Conqueror in 1067,[30] for he received the castellanship of Warwick Castle in 1068.[31] Robert himself had by 1086 acquired some eighty manors worth a total of about £254 a year (including mills and woods): five manors in Leicestershire worth about £35, three in Northamptonshire worth about £10, and sixty-six in Warwickshire worth about £206.[32]

As William distributed the English lands, he made lavish grants to only a few of his magnates, and the Beaumonts were by no means the most richly endowed. Roger of Beaumont's Domesday holdings amounted to a total of slightly less than £80 in Gloucester and Dorset. Henry of Beaumont, castellan of Windsor, held no lands whatever in 1086. And even Robert's estates, worth £254 a year, are dwarfed by those of the Conqueror's greatest Domesday magnates. The pioneering Domesday analysis of William J. Corbett, as expanded by later scholars, has demonstrated that half the lands granted in lay tenure by 1086 were held by only ten or eleven men with estates ranging in annual value from £750 to about £3050, the remainder being held by some 160 favored followers,[33] among whom were Robert and Roger of Beaumont. The process of redistribution resulted in the spectacular enrichment of a comparatively small number of continental magnates, primarily Normans who had risen to power as William secured his ducal rights and hence were great landowners in both realms.[34] Emile Houth alleges that Robert of Beaumont became earl of Leicester shortly after the battle of Hastings, implying that Robert immediately became one of William's great men. The evidence he cites is the Domesday material just listed and a passage in Orderic Vitalis saying that

30. *Regesta* 1, p. xxi: Itinerary of William I.

31. OV 2:218–19. But Henry held no Domesday estates whatever.

32. Cf. *Complete Peerage* 7:523 and n. g. Although Roger of Beaumont was reported never to have gone to England, he received, before 1086, small grants in Gloucester and Dorset, and probably also in Warwick; he grants five hides in Arlescott, Warwick, to the abbey of Préaux (*CDF,* no. 318). But by 1086 Robert held all the Warwick lands.

33. *Cambridge Medieval History,* vol. 5 (Cambridge, 1926, reprinted 1968), pp. 508–11, as amended by C. Warren Hollister, "Magnates and 'Curiales' in Early Norman England," *Viator* 8 (1977): 65; and David Bates, "The Character and Career of Odo, Bishop of Bayeux (1049/50–1097)," *Speculum* 50 (1975): 10. Hollister lists ten magnates holding lands worth £750 or more; he omits William fitz Osbern whom Corbett includes but who was dead in 1086. According to Corbett's classification system of Class A baronies (over £750 per year), Class B baronies (10 at £400–£650 per year), Class C baronies (24 at £200–£400 per year), Class D baronies (36 at £100–£200 per year), and Class E baronies (90/100 at less than £100 per year), Robert of Meulan's Domesday holdings fall toward the bottom of Class C and Roger's are Class E.

34. Douglas, WC, pp. 266, 270.

Robert at some time became earl of Leicester.[35] But nowhere in the Domesday Book does Robert of Beaumont (or of Meulan) appear as earl of Leicester.

William attempted to maintain in his incipient Anglo-Norman state the cohesion among his nobles that he had achieved in Normandy before the invasion. From 1070 to his death in 1087, the same Norman magnates appear in his court on both sides of the channel, and Robert and Henry of Beaumont are among them.[36] Their father Roger, however, remained consistently in Normandy, leaving the exploitation of the new opportunities in England to his sons, while maintaining his close association with William at the Norman court.[37] William entrusted the guardianship of one of his daughters, Adelaide, to Roger[38] and charged him with the imprisonment of Earl Morcar of Northumbria after the earl's rebellion in 1071.[39]

During the remainder of his reign William faced rebellions in England and Normandy and attacks by neighboring rulers. In 1077 Philip I of France took direct control of the French Vexin, succeeding a line of counts of the Vexin who had usually been friendly to the Norman duke.[40] And shortly thereafter the Conqueror's son Robert Curthose demanded that William immediately cede him his inheritance of the duchy of Normandy. Curthose rallied to his cause many of the sons of the Norman magnates associated in William's government, and, with the help of King Philip, tried to take the duchy by force. The rebel force defeated William at Gerberoi in January 1079.[41] Roger's sons Robert and Henry, however, took no part in the uprising. Along with Roger and other Norman magnates, they helped to arbitrate the disagreement, inducing Robert Curthose to repent his

35. Houth, "Robert Prud'homme," p. 804.
36. Douglas, WC, pp. 286–87; Regesta 1, pp. 1–76 (nos. 1–288b). On the attestations of the greatest English landholders, see Hollister, "Magnates and 'Curiales,' " p. 65. Robert of Meulan attested some twenty-three acts of William the Conqueror calendared in the Regesta 1 and identified as authentic, while Henry attested eleven; both rank among the Conqueror's dozen most frequent lay attestors.
37. Douglas, WC, pp. 286–87. William frequently invited Roger to come to England and receive grants of land, as William of Malmesbury reports, but Roger refused to covet foreign possessions (GR 2:482). Roger attests Regesta 1, nos. 2, 25a, 69, 72, 73, 75, 76, 92a, 105, 116–19, 123, 125, 146a, 150, 168, 170, 172, and 173, all certainly or probably issued from the Continent.
38. OV 3:114; "Adelidis"; Douglas, WC, pp. 393–95.
39. OV 2:256–58.
40. Ibid., 4:xxx–xxxiii.
41. Above, Chapter 2 at nn. 179–85. As we have seen, Philip I appears to have shifted to William I's side by the time of the siege of Gerberoi.

errors and implore the royal clemency. In return, William renewed his promise to Curthose of the succession to the duchy of Normandy.[42] The negotiators achieved a finely balanced settlement: William, just defeated, agreed to absolve the rebels (some of whom were sons of the arbitrators), while Robert Curthose gave up the advantage of his victory at Gerberoi. The Conqueror saved face, his son lost nothing by his rebelliousness, and peace was restored with a minimum of discord.

Robert and Henry of Beaumont are notable as the only sons of living magnates cited specifically as not allied with Curthose. They are even more notable as being, along with their father, among the negotiators. Thus at Roger's side, Robert was learning the skills of negotiation, diplomacy, and compromise, and seeing how it was done in the midst of high-level political conflict. Some aspects of international diplomacy are involved in the agreement, for certainly the approval of the king of France, who was at Gerberoi, was necessary to the treaty. As we have seen, Anselm may also have been involved at an early stage in the negotiations.

The documentary evidence provides further indication of the growing involvement of the Beaumont sons in the Conqueror's regime. Henry of Beaumont accompanied his father Roger to William I's court at Le Mans in 1073, and both seem to have been in the Conqueror's company at the dedication of St-Etienne, Caen, on 13 September 1077.[43] Henry of Beaumont also attested a royal grant at St-Georges de Boscherville on 31 January 1080, while his brother Robert attested with the king a charter of Odo bishop of Bayeux, probably in 1079.[44] Roger and Robert attested a royal confirmation for St-Etienne, Caen, sometime between 1066 and 1077, another such confirmation between 1067 and 1079, and a royal grant of 1074 in favor of the bishopric of Bayeux. Robert and Henry attested, without their father, a royal confirmation of 1078–81 on behalf of Cluny.[45] At Easter 1080, after the peace between William I and Robert Curthose, Roger and both his sons were present at the king's court in Normandy, and

---

42. OV 3:110; David, *Robert Curthose*, pp. 28–29. See above, Chapter 2, at nn. 179–85, for Anselm's possible involvement in negotiations with Philip I.

43. *Regesta* 1, no. 69; *Les actes de Guillaume le Conquérant et de la Reine Mathilde pour les abbayes caennaises*, ed. Lucien Musset (Caen, Société des Antiquaires de Normandie, 1967), no. 3, p. 58.

44. *Regesta* 1, nos. 121, 169; *Actes*, ed. Musset, no. 13.

45. *Actes*, ed. Musset, no. 4, p. 62 (cf. 4 A bis, p. 65, where Roger, Robert, and Henry all attest, but on an untrustworthy list); no. 5, p. 67 = *Regesta* 1, no. 116; ibid., nos. 76, 192.

all three Beaumonts attested a royal charter for Lessay issued at Caen on 14 July 1080 and a royal confirmation for Troarn between 1079 and 1081.[46] At about that time, or perhaps somewhat later, the Beaumont abbey of St-Pierre, Préaux, received a royal charter confirming various lands, churches, and tithes in England, the principal donors being the king, Roger of Beaumont, and Roger's two sons.[47] These documents suggest a steady strengthening of the bonds between the Conqueror and the Beaumont sons, associating them more firmly with the friendship between William and Roger.

The Conqueror's charter for Lessay of 14 July 1080[48] is the latest datable document that Robert attests as "Robert of Beaumont." He acquired the county of Meulan shortly thereafter and thenceforth always attested with his comital title. G. H. White's closely reasoned study of Robert's accession to the countship has been accepted by subsequent scholars,[49] and his conclusions remain valid, despite his having based much of his argument on a charter that has since been

46. *Regesta* 1, nos. 123, 125, 173. Robert of Beaumont witnessed another royal act in Normandy in 1080: ibid., no. 127.

47. Ibid., no. 130, dated by Davis about 1080; the Beaumont sons are styled anachronistically Robert count of Meulan and Henry earl of Warwick, which Davis, and the editors of *Regesta* 2 (p. 393), presume to be a copyist's addition. The copyist at Préaux did not include the witnesses, but the death dates of the two addressees, Remigius bishop of Lincoln (1092) and Robert of Oilly (ca. 1093) make it possible that the charter was issued by William II rather than William I. If so, the titles of the Beaumont brothers would be appropriate. Moreover, the charter ascribes the gifts of tithes from a Northampton-shire manor and three Warwickshire manors jointly to Robert "count of Meulan" and Henry "earl of Warwick," implying either that the manors were held in some kind of joint tenancy unnoticed in Domesday Book or that Robert had granted some of the tithes before ceding the manors to Henry about 1088, and that Henry had granted the remainder of them afterward (or, as the current holder, was endorsing his brother's earlier gifts). All four manors — Norton (Northants.), Hill Moreton, Whitchurch, and Harbury (incorrectly identified in *Regesta* 1 as "Great Harborough") — were held by Robert of Meulan in 1086: DB 1, 224b, 239b (bis), 240; and all four passed subsequently to the earl of Warwick: *VCH Northampton* 1, 371; *Liber Feodorum* 1, 508 and passim.

48. Davis, in his notes to *Regesta* 1, no. 125, speaks of a "pretended original" yet accepts the charter's authenticity nevertheless. Many of Davis's critical judgments have since been superseded, but his *Regesta*, if used with caution, will remain indispensable until the publication of a thorough edition of the charters of William I and II based on modern critical standards and an exhaustive search through the French and English archives. Professor David Bates, who is preparing a new and much needed edition of William I's *acta* along these lines, is certain of the authenticity of no. 125: Mathew Bennett, "Poetry as History: The 'Roman de Rou' of Wace as a Source for the Norman Conquest," *ANS* 5 (1983): 38n.

49. G. H. White, "Robert de Beaumont and the Comté of Meulan," *The Genealogist*, N.S., 36 (1919): 173–78; Lucien Musset, for example, uses White's conclusions as a benchmark for dating William I's charters for the abbeys of Caen (e.g., *Actes*, pp. 27, 69, 112), citing *Regesta* 2, p. 393, which itself cites the above article by White. His article is also cited, and its conclusions accepted, in the *Complete Peerage* 7:524 and n. b; 12, pt. 2, app., p. 4 and n. e.

shown to be a forgery. He concluded correctly that Robert inherited Meulan directly from his uncle, Hugh II, who retired from his comital responsibilities to become a monk of Bec. This contradicts the earlier view that Roger of Beaumont succeeded Hugh II as count of Meulan in right of his wife, Adeline of Meulan (Hugh's sister), and that Robert became count only after his mother Adeline's death. White further concluded that Robert inherited Meulan sometime between 14 July 1080 and 25 December 1081.[50] Because White depended on a forged charter and overlooked certain additional evidence bearing on Robert's advancement, the question is worth reinvestigating.

White's *terminus a quo*, 14 July 1080, can be accepted, based as it is on Robert's attestation as "Robert of Beaumont" on William I's authentic charter of that date.[51] White's *terminus ad quem*, however, is insecurely based on Robert's attestation as count of Meulan on a charter for Westminster Abbey purportedly issued by William I at Westminster in 1080 or 1081 "in Natali Domini."[52] As Pierre Chaplais observes, "the paleographical evidence makes its authenticity impossible."[53] Any hope that the charter's dating clause and witness list might be salvaged is dashed by the virtual impossibility of Robert's having attended a Christmas court at Westminster in either 1080 or 1081.

The charter's date range was deduced from the attestations of Odo of Bayeux, who was in captivity between 1082 and William I's death in 1087, and William bishop of Durham, who was elected on 9 November 1080 and consecrated some weeks later at the king's Christmas court.[54] But Simeon of Durham, our best authority on Bishop

50. White's further suggestion, that Robert's advancement probably occurred before 5 June 1081, is doubtful; White guesses that when Orderic reported that Robert ruled Meulan for "more than twenty-seven years" he meant "more than thirty-seven years," and points out that precisely thirty-eight years elapsed between 5 June 1081 and Robert's death on 5 June 1118: op. cit., from Orderic, "Interpolations," *Gesta Normannorum Ducum*, p. 159; Orderic further states that Robert inherited Meulan from his uncle, Hugh.

51. Robert occurs without title on two other, roughly concurrent, *acta: Regesta* I, no. 123, notice of a suit heard by the Conqueror in Normandy at Easter (12 April) 1080, in the presence of Roger of Beaumont and his sons Robert (untitled) and Henry; cf. no. 127, A.D. 1080, attested by "Rotberti Belm[ontensis]."

52. *Regesta* I, no. 143.

53. Pierre Chaplais, "The Original Charters of Herbert and Gervase Abbots of Westminster," in *A Medieval Miscellany for Doris Mary Stenton*, ed. Patricia M. Barnes and C. F. Slade (London, Pipe Roll Society, 1962), p. 95; note the suspicious similarity of the dating clause of *Regesta* I, no. 143, to those of two other Westminster forgeries, nos. 233 and 234.

54. *ASC*, A.D. 1082: *John Le Neve, Fasti Ecclesiae Anglicanae, 1066–1300*, vol. 2, ed. Diana E. Greenway (London, 1971), p. 29.

William's presence at the 1080 Christmas court, reports that the court
met not at Westminster but at Gloucester, where the king participated
in an important ecclesiastical council.[55] We know very little about
William I's itinerary in 1081, and there is nothing to indicate his
whereabouts at Christmas of that year. But Robert attested as count of
Meulan at King Philip I's 1081 Christmas court in France, witnessing
a document dated 6 January 1082.[56] Unless one supposes that Robert
rushed from William's court at Westminster to Philip's court in France
during the twelve-day Christmas season of December 1081–January
1082, or that William I's 1080 Christmas court migrated all the way
from Westminster to Gloucester, the Westminster Christmas charter
can be dismissed on the grounds of its witness list and dating clause
alone. Nevertheless, the dismissal of William's "Christmas charter"
and the addition of Philip's leaves White's *terminus ad quem* essentially unchanged; if Philip's charter can be trusted, Robert was clearly
count of Meulan by 6 January 1082.

Similarly, additional backing can be provided for White's view that
Robert inherited Meulan from his uncle Hugh II rather than his
mother Adeline. Orderic reports that Abbot Mainer of St-Evroul, having obtained a confirmation charter from William I in England about
31 May 1081, returned to St-Evroul and placed the confirmation in
the abbey's archives, after which Queen Matilda came to the abbey
and granted it donations, and Adeline, wife of Roger of Beaumont,
presented further gifts.[57] If Orderic's notices of these benefactions can
be taken to reflect a chronological sequence, or even roughly concurrent gifts, then Adeline, whose obituary is dated in the cartulary of
St-Nicaise de Meulan as 8 April (no year provided), cannot have died
before spring 1082, more than three months after Robert attested as
count at Philip's Christmas court.[58]

---

55. Apart from Simeon, the early sources are utterly silent on the subject of the 1080
Christmas court. Simeon states that Bishop William was consecrated at Gloucester on 3
January 1081 in the presence of the king and all the bishops of England: *Opera Omnia*,
ed. Thomas Arnold, 2 vols. (RS, 1882–85), 1:119, 170; cf. *Fasti* 2, ed. Greenway, p. 29,
and, on the Gloucester council, *Councils and Synods with Other Documents Relating to
the English Church*, 1, ed. D. Whitelock, M. Brett, and C. N. L. Brooke (Oxford, 1981),
pt. 2, pp. 629–32. On William's custom of holding Christmas courts at Gloucester,
ASC, A.D. 1087.

56. *Recueil des actes de Philippe I^e, roi de France*, ed. M. Prou (Paris, 1908), p. 27.

57. OV 3:232–40 and 232 n. 1; *Regesta* 1, no. 140; cf. nos. 137–39.

58. *Recueil des chartes de Saint-Nicaise de Meulan*, ed. Emile Houth (Paris, 1924),
p. 194, for the obituary. White rightly pointed out that Roger of Beaumont never attested
as count of Meulan: "Robert de Beaumont," p. 174.

Robert's predecessor, then, was Hugh II of Meulan, who died as a monk of Bec under Anselm. Hugh was once thought to have entered religious life about 1077,[59] but his probable attestation of an act of Philip I dated 1080 suggests that the date be advanced.[60] Indeed Hugh seems to have died shortly after his retirement to Bec. His obituary was recorded as 15 October,[61] and Abbot Anselm, in a letter from England that was very probably written in spring 1081, compliments the monks of Bec on their handling of arrangements arising from Hugh's death.[62] Thus, in all likelihood Hugh died on 15 October 1080.[63]

A further hint is provided in the statement of William of Malmesbury that Robert "bought from the king of France the castle called Meulan, which Hugh son of Waleran, his mother's brother, had held."[64] This passage, which provides still further confirmation that Robert was Hugh's direct successor, suggests the passing of a period of time between Hugh's retirement and Robert's installation in Meulan on the payment of a relief to Philip I. Robert's attestation of the

59. *L'art de vérifier les dates*, 12:149.

60. *Cartulaire de l'abbaye de Saint-Martin de Pontoise*, ed. J. Depoin (Pontoise, 1901), p. 312, n. 320: "Par une confusion assez explicable, le copiste a écrit HUGO MELEDUNENSIS. Le vicomte de Melun était alors Ourson II, qui souscrit à ce diplôme." The act was issued at Melun.

61. *L'art de vérifier les dates*, 12:149.

62. AEp. 118 (see Chapter 2, n. 220): Anselm sends greetings to Hugh of Gournay, who had participated in the negotiations between William I and Robert Curthose in 1079 but was now evidently a monk of Bec (Robert of Torigni, "Interpolations," in *Gesta Normannorum Ducum*, p. 277, reports that Hugh de Gournay retired to Bec); Anselm also states that he had just recently attended William's Easter court in England and planned to obtain a general confirmation of Bec's English lands at the coming Pentecost court before returning. Anselm and William were both almost certainly in Normandy throughout 1079, as we have seen, and Anselm attested William I's charters at Caen on 7 January, 31 May (probably), and 14 July 1080 (*Regesta* 1, nos. 120, 172, 125; see *Regesta* 2, p. 394, for the dating of no. 172). But William was apparently in England through much or all of 1081 (3 January at Gloucester: Simeon, *Opera*, 1:119, 170; February in London: *Regesta* 1, no. 135; and [probably] 31 May at Winchester: ibid., nos. 138–40). He seems to have been in England during parts of 1082 (ibid., nos. 147, 149) but was apparently in Normandy by 24 June (ibid., nos. 145, 146), twelve days after Pentecost (12 June). It is, of course, possible that William crossed to Normandy during this twelve-day period, or that the Pentecost court in England that Anselm anticipated never occurred. The letter can, nevertheless, be dated most plausibly to 1081, shortly after Easter (4 April). The reference to the general confirmation of English possessions suggests that this was Anselm's first visit to England, again making 1081 the more plausible date (see Chapter 2, n. 220).

63. The evidence for the dating of Epistle 118 makes 15 October 1081 an unlikely but possible alternative, which would also be consistent with the *terminus ad quem* of Robert's advancement to the countship.

64. *GR* 2:483.

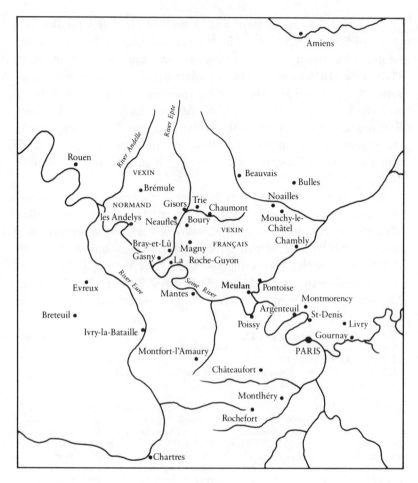

MAP 4.
Meulan, in the French Vexin

charter of 6 January 1082 marks his sole appearance in Philip I's
surviving *acta*, and he may have received his county from Philip at just
that time. His one known attestation of a French royal act may thus have
been his first as count of Meulan.

The county of Meulan, a fief of the king of France, lies on the River
Seine in the Ile-de-France[65] to the northwest of Paris, between the
river fortresses of St-Germain-en-Laye and Mantes.[66] As Freeman

65. Augustin Fliche, *Le Règne de Philippe Ier, roi de France (1060–1108)* (Paris,
1912), p. 105.
66. *Complete Peerage* 7:523 n. d.

describes it, the castle, placed on the steep slope of an isolated hill adjacent to the Seine, dominates a group of islands; bridges join a central island to both banks of the river below the fortress. Recognizing the natural strength of the location, which afforded both an easy crossing of the Seine and an effective position from which to protect it, the French had strengthened Meulan "by all the art of the time."[67] But now this strategic county, adjacent to the demesne of the French kings and very near to Paris, passed to the control of a powerful Anglo-Norman magnate whose primary allegiance was to the *rex Anglorum*.

Augustin Fliche, in his history of Philip I of France, accords the counts of Meulan "the first place" among the counts of Philip's entourage and includes Robert, along with his predecessors Hugh II and Waleran, among the habitual counselors of the French king.[68] Fliche is aware that Prou's collection of Philip I's *acta* contains only the one reference to Robert of Meulan.[69] But since Hugh and Waleran also attest relatively few documents and other counts attest even less frequently, Fliche's conclusion is reasonable in the context of French history. Nevertheless, it seriously underrates Robert's role in Normandy and England, and it obscures the point that Robert's elevation to the countship brought a change in the direction of the loyalties of his predecessors — a change perhaps foreshadowed by the troubles Robert's grandfather Waleran had experienced under King Henry I.[70]

Even when one allows for the many *acta* of Philip I that have not survived, there can be no doubt that Robert devoted his services and allegiance to the Anglo-Norman monarchy, not the French. On 5 September 1082, he was back at the Norman ducal court, where he joined his father and brother as witnesses to a suit adjudicated in the Conqueror's presence.[71] Indeed, Robert's dozen or so attestations of Anglo-Norman royal acts between his elevation to the countship of Meulan (1080–82) and the Conqueror's death in 1087 are exceeded only by those of Roger of Montgomery earl of Shrewsbury, among the lay magnates outside the king's immediate family.[72] Count

---

67. Freeman, *Rufus* 2:183.   68. Fliche, *Philippe Ier*, p. 105.

69. See above, n. 56. Robert attests no *acta* for Philip I's successor, Louis VI (1108–37): Achille Luchaire, *Louis VI le Gros: Annales de sa vie et de son règne* (Paris, 1890).

70. See above, Chapter 3 at nn. 22–23.

71. *Regesta* 1, no. 146a: as "Robert count of Meulan."

72. Ibid., nos. 131, 146a, 150, 168, 170–71, 206, 235(?), 247; *Actes*, ed. Musset, nos. 15, 18. Only eight people attest more of William I's surviving charters (1066–87)

Robert's importance in the Anglo-Norman government was growing swiftly; he had attested only four or five surviving charters between 1066 and 1079, but now he was almost constantly at the Conqueror's side. His brother, Henry of Beaumont, can also be shown to have attended William I's court in the 1080s, but less regularly than Robert and always in Robert's company.[73] As Robert's appearances at William's court increased, those of Roger of Beaumont declined. From 1066 to 1080–82, Roger attested some fifteen royal acts, but from 1080–82 to 1087, he attested only five or six, and he never attested after 1087 for either William Rufus or Robert Curthose.[74] Thus the charters indicate two contributing factors to the growth of Robert of Meulan's importance at the Anglo-Norman court: his own increased status as count of Meulan, and Roger of Beaumont's gradual retirement from court life.

Roger thus appears to have been yielding more and more of the Beaumont political leadership to his eldest son, who was probably about forty at the Conqueror's death in 1087. After a period in which father and sons had combined their efforts in the service of William I, Roger retired from public life to manage his Beaumont estates.[75] Between 1087 and 1088, he formally founded the priory of Holy Trinity, Beaumont, in a charter that renewed all the previous donations he had made with the assent of King William I, in the presence of a large company of witnesses including Duke Robert Curthose, William Bonne-Ame archbishop of Rouen, Gilbert bishop of Evreux, and a number of Roger's vassals.[76] The presence of these vassals,

---

than Robert of Meulan: the Conqueror's wife Matilda, his sons Robert Curthose and William Rufus, his half-brothers Odo of Bayeux and Robert of Mortain, Archbishop Lanfranc, Roger of Montgomery, and Geoffrey bishop of Coutances.

73. *Regesta* 1, nos. 123, 125, 131, 146a, 168, 173, and 192 (Robert occurs on nos. 123, 125, 173, and 192 without his comital title); *Actes*, ed. Musset, no. 15; but Robert joins Henry in only three of Henry's eight attestations for William Rufus: nos. 326, 338a, 372c.

74. *Regesta* 1, passim. While few of the acts calendared in *Regesta* 1 are precisely dated, Robert's accession to the county of Meulan between July 1080 and January 1082 provides a convenient demarcation within the Conqueror's reign.

75. Le Prévost, *Eure* 1:203.

76. Etienne Deville, *Cartulaire de l'église de Sainte-Trinité de Beaumont-le-Roger* (Paris, 1912), pp. ix, 5, 6. Deville says that La Trinité may have existed before A.D. 735, but Roger's charter of 1088–89 is looked upon as a proper charter of foundation. The presence of Gilbert du Pin, killed at Brionne in 1090, is his reason for dating the charter. But see Chapter 4, where I have suggested that the battle of Brionne be redated to about 1088. Thus the most likely date is 1087–88. See Haskins, *Norman Institutions*, p. 68, no. 6, with references.

including William *dapifer* of Formovilla and Morin du Pin with his son Gilbert, suggests that Roger maintained a household to manage his large estates — a miniature version of the household of the king. Robert would inherit this household organization along with the Beaumont estates in Normandy and the Beaumont patronage of both Holy Trinity, Beaumont, and the abbeys of St-Pierre and St-Léger de Préaux. A part of his inheritance, too, was a certain interest in the abbey of Bec, to which Roger had made donations between 1041 and 1066 of the tithe of the forest of Brionne.[77]

But in 1087, Robert's importance as count of Meulan overshadowed his future role as lord of Beaumont. When in late summer 1087 Philip I's garrison at Mantes raided and pillaged Normandy, Robert was in a position to render invaluable aid to William's campaign of retaliation by providing a strategic base of military operations and support at Meulan. William launched his expedition in August 1087 with the purpose, so Douglas believes, of regaining the French Vexin. But in a brutal and devastating attack on Mantes in which he leveled the town, William received a fatal injury and died shortly thereafter.[78] While no account connects Robert of Meulan with William's last venture, the strategic importance of Meulan, Robert's continued close association with William, and the success of the venture itself suggest the possibility of Robert's participation.

Robert of Torigni reports that Robert of Meulan had received from the Conqueror the castellanship of Ivry, a fortress on the frontier between Normandy and the French Vexin.[79] But a charter of 1079 – 82 (probably 31 May 1080), witnessed by Roger of Beaumont as *vicomte*,[80] suggests that the grant was made to Roger, not his son. Nevertheless, the proximity of Ivry to Meulan and the strategic importance of linking Normandy to a base of operations in France in the 1087 campaign suggest that Roger may have passed it on to his son at this time as he gradually retired and withdrew from the court, and probably from active participation in the Conqueror's wars. Whatever the date of Robert's acquisition of Ivry (if we can believe Torigni's statement that Robert indeed gained control of this castle), Beaumont

77. Fauroux, *Recueil*, p. 33, no. 16.
78. Douglas, *WC*, pp. 357 – 58.
79. Robert of Torigni, "Interpolations," pp. 288 – 89; according to Orderic (OV 3: 204), William granted Ivry to Roger of Beaumont, not Robert, and Roger held the castle at the time of William I's death. Whatever the case, the strategic outcome would have been much the same.
80. *Regesta* 1, no. 172. See also OV 4:114.

control of both Ivry and Meulan further suggests that Robert may have played a significant though unrecorded role in the Vexin campaign of 1087.

Having begun his political career during William's English adventure of 1066, Robert of Meulan had thus become by the time of the Conqueror's death in 1087 a major political figure in England and France. He had acquired important lands in England, rewards of the English conquest; he had become the first of the Beaumonts to bear a comital title when he inherited Meulan; and he could expect soon to receive the Norman patrimony. Robert's political importance had grown along with his possessions. Under the tutelage of his influential father, he had secured a place for himself in the Conqueror's inner circle, with the added prestige and power afforded him by a connection with the French court. His father had trained him in the skills of diplomacy and international politics, and he appears to have rendered valuable diplomatic and military aid to his king. While Robert had yet to distinguish himself in the accounts of the chroniclers, he had established himself by 1087 as one of William I's most active *curiales*, had developed the skills necessary for the effective exercise of feudal lordship on an international scale, and had acquired, with his lands, the potential for playing a central role in the government of the Anglo-Norman state.

In accordance with the Conqueror's deathbed bequest, his eldest son Robert Curthose inherited the duchy of Normandy, his second son William Rufus received the kingdom of England, and his youngest son Henry received a large sum of money. While Rufus continued the strong government of his father in the kingdom, the duchy, under Curthose, was torn with disruptive civil strife and private warfare.

One incident involving Robert of Meulan is often cited as an example of this discord in Normandy — the incident with which this book began. Orderic reports that the Conqueror granted to Roger of Beaumont the castellanship of the great ducal stronghold of Ivry, and Robert of Torigni reports that Robert of Meulan held the office of *vicomte* of Ivry under Robert Curthose.[81] But at some time between

81. OV 4:114; Robert of Torigni, "Interpolations," p. 288: note that Roger (not Robert) of Beaumont occurs among the *signa* of *Regesta* 1, no. 172 as *vicecomes;* the document is to be dated 1079–82, and perhaps 31 May 1080: *Regesta* 2: 393, 394. David, *Robert Curthose*, p. 75, cites this incident at Brionne as an example both of the reckless

1087 and 1089, Curthose granted Ivry in fief to William of Breteuil, the great-grandson of Count Ralph of Ivry, half-brother of Richard I of Normandy, and gave the equally important ducal castle of Brionne to Roger of Beaumont to pass on to his son Robert of Meulan. Brionne was conveniently close to the Beaumont lands; Roger of Beaumont seems already to have had some interests in the forest of Brionne, and may even have suggested the exchange. But according to Orderic, Roger was unable to consult his son, who happened to be in England at the time. Returning to Normandy, Robert of Meulan descended on the ducal court in a rage, protesting the duke's failure to consult him and threatening Curthose with vengeance if Ivry were not restored. Duke Robert, with uncharacteristic fortitude, threw Robert of Meulan into prison and took back Brionne, giving it to Robert of Meules.

When this news reached Roger of Beaumont, he came out of retirement, went to the ducal court, and with soothing and conciliatory speeches recalled to the duke his constant fidelity and services to the Conqueror. Guaranteeing Robert of Meulan's good behavior, Roger secured his release, along with the restitution of Brionne, in return for a large sum of money. But Robert of Meules refused to yield the castle, claiming a hereditary right through his grandfather Count Gilbert of Brionne (his great-grandmother Aubrée had built it). Curthose, Roger of Beaumont, and Robert of Meulan then combined forces and took the castle in a very short time, using the novel tactic of shooting burning arrows onto the castle's wooden roof. Robert of Meulan then persuaded Robert Curthose to give Robert of Meules other lands as compensation.[82] This incident, mentioned at the beginning of this book as it appeared in the Bec sources, had even broader implications.

According to Orderic, this is an example of how "the magnates of Normandy expelled the king's [i.e., William I, recently dead] garrisons from their castles."[83] Jean Yver, and Marjorie Chibnall following him, have argued convincingly that Curthose's accession brought

---

grants of castles that Robert Curthose made, which David considers as a contributory factor to the general anarchy in Normandy, and of Robert Curthose's long record of weakness, incompetence, and failure to curb the feudal baronage. Freeman, *Rufus* 1:245, conjectures that Robert of Meulan and Rufus may have planned the incident as a means of increasing the confusion reigning in the duchy.

82. OV 4: 114, 204–10; Le Prévost, *Eure* 1:439–40. Le Prévost dates the seizure of Ivry in 1087 and Robert's return to Normandy in 1090, while David places Robert's return in 1088: *Robert Curthose*, p. 76.

83. OV 4:115.

a revolutionary change in Normandy whereby, through Curthose's weakness, aristocrats asserted their lordship over many formerly ducal castles.[84] As of 1087, Ivry and Brionne were both ducal castles. Roger of Beaumont, while holding Beaumont and Pont-Audemer as fiefs, was merely castellan of Ivry. Brionne, too, was under a ducal castellan (unknown). Since Roger of Beaumont was "gray with age"[85] in 1087, Robert of Meulan may well have been assuming Roger's custodial duties at Ivry by that time. Yver concludes that the exchange of castles was Roger of Beaumont's idea: "By the possession of Brionne, the Beaumonts became masters of the valley of the Risle."[86] The result was that William of Breteuil now held Ivry as a fief, and Brionne became a Beaumont fief. Thus Curthose "diminished his inheritance daily by his foolish prodigality, giving away to everyone whatever was sought."[87] While William of Breteuil had a hereditary claim to Ivry, the Beaumonts had no real claim to Brionne. Roger seems rather to have simply seized his opportunity to strengthen his own position in the Risle valley.

It is difficult to date this event. Curthose and Rufus during these years were engaged in campaigns against each other, culminating in Rufus's conquest of part of the duchy in 1091. Marjorie Chibnall, following Jean Yver, suggests that Robert of Meulan's arrest occurred in 1090, pointing out that Curthose was occupied with hostilities in eastern Normandy in 1089.[88] But Orderic implies that William of Breteuil was in possession of Ivry very shortly after the Conqueror's death, reporting that Ascelin Goel seized the stronghold from William of Breteuil during the second year of Curthose's reign (August 1088 to August 1089).[89] If this is correct, the Beaumonts must therefore have lost Ivry and gained Brionne well before summer 1089. As we shall see in Chapter 4, there were further complications over the castle of Brionne, which add to the complexity of dating the incident.

Robert of Meulan had good reason for being in England in the latter half of 1088. In mid-1088, Rufus had suppressed a baronial

---

84. Ibid.; Jean Yver, "Les châteaux-forts en Normandie jusqu'au milieu du XIIe siècle," *Bulletin de la Société des Antiquaires de Normandie* 53 (1955–56): 67–68.

85. OV 4:207.

86. Yver, "Les châteaux-forts en Normandie," p. 67.

87. OV 4:115.

88. OV 4:204, n. 1; see also Yver, "Les châteaux-forts en Normandie," pp. 66–69, who provides a valuable discussion of the affair and places it in 1090 (without explaining why).

89. OV 4:198.

uprising in England on behalf of Robert Curthose. Rufus then made Henry of Beaumont earl of Warwick in return for his services in putting down the revolt. Henry's elevation, which probably occurred in or shortly after July 1088, was accompanied by a drastic rearrangement of the Beaumont lands in England, in which Henry received Robert's Warwickshire estates.[90] The castle exchange in Normandy, while Robert was in England, thus seems likely to have occurred sometime during the latter half of 1088.

The exchange of Ivry for Brionne may well have seemed more advantageous to Roger of Beaumont than to his son. Brionne, situated on the River Risle midway between the lands of Beaumont and Pont-Audemer, might reasonably have been coveted by Roger of Beaumont, as both Jean Yver and Le Prévost have concluded,[91] in order to consolidate the Beaumont territories into a line of fortifications along the Risle. Ivry-la-Bataille, on the other hand, lies on the River Eure, on the frontier between France and Normandy, south of the Eure's juncture with the Seine. It stands halfway between Beaumont and Meulan, and even closer to the strategic Vexin stronghold of Mantes. Hence for Robert of Meulan, the castle of Ivry represented a link or way station between his Norman and French lands and was likely to be more valuable to him than Brionne in his expected dual role as lord of Beaumont and count of Meulan. Robert's reported, and uncharacteristic, violent outrage suggests a sense of betrayal after his service to Duke William and Duke Robert, and also a feeling of frustration at the thwarting of his plans to connect his two most important domains, Meulan and Beaumont, by means of Ivry.

Robert of Meulan also possessed the means of carrying out his purported threat of vengeance upon Curthose. His position as count of Meulan opened the possibility of an alliance with the king of France at any moment Robert of Meulan might choose. The French kings in this period, with very loose control of their castellans in the Ile-de-France, repeatedly allied themselves with marcher lords along the Norman frontier[92] and frequently supported enemies of the duke of

90. *Complete Peerage* 7:523, n. g; 12: 2; app., pp. 2–3; Fox, "Honor and Earldom of Leicester," pp. 386–87; some or all of Robert's Northamptonshire lands also passed to Henry: *VCH Northamptonshire* 1: 371; see also nn. 32 and 47 above. Henry attests *Regesta* 1, no. 325 (after 24 June 1088), as "de Beaumont," and no. 302 (very shortly after the 1088 siege of Rochester) as "earl of Warwick"; the siege was probably concluded in early July: OV 4:134 ("in inicio estatis") and n. 1.

91. Le Prévost, *Eure* 1:439, 203; Yver, loc. cit.

92. Luchaire, *Louis le Gros*, pp. xxvi ff.

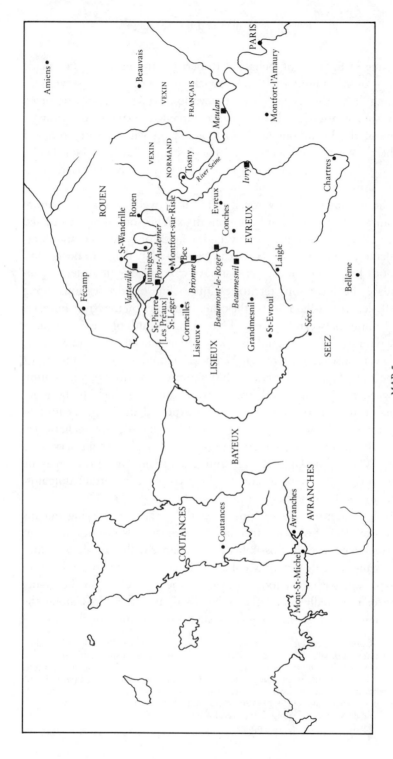

MAP 5.
The Beaumont Castles in Normandy, 1088

Normandy. Robert Curthose or his advisors may have seen the political necessity of limiting this tremendous potential threat to the duchy,
particularly in view of Robert of Meulan's contemporaneous visit to
England, which implied a liaison with Rufus. By transferring the Beaumont holding from Ivry to Brionne, Curthose could more effectively
separate Robert of Meulan's estates, whereas the previous link between
Meulan, Ivry, Beaumont, Pont-Audemer, and Vatteville provided a
direct route into the heart of Normandy for the king of France.

On the other hand, this same link of castles also offered a direct
route into the heart of the Ile-de-France if the Normans chose to use
it. Everything depended on which side Robert of Meulan chose. It
would have been uncharacteristic of Curthose to have providently
foreseen a possible line of military strategy such as that suggested
earlier. If we can credit the descriptions of the chroniclers summarized
in Chapter 1, however, Robert of Meulan would surely have grasped
the strategic implications of the castle configuration. Considering his
continued loyalty to Curthose, despite the Brionne-Ivry incident, he
may well have had the best interests of the duchy in mind when he
objected to the exchange. Curthose's forcefulness in throwing Robert
into prison is highly unusual and, as we shall see in Chapter 4, may
have involved reasons other than the castle exchange. In any event,
having failed to recover Ivry from the duke, Robert of Meulan and his
father decided to a least salvage control of Brionne, with the payment
of a large indemnity.

Although the Conqueror's death resulted in the political separation
of Normandy from England, the aristocracy retained the Anglo-Norman character that William I had given it — a transchannel nobility
with interests in both realms.[93] Immediately the Norman barons faced
the problem of owing fealty to both lords, a situation that Rufus and
Robert Curthose made intolerable by engaging in protracted warfare
until, in 1096, Curthose pawned Normandy to Rufus and departed on
the First Crusade. In the warfare between 1087 and 1096, Robert of
Meulan, like his fellow magnates, had to choose between his English
and Norman lords. Historians have generally agreed that both Robert
of Meulan and Henry of Beaumont sided with William Rufus,[94]
basing their opinions in part on the assumption that the Ivry-Brionne

93. John LePatourel, *The Norman Empire* (Oxford, 1976), passim.
94. *Complete Peerage* 7:524; Le Prévost, *Eure* 1:206–7, 439; Freeman, *Rufus*
1:245.

incident left Robert of Meulan with a permanent grudge against Curthose. But such was not the case, as the documentary evidence reveals.

Although Le Prévost has suggested that Roger of Beaumont retired
from the ducal court at the death of the Conqueror because of his
dislike of Curthose and his followers, nowhere in the chronicles are
these same feelings ascribed to Roger's son.[95] Furthermore, Roger had
been withdrawing gradually from court activities ever since about
1080, as we have seen, and indeed ceased to witness documents from
either court, whereas, as Haskins notes, Robert of Meulan is one of
the most frequent lay witnesses of Robert Curthose's charters from
1087 to 1096. Haskins cautions, however, that the duke's court was
characterized by discontinuity to the point of disintegration.[96] Nevertheless, during the period 1087–93 Robert saw a good deal of Curthose. Despite the paucity of Curthose's *acta*, Robert of Meulan's
attestations place him at the ducal court in autumn 1087,[97] 1088,[98]
1089,[99] 1091,[100] and on three further occasions during the early
1090s.[101] These seven notices of Robert's presence at Curthose's court
exceed those of any of the duke's other followers during the period
1087–96,[102] and they make it clear that Robert of Meulan was repeatedly in attendance at the ducal court until at least 1092.

The charters of William Rufus, although more difficult to date
precisely, indicate that Robert of Meulan was rarely at the English
court during these years. A charter dated 1089 to January 1091, issued
in England, bears the names of both Robert of Meulan and his brother
Henry, now earl of Warwick.[103] Robert's only other possible attesta-

95. Le Prévost, *Eure* 1:203.

96. Haskins, *Norman Institutions*, p. 76. The most frequent lay witnesses are Robert
count of Meulan, William count of Evreux, Robert of Montfort, William of Breteuil,
William Bertran, Enguerran fitz Ilbert, and William of Arques.

97. Ibid., p. 285, reprints a charter dated shortly after September, and witnessed by
Robert of Meulan and "Henricus comes, frater eius."

98. *Regesta* 1, no. 299.   99. Ibid., no. 310.   100. Ibid., no. 317.

101. (1) *Regesta* 2, no. 317b, a charter of Archbishop William of Rouen to Abbot
Anselm, witnessed by Curthose and dated 1091–92, but more probably 1091. (2) Haskins, *Norman Institutions*, pp. 291–92 (no. 7), dated 1091–95, at Lisieux. (3) P. 67
(no. 7), dated 1091–92 (calendared in *Regesta* 1, no. 327, dated February 1092, from the
edition in *Neustria Pia* that omits Robert of Meulan and a number of others from the witness list).

102. Stephanie L. Mooers, " 'Backers and Stabbers': Problems of Loyalty in Robert
Curthose's Entourage," *Journal of British Studies* 21, i (1981): 12; the sixteen men whom
the author regards as "Curthose's *curiales*" each attest between one and four ducal acts
between 1088 and 1095. Robert of Meulan is omitted from the list, perhaps because the
author associates him with William II's court: ibid., p. 7.

103. *Regesta* 1, no. 326.

tion at William's court in this period is on a royal writ issued sometime between 1087 and 1097, and probably toward the end of that date range.[104] Thus the charter evidence places Robert in England on only one occasion between 1087 and 1093, and the visit mentioned by Orderic is otherwise undocumented. Henry of Beaumont, on the other hand, attested for Rufus twice in 1088, again about 1091, and again between 1088 and 1091.[105]

While the small number of surviving documents precludes any firm conclusions, the evidence suggests a possible sequence of events. With Roger in retirement at Beaumont, and Normandy and England now under the rule of separate princes, Robert of Meulan seems to have assumed the responsibility for attending to the family interests at Duke Robert's court while Henry, now earl of Warwick, handled the family's English affairs. It was probably in this period that Robert ceded his Warwick and Northamptonshire lands to Henry. With the Beaumont paterfamilias in retirement, the sons proceeded to divide the family estates. Following more or less the pattern of inheritance that occurs repeatedly in the Anglo-Norman state, the eldest son inherited the Norman patrimony, while most of the family's English acquisitions passed to the second son. The Beaumont's situation was unusual in that Robert received a considerably greater English honor in the course of the Conquest settlement than did his father, but the anomaly was largely rectified when Robert, on inheriting the Beaumont honor in Normandy, granted all or most of his English holdings to Henry.[106]

Roger of Beaumont saw to it that both his sons retained cross-channel footholds: Robert inherited his father's relatively modest Domesday holdings in Dorset (£72 a year) and Gloucestershire (£5 a year), while Henry received from his father a group of estates in southwestern Normandy later known as the barony of Annebecq.[107] Nevertheless, Henry's interests would have centered on his new English

104. Ibid., no. 395. Hugh of Bochland, one of the addressees, occurs only in William II's late or undatable *acta:* nos. 416 (1099), 444 and 455 (1087–1100), and 466 and 471 (1093–1100).

105. Ibid., nos. 302 and 325 (1088: above, n. 90), 320 (ca. 1091), and 326 (1089–January 1091 and witnessed also by Robert of Meulan; above, n. 103).

106. *Complete Peerage* 12: ii, 358–59.

107. Ibid., app., pp. 4–5. The barony included the vills of Rânes, St-Georges-d'Annebecq, and Faverolles (dép. Orne, arr. Argentan, cant. Briouze): according to the Norman Inquest of 1172, the barony enjoyed the service of a fraction over fifteen knights and owed ten knights to the duke: *Red Book of the Exchequer*, ed. Hubert Hall, 3 vols. (RS, 1896), 2:630. Henry also held Norman lands of the bishop of Bayeux: ibid., p. 646.

earldom,[108] whereas Robert count of Meulan and lord of Beaumont[109] concentrated his interests on the Continent. Judging from his
attestations of ducal charters, Robert, following in his father's tradition, served his Norman prince faithfully in the years immediately following the resolution of the quarrel over Ivry.

Robert of Meulan appears to have been firmly on the side of Curthose during the civil wars in Normandy from 1090 to 1092. On 21
April 1090, at the Easter assembly at Winchester, William Rufus declared war on Curthose. His partisans in Normandy instantly rebelled against the duke, winning over a large part of eastern Normandy before June. Robert of Meulan's name does not appear in the
Norman chronicle accounts of this period,[110] but he continued to
attend the ducal court for two more years.

In February 1091, William Rufus crossed to Normandy, and many
of the Norman nobles, including Robert of Bellême, went over to his
side for the gifts and payments that he offered.[111] Philip I of France,
at the appeal of his vassal Duke Robert, had sent an army to the duke's
aid. Philip, however, also abandoned Curthose, accepting a large sum
of money from Rufus and withdrawing.[112] In a desperate position,
Curthose had little choice but to accept a treaty of peace on terms
extremely favorable to Rufus. The duke ceded to Rufus overlordship
of Fécamp, Eu, Aumale, Gournay, and Conches, among others.[113]
The treaty also provided for the elimination of Prince Henry as a
claimant to either realm. According to the anonymous author of the
Brevis Relatio, the two brothers joined forces not only to deprive
Henry of his lands, but to expel him from both realms.[114] They besieged him at Mont-St-Michel and drove him from Normandy, after
which Curthose accompanied Rufus to England to repel an invasion of
England by Malcom, King of Scotland.[115] But finding "little to rely

---

108. The earldom of Warwick included not only the Domesday estates of Robert of
Meulan but also the considerable Domesday holdings of the Englishman Turchill of
Arden (about £120 a year). Altogether it was worth no less than £330 a year exclusive of
gifts that Henry may have received of royal demesne lands; see VCH Northamptonshire
1:387; Judith Green, "William Rufus, Henry I and the Royal Domain," History
64 (1979): 345.

109. The Norman Inquest of 1172 reports that the Beaumont honor had 63½
knights (73½ according to another ms.) and owed 15 to the duke: Red Book of the
Exchequer 2:626.

110. OV 4:220–26.   111. OV 4:236, 250.
112. Fliche, Philippe Ier, pp. 293–94.   113. OV 4:236.
114. "Brevis Relatio," p. 11.   115. OV 4:250–52 and 252, n. 1.

on" in his agreement with Rufus, Curthose left England suddenly, two days before the Christmas festival.[116] He returned to Normandy only to face more rebellions and private wars among his vassals. In short, by 1092 Duke Robert not only had lost the overlordship of a large portion of his duchy, but was visibly failing to maintain control within the remainder.

At this point Robert of Meulan's attestations of ducal charters suddenly cease, and by August 1093 he emerges in the pages of Eadmer's *Historia Novorum* as an adviser of William Rufus.[117] Robert of Meulan's shift in allegiance was evidently motivated not by animosity toward Curthose but by the realization that the duke had proved himself incompetent and was likely to lose the whole of Normandy to his stronger and abler brother. The year 1093 finds Robert of Meulan not only attending Rufus's court in England but playing a major role in the important events surrounding the appointment and consecration of St. Anselm as archbishop of Canterbury.

Robert of Meulan had encountered Anselm long before in Normandy. They appeared as witnesses together on some of the Bec charters, and about 1087–1090 they met in a violent personal encounter involving the liberties of Bec, of major concern to Anselm, and the jurisdiction of the fief of Brionne, which Robert had received in the exchange for Ivry. It was at this first encounter that Robert and Anselm began a period of relations in which Anselm defended the liberties of the church and Robert endeavored to uphold secular political rights. This conflict and its resolution presaged the interplay between *regnum* and *sacerdotium* with which the remainder of the careers of both men was involved.

116. *ASC*, A.D. 1091. The treaty was formally repudiated early in 1094: ibid., A.D. 1094.

117. *HN* 40. See below, Chapter 4 at nn. 165–66.

Four

Private Initiatives:
The Count and the Reluctant
Archbishop-elect at Bec, Brionne,
and Canterbury, 1087–1093

When Robert of Meulan became lord of Brionne in 1087–88, the prosperous and growing abbey of Bec, some three and a half miles from his castle, naturally attracted his attention. He sought to establish his lordship over the abbey, but Bec was by tradition free from ties of subordination to the lord of Brionne. As we have seen, Anselm had been invested and consecrated as abbot of Bec in 1079 without rendering homage to the Conqueror, who then held Brionne in his domain. But Robert of Meulan, when he acquired dominion over Brionne from Robert Curthose, saw an opportunity to bring the monastery under his own jurisdiction, if only Anselm would acquiesce. This issue brought Anselm and Robert into opposition for the first time.

The confrontation was also the first instance in which the private political initiatives of both men emerge clearly from the sources, but it was not to be the last. The tension between Bec and Brionne continued for several years, and was finally resolved only when Anselm had been elected archbishop of Canterbury. In this first confrontation between Anselm and Robert, as in their later ones, the principle of ecclesiastical liberty was pitted against the rights of a lord over the churches in his dominion. The controversy thus prefigured their later and more dramatic conflicts in England.

The only account of this initial confrontation between Anselm and Robert of Meulan is provided in *De Libertate Beccensis Monasterii*. This brief tract was written, as we have seen, by an anonymous monk of Bec shortly after the death of Abbot Boso in June 1136. To a far greater degree than the *vitae* of the abbots of Bec, *De Libertate Beccensis* is narrowly focused on the abbey's liberties and how they were maintained against external challenges.[1]

Chapter 3 discussed the exchange of the castle of Ivry for that of Brionne according to the account of Orderic Vitalis. The Bec monks, however, viewed the exchange from quite a different perspective and added some detail to the account. Lacking the broader political viewpoint of Robert of Meulan, they assumed that Robert would prefer Brionne to Ivry. As the Bec monk Robert of Torigni later relates, Robert of Meulan "by cleverness alone" arranged with Duke Robert Curthose that William of Breteuil might legally be granted possession of the town and castle of Ivry on the condition that Robert of Meulan receive in exchange the ducal castle of Brionne in perpetuity, and Duke Robert receive a very large payment from William of Breteuil.[2] Robert of Meulan also arranged by skillful diplomacy that Roger de Bienfaite, who claimed the ducal castle of Brionne by hereditary right, might receive in exchange for his claim the castle of Le Hommet in the Cotentin — again in exchange for a large cash payment to Curthose.[3] Viewing Robert of Meulan as the shrewd and skillful baron described by the English chroniclers, Robert of Torigni reads purposiveness into Robert of Meulan's arrangements in the Ivry-Brionne exchange. His account sees Robert skillfully gaining Brionne not as a castellanship as he had held Ivry, but as a hereditary fief, and pleasing the spendthrift duke by filling his coffers at the expense of others. From the Bec perspective, Brionne would have seemed more desirable than Ivry, and hence Robert would have bent all his efforts toward acquiring it.

---

1. *DLB* 601.
2. Robert of Torigni, "Interpolations," in *Gesta Normannorum Ducum*, p. 288. Ivry had formerly been held by Count Ralph, half-brother of Richard I of Normandy, and William of Breteuil's great-grandfather, but it became a ducal castle under William the Conqueror.
3. Ibid., pp. 288–89; Thomas Stapleton, *Magni Rotuli Scaccarii Normanniae sub Regibus Angliae* (London, 1840–44), 2: cxxxvi.

De Libertate Beccensis partially confirms Robert of Torigni's account and adds the next chapter. Robert of Meulan wished to possess the abbey of Bec in his own dominion, because it lay within the fief of the castle of Brionne.[4] Once in possession of Brionne, Robert moved at once to secure all of its appurtenances and rights: "being a wily person, Robert first sought the ear of Father Anselm confidentially through messengers, asking for his request to be granted as though he were a suppliant petitioner. He promised a number of enlargements to the church from his own possessions, especially at Brionne."[5]

The petition could have had one of two meanings. Robert of Meulan may have been seeking *avouerie* over the abbey, which would by custom have entitled him to represent the abbot as feudal lord in the abbey's dealings with the secular world, acting in the abbot's place in ducal tribunals and supervising the abbey's own secular jurisdiction over its tenants. Such an official relieved the abbot of much secular responsibility but also deprived him of a great deal of power. Often the *avoué* is the founder of the abbey or his descendant. Yver, in his valuable and detailed study of the problem, has concluded that the practice did not exist in Normandy,[6] But Robert of Meulan, with his widespread associations and contacts outside the duchy, may have been striving to introduce the custom at just this time.

Alternatively, Robert of Meulan may simply have been seeking Anselm's homage and his own recognition as Bec's feudal lord. In view of the *De Libertate*'s concern with homage and professions of obedience throughout, and its repeated insistence that the abbot of Bec traditionally never does homage to anyone for the abbey, homage and fealty were more probably the objectives of Count Robert, although the author never expressly states this. The wording, "he wanted the abbey of Bec to pass into his dominion" (*sub suo dominio*), suggests a

---

4. *DLB* 601: "In the days of this venerable Father Anselm, Robert, count of Meulan, by his own adroitness at the court of Robert, duke of Normandy, gained hold of the castle of Brionne in his own domain. Up to this time it had come under the lordship of the dukes of Normandy." Robert of Torigni did not base his account on *DLB,* for he includes a great deal more detail about the exchange of castles.

5. *DLB* 601: "Voluit Beccense coenobium sub suo dominio possidere, eo quod idem coenobium in fisco Brionensis castri constat aedificatum. Tunc primum, ut astutus homo privatim autem patris Anselmi per nuntios expetiit, rogans et quasi supplex exorans, ut hoc concederet, promittens multas augmentiones ecclesiae de suis rebus, maximeque in eodem castro."

6. Jean Yver, "Autour de l'absence de l'avouerie en Normandie," *Bulletin de la Société des antiquaires de Normandie* 57 (1965): 189–283, esp. pp. 189, 192, 194. Haskins, *Norman Institutions,* p. 36, n. 143, notes the absence of *avouerie* in Normandy.

plea for homage. Moreover, there is evidence from the next generation that Waleran, Robert of Meulan's son and heir, exercised something that he and the monks called *avouerie* over the abbey. He used the title of *advocatus* of Bec in a charter issued in 1131, shortly before the *De Libertate* was written.[7] The author of the *De Libertate* does not mention Waleran's *avouerie* at all, and certainly not as an infringement of Bec's traditional liberties, as we should expect. But the *De Libertate* places great importance on Robert of Meulan's demands on Anselm. Hence it seems probable that Robert demanded Anselm's homage for Bec, and that Waleran's unusual Norman *avouerie* was much more limited in its attributes than was customary in France.

We have already touched on a possibly similar instance when, about 1103, Robert of Bellême demanded homage and fealty of Ralph d'Escures abbot of Séez, and Ralph refused on the grounds of the papal prohibition.[8] But at Bec in the late 1080s, the situation was different in at least two respects. First, and most obviously, the papacy had not yet prohibited the custom. And second, whereas St-Martin of Séez was a Montgomery-Bellême foundation, situated in an area where the churches had long been under the domination of the Bellême family, Bec owed its origin, uniquely, neither to the duke nor to a great aristocratic family. Gilbert of Brionne had been helpful to Herluin, but Bec was Herluin's own foundation and rose gradually through the efforts of its own monks. At Gilbert's death, Brionne had passed into ducal hands, where it had remained throughout the Conqueror's reign. Now, once again, it had become a private lordship, and its new lord, Robert of Meulan, seemed bent on transforming neighboring Bec into a Beaumont family abbey.

Anselm's answer to Robert of Meulan's demand is complex and difficult to interpret. He protested that the abbey was not his to grant but belonged to the lord prince of the Normans.[9] In a general sense this was so. *De Libertate* earlier described the Conqueror as having the authority to "present" the abbacy to Anselm, and affirmed that William "handed over the abbatiate to him by the gift of the pastoral staff as was the custom," but added pointedly that William did not require any homage from him. Nor is it to be supposed that Anselm

---

7. *CDF*, no. 373
8. *GP* 127
9. *DLB* 601: "Hoc non est meum concedere; abbatia ista non est mea, sed domini principis Normanniae, quod illi placuerit, erit."

rendered homage to Curthose, although Anselm would surely have regarded Bec as being under the special protection of the duke. He turned Count Robert aside with the argument that only the duke could act in this matter: "It shall be as it pleases him."

Robert of Meulan's legates replied that the count hoped the grant of the duke would follow easily, but first the count wished to know Anselm's will and to have his assent. The abbot replied, "I can do nothing about this on my own account. But I will tell you that in my opinion the lord count is striving for a difficult goal." When the legates asked why, Anselm at once stated the reasons (which are not given). Apparently Anselm's answer confounded the legates, for they said nothing in reply and returned to Robert of Meulan empty-handed. The count, hearing Anselm's answer, "was astounded at the prudence of the man."[10]

When Anselm told the story to the monks, they were as horrified as if facing total destruction of their abbey. After taking counsel, they went to Duke Robert, clearly with Anselm's knowledge but without the knowledge of the count of Meulan. The arguments that they presented to Curthose are not provided but can be inferred from his reply: "As soon as the duke had heard it all, he shouted in loud rage: 'By God's miracles, what does this mean? What madness is this I hear? Does the count of Meulan want to snatch my abbey from me? Does this traitor wish to take from me by stealth the one thing I love beyond all else? By God's miracles, he won't enjoy the gift I made him for long!' "[11] The monks had thus convinced the duke that the subjection of Bec to the count of Meulan would be a terrible injury to Curthose, even though he had cheerfully permitted Brionne to slip from his grasp into that of the Beaumonts.

The reactions of the magnates at the ducal court were as strong as that of the duke himself. William Crispin, William of Breteuil, and

10. *DLB* 601: "Ille e contra: Concessum principis facile assequi sperat dominus noster, sed voluntatem vestram inde vult scire, et assensum vestrum inde habere. Et abbas: Ego per me de hac re nihil possum facere; dico autem vobis, quod difficilem rem, ut aestimo, elaborat dominus comes. Et legati: Quomodo? Abbas statim edisserit causas: quibus finitis, sine ulla controversia reversi sunt legati ad dominum suum. Comes audiens responsum Anselmi, obstupuit ad prudentiam viri."

11. *DLB* 601: "Cumque haec ad notitiam monachorum venissent, veluti destructionem totius ecclesiae audissent, exhorruerunt, et mature consilium inierunt quidnam contra agerent. Et facillime reperto, ducem Robertum festinanter adierunt, eique causam intimaverunt pro qua venerant. Cumque dux haec audisset, ira commotus magna voce dixit: Per mirabilia Dei quid est hoc? Quae insania est quam audio? Vult comes Mellenti mihi auferre meam abbatiam, illam utique quam super omnes diligo, vult iste traditor mihi subtrahere? Per mirabilis Dei de dono, quod ei feci, non diu gaudebit."

Roger de Bienfaite are reported to have all declared with great and terrible oaths that whatever their parents had given to the church of Bec they would take away, if the count of Meulan held the abbey of Bec in his own dominion, and at the same time they vehemently rebuked the duke because he had handed over "the key to his province [Brionne] to this perfidious creature."[12] The monks, surely coached by Anselm, had convinced the duke and his magnates that Robert of Meulan was a dangerous enemy, who should be not only prevented from extending his dominion over Bec but also stripped of his newly acquired lordship over the castle and lands of Brionne. Although in serious trouble, Robert of Meulan was as yet thoroughly unaware of his predicament.

After a few days, not knowing what the monks had done, the count of Meulan came to Bec with a few men, "wishing to test Father Anselm's feelings on the matter in person." The monks prepared for him as if for the destruction of their abbey. The count began to speak with "affectionate language, in his customary manner." The monks responded that they despised him, and while both sides "strove vigorously in the matter," Anselm intervened, checked their quarreling, and offered himself as a mediator.[13]

Anselm had let the monks take the lead in arguing with Count Robert, and thence intervened seemingly as if a neutral third party. But as one would expect under the circumstances, his mediation was anything but neutral. Seating himself midway between the two contending parties, he said to Robert of Meulan:

My lord Count, you have not the least power to obtain this object you are toiling for, because our lord does not desire it, nor the nobles on whose favors we live, nor, apart from this, have the authorities here and our sons the monks any kind of wish to grant it. This castle [Brionne] is not part of your inheritance, but the gift of your lord prince, who, at any time he wants, may take back his own property. But what need is there to fight between ourselves over this business? Find out the will of our lord and yours, and from this his judgement and orders will follow automatically.[14]

Unlike the count's men or his own monks, Anselm spoke quietly and reasonably — to a man who was himself accustomed to winning his goals through reasonable argument and affectionate language. He

12. *DLB* 601–2: "Simulque ducem vehementer intrepavere, quod clavem suae provinciae homini infideli tradidisset."
13. *DLB* 602.
14. *DLB* 602.

explained to Count Robert, almost as a father to a son, that Robert's objective was hopelessly unrealistic and that to continue to pursue it would not be in Robert's own best interest. Without ever expressing his own opinion on the rights or wrongs of Robert's claim to Bec, Anselm pointed out that it was firmly opposed by the duke, by Bec's aristocratic benefactors, and by the monks themselves. He then reminded Robert, gently but unmistakably, that Brionne itself might be at risk. The Beaumont family had no hereditary claim to it whatsoever, and although Curthose had recently granted it, he might just as readily take it back. Anselm and Robert of Meulan would have been equally aware of the implications and ambiguities of tenurial custom — of the fragility of Robert's lordship over a castlery that until very recently had been ducal and, before that, had been the seat of the Clares. But Anselm turned quickly from his threat to an appeal for peace and mutual affection and ended by suggesting that Robert seek out the opinion of their mutual lord, the duke of Normandy, whose judgment would settle the matter.

Anselm had spoken truly, even warning the count that Curthose opposed his design, but because he said nothing about the Bec delegation to the ducal court, Robert of Meulan would not have realized that the abbot had inside information. Anselm's words, though recorded a half-century later, reflect a style and approach characteristic of many of his letters dealing with issues of ecclesiastical politics. The traits are the composure and quiet reasonableness, the skillful exercise of his responsibilities as God's steward through a penetrating understanding of the situation and its full implications, the plausible and well-aimed threat, and the concluding appeal for friendship and peace.

When Anselm had finished speaking, his monks continued to argue heatedly with the count: "Lord Robert," one of them said, "by that church I swear to you, as long as I and the rest of the monks who now belong to this institution are alive, that by no method or artifice of yours shall the liberty of Bec be subservient to you."[15] Anselm watched in silence while the monks argued further with Count Robert until he went off in a towering rage. After a few days he went to the ducal court.

15. *DLB* 602: "Domine Roberti, per istam ecclesiam juro tibi, quia, quamdiu ego et ceteri monachi, qui modo in hac ecclesia sumus, superstites fuerimus, nullo modo, nulloque ingenio libertas Beccensis ecclesiae per vos ancillabitur . . . Cuius iram pro nihilo monachi duxerunt, ad hoc omnino studentes, ut libertatem suae ecclesiae liberam conservare possent."

The monks well understood that Robert of Meulan would do so. Fearing the duke's fickleness and Count Robert's persuasiveness, they hastened to the ducal court, presumably on Anselm's advice, and warned Curthose that Robert of Meulan was coming, entreating the duke that he not let one word sway him from his promises to Bec. Robert of Meulan arrived in the middle of the interview, and Curthose, greeting him with a laugh, asked how he was getting on with the monks of Bec. Noticing the monks, Robert of Meulan replied humbly that they were on good terms, and that the monks would yield whatever Curthose commanded them to yield. "You lie through your teeth. . . . By God's miracles, you are utterly deceived if you expect me to be so stupid. Would I want to give you my abbey?" Seeing that Anselm had been correct in warning of the futility of his designs, the count abandoned them entirely. A few days thereafter, Curthose revisited Brionne, removed it from the count's hands, and delivered it to Roger de Bienfaite (a Clare descended from Gilbert of Brionne), who claimed it by hereditary right. Thenceforth, "Bec suffered no disturbance from this affair," and Anselm continued to rule the abbey "dextrously."[16]

Anselm's handling of the event demonstrates his diplomatic skill and perceptiveness. Although he had been exercising authority over the Bec monks for more than a quarter century, as prior and abbot, he now permitted them to take the lead — to argue contentiously with the count and his men and to go on secret missions to the duke. The monks, bound to their abbot by the strictest ties of obedience, were not acting on their own, nor do Anselm's words suggest any disinterest or misunderstanding of the issue. The account in *De Libertate Beccensis* demonstrates that he used the very weapons against Count Robert that the count himself was known for: soft and affectionate words, delay, and subtle maneuvers behind the scene. When Robert of Meulan went to the ducal court, he found he had met his equal. Anselm had convinced Curthose that the count was a traitor, and the duke took back the castle of Brionne.

Orderic Vitalis provides another, quite different version of the story. Unaware of Anselm's connection with the event, Orderic begins by saying that Robert of Meulan, puffed up by the gifts and promises of King William Rufus of England, haughtily objected to the exchange

16. *DLB* 602.

of Ivry for Brionne. The count shouted angrily that if Curthose would not rescind the exchange, he would be sorry. Curthose flew into a rage, had the count seized, threw him into prison, and gave Brionne to Robert son of Baldwin (fitz Gilbert of Brionne) to guard.[17] But the Bec account is far more in keeping with the cautious and skillful approach to politics attributed to Robert of Meulan by other sources, and the details of Orderic's account therefore seem improbable. Writing from southern Normandy, Orderic lacked the knowledge of the monks of Bec and hence their understanding of the dispute. But the monks of Bec, vitally concerned with the welfare of their abbey, lacked Orderic's larger perspective. While a dispute over Ivry and Brionne is likely, as we have seen from the strategic importance of the castle of Ivry to Robert of Meulan's holdings, and ultimately to the defense of the duchy, it is probably not the sole cause of Robert's imprisonment. Orderic and the Bec writers are each telescoping events in a different way.

A possible sequence of events suggests itself from the three accounts: William of Breteuil made good his ancestral claim to the ducal castle of Ivry, in exchange for which Curthose granted Brionne to Roger of Beaumont, to be passed on to his son Robert on his return from England. It may well have been left unclear whether Robert was to be castellan or lord of Brionne, since Curthose does not always seem to have thought clearly about such matters. But the proximity of Brionne to the other Beaumont centers would have caused it to drift, under Curthose's sleepy eyes, into Beaumont lordship. Then Robert of Meulan, having negotiated the transfer of his Warwickshire and Northamptonshire lands to his brother Henry, returned to Normandy to assume effective control of his aged father's dominions. While objecting to the granting away of Ivry, Count Robert nonetheless tried to impose his lordship on Brionne — evidently hoping to transform both from castellanships to lordships. Anselm appears to have been more clearly aware of Count Robert's plans than was the duke himself, for he reminded Robert that Brionne was not his hereditary domain, and suggested that his aggression against Bec might cost him the whole lordship. Robert of Meulan, though, seemed confident that the pliable duke would grant his request for authority over Bec. Rather than flying into a rage, which was not his style, Robert of Meulan shrewdly and cautiously approached the duke, just as he had approached An-

17. OV 4:204. Baldwin fitz Gilbert was the brother of Richard de Bienfaite. See Appendix B.

selm. But Anselm outwitted him, and the duke was incited to such a state of rage that he seized Brionne and, as Orderic reports, threw Robert of Meulan into prison.

If Orderic is correct in saying that Robert of Meulan had just returned from England, Anselm and his monks may have played upon the duke's fears of an oncoming invasion of Normandy by King William Rufus — an invasion that did in fact take place in 1091.[18] They may also have played on the resentment of Roger de Bienfaite[19] that Robert of Meulan should be asserting prerogatives of lordship over a castle that had once belonged to Roger's grandfather.[20] William of Breteuil, another of the three barons whom the Bec writer identifies as being enraged at Count Robert's behavior, cannot have been pleased to learn that while the count was seeking the return of Ivry, he was also tightening his grip on Brionne.[21] All three magnates were among the friends of Bec whom Anselm had taken pains to cultivate, and all, for whatever reasons, leapt to Anselm's support. The Beaumonts had to salvage what they could, and that was the castle of Brionne.

Orderic contends that Curthose gave Brionne to Robert of Meules, son of Baldwin, whereas *De Libertate Beccensis* and Robert of Torigni have it passing to his cousin, Roger de Bienfaite. Orderic appears to have named the right family (Clare) but the wrong person. The monks of Bec are unlikely to have mistaken the overlord of the castle continuously threatening them, and their report that Roger de Bienfaite received Brionne therefore seems more creditable. Orderic next tells us that Robert of Meulan's father, "the wily old Roger of Beaumont," came out of retirement and spent some time at Curthose's court ingratiating himself with smooth speeches, so that at length Curthose was persuaded to release Robert of Meulan upon Roger's promise to guarantee his son's good behavior and to pay a large fee. Probably upon payment, the Beaumonts received Brionne in perpetuity. The Beaumonts and the duke then besieged the castle, when its Clare custodian failed to yield it, and won it back for the Beaumont family.

18. Elsewhere Orderic reports that Curthose imprisoned Prince Henry and Robert of Bellême on their return from England in fall 1088, on the suspicion of having joined Rufus in a hostile conspiracy. OV 4:148.

19. Or, as Orderic identifies him, Robert son of Baldwin, Roger's cousin.

20. OV 4:206–8.

21. William of Breteuil himself had possessions in the "banlieue" of Brionne, which he donated to Bec: Porée, *Bec* 1:330.

The Bec-Brionne controversy was thus resolved, at least for the time being, with Anselm victorious in protecting the liberties of Bec, but with Robert of Meulan — chastened yet potentially dangerous — again in control of the neighboring castlery. Although Bec had refused Count Robert's lordship, it was now in Bec's interest to win his friendship. This would be a daunting task, especially if Robert blamed the community for his recent imprisonment. But it was not an impossible task for an abbot so remarkably talented at turning enemies into friends.

Robert of Meulan's transformation into a friend of Bec came as a by-product of a much more celebrated event: Anselm's advancement from Bec to Canterbury in 1093. The sources bearing on his elevation to the archbishopric — Eadmer's histories, Anselm's letters, the *Vita* of Abbot William of Bec, Florence of Worcester, and others — are far richer and more illuminating than the three conflicting narratives of the Bec-Brionne controversy. They permit us an unusually close scrutiny of Anselm's motives and methods during one of the most critical episodes of his ecclesiastical career. To this episode we will now turn.

Eadmer reports that after Archbishop Lanfranc's death in 1089 calamity descended on Canterbury.[22] William Rufus seized its possessions and, reserving only enough for the bare sustenance of the monks, took the rest for himself or let it out at rent. He kept Canterbury and other churches vacant on the deaths of their prelates and offered their lands to the highest bidder, renewing the bidding year by year. He sent out some of the Canterbury monks to other monasteries, and his men intimidated and insulted those who remained. In 1093, Rufus offered the archbishopric to Anselm, who publicly resisted the appointment and repeatedly denied that he desired the office. But his resistance proved futile, and he was consecrated at Canterbury Cathedral on 4 December 1093 as Lanfranc's archiepiscopal successor.[23] The topos of reluctance and unworthiness to accept a high ecclesiastical office has been touched on previously, but the instance of Anselm's elevation to Canterbury requires a fuller discussion.

Clearly Anselm's reluctance was heartfelt, not feigned. But, conversely, it cannot be interpreted simply as the spontaneous response of a particular individual who happened to dislike wealth, power, and

22. *HN* 26–27.   23. *HN* 42–43.

administrative responsibilities, or who, as a monk, had been conditioned to dislike them. Rather, Anselm's behavior was influenced by
the weight of a powerful tradition that stretched back for more than a
thousand years. Even in the lives of the early saints, Angelo Paredi
writes, "flight to escape an ecclesiastical dignity is almost traditional."[24]
In 248 a crowd besieged St. Cyprian in his home in Carthage in
order to make him bishop. In 251, Cornelius had to be physically
forced into receiving the papal office. In 371 St. Martin of Tours fled
from his monastery to avoid being raised to the episcopacy, only to be
carried back to his consecration by a crowd that had discovered his
hiding place. Similarly, St. Ambrose had strongly protested his elevation by popular acclamation to the bishopric of Milan, and Pope
Gregory the Great hid in a water pot in the forest until he was discovered and dragged to his consecration.[25] St. Augustine described
his aversion to episcopal office in these words:

I feared the office of a bishop to such an extent that, as soon as my reputation
came to matter among "servants of God," I would not go to any place where
I knew there were no bishops. I was on my guard against this: I did what I
could to seek salvation in a humble position rather than be in danger in high
office. But, as I said, a slave may not contradict his lord. I came to this city to
seek a friend, whom I thought I might gain for God, that he might live with us
in the monastery. I felt secure, for the place already had a bishop. I was
grabbed. I was made a priest . . . and from there, I became your bishop.[26]

Such examples could be multiplied endlessly; even late Roman emperors routinely protested their accessions on the grounds of humility.[27]

In Anselm's own time, protestations of reluctance and unworthiness had become routine. They abound in the correspondence of
Gregory VII and other reform popes, and William of Poitiers even
claimed that William the Conqueror, after his victory at Hastings, was
reluctant to accept the English crown.[28] Calixtus II was "made pope
in spite of his refusal and reluctance";[29] the great magnate Geoffrey of
Mowbray claimed at the Council of Reims in 1049 that he had been

24. Angelo Paredi, *Saint Ambrose: His Life and Times,* tr. Joseph Costelloe (Notre
Dame, 1964), p. 122.
25. Ibid.
26. Quoted in Peter Brown, *Augustine of Hippo,* p. 138.
27. Raymond Van Dam, *Leadership and Community in Late Antique Gaul* (Berkeley
and Los Angeles, 1985), p. 23.
28. WP 216.
29. HCY 61; cf. 71.

thrust by force into the bishopric of Coutances;[30] Godric was raised
to the abbacy of Peterborough "against his will," only to be deposed
by Anselm at the Council of 1102 — presumably for simony;[31] and in
1114 Ernulf "resisted long and resolutely" before being compelled to
accept the bishopric of Rochester.[32] When Henry I nominated the
royal chancellor William Giffard to Winchester in 1100, William submitted only with the greatest reluctance, assailing the Winchester
monks who had elected him with threats and reproaches.[33] And when
Archbishop Lanfranc and King William raised the Bec monk Gundulf
to the bishopric of Rochester in 1077, Gundulf "was powerless to
resist because the authority of the mighty king and archbishop constrained him. His own plea of unworthiness was silenced, for the more
he protested that he was unworthy, the more worthy he was
acclaimed."[34] Lanfranc himself, as we have seen, raised similar protests to his promotions to both Caen and Canterbury.

Some of these protests were doubtless mere formalities, but many
were genuine. The pattern of resistance followed by forced submission
is best interpreted as the interaction of two fundamental Christian
moral imperatives: humility and obedience. Humility impels the
nominee to affirm his reluctance and unworthiness — by protesting,
weeping, and in some instances fleeing or offering physical resistance.
Obedience, on the other hand, constrains him to yield to God's will,
expressed in such forms as physical coercion, the absolute commands
of lay or ecclesiastical superiors, the manifest will of clergy and laity,
or a combination thereof. A holy man should disdain, both publicly
and in his heart, the role of the ecclesiastical careerist — a type that
abounded in the Anglo-Norman church. He should emulate Christ in
his refusal to accept Satan's offer of worldly wealth and authority.
But, equally, God's church requires the governance of holy prelates.
St. Augustine had argued that the possession of inner peace does not
justify withdrawal from human affairs. On the contrary, as Thomas
Renna has pointed out, Augustine insisted that a Christian possessing
true peace "is obliged to use his personal union with God in an effort
to pacify the world. . . . When men attain peace of heart they are
naturally moved to create social peace, itself a model of the City of

30. John Le Patourel, "Geoffrey de Mowbray, Bishop of Coutances, 1049–1093,"
EHR 59(1944): 133–34.
31. Hugh Candidus, *Peterborough Chronicle*, ed. W. T. Mellows and A. Bell
(London, 1949), pp. 86–87.
32. Ibid., p. 96.   33. *GP* 110.   34. *VG* 39.

God."[35] Similarly, Gregory the Great concluded in his *Pastoral Care* that although the episcopal office should be denied to those who covet it for its distinction and wealth, the truly skillful man cannot justly refuse such office when it is thrust upon him. Although "it is safer to decline the office . . . , we ought not to decline it pertinaciously when we see that God wills us to undertake it."[36]

The Christian emphasis on humility and obedience has deep biblical roots. It echoes the reluctance of Old Testament prophets such as Jeremiah and Jonah to accept their divine commissions. Similarly, St. Paul enjoins the Philippians, "Do nothing from selfishness or conceit, but in humility count others better than yourselves."[37] Again, Paul teaches that Christ "humbled himself" by taking human form "and became obedient unto death, even death on a cross. Therefore God has highly exalted him."[38] In Jesus' own words, "If anyone wants to be first, he must make himself last of all and servant of all,"[39] and "He who makes himself as little as this little child is the greatest in the kingdom of heaven."[40] The ultimate model of the reluctant yet obedient prelate is Christ himself in the Garden of Gethsemane, agonizing over the acceptance of the greatest of all priestly obligations, his own crucifixion: "'Father,' he said, 'if it is possible, let this cup pass me by. Nevertheless, let it be not as I will but as you will.'"[41] Anselm himself explained his reluctant acceptance of the archbishopric with the same words:

Being therefore conquered — not so much by the power of man as by the power of God, against whom no wisdom or strength can avail – I feel constrained to follow this course only: after having prayed as much as I could, and striven that, if it were possible, this cup pass me by — that I should not drink it — then, seeing my prayer rejected and my struggles useless, I should say to God, "Nevertheless, let it be not as I will but as you will."[42]

Anselm, in short, echoing the views of countless predecessors and contemporaries, believed that humility required the Christian to abhor high office and to express his abhorrence publicly, but that obedience required him in the end to submit, as Christ had submitted, to the divine will. Anselm of all people would have understood that despite

35. "The Idea of Peace in the West, 500–1150," *JMH* 6, pt. 2 (1980): 147.
36. *Pastoral Care*, I.1,2; 5.
37. Philippians, 2:3.
38. Philippians, 2:8–9a.
39. Matt. 20:26–27 = Luke 22:26–27.
40. Matt. 18:4.   41. Matt. 26:39.   42. AEp. 148.

the agony at Gethsemane, Christ in the end had no real choice but to drink the cup and fulfill the Father's plan. Anselm, imitating Christ, pleaded for release and then surrendered his will to his Lord's. Canterbury was Anselm's Calvary: a prospect to be dreaded, yet perhaps his very raison d'être.

Anselm expressed his views on holy monks acquiring episcopal office in a letter to his intimate friend Gundulf, monk of Bec and Caen, on Gundulf's elevation to the bishopric of Rochester in 1077.[43] Anselm rejoices that Gundulf has been found worthy to be numbered among the princes of the church but grieves at the knowledge that the more he is raised up, the more he will be weighed down by suffering. Yet Anselm then reflects that "out of suffering is born patience, which leads to perfect work." He concludes:

I know that I should not so much grieve with your holiness at the tribulation you must endure in the labor of your office, as to congratulate you because of the perfection and hope to which you will advance by means of that office. Therefore, glory be to God on high, who has been so pleased with your life that he has raised it up as an example; and glory be to God on high, who has so loved you that he has put you into the fires of tribulation that he may purify your work until it reaches perfection, and your hope until it can be brought to full strength.

To the devout Christian, episcopal office thus brings both the agony and triumph of Christ and the suffering and purification of Job.

With this background in mind, we can understand the motives underlying Anselm's display of reluctance to become archbishop and his subsequent acceptance of the office. Was he seeking its prestige and wealth? Clearly not, as he himself was at pains to explain in his correspondence,[44] and as his two painful exiles demonstrate beyond all question. Did he savor the opportunity to carry on God's work in the arena of administration and politics? Again, clearly not, as he affirms in a letter to the monks of Bec: "If obedience and love . . . allowed it, I would rather serve and live as a monk under a superior, and receive spiritual advice and material necessities from him, than to rule or guide other men, whether by directing their souls or providing sustenance for their bodies, or to possess worldly riches."[45] But

43. AEp. 78.   44. See in particular AEpp. 148, 156.
45. AEp. 156; Anselm makes a similar statement to Fulk bishop of Beauvais: AEp. 160.

Anselm's personal inclinations are quite beside the point. To him, the purpose of human life — and monastic life in particular — was not to do as one pleases but to serve God: "When I professed myself a monk, I surrendered myself in such a way that thereafter I could not be my own man . . ., that is, I could not live in accordance with my own will, but only in accordance with obedience . . . to God or his church."[46] Anselm asks the Bec monks how he could possibly "refuse to accept God's disposal of me, to which I was rightly subject whether I willed it or not, or the obedience to which I had surrendered myself totally?"[47] Thus, if one asks if Anselm sought the archbishopric as an act of submission to God's plan, the answer is clearly yes; he makes the point repeatedly in his correspondence.

When did Anselm come to believe that God had destined him for Canterbury? Was it only in the course of his forced investiture in 1093? Or might it have been earlier, when it became evident that Rufus was plundering the English church? Or earlier yet, while Lanfranc still lived? Anselm's letters, corroborated by the testimony of Eadmer, attest to the first alternative, but other evidence suggests that Lanfranc himself intended Anselm to succeed him and that Anselm was aware of the intention.

The *Vita Lanfranci* reports that Anselm, visiting Archbishop Lanfranc in England shortly after his consecration as abbot of Bec, discovered a gold ring on his bed as he was about to retire after matins.[48] Crossing himself to determine whether it was a diabolical vision, he found that the ring was no illusion. After showing it to all the Christ Church officials and failing to find its owner, he sold it and gave the proceeds to his brethren. Lanfranc, hearing the story, interpreted the ring as a divine portent, prefiguring the gold ring that symbolizes the marriage of the archbishop to his see: "You must understand," Lanfranc said, "that Anselm will quite certainly be archbishop after me."[49]

Even if one dismisses this story as post facto legend, the likelihood remains that Lanfranc would have preferred Anselm as his successor over all others. Having devoted himself single-mindedly to the reform of the English church under the primacy of Canterbury, Lanfranc would surely have hoped that his task might be carried on with similar

---

46. AEp. 156.   47. Ibid.
48. *VL* 57. The story also occurs in *VA* 41, but without the association with Lanfranc.
49. *VL* 57; cf. *VA* 41.

energy and skill after his death. And one might reasonably suppose
that he would have fastened his hopes on Anselm — his handpicked
successor at Bec, his "friend and brother with whom he was of one
mind,"[50] and, next to Lanfranc himself, the foremost exemplar of the
Bec reform tradition. Anselm would have stood out as a man who
could bring to the archbishopric the requisite combination of stead-
fastness, holiness, and commanding intelligence to consummate Lanfranc's work.

Eadmer reports that on Anselm's visits to England during the Conqueror's reign, Lanfranc helped to ensure his warm reception at the
royal court, and that the two prelates jointly counselled the king on
important ecclesiastical affairs:

Anselm . . . was held in great fame in England, and moreover he was linked by
the most sacred friendship to the aforesaid king as well as to Lanfranc. When
he came to the king's court for the diverse affairs of his church and other
business, the king himself, having put aside the savage and formidable ferocity
seen by others, astounded all who knew him by making himself . . . friendly
and affable toward Anselm. And so naturally William always held Anselm and
Lanfranc before him as supports [fultos], as men at the same time divine and
human by their prudence. And in all that pertained to them, in whatever
referred to their offices, in whatever they were doing, he zealously listened to
them before all others. Whence he heeded their advice . . . and strove zealously to see that the observance of religion should increase in his dominion.[51]

Eadmer's words suggest that Lanfranc may have been grooming
Anselm to fill his place as archbishop, associating him in the ecclesiastical affairs of England as he had earlier prepared Anselm to succeed
him as prior of Bec.

During the years following Lanfranc's death, Rufus faced increasing
pressure from his prelates and magnates to fill the vacant archbishopric. And none of the sources bearing on the issue of Lanfranc's successor mentions any potential candidate apart from Anselm. If Lanfranc expected Anselm to succeed him, so too did many of Rufus's
great men. Anselm himself was keenly aware of the possibility when,
in 1092, he refused to journey from Bec to England because, in Eadmer's words, "already a kind of premonition was creeping into the
minds of some — and not a few were saying, not publicly but among

50. *VA* 51.
51. *HN* 23.

themselves — that if Anselm went to England he would become arch-bishop of Canterbury."[52]

Nevertheless, Anselm did cross to England in early September 1092 and tarried there for no less than half a year before being forcibly invested with the archbishopric. Anselm's motives are difficult to discern, not because Eadmer glosses over them but because he dwells on them at such remarkable length as to arouse suspicion. He devotes eleven pages (in the Rolls Series edition) to explaining in painful elaboration that Anselm visited England in 1092–93 for compelling reasons, totally unconnected with the archiepiscopal vacancy, and that he was coerced to accept the office despite heroic efforts to refuse it. Eadmer's account of Anselm's itinerary, and of his display of reluctance, can doubtless be trusted, but his discussion of Anselm's motives cannot.

Eadmer provides us with three distinct reasons why Anselm was compelled to visit England despite the risk of his advancement to Canterbury.[53] First, he was morally bound to visit the bedside of his old friend, Hugh earl of Chester, who had fallen gravely ill and was begging Anselm to come swiftly to care for the welfare of his soul. Second, "certain very pressing affairs" of the church of Bec required Anselm's presence in England. And third, the Bec monks commanded him to go to England "unless he wished to be branded with the sin of disobedience."

The moral obligation to visit a dying friend is the most powerful motive that Eadmer alleges — and the least persuasive. According to Eadmer, Earl Hugh wrote three letters to Anselm — none of which has survived. In the first, Hugh asked Anselm to come to oversee the replacement of secular canons by Bec monks at St. Werburg's, Chester. Anselm declined to set foot in England "lest anyone should suspect that he had done so to obtain this advancement." Hugh then sent word to Anselm that he was seriously ill, begged him to come to his bedside, and assured him that the rumors regarding the archbish-opric were groundless. Still Anselm refused. Hugh then sent a third message: "If you do not come, be assured that in eternal life you will never find repose so deep that it will save you from forever grieving that you do not come to me." On reading this final letter, so Eadmer relates, Anselm was at last moved to depart: "Commending myself

52. *HN* 27.
53. *HN* 27–29.

to God and my conscience, which is devoid of any ambition for worldly honor, out of regard for God's holy love I will go to satisfy my friend." The three letters, mentioned only by Eadmer, echo the topos of the threefold summons to court. That Anselm ignored the second letter, announcing the earl's grave illness, but responded to the third with its threat of eternal grief requires the unlikely supposition that Anselm was moved to action not by the illness of the notoriously worldly Hugh[54] but by his spiritual counsel.

Having departed Bec, Anselm journeyed to the bedside of his dying friend at a most leisurely pace. He traveled northeastward to Boulogne, probably intending to cross from Wissant to Dover, and visited Countess Ida of Boulogne for a number of days—being "unavoidably detained" for reasons unspecified.[55] It was in the course of this visit that Anselm is said to have received the message from his monks commanding him not to return to Bec until he had completed the abbey's business in England. The message is consistent with the Bec tradition of mutual obedience—the monks to their abbot and the abbot to the monks as a group—and it adds some weight to the notion that Anselm was not racing to his sick friend's side. It also embodies the topos of the reluctant holy man being driven toward high office by obedience to legitimate authority. But the message—which Eadmer summarizes but does not quote, and which has not survived independently—is suspiciously inconsistent with the interests of the Bec monks. They would have been as aware as Anselm of the pressure building in England for his advancement, and they subsequently did all in their power to keep from losing him. One cannot dismiss the possibility that the message is a figment of Eadmer's imagination.

According to Eadmer's *Historia Novorum,* the alleged message from Bec prompted Anselm to move with alacrity at last. He crossed to Dover and "came in haste to the earl."[56] But this statement is altogether incompatible with the fuller account of Anselm's English itinerary in Eadmer's *Vita Anselmi.*[57] In fact Anselm went from Dover to Canterbury, arriving on 7 September 1092, and was embarrassed at being prematurely acclaimed archbishop by many of the monks and laity. He tactfully departed the next morning, declining to celebrate

---

54. OV 2:260–62; 3:216.   55. HN 28–29.   56. HN 29.
57. VA 63–64. See also R. W. Southern, "St. Anselm and Gilbert Crispin, Abbot of Westminster," *Medieval and Renaissance Studies* 3 (1954): 87–92.

the Feast of the Virgin's Nativity in Canterbury Cathedral. But Earl Hugh was kept waiting still longer, for Anselm journeyed next to the royal court. There the king and nobility "eagerly met him and received him with great honor."[58] Afterward Anselm requested a private interview with Rufus, and, putting aside the business of Bec, "which was supposed to be his chief reason for coming there,"[59] he chided the king for all the misdeeds that were reported of him — assuming a role more befitting an English primate than a Norman abbot. Only then did he go to Chester, where he found that Earl Hugh had recovered from his illness.[60]

Of the three motives alleged by Eadmer for Anselm's visit to England, by far the most plausible is the "pressing affairs" of Bec. In a later letter Anselm stated that he went to England in 1092 on business concerning church property; he said nothing about Hugh's illness or an order from the Bec monks.[61] William of Malmesbury states that Anselm sought and obtained a geld reduction on the abbey's English lands.[62] And Eadmer is correct in reporting Hugh's intention to fill St. Werburg's with Bec monks under a Bec abbot.[63] These two projects provide a sufficient if less dramatic motive for the visit.

They do not, however, account for its length. After supervising the reestablishment of St. Werburg's, Anselm spent some time visiting his friend and former Bec colleague, Gilbert Crispin abbot of Westminster.[64] Anselm attended the royal court at Christmas 1092, where Rufus grudgingly permitted his bishops to have a prayer said in all the churches of England that God would inspire the king to appoint an archbishop of Canterbury. The bishops, already looking to Anselm as their leader, asked him to compose the prayer, and, after an expression of reluctance, he did so.[65] Eadmer alleges that Anselm now wished to return to Normandy but that Rufus refused to permit him to depart the kingdom. Here again Eadmer's testimony is discredited — both by the unlikelihood of an English monarch forbidding a Norman abbot to return home and by the testimony of Anselm himself. In a letter to Baudry prior of Bec, Anselm reports that Rufus, although showing

58. *VA* 63.   59. *VA* 64.
60. *HN* 29.   61. AEp. 198.   62. *GP* 79.
63. David Knowles and R. N. Hadcock, *Medieval Religious Houses, England and Wales*, 2d ed. (London, 1971), p. 62; *Heads*, 39; Richard of Bec became abbot of St. Werburg's in 1092/3.
64. Southern, "St. Anselm and Gilbert Crispin," pp. 87–88.
65. *HN* 29–30.

him immeasurable love and honor, had not yet granted his request regarding the business of Bec (perhaps the geld reduction), and that Baudry should not expect him to return before the beginning of Lent (2 March).[66] In the same letter Anselm requested copies of his Prayer to St. Nicholas, some of his letters, and the treatise against Roscelinus that he had begun. "Clearly," Frank Barlow concludes, "he was preparing for a protracted stay in England in which he could get down to some devotional and theological work."[67] As his prayer for the filling of the archbishopric rang through the churches of England, Anselm was settling down for a lengthy visit. Eadmer offers the unlikely explanation that he had by now come to feel secure from his former fear of being seized for the archbishopric — implying inadvertently that Anselm doubted the efficacy of kingdomwide prayer. It is difficult to believe that the unfinished business of Bec, whatever its importance, can have seemed worth the risk of remaining so long in England unless Anselm already suspected that God intended him for Canterbury. Obedience to the divine will was Anselm's overriding imperative, and with the English affairs of Bec providing a reasonable justification to remain, he may well have feared that leaving the kingdom might thwart the fulfillment of God's plan.

Rufus, in the meantime, found himself under mounting pressure to raise Anselm to the archbishopric. When one of his magnates lauded Anselm as a holy man devoid of worldly ambition, Rufus replied that if Anselm thought he had any chance of attaining the archbishopric of Canterbury, he would "applaud with hands and feet and rush to embrace it," adding that for the present neither Anselm nor anyone else would be archbishop except Rufus himself.[68] Anselm's protracted visit may well have roused the suspicions of the cynical monarch, but if Eadmer can be trusted, Rufus suffered immediate retribution for his irreverence: at that exact moment he was stricken with a violent illness that left him bedridden and grew worse each day.

Even if Eadmer exaggerated on the matter of the timing, in early March 1093 the king lay ill at Gloucester fearing for his life.[69] Anselm was staying at a neighboring village — "conveniently near the royal sickbed," as Frank Barlow observes.[70] On 6 March, having been

---

66. AEp. 147.   67. *Rufus*, p. 303.   68. *HN* 30; *GP* 80.
69. *HN* 30–31; *VA* 64; *VG* 54; *ASC*, A.D. 1093; Florence, 2:30.
70. Barlow, *Rufus*, p. 303; *HN* 31: "At that time, Anselm, knowing nothing about all this, was staying at a vill not far from Gloucester."

summoned to give spiritual counsel to the dying king, Anselm hastened to his side. He heard Rufus's full confession and obtained his
solemn oath to follow thenceforth the paths of mercy and justice.
Rufus ordered his prisoners released and his fines pardoned and promised all his people righteous laws. His bishops and nobles then urged
him to appoint an archbishop of Canterbury, and he readily agreed,
"saying that he had already been thinking of doing so."[71] Rufus
thereupon named Anselm, and the assembled magnates and prelates
unanimously acclaimed his decision with shouts of joy.[72]

Eadmer states that Anselm was aghast at this development. As he
was being rushed to the king's side to receive the archiepiscopal staff,
he resisted with all his strength.[73] The bishops took him aside and
pled with him to abide by God's will and rescue the English church
from its disorder and oppression. They accused him of caring only for
his selfish ease. Anselm replied that he was unworthy of the office, too
advanced in years, and repelled by worldly affairs, which he alleged he
had shunned ever since becoming a monk. Eadmer quotes the bishops'
response: "Fear not. Simply take on the primacy of the church and
lead us in the way of God, declaring and teaching us what we should
do, and behold, we will pledge never to fail to follow and obey your
directions. Concern yourself with God for us, and we will manage
your worldly affairs for you."[74] This promise of obedience, when
juxtaposed against Eadmer's subsequent account of the bishops abandoning Anselm and adhering to Rufus, seems a deliberate evocation of
Peter's denial, if not Judas's betrayal.[75]

Anselm next raised the objection that as abbot he owed submission
to the duke of Normandy, the archbishop of Rouen, and the monks of
Bec, and could never accept the archbishopric without their permission. "It will be easy," the bishops said, "to obtain the consent of all
of them."[76] Having evidently exhausted his arguments, Anselm sim-

71. *HN* 32.
72. *ASC*, A.D. 1093, adds that Rufus also named his chancellor, Robert Bloet, to the
bishopric of Lincoln and granted land to many monasteries, which he took back after he
had recovered from his illness.
73. *HN* 32–36. Eadmer describes Anselm's reluctance in elaborate detail; the gist of
his account is corroborated in AEpp. 148, 149, 151, and 176; cf. *VA* 65; *GP* 80–83.
74. *HN* 33.
75. Cf. *HN* 54–55: When the bishops abandon Anselm's cause at the Council of
Rockingham in 1095, Eadmer quotes Anselm as reminding them of their having thrust
him unwillingly into the archbishopric.
76. *HN* 33.

ply protested, "It's no good! What you intend is quite impossible." At that, they dragged him to the royal bedside, where Eadmer quotes Rufus as pleading, " 'Oh, Anselm, what are you doing? Remember I beg you the true friendship which my father and mother had for you and which you always had for them. And by that friendship I beg you not to allow me, their son, to perish in body and soul alike. For I am certain that I will so perish if I die still possessing the archbishopric. Help me then, lord father, and take it from me.' "[77]

When Anselm remained obdurate, the assemblage of magnates and prelates turned reproachful, accusing him of tormenting a dying king and warning him that he would bear full responsibility for all subsequent disorders and oppressions of the English church if he continued to refuse the office. Anselm turned for help to the two Bec monks who accompanied him, Baldwin and Eustace, who told him tearfully that God's will was at work and should not be resisted. Eadmer states that Anselm would at that moment have chosen death rather than be made archbishop if he could have done so without transgressing God's will. "I swear before God," Eadmer assures us, "that I am not lying."[78] Rufus ordered the assemblage to kneel in supplication at Anselm's feet. Anselm responded by kneeling at their feet.[79] Growing angry, the crowd cried out, "Bring the pastoral staff, the pastoral staff!" And seizing his right arm, they dragged him back to Rufus's bedside. The king held out the staff to him, but Anselm, weeping and clenching his fist, refused to take it. The bishops tried to pry his fingers up, making Anselm groan in anguish, but they managed only to pull back his forefinger.[80] Finally, they pressed the crosier against his clenched hand, "and staff and hand were pressed and held tightly by the hands of the bishops. Then, while the assembly shouted 'Vivat episcopus! Vivat!,' the bishops and clergy raised their voices to chant the Te Deum and the pontiff-elect was carried, not led, into the nearby church, continually resisting with all his might and saying, 'What you are doing is a nullity, a nullity!' "[81] Nevertheless, once inside the church,

77. HN 33–34.

78. HN 34.

79. HN 35, echoing an earlier episode when Archbishop Lanfranc, visiting Bec, prostrated himself at Abbot Herluin's feet and Herluin thereupon attempted to prostrate himself in return: VH 105.

80. Neither Eadmer nor any other source mentions the episcopal ring. Anselm is not objecting here to the practice of lay investiture, which he accepted without a murmur throughout Rufus's reign, but only to his becoming archbishop.

81. HN 35; cf. GP 82–83; on Anselm's weeping, see AEp. 159.

Anselm underwent "all the ritual which it is the custom to have performed on such occasions"[82] — presumably his installation as archbishop-elect.

Afterward, so Eadmer tells us, Anselm returned to the king and told him that when he had recovered his health, as he surely would, he (Rufus) was free to reverse his decision to make Anselm archbishop, "for I have not consented to its ratification, nor do I now." Anselm warned the bishops that Rufus would crush him, "and not one of you would dare oppose the king." Rufus then commanded that Anselm be invested with all the property of the archbishopric along with the city of Canterbury and the abbey of St. Albans, both of which the archbishopric had previously held of the king as benefices but would thenceforth possess *in allodium*. Thereupon Rufus directed that Anselm take up residence on the estates of Canterbury; Gundulf bishop of Rochester lived with him and saw to it that all of Anselm's necessities were provided from these estates.[83]

Such is Eadmer's account of Anselm's election. He has doubtless reshaped some things to suit his dramatic and didactic purposes, but the main sequence of events and clash of views finds corroboration in Anselm's own letters and in other sources.[84] By a striking reenactment of the age-old topos of unworthiness and reluctance, Anselm had made it as clear as humanly possible that he disdained the wealth and authority of the archbishopric. It was of crucial importance to him that he should demonstrate this point, for Canterbury was by far the richest and most powerful prelacy in the Anglo-Norman world. It was the tastiest of all plums for ecclesiastical careerists, yet, because of its distinctive traditions, virtually out of their reach.[85] Anselm, ever conscious of the importance of appearances,[86] displayed with dramatic force the point that he did not seek the office out of covetousness but was swept into it by the irresistible tide of God's will. The role came easily to him, for he had only to reach inside himself and rediscover the young, "untamed" Anselm who had not yet surrendered himself to God, and who now, at sixty, really did dread the responsibility of

82. *HN* 35.   83. *HN* 37.
84. See especially AEp. 149: Osbern of Canterbury to Anselm.
85. Archbishops of Canterbury were usually monks of some spiritual distinction, and Canterbury was therefore customarily filled "by methods which are quite distinct from those used in any other see": Brett, *English Church*, p. 75.
86. E.g., *HN* 27: Anselm was concerned always to appear honorable "not only in God's sight but also in the sight of all people."

the archiepiscopacy—particularly under an impetuous cynic such as Rufus. But in resisting, Anselm was obliged to conceal his most fundamental moral commitment: the surrender of self to God. "Not until you had given me your permission to be advanced to the archbishopric," Anselm later told the Bec monks, "did I disclose to anyone this surrender of self; rather, I used self as an insuperable obstacle to my being promoted."[87]

By making a secret of his self-surrender, Anselm was reduced to protesting his election on grounds that he himself did not fully believe. His argument that nothing could make him take pleasure in worldly affairs, although literally true, was consciously misleading. Years earlier he had explained to Gundulf that avoiding high office because of a distaste for worldly affairs was little better than seeking high office out of love of them. In both instances, one is permitting worldly affairs to determine one's course of action. The holy man must altogether transcend worldly vanities, neither cherishing them nor permitting the hatred of them to thwart God's plan: "If you are grieved by the contrariness of those things which a servant of God ought to despise, you disclose yourself as preferring transitory things more than is fitting, and eternal things less."[88] By displaying only his untamed self during the climactic events surrounding his forced investiture, Anselm exposed himself to the deserved reproach of the bishops that he was refusing to deliver their church from ruin for the sake of his own selfish ease. His protest that he could not accept the office without permission from the duke of Normandy, the archbishop of Rouen, and the monks of Bec was overcome just as easily. Not only was Anselm overwhelmed by force; he was, for once in his life, outargued.

At whatever point Anselm became inwardly convinced that God intended him for Canterbury, the events of 1093 resulted in God's will being manifested in its three traditional forms: physical coercion, election by the unanimous acclamation of clergy and people, and the commands of superior authorities—in Anselm's case, the Norman authorities to whom his abbatial office bound him.[89] The crowd in Rufus's chamber was taken to represent the clergy and people of England. As Eadmer expressed it in his *Vita Anselmi*, Rufus's nomina-

---

87. AEp. 156.
88. AEp. 78: Anselm to Gundulf.
89. Recall that Lanfranc had reluctantly accepted the archbishopric at the command of Abbot Herluin and Pope Alexander II, and that Gundulf had accepted Rochester at the command of King William and Archbishop Lanfranc.

tion of Anselm was greeted with "universal acclamation, and both clergy and people commended the king's judgment with not a single voice objecting." Despite Anselm's struggles, "the united body of the church of God prevailed."[90] Similarly, Bishop Gundulf wrote to the monks of Bec that God, pitying the plight of orphaned Canterbury, caused the king, at the counsel and petition of his nobles and the election by the clergy and people, to bestow the governance of the Church of Canterbury on Abbot Anselm.[91] Anselm himself, writing afterward to Hugh archbishop of Lyon, explained that his resistance had been overcome "by the command of my archbishop and election by the whole of England."[92]

The topos of obedience to the commands of superiors occurs repeatedly in Anselm's letters discussing his elevation. To Gilbert bishop of Evreux, Anselm protested the charges of ambition and cupidity that were being directed against him by again stressing his tearful submission to God's will, as expressed in direct orders: "Our lord Robert count of the Normans, and our father the reverend Archbishop William, and our brothers of Bec commanded that I could resist no further without falling into sin."[93] And in a letter to the bishops of Ireland summarizing his advancement, Anselm deploys every one of the appropriate topoi. He had journeyed to England in 1092 "by God's secret judgment." He had been "dragged violently" to the archiepiscopal office, "clergy and people shouting together, so that everyone present seemed pleased at what was being done." He protested that he was being removed from the authority of the duke of Normandy and archbishop of Rouen without their knowledge but was afterward compelled by the command of these very men — duke and archbishop — "and obeying, I took on the burden of the office. In this manner I was raised to the pontificate, and I accepted it because I was powerless to resist."[94]

90. VA 64–65.   91. AEp. 150.   92. AEp. 176.
93. AEp. 159. Here Anselm is not only evoking the topos of reluctant submission to lawful authority but also making the correct canonical point, dating from the Council of Nicaea, that an abbot cannot be advanced to episcopacy without the approval of his archbishop: Robert L. Benson, *The Bishop-Elect: A Study in Medieval Ecclesiastical Office* (Princeton, 1968), pp. 36–37.
94. AEp. 198: The omission of the command from Bec probably results from Anselm's habit of teaching only what his audience can understand. The custom of reciprocal obedience between the abbot and his community was peculiar to Bec and would have puzzled the Irish bishops.
It may be significant that these topoi follow to some extent the traditional English methods of "election" to kingship. As Christopher Brooke has discussed (*The Saxon and*

In these accounts of his elevation, as at other critical moments in his career, Anselm is functioning on two distinct levels of reality: the ideal level, where his actions perfectly reflect the due order of God's kingdom and the behavior appropriate to a holy prelate, and the more disorderly level of everyday events. Insofar as he was able, Anselm tried to make the two levels one by living day by day as God's obedient servant. But events sometimes forced Anselm to transgress the narrow path of traditionally correct day-by-day behavior in order to fulfill God's will at the higher, ideal level of reality — which was for Anselm, as it had been for Augustine and Plato, the truer reality. Once God's will had been fulfilled, Anselm would then reinterpret his actions in such a way as to align them absolutely to traditional Christian norms — reshaping some things, editing out others — so that his life might serve as a model for his contemporaries and posterity. Eadmer, as the saint's biographer, wrote with a similar goal in mind, but his idealized interpretation of events is sometimes distinctly different from Anselm's own.[95]

According to Eadmer, Anselm lingered passively in England for the next half year, enjoying Gundulf's good company.[96] Although Eadmer could refer to Anselm at that time as "pontiff-elect,"[97] he portrays him as continuing to have the gravest reservations about accepting the archbishopric from the 6 March election into late August or September.[98] Anselm's own interpretation is similar but not identical. It can be pieced together from the letters preserved at Canterbury in Lambeth ms. 59 — the collection of his archiepiscopal correspondence recorded almost entirely under his personal direction.[99] The earliest

---

Norman Kings [London, 1963], pp. 21ff.), there were three methods of choosing a king in Anglo-Saxon England: designation, inheritance, and election by clergy and people. No single method predominated, and often the king would be chosen by all three methods or some combination of two.

95. Recall, for example, that Anselm explained his trip to England in 1092 without reference to the illness of Earl Hugh or the command of Bec. See below, Chapter 7 at nn. 112–32 for further examples of this thinking. Hopkins (Companion to the Study of St. Anselm, pp. 18–20) notes that the perfect was more real than the imperfect to Anselm, and the perfection of the ideal was thus more real than flawed actuality.

96. HN 37.   97. HN 35.   98. HN 39.

99. Walter Fröhlich, "The Letters Omitted from Anselm's Collection of Letters," ANS 6 (1984): 58–71; "The Genesis of the Collection of Anselm's Letters," American Benedictine Review 35 (1984): 249–66. Fröhlich argues convincingly that Anselm supervised the recording of all the letters in the collection except a handful that he wrote at the close of his life.

relevant letters in the manuscript are from Duke Robert and Archbishop William admonishing Anselm to accept the archbishopric.[100] In
another Lambeth ms. 59 letter Anselm writes at great length to the
monks of Bec, bidding them a tearful adieu, reasserting the theme
of his heartfelt reluctance being overcome by God's will, defending
himself against charges of cupidity, and concluding with a request
that the letter be given the widest possible publicity in order to clear
him of false suspicions.[101]

The collection includes two further letters, already discussed,
wherein Anselm explains and justifies to Fulk of Beauvais and to the
Irish bishops his reluctant surrender to the will of God.[102] One last
relevant item in Lambeth ms. 59 is Anselm's letter to Prior Baudry and
the monks of Bec urging that they elect as their new abbot the Bec
monk William of Beaumont. Collectively, these letters summarize
Anselm's case: having been popularly elected and subjected to physical
coercion, he had continued to resist until receiving direct orders from
Archbishop William, Duke Robert, and the Bec monks. Then he had
reluctantly bowed to God's will, while seeing to the welfare of Bec by
proposing a new abbot.

But a distinctly different picture unfolds when one analyzes the
whole of the surviving evidence. First the crowd around Rufus's sickbed would surely have included many magnates and prelates who
numbered among Anselm's special friends. Shortly thereafter, Anselm
explained to Gilbert of Evreux that until he had totally committed
himself to God's plan to raise him to the archbishopric, he was in
doubt as to "what aid I ought to expect from my friends."[103] One
such friend, Gundulf of Rochester, who was often in the king's entourage in the years around 1093,[104] is described by his biographer as
being "a most willing collaborator" in Anselm's election, "embracing this dearest of friends joyously."[105] As Anselm had earlier rejoiced
at Gundulf's elevation, so now Gundulf rejoiced at Anselm's. Gilbert
Crispin abbot of Westminster, another intimate friend and former Bec
colleague whom Anselm had recently visited, also frequented Rufus's
court and is likely to have been among the cheering crowd at Gloucester.[106] Two of Rufus's most frequent lay attesters, Hugh of Chester and

---

100. AEpp. 153, 154.   101. AEp. 156.   102. AEpp. 160, 198.   103. AEp. 159.
104. Regesta 1, nos. 315, 319, 325, 328, 336, 338, and 341.
105. VG 54.
106. Regesta 1, nos. 315, 328, and 338.

Eudo *Dapifer,* were particularly close to Anselm,[107] while others among Anselm's lay friends and patrons — Walter Giffard, Gilbert fitz Richard of Clare, Ernulf of Hesdin, Hugh of Grandmesnil, and Henry of Ferrers — were also at Rufus's court during these years,[108] and some or all of them were very probably at the king's bedside at Gloucester. Eadmer himself quotes Anselm as telling the bishops that in compelling him to assume the burden of archiepiscopal office, "perhaps you thought that you were doing me a service as I would wish."[109] Anselm's lay friends probably had the same thought. If Anselm was truly determined to avoid the archbishopric, his visit to the bedside of a repentant king surrounded by Anselm's admirers was the walk of a blind man into a visible and obvious trap. His election by the clergy and people of England was a product of his own friendship network.

Depite the testimony of Eadmer and the letters Anselm chose to preserve, from his election at Gloucester onward, if not long before, he accepted his elevation as an expression of God's will. Once he had departed the king's court, he might have fled to the Continent.[110] Indeed the king's subsequent behavior gave him every reason to do so. In a move typical of Rufus, suppressed by Eadmer and ignored in Anselm's surviving correspondence, the monarch quickly reneged on his investiture of Anselm with all the Canterbury lands. Once the king had returned to good health, the Worcester chronicle discloses, his grant to Anselm went the way of his other acts of deathbed generosity: "Anselm was permitted to receive nothing from the archbishopric beyond what the king allowed, until the annual farm which he had been collecting since Lanfranc's death was paid in full."[111] Anselm's investiture had indeed been a nullity. Yet instead of returning to Bec, Anselm settled down with Gundulf as a pensioner on the Canterbury estates, which continued to be administered and exploited by royal officials.

107. Hollister, "Magnates and 'Curiales,' " p. 76; cf. AEp. 163: Anselm to Eudo *Dapifer.*

108. *Regesta* 1, nos. 290, 301, 302, 315, 319, 320, 325, 361, 392, and 474.

109. *HN* 55.

110. In 1097, as archbishop, Anselm threatened to do precisely that, with or without the king's permission. *VA* 92.

111. Florence, 2:31. The passage leaves open the alternate possibility that Eadmer was simply mistaken in crediting Rufus with investing Anselm into the Canterbury lands in March, but Gundulf's statement to the monks of Bec that the afflicted king had granted Anselm the governance (*gubernatio*) of Canterbury suggests otherwise: AEp. 150. Whatever the case, there is nothing to suggest that Anselm either governed Canterbury or controlled its revenues until his enthronement on 25 September 1093.

Eadmer's account and the letters in Lambeth ms. 59 also disguise the fact that during the weeks and months after the 6 March investiture, Anselm was taking active measures to ensure his advancement. As Eadmer portrays it, the releases from Duke Robert, Archbishop William, and the Bec monks were obtained entirely through the king's initiative, and, to prevent Anselm from escaping the burden they imposed, "they laid it on him as a matter of obedience."[112] Anselm himself would later declare that he accepted his archiepiscopal office only after having been ordered to do so by the duke, archbishop, and monks, who "commanded that I could resist no further without falling into sin."[113] His statement is both literally correct and drastically misleading, for when the king's efforts to obtain the releases did not immediately succeed,[114] Anselm took matters into his own hands. He personally requested that his old friend Archbishop William sanction his translation to Canterbury. His letter, now lost, is mentioned in the archbishop's reply: "Regarding those matters that the king had asked of me concerning you, and of which you yourself have written me . . . , I order [*iubeo*] that you accept the pastoral care of the church of Canterbury."[115] Anselm may well have intervened similarly with his old friend Robert Curthose, whom Anselm described shortly afterward as having sent him a letter of great kindness. In the letter the duke apologized if he had "either behaved or said anything about me [Anselm] other than what was fitting."[116] If Anselm wrote to Curthose as he had written to Archbishop William, the letter has perished along with most of the remainder of Curthose's records. Whatever the case, the duke released Anselm only after having been subjected to much persuasion.[117]

Anselm's efforts to persuade the Bec monks are far better recorded, for although he saw fit not to preserve the relevant letters in Lambeth ms. 59, they were preserved at Bec. Four of these letters, all written between 6 March and 15 August 1093, are particularly illuminating.[118] The first is a response by Anselm to letters (now lost) from the

112. *HN* 38.   113. AEp. 159; cf. AEpp. 176, 198.
114. *HN* 37–38.   115. AEp. 154; *HN* 38.
116. AEp. 164; cf. AEp. 153: Duke Robert enjoins Anselm (*commoneo*) to accept the archbishopric; the closing lines of this short letter suggest that Anselm may have conveyed some of his thoughts to the duke.
117. Cf. *HN* 137.
118. AEpp. 148, 150, 151, and 155; for the date range, see *HN* 37 and *VW* 715–16. AEp. 159, also absent from Lambeth ms. 59, includes Anselm's explanation to Gilbert of Evreux of his efforts to persuade the monks of Bec to release him.

monks of Bec urging him not to abandon them.[119] Anselm assures
them in words of great emotional intensity that their separation is as
painful to him as to them, and that he is grief-stricken at the prospect
of becoming archbishop. He evokes the image of Christ in Gethsemane pleading that the cup pass him by. Nevertheless, Anselm expresses his
conviction that God has destined him for Canterbury: "I am compelled
to confess that God's decisions increasingly defy my efforts." Consequently, Anselm expresses his determination to set aside his own wishes
and to abandon himself totally to God. "I therefore advise you," Anselm
continues, "to let nothing make you persistently oppose God's will, for
'rebellion is the sin of witchcraft.' " If the elevation to Canterbury should
be thwarted "through your obstinacy, you would cause me to be worn
down in my old age, and to fail from inconsolable grief because of the
manifold and great evils that would follow. . . . If you knew what evils the
delay has already brought about . . . , and how much the delay and its
perpetrators are detested by the best and wisest of the English — indeed,
by the entire nation — I think you too, if you are not inhuman, would
hate the delay." Protesting once again his contempt for worldly vanities,
he concludes with a further touch of irritation: "Farewell, and may God,
who guides those who are weak in judgment and shows his way to those
who are not stubborn but gentle, direct your minds and wills to a correct
judgment in this matter."

Anselm's companion Gundulf wrote a letter of similar purport to
his former brethren at Bec.[120] He prays and "humbly" orders that
they cease obstructing the operation of the divine will as expressed
through Anselm's election by the English clergy and people, and that,
"acting through the grace of God, you concede what is done with joy
and goodwill." Gundulf tells the monks that the project of Anselm's
elevation has already progressed far and has by now undoubtedly been
brought to the attention of the papal court. The monks should therefore follow the advice of wise men and do what they ought to do
"without obstruction."

The sense of urgency in Anselm's and Gundulf's letters is a reflection
of the fact that Bec's delay was perpetuating Canterbury's bondage
and feeding Rufus's treasury. Having insisted on the releases from
Normandy, Anselm had inadvertently given Rufus an excuse to retain
the lucrative Canterbury lands until the releases were obtained. At this

119. AEp. 148.
120. AEp. 150.

juncture Anselm seems more anxious than the king to complete the archiepiscopal elevation. But the irresolution of the Bec community is equally understandable. Not only was Anselm a beloved and celebrated abbot, he was a teacher and spiritual director of such unique talent that a great many of his monks had taken their lifetime vows at Bec for the express purpose of obtaining his instruction. As their abbot, he was bound by a solemn oath never to abandon them. Now he seemed prepared to subordinate his oath to the higher obligation of fulfilling God's plan. But although he might leave Bec, his monks were bound by their vows to remain.[121]

Bowing to the combined pressures of Anselm and Gundulf, the Bec monks sent a messenger to tell Anselm by word of mouth that they released him. Anselm replied to the monks:

You did well in ordering your concession to me through Dom Tezo, because the matter in question cannot be changed either by you or by me. But you would do better if you order [*mandabitis*] the thing that God deigns to arrange for me, through letters — one to the king and another to me — and the same king and count [Rufus and Curthose], who are the lords of our church, will order it [*ordinaverit*] out of fear of God, and our archbishop will order it [*iusserit*] following religious and ecclesiastical reason.[122]

Anselm then suggests that if the monks remain obdurate they will lose both God's grace and the grace of the king, without which they would suffer "great damage." And he asks them to cease burdening and tormenting his own mind by their dissension.

Anselm's threat of damage through the loss of the king's grace, which is uncharacteristically blunt, apparently angered some of the monks.[123] Nevertheless, the Bec community sent the requested letters. Their letter to Rufus has perished; to Anselm they conceded as one congregation "whatever is required of us."[124] It was hardly the firm command that Anselm had hoped to receive, but it might still have found its place in Lambeth ms. 59, alongside the letters of the duke and archbishop, had it not been that the Bec scribe went on to discuss

121. There were exceptions. As archbishop, Anselm summoned a handful of Bec monks to join his household or otherwise serve him: Southern, *Anselm*, pp. 194–202.
122. AEp. 151; the subsequent orders from the duke and the archbishop suggest strongly that both made their decisions after much deliberation and in consultation with the monks of Bec: AEpp. 153, 154. Archbishop William says explicitly that he has consulted with both his own friends and Anselm's.
123. AEp. 159, lines 56–79.
124. AEp. 155.

in embarrassing detail the conflicting views of factions within the community on the issue of releasing Anselm from his vow. The letter was never enrolled in Anselm's collection, but it was nevertheless sufficient, alongside the amiable commands of duke and archbishop, to permit Anselm to cut his ties with Normandy at last. The components of the obedience topos were all finally in place, and Anselm now returned his abbatial staff to Bec.[125] If the release from Bec was grudging and slightly ambiguous, Anselm could nevertheless maintain without gross exaggeration that the duke, the archbishop of Rouen, "and our brothers of Bec commanded that I could resist no further without falling into sin."[126] Or as Eadmer explained it, the duke, the archbishop, and the monks of Bec "consented to the completion of what had been begun concerning Anselm. And, to prevent him from evading the burden thus imposed, they laid it on him as a matter of obedience. So each of them wrote separate letters, all in the same identical consenting strain, which were sent by messenger to both Anselm and the king."[127]

Anselm sent two further letters to Bec, along with his abbatial staff, and both were recorded in Lambeth ms. 59.[128] One was Anselm's long, comprehensive defense of his behavior during the process of his promotion, ending with the admonition that the letter be widely circulated. Lacking any allusion to dissent within the Bec community, the letter was clearly intended not merely as an apologia but as a statement of the deepest truths of the matter, shorn of all unedifying details: that Anselm loved his monks dearly, that it grieved him to leave them, and that God was raising him to an office that he despised yet must accept. The second letter, in which Anselm urges the monks to accept William of Beaumont as their new abbot, seems at first glance merely the act of a caring former pastor, but in fact it launched another heated controversy.

The conflict over William of Beaumont is not easy to reconstruct. Eadmer says nothing about it, and the two Bec accounts — in the *Vita Willelmi* and *De Libertate Beccensis* — are at once extremely discreet and, at points, mutually contradictory. But when these accounts are correlated with evidence from Anselm's letters, particularly those absent from Lambeth ms. 59, the picture becomes much clearer. *De Libertate* reports that once the Bec monks were resigned to losing

125. *HN* 41; *VW* 716–17.   126. *AEp.* 159.   127. *HN* 38.
128. *AEpp.* 156, 157. See above, Chapter 4 at n. 87.

Anselm they put the election of his successor "under Anselm's judgment and authority" and were "prepared to give total obedience to his will."[129] This is clearly erroneous; it is contradicted by the earlier testimony of the *Vita Willelmi* and by Anselm's letters.

The *Vita Willelmi* reports that the monk Girard arrived at Bec on 15 August 1093, carrying Anselm's abbatial staff and his two letters, the first of which was immediately read aloud to all the monks and moved them to tears.[130] After the community had celebrated mass, Prior Baudry called them into the chapter house, where Girard told them that he had a second letter from Anselm, concerning the election of a new abbot. Before reading it, however, "he wished to hear if they would all concur with Anselm's advice on whom to choose. 'We shall not do so,' the prior said, 'before we hear the letter.' " Girard replied that he was only following Anselm's own instructions, but he was finally persuaded to let the letter be read without the monks' prior commitment. In it Anselm states that if the duke should permit the election of a new abbot of Bec and if the duke and monks wished to follow Anselm's counsel, they would choose William of Beaumont, prior of the Bec dependency of Poissy.[131] And assuming that this is done — "Oh that it would be done!" — Anselm orders William, through holy obedience, to assume the abbatial office. He further asks that the Bec community send letters confirming William's election as swiftly as possible to the duke and other responsible officials, with copies to Anselm. He concludes by ordering Baudry "that through holy obedience you not desert your office of prior, whoever might be abbot, without his consent and mine while I live."[132]

Up to this point the *Vita Willelmi* and Anselm's correspondence tell a consistent and plausible story. When William of Beaumont's biographer admits of certain irregularities in his hero's advancement, he is surely to be believed; and he would not have invented them. But the *Vita Willelmi* seriously misrepresents the community's response to the letter: "Prior Baudry replied that he would gladly undertake the election, and all the other monks were of the same mind."[133] A subsequent letter from Anselm to Bec, absent from Lambeth ms. 59, indicates

---

129. *DLB* 602.   130. *VW* 715–16; AEp. 156.

131. See Porée, *Bec* 1:241–42: Notre-Dame de Poissy was given to Bec in 1077 by Philip I and passed out of Bec's control in the 1090s.

132. AEp. 157; *VW* 716.

133. Ibid. From that time onward William's biographer refers to him as "abbot-elect."

a very different reaction.[134] Anselm reports that Duke Robert had
promised to appoint to the abbacy of Bec whomever Anselm suggested, and that Baudry and his monks would be well advised to
concur. Once again Anselm evokes the menace of Rufus, "who sends
you his greetings, his aid, and the guardianship of your properties under his authority — as long as you act and live by my counsel. But
if you despise it, you have no profit in these things." He then speaks of
a long, secret letter he had received from the Bec community which,
by resisting his advice, caused him many tearful days and nights.[135]

Anselm's letter demonstrates that the monks did not elect William
as their abbot on 15 August. On the contrary, they appear to have
resisted doing so for the next two months, despite all Anselm's efforts.
They had doubtless expected that, as before, their prior would ascend
to the abbatial office. Baudry was senior to William of Beaumont[136]
and had been directing the abbey's affairs during Anselm's long absence. It is probably for that reason that Anselm, in his initial letter
proposing William of Beaumont, ordered Baudry not to desert his
office. The monks may have had the further objection that Anselm
was denying them a free election. When William of Beaumont was
himself asked to select the next abbot as he lay dying in 1124, he
replied, "It is not mine to choose, since the sacred canons order that
no one may nominate his own successor."[137]

As the monks continued to resist, Anselm continued to press them.
Besides writing to Bec and to Duke Robert and enlisting the king's
support, Anselm urged William of Beaumont's candidacy on Eudo
lord of Préaux near Rouen, Rufus's *dapifer* and *curialis*.[138] As a last
resort, Anselm asked his former colleague, the elderly Roger abbot of
Lessay, to go to Bec, take its interests into his own hands, and do what
Anselm himself would do if he were present.[139] Arriving at Bec in
October, Roger brought the grumbling community into line at last.[140]
He persuaded Prior Baudry and some other monks to accompany him
on a mission to inform Duke Robert that they were now prepared to
accept Anselm's instructions.[141] "The duke heard all this with de-

134. AEp. 164.   135. The secret letter has not survived.
136. Porée, *Bec* 1:630: Baudry was the ninth monk to enter Bec during Anselm's
abbatiate, William the twenty-fourth.
137. *VW* 722. William was in fact succeeded by his prior.
138. AEp. 163.   139. AEp. 158.   140. *VW* 716–17.
141. *VW* 717 states that they "informed the duke of Anselm's instructions," but, as
has been seen, Curthose had already been so informed: cf. *VW* 716: "Sed et principem
Northmanniae Anselmus mandando rogavit ut praedictae electioni assensum praeberet."

light" and commanded that William of Beaumont be presented to him. Rushing home, they assembled all the Bec monks and, reporting their interview with Curthose, asked each monk individually how he stood with regard to the election. According to the *Vita Willelmi*, "nearly all" assented to William's election. In the *De Libertate* account they agreed unanimously to follow Anselm's bidding, "though many of them had quite different inclinations."[142] William of Beaumont responded to the news of his election in the appropriate way, hurling himself onto the ground in protest, but his objections were overcome. Roger, Baudry, and others hurried him to the ducal court, and Curthose invested him in the abbacy "according to the custom of his predecessors." Returning to Bec, William took up his abbatial duties on 23 October 1093.[143]

Anselm responded with delight that the monks had elected William, and a touch of irritation that they had taken so long to do so. In a letter to Abbot-Elect William and his monks, not enrolled in Lambeth ms. 59, he rejoices that the monks have been moved by God's grace — a grace too easily driven off "by long delays."[144] He warns the monks to show their new abbot humble obedience,[145] admonishes William to rule with traditional Benedictine moderation, and urges the community to acquire friends from all sides.[146] In conclusion he reports that he has sent messengers to Duke Robert and Archbishop William Bonne-Ame on the subject of the abbot-elect's consecration by the archbishop, "asking that all things be done fittingly" — a veiled but unmistakable reference to the profession of obedience issue. As a result of Anselm's efforts, strenuously seconded by Bec, Curthose commanded his archbishop to consecrate William without demanding his profession, and the archbishop grudgingly complied.[147] Anselm had thus chosen his own successor, imposed him on the prior and monks of Bec in the face of heated resistance, and helped steer him through

142. *DLB* 602, where we are also told that Anselm had written confidentially to Baudry warning him "not to allow the monks to hold any secret conferences among themselves."

143. *VW* 717–18.

144. AEp. 165.

145. Obedience to Abbot William seems to have been something of a problem in his initial years: Anselm again urged the Bec monks to obey him in AEp. 179 and still again in AEp. 199.

146. Above, Chapter 1 at n. 44.

147. *VW* 718; *DLB* 603: the duke was also lobbied by Baudry and by the former Bec monk William abbot of Cormeilles. The consecration occurred, after considerable delay, on 10 August 1094.

the hazardous shoals of the archiepiscopal consecration. The significance of the episode far transcends the precincts of Bec: it demonstrates that the politics of the abbey could sometimes interpenetrate
the politics of the ducal and royal courts, and that Anselm was capable
of directing the powers of both duke and king to his own end.

Why did Anselm insist so adamantly on William of Beaumont?
William emerges from the pages of his biography as a pious and
learned monk, but not to any extraordinary degree by Bec standards.
Nor is it likely that Baudry was passed over because of his cumber-
some handling of Anselm's letter of release; Anselm could be surprisingly firm, but he was always quick to forgive. The answer must surely
lie in William's aristocratic connections, as a kinsman of both the
Beaumonts and the Montforts. His father, Turstin of Montfort, was a
relative of the great English magnate Hugh III of Montfort, lord of
Haughley and royal constable of Dover castle, and of Hugh's brother
Robert of Montfort, lord of Montfort-sur-Risle—a major castle
located less than six miles from Bec.[148] His mother, Aubrée, was
Roger of Beaumont's niece and Robert of Meulan's first cousin.[149]
(Figure 2 shows the abbot's Beaumont connection.) By going to such
efforts to raise William of Beaumont to the abbacy of Bec, Anselm
was rendering a great service to both the Montfort and Beaumont families, and was thereby winning additional powerful friends at court.[150]

Robert of Meulan's interest in his kinsman's advancement is made
clear in the *Vita Willelmi*. Crossing from England to Normandy,
Count Robert was at Curthose's court in October when Prior Baudry
and Roger of Lessay presented William of Beaumont for the ducal
investiture.[151] Overjoyed at his cousin's preferment, Robert of Meulan arranged for an escort to conduct the new abbot-elect back to
Bec and commanded his own servants not to annoy the abbot or his
monks in any way. Robert also freed the monks of Bec from all custom-

148. For the Montfort family and genealogy, see David C. Douglas, ed., *The Domesday Monachorum of Christ Church Canterbury* (London, 1944), pp. 65–70: The precise
connection between Turstin of Montfort and the main Montfort lines in England and
Normandy cannot be established, but "Turstin" is a Montfort family name. Robert and
Hugh's ancestor, Turstin of Bastembourg, is the first known lord of Montfort-sur-Risle, the
family's Norman *caput*, and William of Beaumont was born and reared there: VW 713.
149. Porée, *Bec* 1:240 and n. 3.
150. A link already existed between Bec and the Montforts: Hugh II of Montfort,
father of Robert and Hugh III, had retired to Bec about 1088 to spend his last days as a
monk: *Gesta Normannorum Ducum*, p. 260.
151. VW 717; cf. *HN* 40, where Robert of Meulan is serving as Rufus's advisor in
mid-August.

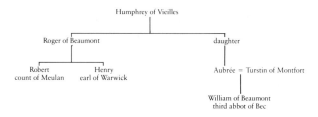

2.

William of Beaumont's Lineage

ary food taxes, which had previously been exacted by his officials at Brionne, and he later granted the monks an exemption from all customary taxes and tolls on their household goods throughout the lands under his authority. "This he did for the love of God and of William his cousin, abbot of Bec. He also conferred many other kindnesses on the community of Bec while he lived, for the sake of this abbot."[152]

By no later than summer 1093, as we have seen, Robert of Meulan had abandoned Curthose's court to become a member of Rufus's inner circle of advisers.[153] His visit to the ducal court in mid or late October was thus a departure from his usual pattern of behavior and may well have been undertaken for the primary purpose of ensuring and overseeing his cousin's advancement to the abbacy of Bec. One can hardly suppose that Anselm had kept his nomination of William a secret from the count; Anselm himself had warned the monks of Bec that Rufus supported William of Beaumont's candidacy to the point of refusing to safeguard Bec's English lands unless the monks elected him.[154] Rufus's active support is difficult to explain unless it was an effort to serve the interests of William's Beaumont and Montfort kinsmen in the royal curia. The *Vita Willelmi* account suggests that the magnate with the greatest interest in the matter was Robert count of Meulan. Indeed the likelihood is that Anselm consulted with Count Robert before choosing William. It could well have been Robert's idea to begin with.

The details of the arrangement between Robert and Anselm are hidden from us, but a concurrent letter from Anselm to Bec provides a

152. Ibid. Robert of Montfort also gave generously to Bec: Douglas, *Domesday Monachorum*, p. 67, n. 6.

153. Above, Chapter 3 at nn. 95 – 106. Of Robert's seven Norman attestations under Curthose, six can be dated in or before 1091; the seventh is 1091–95.

154. AEp. 164.

strong hint that the two men were in touch during the spring or summer of 1093.[155] In it Anselm enjoins the monks to welcome the countess of Vermandois "who, so I have heard, will be visiting you." He asks that they honor her in every possible way, caring for her tenderly with their hospitality and goodwill, and suggests that their kindnesses to her will benefit the church of Bec in many ways. The woman in question was Adelaide, daughter and heiress of Herbert IV, count of Vermandois (d. 1086) and wife of King Philip I's younger brother, Hugh "the Great," count of Chaumont-en-Vexin. The most likely reason for her visit to Normandy and sojourn at Bec is suggested by the fact that in 1096 Isabel of Vermandois, daughter of Hugh the Great and Countess Adelaide, married the lord of nearby Brionne, Robert of Meulan.[156] The marriage represented a dazzling triumph for the Beaumont family, ensuring that Robert of Meulan's children would be direct descendants of the Capetian royal house and, more distantly, Charlemagne.[157] If Countess Adelaide's purpose was indeed to discuss marriage arrangements, the person who informed Anselm of her intention to visit Bec was very likely Robert of Meulan himself.

These tantalizing glimpses suggest the possibility that Anselm and Robert of Meulan could cooperate as well as contend. Anselm, ever seeking friends, may well have pressed William of Beaumont on Bec in the hope of winning Robert of Meulan's goodwill, along with the gratitude of Henry earl of Warwick and the Montforts. And although Robert of Meulan always reserved his ultimate loyalty to the king, as did Anselm's other friends among the curial magnates, the affection and gratitude of these men toward Anselm does much to explain the otherwise puzzling fact that, at critical moments in his subsequent struggles with Rufus, Anselm enjoyed stronger support from the king's magnates than from the bishops.[158]

William of Beaumont's election also marked the ultimate resolution of the Bec-Brionne controversy. With a Beaumont abbot governing Bec, the castle of Brionne ceased to be a menace. Robert of Meulan had failed in his attempt to assert his lordship over Bec, but he now

---

155. AEp. 151: well after 6 March and before 15 August.
156. OV 5:30.
157. The marriage took place before Hugh the Great's departure on the First Crusade in fall 1096, at which time Isabel was very young: *Complete Peerage* 7:526 and n. Her youth could well account for a three-year lapse between the initial marriage negotiations and the marriage itself. Evidence for the date of the betrothal is lacking.
158. See Chapter 5.

had the security of a kinship bond with its abbot. The arrangement benefited both the count and the abbey: the monks continued to safeguard their liberties while at the same time enjoying the count's friendship and generosity. And Robert, satisfied that his kinsman would be sensitive to Beaumont family interests, never pressed for tighter control.

Although resigned to assuming the archbishopric, Anselm had no intention of abandoning the Bec community altogether. In their desperate efforts not to lose him, the monks had at one point asked him to continue serving as their abbot even after his promotion to Canterbury.[159] Predictably, Anselm declined their request, but he did in fact continue to exercise some authority over Bec: "I will never relinquish the power I had over you of binding and loosing, so long as the abbot who succeeds me, and you who will be under him, shall yield it to me."[160] That these were more than mere words is suggested by his all-out effort to make William of Beaumont his successor. In his letter nominating William, he exercised authority despite his having vacated the abbatial office. Having returned his crozier, Anselm, "who until now served . . . as abbot," commanded William of Beaumont to accept the abbacy and ordered Baudry not to desert his office.[161] After William's installation Anselm continued to watch over Bec, urging William to govern justly and instructing him in some detail how to proceed, so that "on all sides the inviolate order of the abbey can be preserved rightly."[162] Informally, Bec and Canterbury remained sister houses: Anselm would always receive a lordly and loving welcome at Bec, and he often depended on Bec monks as messengers and envoys in the affairs of his archbishopric. The quarrels of 1093 were put to rest, and throughout the remaining years of Anselm's life he and the Bec monks remained mutually devoted.

But with respect to his primary responsibilities, so Anselm informed the monks, "I am absolved from your care and involved in greater things."[163] Having resigned his abbatial office, he turned to the completion of the process of his elevation to the archbishopric and the restoration of the Canterbury lands.

159. *DLB* 602.
160. AEp. 156.
161. AEp. 157.
162. AEp. 165.
163. AEp. 157.

Immediately after returning his abbatial staff, Anselm conferred privately with Rufus at Rochester. Eadmer quotes Anselm as saying: "My lord king, I continue to remain in doubt as to which course I ought to follow, whether I should consent to undertake the archbishopric, or whether I should not. But in case on further consideration I should be let to undertake it, I want to make known briefly to you in advance the treatment I would have you accord me."[164] If Eadmer's quotation is correct, then Anselm can only have been bluffing. That his doubts had by then been fully resolved is evident from his correspondence, his return of the crozier, and his nomination of William of Beaumont to succeed him. At one level Anselm appears to be alleging his continued indecision as a bargaining device. At a deeper level he seems to be striving to effect God's will not only by accepting the burden of the archbishopric but now, for the first time, by undertaking to exercise his archiepiscopal authority as God would wish, in accordance with divinely sanctioned due order and on the model of Lanfranc. As one who had accepted the office in regretful obedience to God, Anselm thenceforth had the freedom to act as he believed God intended him to act, taking personal and political risks impossible to a careerist. As a truly reluctant prelate-elect, he could threaten even yet to decline the office unless Rufus offered it on terms that Anselm regarded as satisfactory to his divine commission.

Anselm asked Rufus to restore all the estates that Canterbury had held at Lanfranc's death, to grant a lawful hearing with regard to other estates that Canterbury claimed but Lanfranc had failed to recover, and to accept Anselm as his spiritual father and guardian of his soul.[165] Rufus responded by summoning two counselors, William bishop of Durham and Robert of Meulan, and at the king's command Anselm repeated his conditions in their presence. On their advice, Rufus conceded to Anselm the lands that Lanfranc had held. The king made no commitment regarding other lands that Canterbury might claim but promised that in that matter and in others he would be guided by Anselm as he ought to be. In essence, if a bit vaguely, Rufus had submitted to Anselm's terms; and he had done so on the advice of a counselor who had his own reasons to support Anselm's translation from Bec to Canterbury.

164. *HN* 39.
165. *HN* 39–40. Anselm's terms will be examined more carefully in the next chapter.

Eadmer claims that shortly thereafter, at Windsor, Rufus and his men once more pressed Anselm for his decision.[166] Again Eadmer's account conflicts with Anselm's repeated assertion that he reached his decision after having received the orders from the duke, archbishop, and monks. And it seems most improbable that by this late date the king and count were unaware of the return of Anselm's staff and his nomination of William of Beaumont — a nomination of keen interest to Count Robert and enjoying Rufus's strong backing. The king now qualified his pledge to restore the Canterbury lands, asking Anselm to relinquish claim to certain estates on which Rufus had enfeoffed his men after Lanfranc's death. Anselm's flat refusal moved the king to such anger that he suspended the process of Anselm's elevation.[167] Describing Anselm's response, Eadmer pushes the reluctance topos to a point that does credit neither to Anselm's practical intelligence nor to the seriousness of his commitment to the divine will: "At this Anselm rejoiced greatly, hoping that by God's grace this turn of events would open the way to his being unburdened with any preferment at all." Having resigned his abbatiate, he hoped that by refusing to condone the wrongful alienation of Canterbury lands "he had escaped the burden of episcopal office."[168] Whatever the truth of this — and it is utterly inconsistent with the views expressed in his unenrolled letters to Bec — Anselm was hardly the man to be pressured by Rufus's threat. The king, bowing to "the general outcry of complaint," dropped the matter. At a royal court at Winchester in September, comfortably close to the end of the fiscal year at Michaelmas, Anselm was "inducted in the manner and on the precedent of his predecessors." He rendered homage to the king and was seised of all the lands of the archbishopric "as Lanfranc had been in his day."[169] Anselm thus seems to have undergone a second investiture ceremony, less ambiguous and more dignified than the first, permitting him at last to take custody of the archiepiscopal property that Rufus had granted and then denied him the previous March.

Next Anselm went to Canterbury where, on 25 September 1093, he was raised to the archiepiscopal throne amidst tremendous rejoicing

166. *HN* 40.
167. *HN* 40–41.
168. *HN* 41.
169. *HN* 41.

by the monks, clergy, and people. The festivities were marred, however, by Rufus's principal administrator, Ranulf Flambard, who instituted a lawsuit against Anselm on a matter that Eadmer describes only as being related to ecclesiastical, not royal, law.[170] The suit may well have had to do with the king's claim to revenues during the vacancy, since, as Frank Barlow has suggested, Ranulf's main purpose at the occasion was to supervise the transfer of the archbishopric from the king's custody to Anselm's.[171] Although deeply grieved, Anselm would not now permit a lawsuit to deflect him from his course. On Sunday, 4 December 1093, he was consecrated at Canterbury Cathedral by Thomas archbishop of York, Lanfranc's former student. This occasion, too, was marred by a dispute — as to the title with which the archbishop of York should consecrate Anselm. The issue appears to have been resolved without great difficulty, but on terms that will always be unclear because Eadmer of Canterbury and Hugh the Chantor of York provide conflicting accounts. According to Eadmer, Anselm was consecrated "Primate of all Britain"; according to Hugh, he was consecrated with the far less exalted title "Metropolitan of Canterbury."[172] Hugh adds, probably with Eadmer in mind, "A false report and a wicked denial of what was done in the sight of so many important people is disgraceful in men's eyes and criminal in God's."[173]

Eadmer declares that during the consecration the bishops in attendance performed the traditional ritual of holding an open Bible over Anselm's head and, after the ceremony, reading the beginning of the page that they had earlier opened at random. The text perfectly embodied one of Eadmer's major themes — that the crowds of nobles and prelates who had coerced the reluctant abbot to become archbishop, rejoiced at his election, cheered tumultuously at his enthronement, and flocked to his coronation, would afterward desert him in his time of need: "He invited many people. And at the time for the feast he sent his servants to tell his guests that they should come, for everything was now ready. But they all, one after another, began to make excuses."[174]

170. *HN* 41.
171. *Rufus*, 307–8.
172. See Barlow, *English Church*, pp. 42–43.
173. *HCY* 8.
174. *HN* 43; Luke 14:16–18.

Five

Regnum and *Sacerdotium:*
The Archbishop, the Magnate,
and the King, 1093–1100

Looking back on his enthronement, Archbishop Anselm wrote to the bishops of Ireland: "Being therefore crowned episcopally, I began carefully to consider what was my duty to Christ, to his Church in this land, and to my office; and I tried to repress evils by pastoral rule, to coerce those who had unjustly taken possession, and to lead everything irregular back to due order."[1] Such, in essence, was the mission to which Anselm would thenceforth devote himself. Although his subsequent disputes with William Rufus might appear trivial and inconclusive,[2] they all arose from Anselm's unwavering commitment to his stewardship of Canterbury. In Anselm's mind nothing, not even the Investiture Controversy, took precedence over his God-given obligation to rule Canterbury and the churches of all Britain as a model archbishop and primate. Perhaps Canterbury's destiny was not the most important issue in Christendom, but because God's power had brought Anselm to the archbishopric and committed it to his care, Canterbury, like Bec beforehand, became his primary responsibility. His determination to exercise his archiepiscopal duties properly provides the connecting link between his various quarrels with Rufus and his very different conflict with Henry I.

1. AEp. 198.
2. Southern, *Anselm*, p. 150; cf. p. 165.

What, in Anselm's mind, were the specific components of the "due order" that he sought and the stewardship that he endeavored to exercise? The answer is to be found in the Canterbury traditions that had developed gradually over the centuries but were refashioned by Lanfranc into principles of unprecedented clarity and force. The first such principle was the integrity of Canterbury lands — a matter on which Anselm had sought and obtained Rufus's guarantee as a sine qua non for accepting the archiepiscopal office. It might seem odd that a question of real estate should be of such vital importance to the spiritual leader of Britain. But Anselm, like all responsible prelates of his age, felt a profound obligation to safeguard the lands that his church had received through divine grace.[3] As his contemporary, Pope Urban II, expressed it, the church's property, like the Holy Spirit, is the "gift of God."[4]

Another important component of the Canterbury tradition was the idea that the king and archbishop should work harmoniously together as corulers of the Christian realm, each in his proper sphere.[5] The archbishop ought to be the king's loyal supporter; the king ought to take the archbishop as his most intimate counselor and heed his advice on all spiritual and moral issues. This ideal is epitomized in the opening paragraph of Chapter 1 of Eadmer's *Historia Novorum:*

In the reign of the most glorious King Edgar, as he diligently governed the entire realm with righteous laws, Dunstan prelate of Canterbury, a man of limitless virtue, ordered the whole of Britain by the administration of Christian law. Under his influence and counsel, King Edgar showed himself to be a devoted servant of God. . . . All England enjoyed peace and felicity so long as it was fortunate enough to have that king and Father Dunstan in bodily presence.[6]

The ideal reemerges in Eadmer's discussion of William the Conqueror's relationship with Archbishop Lanfranc:

William heeded his counsel not merely as one of several advisers but rather as his chief adviser. And since Lanfranc was at the same time totally and extraordinarily devoted to the service of God, he always took pains both to make the king a faithful servant of God and to renew religion and righteous living throughout

---

3. See, for example, *HN* 41.
4. Benson, *Bishop-Elect*, p. 211 and n. 25; cf. Margaret Howell, *Regalian Right in Medieval England* (London, 1962), p. 12; Southern, *Anselm*, pp. 127, 141–42.
5. The lay and ecclesiastical spheres were not, however, clearly divided. The king might participate in primatial councils; the primate might assume a military role in the kingdom's defense.
6. *HN* 3.

the whole kingdom. Nor was his wish denied him. His teaching and perseverance brought a great increase of religion throughout the land.[7]

The same principle was in Anselm's mind as he negotiated with
Rufus prior to his archiepiscopal enthronement and consecration:
"Furthermore, I ask that in all matters pertaining to God and Christianity you accept my advice before anyone else's and, just as I am
willing to hold you as my earthly lord and protector, so you should hold
me as your spiritual father and the guardian of your soul."[8] Anselm had
previously expressed the idea metaphorically: "You must think of the
church as a plow. . . . In England this plow is drawn by two oxen
outstanding above the rest, and these two, by drawing the plow, rule the
land: the king and the archbishop of Canterbury. The former rules by
secular justice and sovereignty [*imperio*], the latter by divine doctrine
and authority [*magisterio*]."[9]

Anselm's two-oxen metaphor reminds one of Gelasius's well-known
theory of the two swords, but the apparent similarity is deceiving. To
Gelasius, the spiritual sword was superior to the secular sword, and by
Anselm's time the Gregorian papacy was stressing this superiority as
never before. The Canterbury idea of corule, on the other hand, was one
of equality, thus differing from both the papal concept and the concept
of unrivaled royal authority upheld by William Rufus. The Canterbury
theory of corule under God was expressed diagrammatically by one of
Anselm's beloved friends and obedient bishops, Gilbert of Limerick. He
pictured the world as a vast pyramid under Christ — with the pyramid
expressed interestingly and medievally as a vast Gothic arch containing
within it smaller Gothic arches pyramided in a descending scale. The
vast arch seems to represent Christendom, which is ruled jointly by
pope and emperor, whom Gilbert placed on an equal level. Contained
in this arch are two smaller arches of equal size with king and
primate at an equal level at their apexes. And beneath these are pyra-
mids of authority equating archbishop with duke, bishop with count,
and priest with knight. Each secular office is thus made exactly equal to
a corresponding ecclesiastical office.[10]

---

7. *HN* 12.　　8. *HN* 40.

9. *HN* 37: although Anselm goes on to complain that he is a feeble old sheep about
to be harnessed alongside an untamed bull, his conception of the proper royal-
archiepiscopal relationship emerges nonetheless.

10. Durham Cathedral ms. B. II. 35, fol. 36v, printed in R. A. B. Mynors, *Durham
Cathedral Manuscripts to the End of the Twelfth Century* (Oxford, 1939), pl. 47; see
p. 268. On Gilbert, see below, Chapter 5 at nn. 230–31; and Chapter 8 at nn. 109–16.

3.
Gilbert of Limerick, "The General Image of the Church."
Durham Cathedral ms. B. II. 35 fol. 36v. Reproduced by permission of the
Durham Cathedral Chapter Library.

A third component of the tradition that Anselm strove to uphold was
Canterbury's proper position in the ecclesiastical hierarchy of Britain
and Christendom. Like Lanfranc, Anselm was intent on establishing
Canterbury's supremacy over the churches of Britain — the Canterbury
primacy — and direct lordship over the bishopric of Rochester and the
abbeys of St. Augustine's Canterbury and St. Albans.[11] He was also
intent on maintaining a correct posture toward the papacy, which was
an immensely greater international force in 1093 than it had been a few
decades earlier. Anselm has sometimes been viewed as a Gregorian who
veered from Lanfranc's royalist path to support the papal reform movement. But a closer inspection of the evidence discloses that the two
men entertained quite similar ideas about Canterbury's relationship to

11. R. A. L. Smith, "The Place of Gundulf in the Anglo-Norman Church," *EHR* 58
(1943): 261–63; *HN* 15–16, 37, 188–91.

Rome. Both viewed it as one of respectful but strictly limited subordination — obedience from a distance. The archbishop would receive his pallium from the pope and would obey him on matters of broad significance relating to the whole of Christendom; but on more specific matters involving the English church, Canterbury expected somewhat free rein. The primate of Canterbury might turn to the pope for a confirmation of his primacy and support against York, but from Canterbury's point of view, papal legates were usually unwelcome in England and ought never to usurp Canterbury's prerogative to preside at English synods.[12]

Canterbury's relative autonomy from Rome was evidently conceded by the papacy itself. As Eadmer proudly reports, Pope Urban II welcomed Archbishop Anselm to Rome in 1098 with these words: "We regard him as if he were our equal, just as by right he should be venerated like the apostle and patriarch of another world."[13] At the Council of Bari in 1098, so William of Malmesbury relates, Urban stated: "We include this man in our world as if he were pope of another world."[14] This concept suggests the archbishop of Canterbury's singular status in relation to the pope, who in the eyes of the Anglo-Normans properly regarded Anselm as a pontiff of almost equal dignity to his own. There was a consciousness in England of Britain being a world apart. Eadmer conceived of Canterbury as "totius Brittanie mater," and the Winchester annalist speaks of "Anselmus Papa" in 1102.[15]

All these elements in the Canterbury tradition — the integrity of its properties, its ideal of joint governance with the king, its primacy over all Britain, and its wide discretionary authority under the papacy — were regarded as the essential means by which the archbishops could fulfill

---

12. The one obvious exception is the altogether unique legatine council of 1070 that deposed Archbishop Stigand and cleared the way for Lanfranc's advancement; Lanfranc took the position that Stigand was not a true archbishop but a usurper. On the matter of Canterbury's views on legates and legatine councils, see Brett, *English Church,* pp. 35–36; Southern, *Anselm,* p. 132; Barlow, *English Church,* p. 107. William I's ban on unlicensed legates "protected his church" and would surely have had the support of Lanfranc, who in 1071 had been granted de facto legatine powers by Alexander II: LEp. 7, lines 41–44.

13. *VA* 105: "Et quasi comparem velut alterius orbis apostolicum et patriarcham jure venerandum censeamus."

14. *GP* 100: " 'Includamus,' inquit, 'hunc in orbe nostro: quasi alterius orbis papam.' " See Southern's valuable observations in *VA* 105, n. 2.

15. Brett, *English Church,* pp. 12, 14, 69 n. 2.

their central responsibility: "To renew religion and righteous living throughout the whole kingdom."[16] And the chief instruments by which such reforms could be promulgated were kingdomwide synods summoned and supervised by the archbishop of Canterbury with the king's backing. It was in presiding effectively over reforming synods that the archbishops manifested most forcefully their corule, their primatial authority, and their freedom from close papal supervision. Rufus's refusal to permit such synods constituted one of Anselm's deepest grievances. It was a denial of one of the primate's most essential traditional rights.

But as has been observed, the principles that Canterbury had come to regard by 1093 as its traditional rights had been restructured and meticulously redefined during the pontificate of Archbishop Lanfranc. Thus we must examine Lanfranc's activities as archbishop to discern the model he provided Anselm. It was Lanfranc who made Rochester an *eigenkirche* of Canterbury and its bishop an archiepiscopal vicar.[17] And it was through Lanfranc's lawyerlike efforts that Canterbury recovered most of its previously alienated lands and jurisdictional privileges. He pursued these claims in case after case, the court at Penenden Heath being only the most famous of many, with the result that the annual value of the archiepiscopal demesne rose by nearly £500 between 1066 and 1086 to about £1250.[18] And the figure of £500 probably underestimates Lanfranc's success: Canterbury had not only lost lands to the Godwines but had suffered further losses between 1066 and 1070 as a result of the land-grabbing of Odo of Bayeux and other newly established Conquest magnates.[19] The figure of £1250, moreover, represents only the value of the archbishop's demesne. If one includes enfeoffed lands and *terrae militum,* the figure rises to about £1600 a year, with further manors worth an additional £600 a year reserved for the Canterbury monks.[20]

---

16. *HN* 12, from the passage earlier quoted.

17. Smith, "Gundulf," pp. 261–63.

18. DuBoulay, *Lordship,* pp. 37–42, 243; cf. David Bates, "The Land Pleas of William I's Reign: Penenden Heath Revisited," *BIHR* 51 (1978): 1–19.

19. DuBoulay, *Lordship,* pp. 37ff.; cf. *HN* 22. Bates argues, however, that Odo's depredations have been exaggerated ("Land Pleas," pp. 18–19), and that some of the increased values between 1066 and 1086 resulted from a significant rise in the profitability of Canterbury's TRE estates (i.e., those listed as Canterbury possessions Tempus Edwardi, or 1066).

20. DuBoulay, *Lordship,* p. 58.

Having taken the leadership of a ravaged archbishopric, Lanfranc brought it to the point where its estates were far more valuable than those of any other church in England and were more than twice as profitable as the English lands of such dominating curial magnates as Geoffrey of Coutances (£788) and Richard fitz Gilbert of Clare (£794).[21] Lanfranc's estates in 1086 were surpassed in value only by those of Roger of Montgomery (£2100) and the king's two half-brothers, Robert of Mortain (£2100) and Odo of Bayeux (£3050), the latter being disseised and in prison at the time of the Domesday inquest.[22] If one adds the £600 of lands assigned to the Christ Church monks (and excludes the captive Odo), the Canterbury estates constituted the most profitable tenancy-in-chief in all of Domesday England.[23] In short, when Anselm negotiated with Rufus over the restoration of Canterbury's lands in 1093, the stakes were very high.

While working indefatigably through the courts to recover his own lost properties, Lanfranc also strove for the recovery of the lands and rights alienated from Canterbury's suffragan bishopric of Rochester and from many other churches as well.[24] His skill at dealing with land cases is suggested by the fact that his name occurs as a witness or addressee in no less than nineteen of the Conqueror's thirty-four extant charters reporting meetings of shire or hundred courts that determined rights to land, or confirming lands held "at the time of King Edward."[25] In one writ, probably from 1086, William orders Lanfranc to inquire through Geoffrey of Coutances and Walchelin bishop of Winchester "who it was that caused the abbey of Ely's estates to be enrolled and sworn, how they were sworn, by whom, before what witnesses, and what are the lands and their names and size, and who holds them."[26] This last charter suggests Lanfranc's involvement, at least indirectly, in the Domesday survey; E. O. Blake has argued persuasively that portions of the *Inquisitio Eliensis* constitute Lanfranc's responses to the

21. These figures represent totals of demesne and enfeoffed estates and are thus directly comparable to the archbishop's total of £1600.

22. The values are taken, with some minor corrections, from C. W. Hollister, "Magnates and 'Curiales,' " pp. 72, 75.

23. See DuBoulay, *Lordship*, p. 21: "Not until Anselm's time were the monks granted power to administer their own lands separately."

24. DuBoulay, *Lordship*, pp. 38–42.

25. *Regesta* 1, nos. 151–57, 162–63, 166–67, 177, 184–85, 200, 206, 210, 220, 222, and 261 — of which nos. 167 and 222 are spurious, and 261 is suspicious.

26. *Regesta* 1, no. 152; for the date, see *Regesta* 2, p. 394, and *Liber Eliensis*, ed. E. O. Blake (RHS, London, 1962), pp. 206, 426–32.

king's instructions.[27] The expertise that Lanfranc had developed in recovering the lands of Canterbury could thus be put to valuable use in the king's service.

Although Eadmer may well have exaggerated in singling out Lanfranc as the chief royal adviser, other sources place him unmistakably within the innermost circle of the king's counselors. His twenty-two attestations of William I's surviving charters[28] far exceed the attestation totals of any other English churchman and are exceeded only by the attestations of the two great curial magnates, Roger of Montgomery (40) and Geoffrey of Coutances (34), and by those of the Conqueror's immediate family — his wife, two eldest sons, and two half brothers.[29] Lanfranc's attestations as archbishop are all the more significant when one recalls that he had a late start (1070), spent the better part of 1071 on a journey to Rome, and, unlike William I's other frequent attestors, seldom crossed with the king to Normandy.[30]

Lanfranc's service to the Conqueror was by no means confined to spiritual guidance, ecclesiastical reform, and the recovery of church lands. On the king's visit to Normandy about 1073–75, he left Lanfranc in charge of the English administration as the kingdom's "prince and guardian" (princeps et custos Angliae), and Lanfranc may have done similar service on other occasions as well.[31] In 1075, he oversaw the royal military campaigns against the rebellion of the earls while the king remained in Normandy. "We would welcome seeing you as we would God's angel," Lanfranc wrote to William, "yet we don't want

27. Blake, Liber Eliensis, pp. 426–32; cf. V. H. Galbraith, "The Making of Domesday Book," EHR 57 (1942): 167n. Lanfranc's familiarity with the Domesday survey is suggested by the fact that his last primatial council was held in conjunction with the king's 1085 Christmas court at Gloucester at which the great inquest was undertaken, and by the probability that the nearly concurrent Domesday Monachorum of Christ Church Canterbury, ed. D. C. Douglas (London, 1944), was prepared during his pontificate. The absence of Archbishop Stigand's name in Domesday descriptions of TRE archiepiscopal holdings in Kent reflects Lanfranc's own policy of regarding him as a usurper: see Canterbury Professions, p. lvii.

28. Gibson, Lanfranc, pp. 208–10; I am including Regesta 1, no. 218, which Gibson omits: see Regesta 2, p. 396.

29. Robert of Meulan's attestations equal those of Lanfranc.

30. Only six of Lanfranc's twenty-two attestations occur in charters definitely or probably issued in Normandy: Regesta 1, nos. 96, 105, 125, 150, 168, and 170.

31. Our information on William I's regency governments is very thin. The Vita Lanfranci implies that Lanfranc functioned as princeps et custos Angliae whenever William was in Normandy, but this statement must be qualified by the fact of Lanfranc's occasional appearances at William's Norman courts: see n. 30. On the issue of William's regency governments, see Francis West, The Justiciarship in England, 1066–1232 (Cambridge, England, 1966), pp. 1–10.

you to cross the sea at this moment, for you would be insulting us gravely if you should come to our assistance in subduing such perjured brigands."[32] Lanfranc goes on to report that the rebellious Ralph earl of Norfolk and his army have been put to flight: "Our forces are pursuing them . . . and within a few days, as our commanders have informed me, either these oath-breakers will be fleeing from your land by sea, or our men will have them alive or dead."[33] Shortly thereafter Lanfranc reported to William that the rebels had surrendered Norwich castle: "Glory be to God on high, by whose mercy your kingdom has been purged of its Breton dung."[34] And to the bishop of Durham Lanfranc wrote triumphantly: "Now that the Bretons are banished and all warfare is suppressed, we live in a tranquillity greater than we can recall ever experiencing since the king crossed the sea. Be assured that the affairs of our lord king are prospering and that he himself is crossing to England without delay."[35]

The bonds of trust and mutual understanding that linked Lanfranc and William help explain the otherwise puzzling evidence that during the pontificate of one of Canterbury's most vigorous and powerful archbishops, the king was enforcing a series of "customs" on the English church that would seem to have restricted its liberty to a significant degree. As Eadmer reports it, the Conqueror's customs touched on four distinct matters: (1) he forbade anyone in his kingdom to recognize a Roman pontiff except on royal instructions; (2) he forbade anyone to accept a papal letter unless it had first been submitted to the king; (3) the archbishop of Canterbury, when presiding over a synod, was to issue no order or prohibition contrary to the king's wishes; and (4) no bishop was to excommunicate or otherwise discipline any of the king's barons, no matter what his offense, except at the express instructions of the king.[36] Since Eadmer discusses these usages before turning to Lanfranc's election to Canterbury, the last two of them may well have been addressed to an episcopate that was still largely Anglo-Saxon, and to an unsavory primate—Archbishop Stigand—soon to be deposed. It is difficult to imagine Lanfranc's synods producing any canons distasteful to the Conqueror, and when Lanfranc excommunicated the rebel Earl Ralph during the king's absence in

32. LEp. 34
33. Ibid.
34. LEp. 35.
35. LEp. 36.   36. *HN* 10.

Normandy, William can hardly have objected.[37] Indeed the Conqueror's power over the English church strengthened rather than weakened Lanfranc's archiepiscopal authority. When a recalcitrant bishop of Chester ignored Lanfranc's command to respect the liberties of Coventry Abbey, Lanfranc sent him a second command "in the king's name and my own."[38] Similarly, when advising Gundulf of Rochester on the treatment of professing and nonprofessing inmates of nunneries, Lanfranc concludes, "This is the king's policy and my own."[39]

Lanfranc's interests were also served by the Conqueror's prohibitions against recognizing Roman pontiffs or receiving papal letters without royal approval — and, as Eadmer later makes clear, by a further prohibition of unlicensed episcopal visits to the papal court.[40] All these customs would have had the effect of shielding Lanfranc from the insistent demands of Gregory VII,[41] and the further effect of solidifying his primatial authority by limiting direct intercourse between the pope and other English bishops.[42] That Lanfranc did in fact accept papal letters before submitting them to the king is demonstrated by his remark to Pope Gregory: "I presented the text of your message and your abovementioned legate to my lord king with what skill I could; I commended it to him, but without success. Why he has not complied with your wishes in all respects the legate himself is explaining to you both orally and in a letter."[43] Lanfranc was writing in response to a dressing down from Pope Gregory: "Throughout almost its entire length," Lanfranc complained, "you were concerned to rebuke me."

Under the circumstances Lanfranc would have regarded the royal will less as a threat than as a shelter.[44] Similarly, in answer to an unwelcome and embarrassing appeal for support from a cardinal who backed the antipope Clement III, Lanfranc equivocated and urged that the cardinal not come to England "unless you first get permission from

37. LEp. 33.   38. LEp. 27.
39. LEp. 53.   40. HN 83.
41. See, for example, Lanfranc's cautious response to Gregory's complaints (LEp. 38), promising to obey the pope in all matters "in accordance with canon law"; on the general subject of royal policies against papal intervention serving Canterbury's interests, see H. E. J. Cowdrey, *Popes, Monks, and Crusaders* (London, 1984), pp. ix, 94–95; Southern, *Anselm*, p. 130.
42. Cowdrey, *Popes, Monks, and Crusaders*, pp. ix, 94, 104–5.
43. LEp. 38; cf. 39: two of Gregory's demands to which Lanfranc is responding are the payment of Peter's Pence, to which William agreed, and the king's homage, which he refused. Gregory was also pressing Lanfranc to visit Rome.
44. Cf. Barlow, *Rufus*, p. 338: "Lanfranc, who had not had an easy time under Gregory, was not sorry to escape from papal interference."

the king of the English."[45] William's "wall around England" could be attractive to a primate who was wary of a tightening papal grip and who was working with a cooperative king open to reform.

But while maintaining an appropriate distance from the Gregorian papacy, Lanfranc was establishing an unprecedented degree of primatial control over the English church — a project that Sir Richard Southern has aptly termed "the great design."[46] As Michael Richter has shown, Lanfranc brought with him to England a redaction of the pseudo-Isidorian collection of canon law, a collection that included a considerable body of genuine Visigothic ecclesiastical legislation along with the False Decretals.[47] The collection demonstrates that the archbishop of Toledo enjoyed sweeping powers over the Visigothic church, including the right to approve all episcopal elections jointly with the king, to consecrate all new bishops (by implication), to consecrate the king, and to receive professions of obedience.[48] The canons of the councils of Toledo reflected the exceptional political pressures on the Visigothic kingdom, particularly at the time of the Twelfth Council in A.D. 681, and the broad primatial powers conferred on the archbishop of Toledo at that time were probably never enforced with any consistency. But Lanfranc seems to have regarded the conciliar legislation simply as canon law, uncontaminated by its historical context. "The conclusion seems inescapable," Richter states, "that, as far as canon law was concerned, Lanfranc based his claim to primacy on the legislation of the Visigothic Church."[49]

More broadly, Lanfranc used every legal text and precedent at his disposal to buttress Canterbury's primatial claim, including the Benedictine Rule; the writings of the church fathers; the canons of councils at Carthage, Nicaea, and Antioch; Bede's account of the papal privileges granted to Augustine of Canterbury; accounts of past kingdomwide councils presided over by Canterbury archbishops; other instances of Canterbury having asserted authority over York; and a series of papal

45. LEp. 52, A.D. 1080–85: Lanfranc to Cardinal Hugh Candidus.
46. *Anselm*, p. 129.
47. Richter, *Canterbury Professions*, p. lxvi and passim.
48. Ibid., p. lxvii, particularly from XI Tolet. c. 11 (*recte* 10) and XII Tolet. c. 7 (*recte* 6), both of which were singled out by a marginal sign in Lanfranc's manuscript; cf. Richter, "Archbishop Lanfranc and the Canterbury Professions — Some Suggestions," *Downside Review* 90 (1972): 117.
49. *Canterbury Professions*, p. lxviii. The statement may perhaps be too strong; Lanfranc does not often refer explicitly to the Toledo canons in his own correspondence about the primacy: ibid., pp. lxv–lxvi. (But see LEpp. 10, 11, 12, 14, 46, and 47.)

privileges that Lanfranc referred to in a letter to Alexander II but did not quote. These privileges were in all probability the celebrated Canterbury forgeries, which appear to have been fabricated toward the beginning of Lanfranc's pontificate.[50] Lanfranc thus employed his lawyer's skill, as he had done at Bec and Caen, to magnify and define Canterbury's primatial authority to the fullest possible extent.[51]

In doing so, Lanfranc doubtless enjoyed the enthusiastic support of the Canterbury monks, but judging from the new course that he steered, the monks probably learned more from Lanfranc than he from them. He did encounter at Canterbury a collection of some thirty written professions of obedience from various Anglo-Saxon bishops to the archbishop of Canterbury, which provided some backing to his contention that bishops had traditionally professed in writing to the English primate.[52] But this collection was flawed in two vitally important respects: (1) the great majority of the written professions date from the ninth century or earlier, and none date from the century prior to Lanfranc's accession — the practice having evidently gone out of style long before Lanfranc's time;[53] and (2) only one of the thirty professions purports to be from a prelate outside the province of Canterbury, and that one exception, a profession from "Eadulf" archbishop of York, was either forged or interpolated.[54]

Richter thus views Lanfranc's aggressive advancement of the Canterbury primacy as unprecedented — a drastic measure, ruthlessly applied.[55]

50. Ibid., pp. lxv, lxviii; LEpp. 3, 4; Gibson (*Lanfranc*, pp. 231–37) argues persuasively that the forgeries, although put to momentary use by Lanfranc in 1072 to advance the primatial claim, were directed primarily against St. Augustine's Abbey. Lanfranc's uncharacteristic act of mentioning but not quoting from them suggests deliberate caution and awareness of the deception. Privilege VII, Gregory III to the bishops of England, would have supplied Lanfranc with some particularly apt passages had he chosen to use them. In 1123 the Canterbury monks presented the forgeries to the papal curia and were laughed out of court: HCY 114–15.

51. As abbot of Caen, Lanfranc had secured a sweeping papal privilege from Alexander II (1068) largely exempting the abbey from the authority of its diocesan bishop of Bayeux: Lemarignier, *Privilèges d'exemption*, pp. 141–45; cf. Gibson, *Lanfranc*, p. 109.

52. *Canterbury Professions*, nos. 1–30.

53. Ibid., pp. xxxvi–xlvii; cf. Denis Bethell, "English Monks and Irish Reform in the 11th and 12th Centuries," *Historical Studies, 8: Papers Read before the Irish Conference of Historians*, ed. T. Desmond Williams (Dublin, 1971), pp. 131–33.

54. *Canterbury Professions*, no. 1 and p. xl: Eadulf was consecrated archbishop of York in 992; the profession should probably be attributed to Eadulf bishop of Lindsey, consecrated 796x798; it is headed by the words "Eadulfus Eboricensis archiepiscopus," but in the body of the profession he is titled simply "episcopus."

55. Ibid., pp. lviii, lxii.

Perhaps this judgment is too harsh, for Lanfranc would also have been aware of the emergence of primacies at Trier and elsewhere on the Continent with the guarded backing of the early reform papacy.[56] But it remains clear that Lanfranc — backed by King William, inspired by the model of Toledo, and employing every papal privilege and relevant historical text at his disposal — reintroduced the written profession within the province of Canterbury and did all in his power to extend the custom into the province of York and throughout all Britain. In doing so, he launched the conflict between Canterbury and York that echoed across future generations and embittered Anselm's last days. Canterbury's provincial bishops began rendering their written professions without apparent murmur, and Lanfranc even obtained written professions from two successive bishops of Dublin,[57] but York resisted with all its strength.

The trouble began in autumn 1070, when the newly consecrated Lanfranc was called upon to consecrate his former student, Thomas of Bayeux bishop-elect of York. Lanfranc made Thomas's consecration contingent on the rendering of a written profession of obedience. Thomas angrily refused and departed, insisting correctly that Lanfranc's demand was unprecedented.[58] Afterward, however, Thomas compromised, professing obedience to Lanfranc personally but not to his successors, and in return Lanfranc consecrated him. Lanfranc then persuaded William I to lower his wall and refer the dispute to the papal court, which each archbishop had to visit in any case to receive his pallium. At Rome in autumn 1071, Alexander II bestowed pallia on the two archbishops and heard their arguments.[59] They not only differed on the profession issue but also asserted conflicting claims to authority over three disputed bishoprics: Lichfield, Worcester, and Dorchester-Lincoln. The pope conferred all three sees on Lanfranc, leaving York with only authority over Durham and a vague claim to the bishopric of the Orkneys, and referred the profession issue back to the court of William the Conqueror.[60] Pope Alexander also conferred on Lanfranc

56. Richter, "Archbishop Lanfranc," p. 115.
57. Gibson, *Lanfranc*, pp. 122–24, where it is observed that Dublin was by no means the dominant Irish bishopric at the time.
58. Ibid., pp. 117–18: some archbishops of York had professed to Canterbury as bishops of Worcester before being elevated to York, but, as Gibson points out, Lanfranc did not argue that point.
59. Alexander rendered Lanfranc special honor by giving him two pallia; Thomas received only one.
60. Gibson, *Lanfranc*, pp. 118–19, with references.

broad though unofficial legatine powers in England, delegating to him "personal and apostolic authority" to settle major ecclesiastical disputes. As Alexander told William I, "whatever he may decide in these affairs, so long as it is just, can thereafter be considered no less firm and binding than if the matter had been concluded in our own presence."[61]

The two archbishops returned to England accompanied by the papal legate Hubert, who was to attend the royal court and report its decision back to Rome. The profession issue was judged and settled, after considerable debate,[62] at King William's Easter court at Winchester in 1072 and was confirmed by a large gathering at the Whitsun court at Windsor. Marshalling all his arguments,[63] Lanfranc persuaded the king and his counselors to confirm the Canterbury position. They ratified the papal decision to place Lichfield, Worcester, and Dorchester-Lincoln firmly within the province of Canterbury and forced Archbishop Thomas to profess his obedience in writing not only to Lanfranc but to all Lanfranc's successors as well.[64] "Misled by bad advice and terrified by threats," the York writer grieves, Thomas "at last sadly and unwillingly yielded."[65]

Lanfranc then wrote to Alexander II rehearsing his entire case and requesting that Canterbury's primacy over York and all Britain be confirmed by a papal privilege "in due form and without delay."[66] But unfortunately for Canterbury, Alexander II did delay. As Archdeacon Hildebrand explained in a letter of summer 1072, there could be no papal privilege until Lanfranc once again came personally to Rome and resubmitted his case to the papal court. Alexander II died the following spring, to be succeeded by Hildebrand as Pope Gregory VII. The papacy turned more strongly against the concept of primacies, viewing them as impediments to Gregorian ideas of papal monarchy,[67] and Lanfranc never returned to Rome. His triumph was thus marred in two respects: he had won the support of the king but not of the pope; and Thomas of York, although bound by a written profession to Lanfranc and his

61. LEp. 7.
62. GP 40–65; Vita Wulfstani, pp. 24–25.
63. LEpp. 3, 4.
64. LEp. 3; Canterbury Professions, no. 34: Thomas's previous profession to Lanfranc is missing from the collection; Richter suggests that it may have been discarded deliberately by the Canterbury community so as not to weaken the impact of Thomas's later, stronger profession.
65. HCY 4.
66. LEp. 4.
67. Richter, Canterbury Professions, p. lxviii and n. 1.

successors, had not committed his own successors at York. The profession issue was therefore certain to reemerge when the next archbishop-elect of York sought consecration. But since Thomas (d. 1100) far outlived Lanfranc, the Canterbury-York relationship remained essentially unchanged from 1072 until long after Anselm's accession.

For the time being, then, Lanfranc had won his battle for Canterbury's primacy, and he proceeded to put the principle into action. Between 1072 and 1085 he held at least six and probably seven kingdom-wide councils, all but one of them in conjunction with meetings of the royal court.[68] With royal backing and full primatial authority, he seized the opportunity to reform the English church, as Richter expresses it, "more drastically than any of his predecessors since the days of the conversion of the Anglo-Saxons."[69] His councils consolidated the powers of bishops over the clergy and laity of their dioceses, supervised and endorsed the transfer of an unprecedented number of episcopal sees from smaller to larger towns, and echoed contemporary reform councils in Normandy and elsewhere on the continent by repeatedly condemning clerical incontinence and all forms of simony.[70]

It is one of the tragedies of Anselm's pontificate that, although he pursued the goals of his predecessor and eventually achieved most of them, he was obliged to do so in far more difficult political circumstances than Lanfranc had known. Anselm regarded William Rufus as an "untamed bull,"[71] and in some respects the description is apt. Frank Barlow, Rufus's most recent and ablest biographer, can admire his "slightly diabolical charisma."[72] But when this quality was combined with his extortionate fund-raising methods, his fierce determination to exercise his royal rights without challenge, and his often explosive temper, Rufus was not the sort of king who would quietly submit to sharing the plow of his sovereignty with Anselm.[73]

Lanfranc, too, had experienced difficulties with Rufus. Before crowning him, the old archbishop, then in his late seventies, had made Rufus promise to rule justly, equitably, and mercifully; to defend the peace

---

68. Barlow, *English Church*, p. 124; *Councils and Synods* 1, pt. 2: 591–634 passim.
69. *Canterbury Professions*, p. lviii.
70. Barlow, *English Church*, pp. 123–28; *Councils and Synods* 1, pt. 2:591–620.
71. *HN* 36.
72. *Rufus*, p. 436.
73. Southern, *Anselm*, p. 145, describes Rufus as "the most secular of all medieval kings, the one who used the Church most consistently for his own material ends."

and liberties of all English churches; and always to follow Lanfranc's bidding and counsel.[74] Afterward, when Lanfranc reproved him for violating these commitments, Rufus is quoted as responding in anger, "Who is there who could fulfill all that he promises?"[75]

Anselm was also confronted with the considerable political talents of Robert of Meulan, with whom he had at first contended and later, seemingly, cooperated in the Bec-Brionne controversy and its resolution. From 1093 through the end of Rufus's reign, Robert of Meulan's frequent attestations place him among the king's most intimate advisers,[76] and Eadmer strongly implies that Robert was Rufus's chief lay adviser on matters relating to Anselm. When describing these matters, Eadmer usually divides the royal advisers into two, often nameless, groups: the bishops and the lay nobles. When Eadmer does name a bishop, it is almost invariably William of St-Calais bishop of Durham[77] or, after William's death on 2 January 1096, Walchelin bishop of Winchester.[78] Among the lay magnate group Eadmer names no one except Robert of Meulan, whom he singles out on four occasions as the magnates' spokesman or as Rufus's chief counselor.[79] Eadmer's customary technique of having the magnates express their views either collectively in an anonymous chorus or through Count Robert's mouth suggests that both modes of address reflect the same guiding intellect — that the magnates in Eadmer's history spoke for Robert just as he spoke for them.

Robert of Meulan had developed a method of dealing with political opponents that was, by the standards of the times, precociously sophisticated. That he had long been developing this approach to politics is clear from earlier events in his life, particularly the Ivry-Brionne-Bec

74. *HN* 25.
75. Ibid.
76. His attestation rate is exceeded only by three laymen: the two royal stewards, Eudo and Roger Bigod, and Robert fitz Hamon: Hollister, "Magnates and 'Curiales,' " p. 76; Robert of Meulan attests *Regesta* 1, nos. 326, 395, 397, 416, 423, 427, 451, 460, and *Regesta* 2 (*addenda* to *Regesta* 1), nos. 338a, 372c, and 414a; all are charters of William II, and all of these charters but no. 326 are dated by the *Regesta* editors as either probably or certainly within the date range 1093–1100; Orderic (5:26) identifies Robert as a supporter of Rufus against Curthose during their struggle for Normandy in about 1092–95.
77. *HN* 40, 59–62.
78. *HN* 75, 81, 82: in the latter reference Walchelin is accompanied by three other named bishops — Robert of Lincoln, Osmund of Salisbury, and John of Bath; cf. *VA* 91 n.
79. *HN* 40, 62, 82 bis.

controversy. He expressed it publicly only after Rufus's death, in the form of advice to Henry I in the invasion-rebellion crisis of 1101:

We . . . to whom the common utility is committed by Divine Providence, ought to seek after the safety of the kingdom and of the church of God. Let our chief care be to triumph peacefully without the shedding of Christian blood, and so that our faithful people may live in the serenity of peace. . . . Speak gently to all your knights; caress them all as a father does his children; soothe them with promises; grant whatever they might request, and in this manner cleverly draw all to your favor. If they should even ask for London or York, do not hesitate to make magnificent promises, as is fitting to the royal munificence. It is better to give away a small portion of the kingdom than to lose both victory and life to a host of enemies. And when, by God's aid, we have come safely to the end of this business, we will suggest useful measures for recovering the demesnes usurped by rash deserters in time of war.[80]

Since Robert's speech is quoted by Orderic Vitalis writing a generation later, it obviously cannot be taken as a verbatim record of the count's words but only as Orderic's reconstruction of what he thought Count Robert might have said. Yet Orderic had a singularly reliable source of information in the person of his fellow monk and subsequent abbot of St-Evroul, Richard of Leicester. As a young man, Richard had spent some years at Robert of Meulan's court, "where he had been admitted to his most intimate counsels and had taken a leading part in judging cases and in carrying out business as the count's close adviser."[81] So even if not a verbatim transcript, this account of Robert's advice can almost certainly be trusted as an accurate expression of his political viewpoint. It perfectly describes Henry's conduct during the civil war of 1101, and it is also consistent with Robert's own inclination throughout his career to gain his desired ends through diplomatic negotiations, alliances and treaties, eloquence, and affectionate persuasion rather than force of arms. Unlike most of his contemporaries, Robert would analyze the various possible responses to every situation to take into account not only their immediate impact but also their long-range effects — as in his confrontations with Anselm and Count Elias of Maine. Robert was acknowledged by contemporaries to be shrewd, subtle, and eloquent — the persuader of peace and the dissuader of war — and in his speech to Henry I in 1101 he put these qualities into the larger framework of an embryonic theory of state.

80. OV 5:316.
81. OV 6:488.

Robert's advice that Henry keep his temper in the face of impending revolt, drawing potential enemies to his side not by force but by loving persuasion and generous promises that could afterwards be broken, embodies a theory that would later be termed *raison d'état*. The king as God's steward is permitted to transcend conventional morality when the safety of God's realm and church are at stake. For as a divinely commissioned steward, he bears responsibility for the common welfare, and he is therefore duty bound to keep the peace so that his faithful people can live in tranquillity. This formulation implies a subtle change in the relationship between king and people: kings had long ruled by the grace of God and had been enjoined to keep the peace and enforce just laws, but now these responsibilities were becoming more explicit and increasingly dependent on royal policies carefully calculated and effectively enforced. Moreover, the king's vassals and subjects were characterized now as a kind of commonwealth, embracing both the church and secular society. Orderic's use of the term *communis utilitas* in association with the duties of the king is made clear by his description of the more traditional activities and motives of Norman barons, of which he disapproved: "And they [the barons] strove more for their own private welfare than for the public welfare [*publicae commoditati*]."[82] Thus the king had acquired more concrete responsibilities in Orderic's eyes, and the state was coming to resemble the later "community of the realm" — or such is the implication of the words that Orderic attributes to Robert of Meulan. And if the fulfillment of these responsibilities sometimes required deliberate deception, such deception might properly be practiced in the service of a higher good. Kings had been breaking promises since the dawn of time; the novelty in Count Robert's advice is that they might sometimes, as God's stewards, be morally bound to make promises that they do not intend to keep.

As against Robert's concept of *communis utilitas*, Anselm stressed the *utilitas ecclesiae*. We have seen how he admonished William of Beaumont in 1093 to acquire friends through hospitality, kindness, and affable words for the utility of his church of Bec.[83] There is a certain similarity in style between Anselm's words to Abbot William and Count Robert's advice to King Henry to draw all to the royal

82. OV 5:318.
83. AEp. 165, above, Chapter 1 at n. 44: "Et ad vestrae ecclesiae utilitatem proficere et ad eorum quos diligitis salutem valeat pertingere."

favor through gifts and gentle speech. But although Anselm's political behavior was carefully calculated and could sometimes involve a degree of pious deceptiveness, he would never follow Robert in suggesting a policy of promising and then reneging and punishing. Yet Robert, in all fairness, advocated royal promise-breaking only in the pursuit of the king's higher, God-given responsibility to avoid the shedding of Christian blood. And although Anselm would not make a promise that he intended to break, he did share the belief that oaths might be broken out of devotion to the greater good of surrendering oneself to the divine plan — as the monks of Bec discovered to their sorrow in 1093. And he further believed, as we have seen, that historical details might be suppressed or rearranged for the sake of creating an edifying public image.

Unlike Robert's *raison d'état,* Anselm's policy was directed toward the utility, expansion, and liberties of the Church of Bec, and later the Church of Canterbury. But both men were alike in seeking ways to promote the utility of divinely sanctioned institutions. In the very year that Robert advised Henry how to provide for the *communis utilitas,* Anselm warned Pope Paschal II that to withhold from Canterbury its "traditional" legateship in England would be "contra utilitatem ecclesiae Romanae et Anglicae."[84]

These concepts, well known to later generations, were just emerging in the world of Anselm and Robert of Meulan. Gaines Post, drawing on legal sources and the writings of political theorists, has traced such ideas as *utilitas publica* and *utilitas ecclesiae* back to the last half of the twelfth century but no farther. He ascribes their emergence to the influence of the universities and the revival of Roman law.[85] Post traces back to John of Salisbury (ca. 1115 – 80) the idea of "reason of the public welfare" as distinct from the king's private right or self-aggrandizement; and the elevation of "reason of the common welfare" into a principle of law and equity. Post describes John of Salisbury's thought in these words: "The 'reason of defense' . . . justified deceit against the enemy and made *dolus bonus,* the 'good deceit,' a lawful principle of government. The moral law of God was always fundamental. But . . . in case of emergency, or of 'just cause,' when the *status*

---

84. AEp. 214.
85. Gaines Post, "Law and Politics in the Middle Ages: The Medieval State as a Work of Art," in *Perspectives in Medieval History,* ed. Katherine Fischer Drew and Floyd Lear (Chicago, 1963), p. 60.

regni ... was in danger, a compromise [the choice of a lesser evil or a lesser good for the sake of a greater good] was lawful."[86] Post finds germs of these ideas in the writings of St. Bernard of Clairvaux (1112 – 53) and of Richard fitz Neal, author of the *Dialogue of the Exchequer* under Henry II, and believes them to have been put into practice by the French king Philip Augustus.[87] Post surmises that political theory preceded political practice, for he implicitly connects the actions of kings in the next generation to these legists and philosophers.

But the seeds of such concepts as "public utility" and "bonus dolus" are clearly to be found in the words attributed to Robert of Meulan and the words of Anselm himself, as well as Eadmer's description of his actions. And Anselm, as we have seen, was probably influenced by Gregory the Great's advice to tolerate lesser sins until the greater ones are extinguished, and to correct some wrongs strictly while permitting others out of leniency.[88] These notions can thus be found at least by implication not only in Roman law but in patristic writings as well. Yet they seemed to have reentered the world of European politics not so much through the universities as through the traditions and practices that were developing in the Anglo-Norman court and the archbishopric of Canterbury. John of Salisbury was not only a scholar at Paris; he was also a product of the household of Archbishop Theobald of Canterbury, former abbot of Bec, and he enjoyed a friendship with Robert earl of Leicester, the well-educated son and English heir of Robert count of Meulan.

The roots of such ideas as "public utility," "utilitas ecclesiae," and "bonus dolus" could be traced even further back in medieval history than the generation of Anselm and Robert of Meulan. Lanfranc himself, for example, when he listed forged or nonexistent papal privileges in his letter to Alexander II, might well have regarded his act as a "bonus dolus." But Anselm and Robert seem to have applied these principles with a greater consistency than their predecessors, as is suggested by their activities in behalf of church and monarchy in the reign of William Rufus.

Throughout his archiepiscopate, Anselm firmly upheld the tradition of the Canterbury primacy as redefined by Lanfranc. Whether

---

86. Ibid., pp. 68 – 69.
87. Ibid., pp. 69 – 70.
88. Above, Chapter 1 at nn. 52 – 57.

Thomas of York consecrated him "primate of all Britain" as Eadmer reports, or merely "metropolitan of Canterbury" as Hugh the Chantor asserts, the term "Primate of all Britain" occurs in every written profession rendered to Anselm during his archiepiscopate.[89] And although Anselm continued to assert his personal unworthiness,[90] he also stressed the grandeur of his primatial office. He styled himself "archbishop of Canterbury and primate of all England, Scotland, Ireland, and the adjacent isles"[91] and called the Church of Canterbury "the first of all the churches in all England."[92]

Anselm strove to exercise this primacy forcefully and, as he believed, correctly with respect not only to the monarchy and the archbishopric of York — his two best-known opponents — but also with respect to the papacy and the episcopal sees within the province of Canterbury. Routinely he obtained written professions of obedience from his suffragan bishops at the time of their consecrations, employing a format that was simpler but no less binding than Lanfranc's.[93] And when Maurice bishop of London objected to Anselm's consecrating a new church built on a Canterbury estate within the diocese of London, Anselm inquired of the aged Wulfstan bishop of Worcester and was assured that archbishops of Canterbury had traditionally consecrated churches on their lands in whatever diocese they might lie. Thereafter, Eadmer states, "Anselm followed without scruple his predecessors' practice, not only by consecrating churches without consulting the bishops but also by dispensing personally or through his representatives all sacred offices throughout the whole of his lands."[94]

89. *Canterbury Professions,* nos. 50a – 61; cf. p. lxix, n. 2. Richter takes this fact as tipping the balance toward Eadmer's version of the consecration; Southern, conversely, favors Hugh the Chantor's version: *Anselm,* p. 303.

90. E.g., AEp. 193 to Urban II: Anselm, not by his own merits but with the divine assent called Metropolitan Bishop of Canterbury . . . phrases of this sort of course occur repeatedly in medieval ecclesiastical correspondence.

91. Quoted by Eadmer, *HN* 189, in keeping with the Canterbury tradition: Ibid., p. 26.

92. *The Charters of Norwich Cathedral Priory,* pt. 1, ed. Barbara Dodwell (Pipe Roll Society, London, 1974), no. 260: Anselm, in a charter to Norwich Cathedral Priory, refers to himself as "Cantuariensis archiepiscopus et majoris Britannie atque Hybernie primas," and to Canterbury as the see "que omnium ecclesiarum totius Anglie prima est."

93. *Canterbury Professions,* p. lxxvi: Anselm's profession form continued to be employed throughout the twelfth century. Eadmer reports that on at least one occasion Anselm's suffragan bishops complained about his demanding their written professions, but they nevertheless submitted to his demand: *HN* 47; cf. AEp. 200.

94. *HN* 47; cf. AEp. 200: Maurice bishop of London informs Anselm that he does not oppose these practices.

In matters great and small Anselm devoted the administrative experience he had acquired at Bec to the achievement of due order in Britain. The establishment of the primacy of Canterbury and the liberties of his see vis-à-vis the king, the pope, and the prelates of the *orbis Britanniae* guided Anselm's actions throughout Rufus's reign and into Henry I's. Anselm was attempting to institutionalize for posterity the reforms begun by Lanfranc.

Anselm's initial conflict with Rufus involved a question of simony — a practice that had been condemned repeatedly at Lanfranc's primatial councils and at similar councils in Normandy and throughout Western Christendom.[95] A week after his consecration on 4 December 1093, Anselm departed Canterbury to attend Rufus's Christmas court at Gloucester.[96] Besides Anselm the court included many other of the king's tenants-in-chief, among whom were Robert of Meulan and his brother Henry earl of Warwick, William bishop of Durham, and Anselm's close friends and fellow Bec alumni, Gundulf bishop of Rochester and Gilbert Crispin abbot of Westminster.[97] With the question of Canterbury resolved for the moment, Rufus had at once begun preparations for a second Norman campaign against Robert Curthose. The king was already well entrenched in Normandy. Duke Robert's remaining territories, torn by private war, were in great disorder; Norman magnates were defecting to Rufus in increasing numbers. Rufus had made it clear that he expected "voluntary" gifts from his vassals for the coming campaign, but the newly consecrated Anselm feared that such a gift from his own hand would be viewed by ill-disposed people as having been promised beforehand as the price of the archbishopric — as simony.[98]

At Rufus's court everything, including the king's love, was for sale,[99] and he was here making what must have seemed to him a reasonable request for financial aid to support a military campaign — a practice that would later be systematized under the name of "scutage."[100] To

95. Barlow, *English Church*, pp. 123, 126.
96. *HN* 43.
97. *Regesta* 1, no. 338; 2, p. 408, no. 338a.
98. *HN* 44–45.
99. *HN* 50–51, 65; cf. *HA* 216–17. In 1093–94, Robert Bloet bishop of Lincoln had to pay Rufus £5000 to secure the liberties of his church; the guilt of simony, Henry of Huntingdon hastens to explain, lay with the king, not with the bishop.
100. But the level of support that Rufus expected was enormously higher than the scutages of Henry II, which often ran at a mark or a pound per knight's fee: Thomas K. Keefe, *Feudal Assessments and the Political Community under Henry II and His Sons* (Berkeley and Los Angeles, 1983), pp. 24–37 passim.

Anselm, it was essential to avoid even the appearance of simony in order to function effectively in the advancement of ecclesiastical reform,[101] yet reform could not be advanced without the king's support. Anselm compromised, offering Rufus £500, which Rufus immediately accepted. But, according to Eadmer, "certain men of malignant mind" advised the king to refuse the gift and demand much more: "You have honored him, enriched him, and raised him above all other princes of England, and now, when considering your need, he should give you two thousand pounds or at least one thousand as a thank offering for your munificence."[102]

Norman Cantor suggests that the "men of malignant mind" may well have been William bishop of Durham and Robert of Meulan, who had earlier counseled Rufus in his dealings with Anselm and would do so in the future.[103] Of the two, William of Durham seems much the likelier candidate. As we shall see, Count Robert's advice could differ markedly from Bishop William's, and Eadmer later identifies the bishop, not the count, as the instigator of the dispute between Anselm and Rufus.[104] Anselm declined to pay more than £500. He was, according to Eadmer, astonished when Rufus refused his gift: "Do not, I pray you my lord, refuse to accept what I now offer you for your immediate needs. Although it is the first gift from your archbishop, nevertheless it will not be your last." "Keep your goods to yourself," Rufus replied, and dismissed Anselm angrily.[105]

Eadmer relates that Anselm subsequently thanked God for protecting him against ill repute by having Rufus refuse his gift, and Anselm himself analyzed the event in a letter to Hugh of Lyon:

Before he might ask something from me, I promised with the counsel of my friends a not inconsiderable sum of money — God knows with what intention. He rejected it as too little, that I might give more; but I would not. Thanks be

101. Bishop Herbert Losinga of Thetford-Norwich was suspended from office on a charge of simony in February 1094: *ASC*, A.D. 1094; Florence, 2:3.

102. *HN* 43: the figure of £2000 approximates the annual value of all Canterbury lands and would thus have had much the same effect on the royal treasury as if Rufus had extended the Canterbury vacancy an additional year.

103. Cantor, *Church, Kingship, and Lay Investiture*, p. 71. Cantor's slight worry that Count Robert did not attest at the Christmas court is put to rest by *Regesta* 2, p. 408, no. 338a.

104. *HN* 59; below, Chapter 5 at n. 158; note that it is "the bishops" who afterward press Anselm to recover Rufus's favor with a payment of £1000 (*HN* 50–51) or with a similarly generous gift (*HN* 70–71).

105. *HN* 44; besides the matter of principle, Anselm was desperately short of money because of his lands having been "laid waste" by royal officials during the long vacancy: *HN* 218.

to God who, pitying the simplicity of my heart, caused it to happen thus, lest if I had promised nothing or little, there might have seemed a just cause for anger; or if he had accepted it, it might have turned into an accusation against me and a suspicion of nefarious purchase.[106]

Anselm ascribes the outcome to God's will, but his words to Hugh of Lyon suggest at the very least that Anselm understood the situation with complete clarity. They raise the possibility that he may once again have been committing himself consciously to the divine plan — anticipating the reactions of Rufus's advisers and calculating the size of his gift accordingly.[107] When Rufus refused the money, Anselm resolved on giving it to the poor. He had avoided the appearance of simony but at the cost of the king's favor, and Rufus refused to restore his love unless Anselm doubled his offer.[108]

Rufus, however, was himself on rather thin ice. His coming Norman campaign required both a large war chest and a plausible justification to take up arms against Duke Robert. According to Orderic, he had justified his campaign of 1091 as a response to "a cry of distress" from "the holy Church in Normandy" seeking a patron and defender against baronial depredations under Curthose's weak rule,[109] and he may have justified his 1094 campaign on similar grounds.[110] The appointment of an internationally renowned scholar-saint to the archbishopric of Canterbury would have added considerable credibility to Rufus's self-appointed role as a defender of churches, whereas an open break with Anselm would have been embarrassing.

Accordingly, Rufus included Anselm among the bishops whom he asked to assemble at Hastings in early February 1094 to bless the king before his crossing to Normandy.[111] On 11 February, Rufus attended

106. AEp. 176.
107. Cf. Barlow, *Rufus*, p. 327: "Anselm's scruples in this affair are less attractive in the light of his cool and calculating analysis of his action." But if Anselm's analysis was calculating, it was also accurate. A gift equivalent to Canterbury's entire annual revenues, and rendered within three weeks of Anselm's consecration, would have constituted a grave affront to the ecclesiastical reform movement, not to mention Anselm's own conscience.
108. *HN* 44–45.
109. OV 4:178–80.
110. These were also the grounds on which Henry I justified his campaigns of 1105 and 1106 against Curthose: OV 6:284–86; cf. *ASC*, A.D. 1094: messengers from Curthose announced to Rufus at his Christmas court at Gloucester that the duke utterly repudiated their previous truce; Florence (2:33) adds that in 1093 William count of Eu was won over to Rufus's side by a bribe.
111. Rufus went to Hastings on 2 February: *ASC*, A.D. 1094.

the consecration of his father's foundation, Battle Abbey, by Archbishop Anselm, Bishop Gundulf, and six other bishops.[112] It was probably on the following day that Rufus supported Anselm's demand that Robert Bloet, elect of Lincoln, profess obedience to Canterbury before being consecrated — against the contention of some of the bishops that Anselm should consecrate Robert unconditionally.[113] Rufus could uphold the rights of Canterbury when it cost him nothing and when Anselm's support could be useful to him. But contrary Channel winds delayed Rufus at Hastings for more than a month.[114] During this time Anselm pressed him with regard to several matters of central importance to the Canterbury conception of due order, and Rufus resisted with increasing vexation at what he regarded as assaults on his royal prerogatives.

Anselm and Rufus saw much of each other during this month,[115] and in their discussions Anselm dwelt on three abuses above all others: Rufus's unwillingness (1) to permit Anselm to journey to the court of Pope Urban II to receive the archiepiscopal pallium;[116] (2) to work with Anselm toward reform through the agency of primatial councils;[117] and (3) to fill remaining ecclesiastical vacancies.[118] Anselm raised the further complaint that Rufus was continuing his effort to install his own knights as tenants on Canterbury estates, an issue that had earlier caused Rufus to consider halting the process of Anselm's elevation.[119]

The pallium issue was a matter of urgent importance to Anselm. It had long been accepted practice in England that the archbishops of Canterbury and York must receive from the pope a white woolen stole — a pallium — as a symbol of metropolitan authority. New archbishops of Canterbury had regularly traveled to Rome to receive their pallia since at least 927, and archbishops of York had been doing so since 1026.[120] Lanfranc and Thomas of York had been given their pallia, as we have seen, by Alexander II in 1071. To Anselm, then, the

---

112. *The Chronicle of Battle Abbey*, ed. Eleanor Searle (Oxford, 1980), p. 96 and n. 3.

113. *HN* 47; on the date, see John Le Neve, *Fasti Ecclesiae Anglicanae, 1066 – 1300*, 3, *Lincoln*, ed. Diana E. Greenway (London, 1977), p. 1.

114. *HN* 47.   115. *HN* 48.

116. AEp. 176.   117. Ibid.; *HN* 48.   118. *HN* 49.

119. AEp. 176; cf. *HN* 40; *VA* 81 – 84. The list of Canterbury knights in the *Domesday Monachorum*, p. 105, discloses that in about 1090 the archiepiscopal estates were already heavily overenfeoffed, with a total of 98¼ fees to meet a quota of sixty knights. The names of the knights are predominantly Norman.

120. Barlow, *English Church*, p. 298.

pallium represented the final and essential step in his elevation to the archbishopric, empowering him to govern the province of Canterbury and its diocesan bishops.[121] Rufus firmly objected to Anselm's going to the papal court, not because it would breach his wall around England, but because he had not yet chosen to recognize either of the two contenders for the papal office — Urban II and Clement III. Anselm had raised this difficulty previously during his negotiations with Rufus, William of Durham, and Robert of Meulan prior to his consecration, when he had warned them that as abbot of Bec he had already recognized Urban's claim to the papacy and was morally bound to continue yielding him "due obedience and submission."[122] Eadmer does not record Rufus's response, if any, to Anselm's warning. But when the issue reemerged in the context of the pallium dispute, Rufus insisted that in his father's days and his own it was the king's prerogative alone to choose between contending popes. If Anselm usurped that prerogative, Rufus said, it would be the same as robbing him of his crown.[123]

Anselm had no better success persuading Rufus to permit a primatial council. Anselm urged that many years had now elapsed since Lanfranc's last council, and that the calling of a new council was essential "so that some things in that kingdom that seemed unendurable might be corrected."[124] According to Eadmer, Anselm raised the issue in the context of his ideal of corule: "I beg you, let the two of us make a united effort, you with your royal power [potestas] and I with my pontifical authority [auctoritas]."[125] When the king inquired what abuses such a council might address, Anselm stressed the crime of sodomy — perhaps tactlessly if indeed Rufus was himself a sodomite — and also

121. Ibid. "Without it," Barlow adds, "no bishop could exercise that authority." Anselm at first took the position that he must receive the pallium within a year of his consecration or at least send the pope formal notification of his installation and a reasonable explanation of his delay: AEp. 176; see Southern, *Anselm*, pp. 154–55.

122. *HN* 40; Eadmer implies that Anselm did not raise the pallium issue until January 1095 (*HN* 52), but Anselm (AEp. 176) makes it clear that he was pressing Rufus on the matter in February or March 1094 and perhaps earlier.

123. *HN* 53.

124. AEp. 176. Lanfranc had held no council under Rufus, as Anselm reminded the king: *HN* 48; Southern (*Anselm*, p. 158) states that Anselm had no power to hold a council until he had received the pallium; but Barlow points out that from the time of his consecration Anselm exercised all the usual metropolitan powers "without scruple or hindrance": *Rufus*, p. 358, n. 10.

125. *HN* 49.

raised the problem of consanguineous marriages. "Enough," the king replied, "say no more about it."

Anselm next brought up the numerous abbeys for which Rufus was refusing to appoint abbots.[126] Prolonged abbatial vacancies and the diversion of their revenues into the royal treasury had become a systematic royal policy, and it was at variance with the practice of William the Conqueror.[127] The former abbot of Bec, now primate of England, could hardly have ignored it. Canterbury itself had suffered gravely during its recent leaderless years, and in early 1094, St. Albans Abbey, which had been placed under the archbishop of Canterbury's direct lordship, was without an abbot and suffering grievous damage from royal officials who cut down its orchards and robbed its monks of their property.[128] But Rufus once again responded that Anselm was trying to usurp a royal prerogative: "What business is that of yours?" he shouted. "Are not the abbeys mine? You do as you like with your estates, and shall I not do as I like with my abbeys?" Anselm replied, "They are yours to guard and defend as their patron, but not yours to attack and lay waste." "Be certain," Rufus said, "that everything you say is utterly repugnant to me. Your predecessor would never have dared say such things to my father, and I shall do nothing for you."[129]

Having been frustrated at every turn, Anselm afterward summoned the bishops and asked them to deliver his humble petition to the king that he might be restored fully to the royal friendship. "If I have done him any wrong," Anselm told the bishops, "I am ready to make amends." Once again Anselm was endeavoring to rectify a difficult situation by responding to his opponent's hostility with love. But Rufus replied that his friendship was available to Anselm only for a price, thus returning full circle to the initial controversy over the £500. The bishops recommended to Anselm that he do exactly as they did in such cases: "Give the king that £500 immediately, and promise him

126. *HN* 49.

127. Barlow, *Rufus*, pp. 184–85; cf. Howell, *Regalian Right*, p. 12: "The difference between the practice of William I and that of William II in respect to vacant sees and abbeys was the difference of use and abuse."

128. Abbot Paul of St. Albans died on 11 November 1093, and his office remained vacant until 1097: Knowles, *Heads*, p. 66. On the depredations following Paul's death, see *Gesta Abbatum Monasteri S. Albani a Thoma Walsingham,* ed. H. T. Riley (RS, London, 1867–69), 1:65; cf. OV 5:202, modified by Howell, *Regalian Right*, pp. 14–19.

129. *HN* 49–50.

as much again, which you will collect from your men." Anselm firmly declined, asking the bishops to beseech the king "to love me freely and honorably as archbishop of Canterbury and as his spiritual father, and I in return will devote myself and all that is mine unstintingly to his service and to his will as I should." Anselm added that he was no longer prepared to give Rufus even £500 because he had already given most of it to the poor.[130] Anselm had thus avoided the hint of giving simony, and the royal war chest was £500 poorer than it would have been had Rufus accepted his initial offer.

Rufus was not a good loser: "Yesterday I hated him with great hatred; today I hate him with even greater hatred; and he can be certain that tomorrow and thereafter I shall hate him continually with ever fiercer and more bitter hatred." Rufus refused to accept Anselm's blessing for his Norman expedition and dismissed him from court.[131] The king departed for Normandy and campaigned there until the close of 1094, but with little success.[132] Eadmer stresses the fact that Rufus, despite the expenditure of vast sums of money, failed utterly to subdue the duchy, clearly intending to suggest to his readers that the want of Anselm's blessing was the cause of his defeat.[133] And Rufus's army, unblessed and unprayed for, may indeed have departed with dampened morale.

The issues that divided Anselm and Rufus, and that cost Anselm the royal love, were far from trivial. Anselm's insistence on receiving the papal pallium, holding councils, and protecting the lands of his see was absolutely consistent with the Canterbury tradition that he felt the deepest responsibility to uphold. And his disinclination to offer a substantial gift to Rufus within a few weeks of his consecration is in keeping with his conviction that a godly priest must maintain a spotless public reputation. Rufus was equally correct in his assertions that Anselm had challenged his royal sovereignty. The king obviously found Anselm a major irritant, a unique and infuriating nonconformist in an otherwise subservient court—a man without greed or fear, who could neither be intimidated nor lured by the ebb and flow of royal patronage. This total immunity to the attractions of personal wealth and power made Anselm a dangerous antagonist to the Anglo-

130. *HN* 50–52.
131. *HN* 52; Anselm attested no surviving charter of William II after *Regesta* 1, no. 361: 1093–94.
132. Barlow, *Rufus*, pp. 331–36.
133. *HN* 52.

Norman monarchy. He simply could not be manipulated in the usual ways. Yet for Anselm, the situation remained gravely unsatisfactory. He continued to lack the pallium and the royal love, both of which were essential to the realization of his vision of corule in the service of reform. For his part, Rufus saw Anselm as a major obstruction to his goals of imposing his absolute and unquestioned rule on England and extending it to Normandy and perhaps beyond.

Rufus returned to England in the closing days of 1094 to face a Welsh uprising. In Janurary 1095, Anselm came to the king at Gillingham, Dorset, and again expressed his wish to visit Urban II and petition him to grant the pallium.[134] With the passing of time, the pallium issue was acquiring ever greater urgency in Anselm's mind, but Rufus continued to deny it on the grounds that the king alone had the right to choose between rival popes, and that a visit by Anselm to Urban II's court would, in effect, commit England to Urban. To Rufus the question was not whether Urban was the rightful pope, but whether the royal prerogative would remain undiminished. As Southern has pointed out, Rufus would never have chosen Urban's rival, Clement III, because France and Normandy were already committed to Urban. The recognition of one pope in Normandy and another in England would have impeded Rufus's driving ambition to unite the two lands.[135] But Rufus refused as a matter of principle to be rushed into the decision by his archbishop. Anselm responded by proposing a compromise — that the issue be postponed until it could be decided by a council of all the bishops, abbots, and magnates (*principes*) of the realm. Anselm added that if such a council were to decide that he could not go to the papal court without violating his allegiance to the king, he would absent himself from the kingdom until Rufus recognized Urban II.[136]

The truce lasted until 24 February 1095, when the great men of the kingdom assembled at Rockingham, a royal castle in Northamptonshire near the Leicestershire border.[137] The Council of Rockingham lasted four days — Sunday, 25 February, through Wednesday, 28 February[138] — and Eadmer's meticulously detailed account of it fills

134. HN 52–53.   135. *Anselm,* p. 154.
136. HN 53; VA 85. Notice that Anselm did not yet threaten to go to the papal court of his own accord.
137. VA 85 and n. 4.
138. Four days by my count; Southern (VA 85, n. 4) and Barlow (*Rufus,* p. 339), following VA 86–87, count only three days.

more than thirteen pages of the Rolls Series edition of his *Historia Novorum*.[139] He does not make it clear, however, that Rufus was negotiating from a position of relative weakness because of military reverses and the stirrings of baronial rebellion. Between Gillingham and Rockingham, Rufus campaigned against the Welsh with the same lack of success that had plagued his Norman campaign of 1094.[140] By Easter (25 March) at the latest, Rufus was alerted to the danger of a baronial rebellion by the refusal of Robert of Mowbray, earl of Northumberland, to answer a summons to the royal court at Winchester. By summer Rufus was campaigning against the earl and trying to prevent a large-scale baronial conspiracy from erupting into general rebellion. Among the conspirators were Gilbert fitz Richard of Clare, Hugh of Montgomery earl of Shrewsbury, and Ernulf of Hesdin — all representing families closely connected with Anselm. Another conspirator was William count of Eu, enfeoffed with Canterbury lands, who had previously defected from Curthose to Rufus and had been one of the king's chief allies during his Norman campaign of 1094.[141] Rufus may have known of or suspected the oncoming rebellion at the time of the Council of Rockingham, a month before Robert of Mowbray's conspicuous absence from the Easter court. In either late 1094 or early 1095, Robert of Mowbray had robbed four Norwegian merchant ships and then refused to obey Rufus's order to make restitution to the merchants.[142] Barlow suggests that Rufus may have selected Rockingham as the site of the 25 February council in order to threaten the recalcitrant earl.[143] Whatever the case, Anselm was in a position of considerably greater strength than is apparent from Eadmer's account. And it seems reasonable to suppose that potential baronial conspirators, some of whom numbered among Anselm's friends and benefactors, might have taken Rufus's treatment of his archbishop into account as they weighed the pros and cons of rebellion. In the

139. Pp. 53–67; cf. *VA* 85–87; the Council of Rockingham is mentioned by no contemporary writer apart from Eadmer and those who depended on him as their source.

140. Florence, 2:35; Barlow, *Rufus*, p. 338; cf. p. 337: "In the years 1094–5, William's fortunes reached their lowest ebb."

141. Hollister, "Magnates and 'Curiales,' " pp. 68–69; Barlow, *Rufus*, p. 347; others in the conspiracy included Philip of Montgomery, Roger of Lacy, Odo of Champagne, lord of Holderness, and his nephew Stephen of Aumale, whom the conspirators hoped to enthrone in Rufus's place. For William of Eu's Canterbury fiefs, see *Domesday Monachorum*, p. 105.

142. OV 4:280; Barlow, *Rufus*, p. 347.

143. Barlow, *Rufus*, p. 338; if, as seems highly probable, Robert of Mowbray did not attend the Rockingham council, his absence would have been noticed.

course of his description of the Council of Rockingham, Eadmer states, "A murmur of indignation now arose from the entire crowd at the wrong being done to so great a man as Anselm, but such protest was only whispered among them. Nobody dared speak openly in his defense out of fear of the tyrant [*tyrannus*]."[144]

Whether aware of the full extent of Rufus's predicament or not, Anselm remained immovable on the issue of the pallium and the inseparably related issue of his recognition of Urban II. It was not a question of Anselm supporting the reform papacy and Rufus opposing it, or of Anselm reversing Lanfranc's policy and favoring the pope over the king. Nor was it Anselm's purpose to force Rufus to recognize Urban, except insofar as such recognition would clear Anselm's path to the pallium. His previous and continuing recognition of Urban might, with appropriate discretion, have precipitated no crisis were it not for the urgency of his obtaining the symbol of his metropolitan authority. Here, as always, Anselm's overriding commitment was to Canterbury, and he was expressing the tradition of his see when he told the bishops at Rockingham, "It is, to me, a terrible thing to dishonor and disavow the vicar of St. Peter, a terrible thing also to transgress the allegiance which, under God, I have pledged to the king, and most terrible of all to be told that it would be impossible for me to be true to one of these allegiances without being false to the other."[145]

Rufus, too, held to his position: while Anselm might maintain a quiet allegiance to Urban,[146] to make a public display of it by visiting the papal court would be to force the king's hand and rob him of the crown and the jewel of his sovereignty. Although Rufus may earlier have settled the matter merely by recognizing Urban and claiming the decision as his own, such a decision at this late juncture would represent a humiliating public surrender.

As the council commenced, the king and archbishop were at an impasse. Both had adopted positions that they regarded as fundamental to their conceptions of their respective offices, and the two positions seemed irreconcilable. Throughout the pallium debate—

---

144. *HN* 61; Eadmer's discussion of the council makes it clear that the bishops were not among the murmurers and suggests that the indignation was limited largely to the lay nobility: Ibid., p. 64; cf. *VA* 86, where the bishops are singled out as "wishing to be on the king's side and having no regard for justice and equity."

145. *HN* 55–56.

146. At his consecration Anselm had promised obedience "to the Roman pontiff" (unnamed): AEp. 192.

before and during the council — Anselm's attitude was a characteristic
blend of firmness, persistence, and love, whereas Rufus often exploded
in rage against Anselm's patient but unyielding demands. The king
had by now grown to hate Anselm, and historians have ascribed this
hatred to Anselm's stubbornness and tactlessness. As an ecclesiastical
statesman, Anselm has been compared unfavorably with both Lanfranc, who worked extremely effectively with William I, and Gundulf of Rochester, who enjoyed excellent relations with both Williams while also maintaining a warm friendship and unswerving faith
toward Anselm.[147] But William I permitted Lanfranc to receive his
pallium from the pope and to hold frequent reforming synods; and
Gundulf, having won Rufus's gratitude by mediating between the royalists and rebels during the revolt of 1088, was spared the financial exactions with which Rufus "oppressed the other churches."[148]
Anselm was fully prepared to assume a major military role in the
defense of the monarchy against rebellion, as Lanfranc had done in
1075,[149] and to negotiate in the king's behalf with potential rebels.[150]
By always responding to Rufus's anger with love, he was doing all in
his power — consistent with his deeply felt principles — to keep open
the door to reconciliation, which might all too easily be closed by
mutual hatred. The hostility that divided Henry II and Becket provides
an illuminating contrast. The conflicts between Anselm and Rufus
resulted as much from an unfortunately timed sequence of events —
which greatly intensified the contrast between royal and primatial
concepts of due order — as from a clash of personalities.

On Sunday, 25 February 1095, the first day of the Council of
Rockingham, Anselm seized the initiative by calling the bishops,
abbots, and magnates (*principes*) into his presence. After providing a
clear summary of Rufus's and his positions, Anselm asked them to
advise him how he might resolve the enigma of acting with due loyalty
toward both pope and king. He asked for the advice of all three
groups, "but most of all my brothers and fellow bishops," who, he
pointed out, had led the clamorous effort to drag him unwillingly into

147. *VG* 55.
148. *VG* 50–51: with an annual Domesday value of only £220 (Brett, *English Church*, p. 103, n. 1) the Rochester estates were far less tempting than those of
Canterbury.
149. Anselm acted as a royal commander later in 1095 and again in 1101: AEpp.
191–92; *HN* 127.
150. *HN* 127.

his present office.[151] The bishops (alone) advised him to devote him-self single-mindedly to the king, but this advice did not answer the question that Anselm had skillfully posed. Realizing this, the bishops agreed to report to the king the gist of what Anselm had told them; when they had done so, Rufus adjourned the council until the next day.

On the second day of the council, Monday, 26 February, the king's magnates and prelates (*proceres*) again gathered around Anselm.[152] He opened the proceedings by repeating his question: how might he render proper service to his two lords? "The answer we gave you yesterday we give you again today," they replied. According to Ead-mer, they declined to advise Anselm in accordance with God's will if it should be in any way contrary to the will of the king.[153] Anselm then addressed both the bishops and the princes. He lectured them on the Petrine theory, quoted Christ's words ("Render unto Caesar the things that are Caesar's and to God the things that are God's "), and proceeded to release his bombshell. Since the bishops and magnates offered him no advice as to how he might serve *both* Caesar and God, he would, of his own volition, hasten to the pope and "obtain from him the advice that I am to follow."[154] Anselm continued to make it clear that he was not elevating the pope over the king. He would obey the pope regarding the things that are God's, while yielding to the king loyal counsel and all possible help in matters pertaining to his earthly sovereignty. Nevertheless, his threat to seek Urban's counsel face-to-face threw the crowd into a tumult of shouts and accusations. "You can be sure," they said, "that we will never bear such a message to our lord king."[155] Consequently Anselm fearlessly approached Rufus and repeated his threat.

Astonished and enraged, the king consulted with his bishops and magnates to seek an effective rejoinder, but they could find none. Anselm, meanwhile, leaned back against the wall and dozed off. After much anxious consultation, the bishops, "accompanied by some of the magnates," returned to Anselm with Rufus's ultimatum. They told him in words that will by now be familiar, "You are trying to steal from the king, whom we all recognize as our lord, his crown and the jewel of his sovereignty." They attempted to intimidate Anselm by

151. *HN* 54–55.
152. In the chapel of Rockingham Castle.
153. *HN* 56.   154. *HN* 57.   155. *HN* 58.

observing that Rufus could hurt him whereas Urban had no power to help him. Anselm refused to abjure his obedience to Urban but requested that the council be adjourned to the following day so that he might think and pray further on the matter. Eadmer reports that the bishops and magnates took this request as a sign that Anselm was either frightened or at a loss for further arguments. Smelling victory, they returned to the king and urged him not to adjourn the council but to command that it pass judgment on Anselm — thus transforming the proceeding from a conference into a judicial process. Anselm was to be put on trial for disloyalty toward his lord king.[156]

Although obviously biased toward Anselm, Eadmer's account of the council is surely correct in disclosing a king who is at once strong-willed and very dependent on the mediation and advice of his counselors — whom Eadmer divides into bishops (*episcopi*), magnates (*principes*), and, rarely, abbots. The bishops,[157] the majority of whom had risen from the royal chapel, are given the leading role among these groups. Eadmer clearly identifies William of St-Calais bishop of Durham as their leader and Rufus's principal adviser.[158] Although exiled for his disloyalty to Rufus in the rebellion of 1088, Bishop William had been restored in 1091 and had since risen high in Rufus's entourage. Ironically, Bishop William had himself appealed to papal authority when on trial for treason in 1088, but he was by now a devoted royalist. Eadmer singles him out at Rockingham as the leader of the opposition to Anselm and the king's spokesman,[159] and reports that Bishop William had promised Rufus that he would compel Anselm either to renounce absolutely his obedience to Urban or to surrender his archbishopric and return the ring and staff. Eadmer, who believed that Rufus preferred the latter alternative, being determined to brook no rival within his kingdom, relates the rumor that William of Durham himself coveted Anselm's office.[160]

At this point in the council proceedings Eadmer shifts from the plural *episcopi* and places the negotiations directly in William of Dur-

---

156. Barlow, *Rufus*, p. 340.
157. Always excluding Gundulf: *VA* 86; *VG* 55.
158. On the backgrounds of the bishops see Southern, *Anselm,* pp. 146 and n. 3, 147; Worcester was vacant at the time of the Rockingham Council, Wulfstan having died on 18 January 1095; the scholarly Robert bishop of Hereford, who attended the council and sided with the king (*HN* 72), died the following June. On William of Durham, see ibid., pp. 147–50.
159. *HN* 59: "quasi praevius et praelocutor regis in hoc negotio."
160. *HN* 60.

ham's hands. Having counseled Rufus to put the archbishop immediately on trial, "the bishop returned to Anselm, taking with him
several witnesses to corroborate his words."[161] He told the archbishop that there would be no adjournment, and that unless he renounced Urban and professed undivided loyalty to Rufus, "you will
most certainly receive immediately the sentence that your presumption
deserves." Having listened with his accustomed patience, Anselm then
replied that an archbishop of Canterbury can be judged by no man
save the pope.[162] At this point the magnates began quietly to protest
against Bishop William's hard line, and the bishop himself seems to
have been daunted by Anselm's defense—embarrassingly reminiscent
of his own defense when on trial in 1088—that only the pope could
judge such a case.[163] When William of Durham returned and explained matters to Rufus, the king was furious. "What is this?
Didn't you promise me that you would judge and condemn him just as
I wished?" The bishop admitted to having been outmaneuvered by
Anselm, who had at first spoken so softly and hesitantly as to seem a
fool "devoid of all human shrewdness."[164] William of Durham now
advised Rufus to adjourn until the next day after all, so that the royal
counselors, now that they fully understood Anselm's strategy of defense, could devise an effective counterargument on the king's behalf.

Next morning, Tuesday, 27 February—the third day of the council
—Bishop William admitted to Rufus that he was helpless to invalidate
Anselm's argument and recommended that the archbishop be crushed
by force. "If he will not give in to the king's will, then the staff and
the ring must be taken from him and he must be driven from the
kingdom." The magnates objected to this course, and "a certain
Robert, who was much in the king's confidence," spoke on their behalf. He observed that as the royal counselors busied themselves all
day devising arguments against Anselm, the archbishop would fall
into untroubled sleep. When finally presented with the arguments,
Anselm would sweep them away like cobwebs with a few words. The
bishops then confessed to Rufus that they had no power to judge
Anselm, but they agreed, at Rufus's urging, to renounce their loyalty
and obedience toward their primate.[165] Rufus himself thereupon deprived the archbishop of all royal protection and support throughout the kingdom, adding, "I refuse to trust his advice in any matter

161. Ibid.   162. *HN* 61.   163. Southern, *Anselm*, p. 149.
164. *HN* 62.   165. *HN* 63; *VA* 86, corroborated by *VG* 55.

whatever, or to regard him any longer as archbishop or spiritual father."[166]

The bishops, acting with the abbots (but no longer with the magnates), reported this news to Anselm, saying that they would indeed desert him in order to satisfy the king. Anselm reproached them gently, and promised to seek to restore them to the path of righteousness. In return for Rufus's hatred and withdrawal of the royal protection, Anselm offered "faithful service and, so far as it is within my power, full protection."[167] Anselm would continue to care lovingly for Rufus's soul if the king would permit it, but would also continue to act in God's service as an archbishop of Canterbury must, regardless of all harassment. On hearing of this, Rufus angrily challenged his magnates to follow the example of his bishops in refusing any loyalty or friendship toward Anselm. The magnates demurred: not being Anselm's vassals, they had no allegiance to renounce, and they would continue to recognize his spiritual authority because of his primatial office and his innocence of any wrongdoing. With rebellion brewing, Rufus concealed his anger, "being careful not to oppose their contention openly lest they be too deeply offended."[168] The bishops thus found themselves in the embarrassing position of having renounced Anselm while the magnates stood by him, and Rufus tightened the screws by questioning each bishop individually as to whether he had renounced Anselm absolutely or only when he acted in the pope's name. Rufus branded the latter group as traitors and forced them to pay a stiff price to repurchase the royal favor.

The royal position was now crumbling. Since Anselm could be neither intimidated nor formally prosecuted, what was to be done with him? William of Durham's plan to deprive him of the archbishopric by brute force — if Eadmer can be trusted on this point — would have affronted the magnates and produced an international scandal, putting at risk Rufus's designs on Normandy and perhaps even his throne. Anselm now made matters worse by asking the king, in view of the withdrawal of royal protection, to grant him safe conduct to a seaport so that he might leave England. At this, Rufus was greatly troubled. He would love to be rid of Anselm but feared the resulting scandal. Having now completely lost confidence in William of Dur-

166. HN 63.
167. HN 64.
168. HN 64.

ham's plans, "he forsook the council of the bishops, to whom he complained bitterly for having led him into this predicament, and took council with the magnates, asking them what should be done."[169]

The passage just quoted has far greater significance than has been ascribed to it by previous historians. It marks a fundamental shift in power among the king's advisers and a dramatic redirection of the royal policy toward Anselm. No longer was Robert of Meulan superseded in the king's council by William of Durham. Thenceforth, at least as regards the conflict with Anselm, Count Robert became Rufus's foremost adviser. Making all allowances for the king's strong will and forceful personality, royal policy reflected thereafter, as it had not before, the political intelligence and cunning of the count of Meulan.[170] Until this shift Rufus had consistently dealt with Anselm by shouting, blustering, making impossible threats and even contemplating Anselm's destruction. Anselm had easily turned aside this behavior with logic, fearlessness, and love, so that Rufus found himself backed to the wall. But as the third day of the Rockingham Council drew to a close, everything changed. The magnates advised Rufus to drop all his threats and leave Anselm unmolested. Anselm was told to return to his lodging place with the promise that the king would reply on the following day to his request for safe conduct to a port. That very night Robert of Meulan probably persuaded Rufus to adopt an audacious secret plan to resolve the controversy.[171]

On the morning of the council's fourth day, Wednesday, 28 February, "the magnates" came to Anselm and addressed him in words markedly different from William of Durham's. But to those who have followed Robert of Meulan's career, the words will have a familiar ring:

Remembering our long-standing friendship with you, we are distressed that this quarrel has arisen between you and our lord king. We are anxious to bring the two of you back to your former state of amity, and we have concluded that for now it would be helpful if both sides agreed to a truce in this conflict so that peace might be established between you, to continue until some fixed

169. *HN* 65; similarly, *VA* 87.
170. Cf. *HN* 66 ("the magnates" now speak for the king), 71 (Rufus resolves the conflict with Anselm on the advice of his magnates), 86 (Rufus and Robert of Meulan speak with one voice, and afterward Robert speaks for the king); William of Durham died within the year, on 2 January 1096.
171. Although Eadmer ascribes the plan to "the magnates," its boldness and relative complexity suggest a single intelligence rather than a group decision.

date, and that meanwhile you do nothing to him or his, or he to you or yours, that might break the ties of concord.[172]

Anselm was doubtless surprised to hear soothing words, rather than threats of destruction, from the king's advisers. Despite a healthy measure of skepticism, he agreed to the plan: "Peace and concord I do not reject."[173] A truce was then approved to last until Whitsun week (13–20 May), with the king's assurance that if the conflict should not then be resolved he would grant Anselm the requested safe conduct to the sea.[174]

Despite the truce, Rufus began harassing Anselm almost immediately. A few days after his return to Canterbury, Anselm lost his beloved chief counselor and household manager, the former Bec monk Baldwin of Tournai, whom Rufus banished from England along with two of Anselm's clerks. Afterward Anselm's chamberlain was arrested before his eyes, and others of his men were unjustly condemned by royal tribunals.[175] Whether these acts reflect Robert of Meulan's views about royal promises or sheer vindictiveness on Rufus's part, they had the effect of isolating Anselm from advisers and household officers on whom he was accustomed to depend.

The second phase of the "magnates' plan" may well have been set in motion during the closing hours of the Council of Rockingham. Two royal chaplains, Gerard and William Warelwast, were dispatched on an urgent secret mission to the court of Pope Urban II, probably at Cremona or Piacenza, to offer some kind of conditional recognition on Rufus's behalf and to obtain the pallium to bring back to the king — not the archbishop.[176] Eadmer's statement that the two envoys were under royal instructions to determine which of the two popes had been elected canonically cannot be taken seriously. In stressing Rufus's freedom of choice, the statement may represent a cover story circulated by the royal court. But for Rufus to opt for Clement III

---

172. *HN* 66; *VA* 87 adds that Rufus promised Anselm "some considerable concession" at the end of the truce.

173. *HN* 66.

174. *HN* 70.

175. *HN* 67.

176. Barlow, *Rufus*, p. 342; *VA* 87 and n. 2. Eadmer reports that the two royal envoys were secretly dispatched as soon as the king realized that Anselm would not yield to his wish in the Rockingham dispute: *HN* 68. Gerard was a former chancellor of William I and II and future bishop of Hereford and archbishop of York; William Warelwast served frequently as a royal envoy to the pope and was later promoted to the bishopric of Exeter.

would have been utterly self-defeating with regard to both his quarrel with Anselm and his hunger for Normandy. Also, with the Whitsun deadline looming, the envoys had no time for an investigation of rival claims. They can hardly have left Rockingham before 28 February, and they were back in England shortly before Whitsunday (13 May) accompanied by a papal legate, Walter cardinal bishop of Albano, who carried the requested pallium. The envoys conducted the mission with astonishing speed and total secrecy.[177] Eadmer reports that it caught Anselm completely by surprise. By rushing to make terms with Urban, Rufus had seized the initiative, and when the legate arrived, "passing through Canterbury without a word and avoiding any meeting with Anselm, he went straight to the king, saying nothing to anyone about the pallium."[178] At that moment, Eadmer declares, Rufus had every hope of having Anselm deposed and the pallium bestowed on another churchman of the king's choice.[179]

Rufus kept Walter of Albano's arrival a secret from all but his most intimate counselors in a determined effort to prevent his plan from being made public.[180] Walter did not intercede on Anselm's behalf but instead suggested that the king could expect a successful outcome if he gave his personal recognition to Urban II. In return for such endorsement Walter promised that Urban would sanction the royal customs, presumably the Conqueror's usages with respect to the English church — his "wall around England."[181] Hugh of Flavigny, a member of a papal legation to England the following year, asserts in his chronicle that Walter of Albano promised that no papal legate would thereafter be sent to England during Rufus's lifetime except on the king's express order, and that no English prelate could, without royal sanction, receive or obey a papal letter.[182] Accordingly, Rufus acknowledged Urban II and sent commands throughout the kingdom that Urban should be recognized and obeyed as the vicar of St. Peter.[183] The king also agreed to the resumption of the payment of Peter's

177. Approximately ten weeks for the journey to Italy, negotiations with Urban II, and the journey home. The time normally required for journeys between England and Rome is discussed by R. L. Poole, *Studies in Chronology and History* (Oxford, 1934), p. 264: in the twelfth century, an "express courier" could make the one-way trip in a little less than five weeks, or, in cases of extreme urgency, a little more than four.

178. *HN* 68.   179. *HN* 69.
180. *HN* 69.
181. *GP* 89; *HN* 69.
182. Hugh of Flavigny, *Chronicon, MGH, Scriptores*, 8:475; Barlow, *Rufus*, p. 342.
183. *HN* 69.

Pence, an annual tax of about £200 assessed on the English bishoprics.[184]

Rufus then tried to persuade Walter to depose Anselm, promising a huge bribe in return. At Rockingham Anselm had argued with decisive effect that an archbishop of Canterbury could be judged by the pope alone; now Rufus had at his side a legate empowered to act with full papal authority. But once Rufus's recognition of Urban had been obtained and publicized, Cardinal Walter firmly refused to consider deposing Anselm. Eadmer states that Rufus was abashed to discover that he had gained nothing from acknowledging Urban. But, as Barlow points out, Eadmer overlooks Rufus's considerable diplomatic gains.[185] It would have been rather naive to expect a legate of the reform papacy to preside over the deposition of the renowned philosopher-saint, and few of Rufus's advisers can have regarded such an outcome as anything more than a remote possibility.[186] The presence of a legate with a pallium at Rufus's court opened other possibilities as well. Anselm had long been seeking the pallium; what would he now concede in order to receive it?

Rufus, presiding at his Whitsun court at Windsor, now sent a delegation to Anselm consisting of "almost all the bishops of England."[187] They made their peace with the archbishop and then tried to bargain with him. But with Rufus now facing a far-flung baronial conspiracy and about to raise an army against the impending Mowbray rebellion, Anselm was in a powerful negotiating position.[188] The bishops once again, "even at this late hour," asked Anselm to give money to recover the king's friendship. Anselm refused, as before, to purchase the royal love. They then disclosed to Anselm for the first time that Rufus had obtained the pallium, and Anselm at last perceived "how tangled a plot had been set against him."[189] They asked him how much he would pay to receive it; he answered by asserting once more his hatred of high office and refused to pay anything for its ultimate

---

184. ASC, A.D. 1095; cf. Barlow, English Church, pp. 295–97.
185. Barlow, Rufus, pp. 342–43.
186. William of Durham, who continued to seek Anselm's expulsion from office, seems to have believed that Walter would comply: GP 89; but cf. Anselm's subsequent letter to Walter (AEp. 192), stating that Urban had intended the pallium expressly for Anselm.
187. HN 70.
188. ASC, A.D. 1095; cf. Barlow, Rufus, p. 347.
189. HN 71.

symbol. They asked him to give the king at least the sum that he himself would otherwise have spent on the journey to the papal court. "No," he replied, "not even that, or anything at all." Intent on settling the matter before the baronial conspiracy exploded on him, the king submitted. He agreed to give Anselm, free of charge, both the pallium and his royal love, asking only the privilege of conferring the pallium personally on Anselm. But to Anselm that would have constituted a gross violation of correct procedure. The pallium must be given by the pope, not the king. Rufus again backed down. "Adopting, as we have said, the advice of his magnates," he restored his favor to Anselm, recognized him as the kingdom's spiritual father, and permitted him to exercise full primatial authority throughout England.[190]

Anselm was now welcomed to the king's Whitsun court, where Rufus was making preparations for his campaign against the earl of Northumberland. Eadmer hints that the archbishop treated the legate, whom he now met for the first time, with guarded courtesy rather then warm affection. Anselm promised to observe the royal customs and usages and to defend them against all men,[191] thus echoing Urban II's previous concessions to Rufus. The king, on his part, permitted Baldwin of Tournai to return to Anselm's side.[192] Afterward, at Canterbury on 27 May before a great assemblage of bishops, abbots, and laity, Walter of Albano removed the pallium from its silver casket and laid it upon the high altar, and Anselm took it from the altar "as though from the hand of St. Peter."[193]

Thus the "magnates' plan" brought a degree of success to all sides. The papacy won Rufus's recognition and the resumption of Peter's Pence, which had not been collected since the mid-1080s. Anselm at last obtained the pallium on canonically satisfactory terms, along with the considerable convenience of Rufus's recognition of the pope whom Anselm had previously acknowledged. The magnates' tangled plot had caught Anselm off guard, but he avoided the trap with his accustomed

190. *HN* 71.
191. *HN* 83: Eadmer, who refers to this concession only later in connection with events of 1097, states that Anselm made his promise not at the Whitsun settlement but at the close of the Council of Rockingham. But such a promise would be inconsistent with Eadmer's previous account of the Rockingham Council, and I am therefore following Barlow (*Rufus*, pp. 343–44) in redating it to the Whitsun Council and the general settlement of royal-archiepiscopal conflicts.
192. *HN* 73, leaving us to assume that Anselm's chancellor and clerks returned as well.
193. *HN* 72–73; *GP* 91; cf. *VA* 87 and n. 2.

fearlessness and disdain for worldly wealth and honor. Barlow describes Anselm at this point as "intransigent and quite reckless because he was prepared to surrender his office."[194] But if he was planning to resign, the royal curia was quite unaware of it. Also, Anselm had surely received news by now of Robert of Mowbray's defiance and the stirrings of rebellion. Anselm's friends at court included the holy and astute Gundulf of Rochester and several great magnates, and the primate would have understood the pressures that were forcing Rufus toward a settlement. That Anselm was prepared to compromise is made clear by his promise to observe the royal customs, but not even for the pallium would he bribe the king or otherwise violate the due order envisioned by the Canterbury tradition. In the end he won all that he had been seeking at Rockingham including the king's love and the hope of corule, although he remained uncertain as to whether the hope would be fulfilled or the royal love endure.[195] If it did endure, then Anselm, in promising to observe the king's customs, was losing no more than Lanfranc had lost in abiding by those same customs.[196] Indeed the papal legate presently at large in England was, to Canterbury, a loose cannon on a rolling deck, and the pope's concession to send no further legations would have served the interests of Anselm and the Christ Church community even more than the king's.

For Rufus, the pope's concession of the customs was a victory, although it is most unlikely that the customs in question barred his archbishops from going to Rome for their pallia — the primary issue at Rockingham.[197] The resumption of Peter's Pence put a financial obligation on the bishops, not the king.[198] But perhaps more importantly, Rufus had saved face. By seizing control of events, he had escaped from the box into which Anselm had put him at Rockingham and had

194. Barlow, *Rufus*, p. 343.
195. See AEp. 193, about 1095. Anselm implores Urban II that "If in need of your aid from the rushing of the winds, I may flee to the bosom of Mother Church"; Anselm makes a similar plea to Urban indirectly through Walter of Albano: AEp. 194.
196. Like Lanfranc, Anselm corresponded with the pope (and his legates) without apparent royal supervision: AEpp. 191–94.
197. Anselm was the first and only Anglo-Norman archbishop to have been refused permission to receive the pallium.
198. The bishops passed the obligation on to their tenants and parishoners and usually collected substantially more money than they paid to the papacy: in Anselm's time the archbishopric of Canterbury appears to have been making a considerable profit in the process of collecting Peter's Pence: Brett, *English Church*, p. 170, suggests that it may have exceeded 100 percent.

avoided public humiliation. He could now, with Anselm's full support, turn to the matter of the rebellion.

I noted earlier that the audacity and cunning of the "magnates' plan" bears the mark of Robert of Meulan — the magnates' spokesman and Rufus's foremost lay counselor on matters relating to Anselm. The fact that the pallium that Cardinal Walter bore and the cardinal's very identity were kept a secret from both Anselm and the king's own court[199] suggests that the plan was neither devised by nor made known to the magnates as a group, but was known to only the king, his envoys, and a few trusted counselors. Insofar as these counselors can be identified in the pages of Eadmer, they consisted of two or three curialist bishops (William of Durham, Walchelin of Winchester, perhaps Robert of Lincoln) and a single magnate, Robert of Meulan. Although many magnates at Rockingham may have endorsed the truce with Anselm, probably Robert of Meulan alone advised the king to exploit it by swiftly squaring matters with Urban II. Indeed, as the rebellion-conspiracy unfolded,[200] the uncompromisingly royalist count of Meulan may well have been the only great magnate in whom Rufus could place complete trust.

For the time being, however, the disputes were resolved, and Anselm enthusiastically took up his role as the king's loyal supporter. At Rufus's request and by royal writ, Anselm assumed command of the defense of Canterbury and the southeast coast against a threatened invasion (which never materialized), while Rufus campaigned in the north.[201] Barlow remarks, "It was almost as though Anselm had now been girt with the mantle of Lanfranc rather than with the pall of Pope Urban."[202] But ever since the beginning of his pontificate Anselm had been seeking both. Having received the pallium and the king's love, he at once adopted the traditional Canterbury position of cooperating with the king and obeying the pope only from a distance. He wrote to Osmund bishop of Salisbury requesting that prayers be said throughout his diocese on behalf of the king and his northern campaign, "so that God may guard him with his continual protection

199. *HN* 68–69: Walter said nothing to anyone about the pallium he carried, and had no open conversations with anyone at Rufus's court, because the king did not wish the secret of what he was planning to be made public.
200. OV 4:284.
201. AEpp. 191, 192.
202. Barlow, *Rufus*, p. 349.

and, in his kindness, favorably direct all the king's actions to a prosperous end. For indeed, his prosperity is our prosperity, just as his adversity is our adversity."[203] And in a subsequent letter to the same bishop, Anselm echoed Lanfranc in ordering Osmund, "on behalf of the king and on our own behalf," to prevent the abbot and monks of Cerne (Dorset) from joining Peter the Hermit's vast, disorganized campaign to liberate Jerusalem from the Muslims. Anselm further ordered Osmund to forbid any other monks in the diocese of Salibury from joining the enterprise and asked him to pass the order on to the bishops of Exeter, Bath, and Worcester, again "on behalf of the king and on our behalf."[204]

Meanwhile, Anselm used his military responsibility as a pretext to fend off the unwelcome efforts of Cardinal Walter to join him in taking measures to reform the English church. Anselm himself, obviously, was eager to effect such reform but never in company with a legate whose delegated papal authority exceeded that of the primate himself. In Anselm's view, the legate's business in England ended with the conferral of the pallium. To Cardinal Walter's request to consult with Anselm on the matter of reform and to correct what was in need of correction, Anselm responded, "We two can effect nothing except at the king's suggestion."[205] The primate further argued that because of his military commission he dared not leave Canterbury except to go to the Channel ports on news of an invasion. Moreover, the king was campaigning in the north in company with many bishops. Anselm shared with Walter a commitment to church reform, but nothing could be done until the king and bishops' return, and even then it had to be done "reasonably and fittingly." Anselm did not invite Walter to Canterbury; if the legate had any advice about "what matters I should discuss with the king," he was welcome to send it "through our beloved brother the reverend Abbot G."[206]

A further plea by Cardinal Walter provoked Anselm to a testier reply: "After you had received license from the king to return to Rome, and the king left on his expedition . . . , you and I parted expecting never to meet again in this land."[207] Anselm followed this broad hint by asserting that he knew perfectly well what abuses

---

203. AEp. 190.   204. AEp. 195.   205. AEp. 191.
206. AEp. 191: probably Gilbert Crispin; Walter may well have been in London at the time collecting Peter's Pence: Barlow, *Rufus*, p. 348.
207. AEp. 192.

needed correcting, and that he required nobody's help in seeing to their correction "with the aid of God and the assent and aid of my lord the king and of others *to whom it pertains.*"[208] He then proceeded to demolish a series of charges that Walter claimed had been made against Anselm by certain bishops. Among these was the charge that since the English king and episcopate had not acknowledged Urban at the time of Anselm's consecration, Anselm had therefore permitted himself to be consecrated by schismatic bishops and invested by a schismatic king to whom he then rendered homage and fealty.[209] Anselm replied that England was not in schism in 1093. He said that if Urban was not acknowledged neither was he denied, and that at his consecration Anselm had professed obedience "to the Roman Pontiff." Anselm asked why, if Urban thought otherwise, did he send the pallium for Anselm, and why, if Walter himself had any doubts, did he lay it on the Canterbury altar for Anselm to take up? He concluded by requesting Walter's prayers that God "may direct me in all my actions." As far as the surviving evidence discloses, that seemed to close the matter. Walter returned to Rome, bearing a "small gift" from Anselm for the pope, along with a letter apologizing for not having paid him a personal visit and thanking him for the pallium.[210] Due order had at last been achieved, and there was no need for recriminations.

Anselm's ardent wish to preside at a reform council remained unfulfilled, although Rufus may have given him at least vague assurances on this point.[211] But for the next two years Anselm refrained from pressing Rufus because the king was almost continually absorbed in warfare and cross-channel diplomacy. From his settlement with Anselm at Windsor on 13 May 1095 until the end of November, Rufus was engaged in putting down the Northumberland revolt — interrupted briefly by a foray into Wales in response to the fall of Montgomery

208. AEp. 192, my italics.
209. Walter's letter has perished, and we know of these charges only through Anselm's reply, from which it would appear that the alleged offenses involved Rufus's isolation from Urban rather than investiture, homage, and fealty, as such.
210. AEp. 194: the message to Urban was conveyed through Walter, in an apparent gesture of respect for the papal legate.
211. So Eadmer seems to be implying when he writes (re 1097): "Many had high hopes . . . that the archbishop, with the king's approval, would proclaim some great move for the reform of the Christian Church": *HN* 78.

Castle.[212] His Christmas court of 1095 at Windsor was preoccupied with the punishment or fining of the defeated rebels and their sympathizers, and was darkened further when William bishop of Durham fell gravely ill on Christmas day and died on 2 January 1096. Anselm, characteristically, provided his dying antagonist with prolonged spiritual consolation and a final blessing.[213] The trying and punishing of rebels continued at Salisbury in mid-January, where William count of Eu was found guilty of treason, blinded, and castrated.[214] Probably in February Duke Robert Curthose took the Cross. Curthose launched a series of negotiations that resulted in Rufus obtaining all of Normandy in pawn and establishing his authority throughout the duchy, while the newly enriched Curthose departed for the First Crusade.[215] There was no time for Rufus and Anselm to plan a primatial council.

Nevertheless, the king was beginning to show favor to Anselm in a variety of subtle ways. During the Northumbrian campaign Rufus's court had decided against William of Durham's claim to the disputed church of Tynemouth and had awarded the church to St. Albans Abbey, vacant at the time but under the general authority of Canterbury.[216] Two years later, in 1097, Rufus filled the St. Albans vacancy, probably on Anselm's advice, with Richard d'Aubigny from the Bec-related abbey of Lessay.[217] Following the death of Gausbert of Marmoutier abbot of Battle on 27 July 1095, Rufus replaced him in less than a year with Henry, a former Bec monk and Anselm's prior at Canterbury.[218] Rufus was almost equally prompt in replacing Wulfstan (d. 1095) at Worcester with Samson, a royal chaplain and brother of Archbishop Thomas of York; and in replacing Robert (d. 1095) at Hereford with another royal chaplain, Gerard (1096–1101), one of the king's fleet-footed envoys to the papal court. Meanwhile, Anselm may have been functioning throughout the period between Whitsun 1095 and Whitsun 1097 as a royal justiciar.[219] And in 1096, when Rufus laid a large levy on his English landholders to raise the 10,000

212. Barlow, *Rufus*, pp. 348–55, 361.
213. *Historia Dunelmensis Ecclesiae*, in Simeon of Durham, *Opera* 1:133–34.
214. Barlow, *Rufus*, pp. 356–59.
215. Ibid., pp. 361ff.
216. *Regesta* 1, no. 368; *HN* 37, cf. 73.
217. Knowles, *Heads*, p. 66; cf. AEp. 203: Anselm to the prior of the monks of St. Albans during the vacancy (1094–97), assuring them that although God seems to delay, "await him, since he will not tarry."
218. *Heads*, p. 29.
219. So Barlow suspects: *Rufus*, p. 360.

marks that he had promised Curthose for the custody of Normandy during the Crusade,[220] Anselm concluded that "both reason and honor" required him to contribute.[221] He gave all that he could from his personal resources and added 200 marks from the sale of precious objects in the Christ Church treasury, assigning to his monks in return his own manor of Petham for a period of seven years.[222] He was thus able to contribute not only to the realization of his king's most cherished goal but to the Crusade as well.[223] The two years of peace with the king also permitted Anselm to advance the construction of the new Canterbury Cathedral and to finish his *De Incarnatione Verbi* and begin his *Cur Deus Homo*.[224]

In these same years, 1095–97, Anselm had notable success in making good his claim to be primate of all Britain—a claim that he had been asserting strongly since the beginning of his pontificate at Canterbury. Shortly after his consecration, Anselm had undertaken Canterbury's first tangible act of jurisdiction over Wales by suspending two of its three bishops, both Welshmen, for canonical irregularities.[225] One of the two, Wilfred bishop of St. David's, came to Anselm at Rufus's 1095 Whitsun court to seek absolution and Anselm restored him to his see, thereby exercising power over the Welsh church such as none of his predecessors had done.[226] The other suspended bishop, Herewald of Llandaff, is not known to have sought Anselm's pardon. Since Herewald is reputed to have lived to 100, Anselm was obliged to wait until 1107 before placing a loyal prelate in the see of Llandaff and obtaining his written profession.[227] Nevertheless, the years 1093–95 saw the real commencement of Canterbury's authority over the Welsh church, and within the following generation all three Welsh bishops—

220. Ibid., p. 363.
221. *HN* 74–75; cf. Cowdrey, *Popes, Monks, and Crusaders*, pp. xv, 306–7.
222. *HN* 75; it was about this time, too, that Anselm separated the administration of his monks' estates from that of his episcopal lands: Ibid., pp. 75, 219.
223. We are not told the total amount of Anselm's contribution; it probably fell considerably short of the £1000 or £2000 that had been demanded of him in 1093.
224. *HN* 219; *VA* 88, n. 1, 107; AEp. 207.
225. AEp. 175.
226. *HN* 72; cf. AEp. 270 (A.D. 1100–2): Anselm to Robert of Bellême earl of Shrewsbury, Arnulf of Montgomery earl of Pembroke (Anselm's good friend), Ralph of Mortemer, Philip of Briouze, Bernard of Neufmarché, and others holding land in the diocese of St. David's, urging them to show reverence and obedience to Bishop Wilfred and to return any lands, tithes, or churches that rightfully pertained to his bishopric.
227. Urban of Llandaff, 1107–33; *Canterbury Professions*, no. 59; the third bishop in Wales, the Breton Hervey bishop of Bangor, was consecrated by Archbishop Thomas of York in 1092 during the Canterbury vacancy.

Llandaff, St. David's, and Bangor — were regularly giving written professions to Canterbury.[228]

Anselm moved aggressively to exert his authority over Ireland as well. We have already noted in another context his letter of 1093 – 94 to the Irish bishops Donatus bishop of Dublin, Domnall bishop of Munster, "and all others in high Church office in Ireland," in which Anselm explained the circumstances of his elevation.[229] In this same letter he exhorted the bishops to "restrain with canonical severity any teaching which may be found within your provinces that runs contrary to that of the Church." If any question should arise concerning ecclesiastical usages or laws, "we admonish you in the bonds of *caritas* to bring it to our notice so that you can receive advice and comfort from us." Whereas Lanfranc had exercised authority over Dublin alone, Anselm endeavored to expand it across all Ireland, and in 1096 he advanced significantly toward this goal. Not only did he consecrate and receive the profession of a new bishop of Dublin; at the written request of the High King Murchertach and the bishops of Munster, Meath, Dublin, and Leinster, he also consecrated and received a written oath of obedience from the bishop of the newly established see of Waterford.[230] In subsequent correspondence Anselm manifested his primatial rights and responsibilities by sending commands and exhortations on a variety of matters to the bishops of Dublin and Waterford, King Murchertach, and Gilbert bishop of Limerick, to whom Anselm described himself as being "bound by love."[231] In Ireland, as in Wales, Anselm advanced the authority of Canterbury far beyond the point where Lanfranc had left it. When one considers that the churches of neither land had been subject to Canterbury before the Norman Conquest, Anselm's achievement is unparalleled.

While Anselm advanced the limits of the Canterbury primacy and Rufus assumed the rule of Normandy, Robert of Meulan, now in his fifties, was bringing glory to the house of Beaumont by his dazzling marriage to the young Isabel of Vermandois, niece of the king of

228. Ibid., nos. 64, 67; cf. Southern, *Anselm*, pp. 132 – 33.
229. AEp. 198.
230. *HN* 73–74, 76–77; AEpp. 201–202: Samuel of Dublin, former monk of St. Albans; Malchus of Waterford, former monk of Worcester; cf. *Canterbury Professions*, nos. 51, 54; AEp. 207.
231. AEp. 429; also AEpp. 277–78, 427–28, 435; cf. Southern, *Anselm*, pp. 133–35.

France and a direct descendant of the Carolingian emperors. Although Orderic states explicitly that Robert of Meulan held his Norman castles in strict allegiance to the king during the final years of Rufus's struggles with Robert Curthose,[232] the count attested at Curthose's court in mid-August 1095,[233] during a lull in the warfare between king and duke. Robert might have been there for any of several reasons: to persuade Curthose not to involve himself in the baronial conspiracy against the king; to see to the protection of his own Norman dominions in a period of civil turbulence; or to coax Curthose to support his marriage plan. Isabel of Vermandois would have made a splendid match for the duke himself, cementing his on-and-off alliance with the Capetian family, and Robert of Meulan's designs might well have evoked jealousy and apprehension at the ducal court.

The projected marriage was indeed opposed, not by Curthose (so far as we know) but by Ivo bishop of Chartres — Christendom's foremost expert on incestuous marriages. In a letter to the clergy of Meulan, Ivo denounced the marriage on the grounds of consanguinity, "nec ignota, nec remota." He demonstrated that Walter "Albus" count of Valois was both the great-great-grandfather of Count Robert (through the line of the counts of Meulan) and the great-great-great-grandfather of Isabel (through the line of the counts of Crépy-en-Valois).[234] But although Ivo described the relationship as well known, he failed to prevent the marriage. It occurred in 1096, as Isabel's father, Count Hugh, was about to depart on Crusade,[235] and one is tempted to suspect that the marriage might have been accompanied by some sort of agreement on the part of King Philip I, Isabel's uncle, to endorse the crusading vow of his *fidelis,* Robert Curthose, and the pawning of Normandy to Rufus. The marriage would have offered the hope — though it was never realized — of drawing Rufus's intimate counselor into the Capetian court circle. Although Philip I had been excommunicated at Clermont the previous year for his "adulterous" marriage to his second wife, Bertrade of Montfort, his certification of the new arrangement in Normandy would have been useful nonetheless.[236] But the sources are mute on any such arrangements. Although Philip I was a party to the

232. OV 5:26, ca. 1092–95.
233. *Regesta* 1, no. 384; cf. *Regesta* 2, p. 403.
234. *PL* 162: Ep. 45.
235. OV 5:30.
236. Barlow, *Rufus,* p. 364 and references.

peace treaty of 1091 between Rufus and Curthose,[237] there is no express testimony as to whether he approved, opposed, or ignored their
agreement of 1096. Nor is there any report on the activities or
whereabouts of Robert of Meulan — except his 1095 visit to Curthose's
court. We only know that, despite Ivo of Chartres's prohibition, he
married Isabel.

It is again both tempting and hazardous to suppose that the marriage
was made possible by a dispensation from the pope or his legate. Urban
was in France from late 1095 throughout most of 1096[238] and was
prepared to concede much for the sake of the Crusade, perhaps including a dispensation for the marriage of a great crusader's daughter.
Urban had dispatched another legate to Normandy and England,
Jarento abbot of St-Bénigne, Dijon, for the twofold purpose of negotiating a settlement between the duke and king and correcting the abuses
in the English church that had doubtless been described in detail to the
papal curia by Walter of Albano the previous year. Jarento's companion, Hugh abbot of Flavigny, describes the legation in these words:

> At that time, in order to compose peace between . . . King William of the English
> and Robert count of the Normans, Jarento crossed the sea by papal order so
> that the aforesaid king might be warned about the many illicit things which
> were done by him, that is, about the bishoprics and abbeys held in his hands, for
> which he had provided no pastors and in which he had assumed to himself the
> rents and proceeds; about simony; and about the fornication of clerics.[239]

Whether or not this renewal of papal intervention proved helpful to
Robert of Meulan, it was a grave threat to Anselm and the Canterbury
primacy. Jarento and his companions arrived in England before Easter
(13 April 1096) — surely at Rufus's invitation — and were warmly received at the king's Easter court. Anselm, through his envoy Boso of
Bec, who was present at Clermont,[240] would have received news of the
Crusade and perhaps of the legation as well. As in 1095, Rufus and
Anselm normally would have been jointly opposed to a legate endeavoring to reform the English church — Rufus because he welcomed neither
reform nor papal interference in his kingdom (except to serve his
express political goals); Anselm because the reform of England was
Canterbury's responsibility alone. Neither would have taken comfort in

237. *Gesta Normannorum Ducum*, p. 270.
238. Jaffé-Wattenbach 1: 681 – 90.
239. *MGH, Scriptores* 8:474.
240. *VB* 726.

Hugh of Flavigny's remark that on Jarento's arrival "the honor and vigor of the Church of England and the liberty of Roman authority resurged as if it breathed again."[241] Seeking Jarento's diplomatic assistance, and only that, Rufus repeated his strategy of the previous year. While welcoming Jarento with affectionate regard, he had already sent an envoy on a secret mission to Urban who "placed in his hands ten marks of the purest gold," thus feeding "the insatiable whirlpool of Roman greed."[242] The pope in return granted a postponement of the matter of legatine reform until the following Christmas, by which time the bargain with Curthose had been struck, Rufus ruled Normandy, and the matter was quietly dropped. Jarento had remained in England for less than two months, departing by the end of May to negotiate with Curthose. He remained in Normandy until September, when he accompanied the duke and his fellow crusaders on the first stage of their journey — leaving Rufus in Rouen.[243] Since Eadmer tells us nothing about Jarento's visit, we do not know Anselm's exact response to it, but he probably remained of one mind with the king.

Anselm continued to wait and hope for an opportunity to preside at a great reform council. He had spoken to Rufus from time to time about the question of reform, but the king had always replied "that he could not attend to that because of the enemies that surrounded him on all sides."[244] When Rufus finally returned from Normandy at Easter (5 April 1097), with Robert of Meulan once more at his side,[245] Anselm hoped to persuade the king at last to fulfill what Eadmer describes as Anselm's "heart's desire."[246] But the matter of the council was again postponed, when Rufus almost immediately launched an invasion of Wales. Anselm dutifully supplied a contingent of knights from Canterbury.

On the king's return before Whitsun (24 May), Eadmer states, all hopes and expectations of reform were suddenly shattered by a letter from the king charging Anselm with having sent knights to the royal host who were neither properly trained nor suitable for the campaign.

241. *MGH, Scriptores* 8:474.
242. Ibid., 474–75; Barlow (*Rufus*, p. 364) suspects that Rufus's envoy was, as in the previous year, William Warelwast.
243. Haskins, *Norman Institutions*, pp. 75–76; David, *Robert Curthose*, pp. 90–91.
244. *HN* 78.
245. *Regesta* 1, no. 397.
246. *HN* 78.

Anselm was warned to be prepared to pay reparation at the judgment of the royal court whenever the king should choose to arraign him.[247] Eadmer regarded the charge as totally unfounded, and so clearly did Anselm. Their opinion is corroborated by the predominantly Norman names on the more or less contemporary list of Canterbury knights in *Domesday Monachorum*. This list includes not only a number of important local men who held elsewhere as tenants-in-chief of the king, but magnates and *curiales* as well: Hamo *Dapifer* sheriff of Kent (six knights), the royal constable Hugh of Montfort (four knights), Gilbert fitz Richard of Clare (four knights), the count of Eu (four knights), William Peverel (two knights), Hugh of Port (two knights), and William of Briouze.[248] Rufus's complaint was more likely intended as a thrust in his duel with Anselm over the issue of enfeoffing the king's knights on Canterbury estates — an issue that antedated Anselm's consecration and had never been resolved.[249] Regarding Rufus's accusation as an indication that he was being wronged "by the mere whim of the king's malice," Anselm chose to ignore the charge. The episode, however, prompted him to conclude that he would probably not realize his goal of cooperation and corule with Rufus. "We looked for a time of peace," he exclaimed, "and nothing good comes of it; we looked for a time of healing, and behold, confusion."[250]

At Rufus's Whitsun Council at Windsor (24 May 1097), Anselm made a final effort to persuade Rufus to cooperate in the cause of reform. Finding the king as opposed as ever to a primatial council, "he lost all hope of his future amendment" and asked permission to go to Rome and seek the pope's advice.[251] Astonished, Rufus absolutely prohibited the journey, remarking in grudging admiration of Anselm's political skill, "When it is a matter of giving advice, he is better able to help the pope than the pope to help him."[252] But in response to this archiepiscopal counterthrust, Rufus quietly dropped the charge regarding the ill-trained knights. Anselm persisted, repeating his request at a royal council in August, and again in October at Winchester. On this

247. *HN* 78; *VA* 88.
248. *Domesday Monachorum*, p. 105; cf. pp. 36–63 for an analysis of the list.
249. *HN* 40–41; cf. *VA* 81–84, 88, n. 2; *AEpp.* 176, 206, 210: Anselm complains, in his first letter to the new pope, Paschal II, that the king *continued* to place his knights on Canterbury lands.
250. *HN* 98; cf. *VA* 88; *GP* 91–92.
251. *HN* 79.
252. *HN* 80.

last occasion Rufus, moved to anger, ordered Anselm to ask no further and to pay a fine "such as the court shall decide" for continually vexing him. The king further threatened, if Anselm should depart for Rome, to seize the whole of his archbishopric and never again receive him as archbishop, thus presenting Anselm with the choice of total submission or the loss of all his lands. Undaunted, Anselm asserted that he was determined to go to the pope with or without Rufus's permission. When Walchelin bishop of Winchester expressed disbelief that Anselm would remain adamant, Anselm looked him in the eye: "Yes, adamant!"[253]

While Rufus continued to deliberate with his counselors, Anselm summoned four of the curial bishops to his side and challenged them to support and advise him, following divine justice rather than secular royal authority.[254] They declared: "Encumbered as we are by our kinsfolk whom we support, and by many worldly things that are dear to us, we cannot, we confess, rise to the sublime heights of your own life and scorn this world. . . . If you still choose to hold fast to God, [then] you are alone. . . . We owe allegiance to the king, and from that allegiance we shall not depart." "Go to your lord, then," Anselm told them; "I shall hold fast to God."[255] The bishops consulted with Rufus and then returned to Anselm with the ultimatum that he either leave the kingdom immediately or make restitution for having troubled the king and swear never again, under any circumstances, to appeal to the pope.

Anselm then returned to the king's presence. Reminded by the royal counselors that he himself had earlier sworn to uphold the royal customs and usages, which prohibited unlicensed visits to Rome, Anselm answered that he had promised to uphold only such customs as were rightful and in accordance with God's will. He was accused of having neglected to mention this mental reservation when he took the oath. Anselm replied that it didn't matter what he had said: "God forbid, God forbid, I say, that any Christian should hold or defend laws or customs known to be contrary to God and rightfulness."[256] Although logically unassailable, Anselm's argument was at odds with contemporary conceptions of the meaning of oaths. It echoed his earlier reinterpretation of his oath never to abandon his rule of Bec. And few of Rufus's

253. *HN* 81.
254. *HN* 82–83: the bishops were Walchelin of Winchester, John of Bath, Robert Bloet of Lincoln, and Osmund of Salisbury. The last two were former royal chancellors: *Regesta* 1, p. xviii.
255. *HN* 82–83.   256. *HN* 84–85.

counselors would have shared Anselm's certainty that God was calling him to Rome. If Anselm alone could discern the divine will, his promises would have seemed to carry unspoken reservations not altogether unlike the royal promises recommended by the count of Meulan.

Rufus and his counselors well understood that Anselm's threat to depart was far less dangerous to them in the relatively secure political circumstances of 1097 than in the hazardous times of early 1095, and they were now quite prepared, if he could not be humbled, to let him depart. As Anselm continued to argue the priority of obedience to God over obedience to men, Rufus and Robert of Meulan finally interrupted in exasperation, speaking as one voice: "Oh! Oh! Words, words! All he is saying is only words!" The nobles shouted in agreement, and when Anselm resumed his argument, the count of Meulan again interrupted, assuring him that he could indeed go to Rome, for "what we have in mind will lose nothing by it."[257]

Robert of Meulan had reached such a state of authority that he spoke not only with the king but for him.[258] Count Robert evidently concluded that there was now no stopping Anselm, but that with Normandy won and England at peace, the king would no longer be hurt by the spectacle of the archbishop of Canterbury going into exile. On the contrary, the Canterbury revenues might then be diverted to Rufus's projected campaigns to recover Maine and the French Vexin — lands that he claimed by hereditary right and whose conquest required no elaborate religious justification. But Rufus determined to make Anselm's departure as humiliating as possible, forbidding him to take with him any treasure or possessions from his see. Anselm replied that he would make the journey on foot and naked if necessary. The king could not permit Anselm to cast him in such a light and made it clear that the archbishop could take horses and baggage. Anselm afterward returned to Rufus to bid him a characteristically cheerful and affectionate farewell: "I commend you to God," he told the king, "and as a spiritual father to his beloved son, as archbishop of Canterbury to the king of England, I would give you God's blessing and my own before I go, if you do not refuse it." The king answered, "Your blessing I do not refuse."[259] Rufus bowed his head and received from Anselm the sign of the Cross, and they parted, never to meet again.

257. *HN* 86.
258. Cf. OV 5:248, writing of Robert of Meulan in the following year: "Callidus enim senex regalibus consiliis et iudiciis praeerat."
259. *HN* 87.

Anselm returned to Canterbury to bid a tearful adieu to his monks, clergy, and people,[260] and then traveled to Dover for the Channel crossing. There he encountered the royal chaplain William Warelwast, who paid him the final indignity of searching his baggage in the vain hope of finding money.[261] Anselm set off at last in late October 1097, accompanied by two of his most faithful monks, Baldwin of Tournai and Eadmer.[262] At the news of his departure, Rufus immediately had the properties of the archbishop and monks taken into the royal hand.[263]

Anselm explained his reason for choosing exile in one succinct sentence: "I saw in England many evils whose correction belonged to me and which I could neither remedy nor, without personal guilt, allow to exist."[264] The evils Anselm had in mind will be obvious from the foregoing discussion, and he summarized them once again in a letter to Pope Urban written from Lyon in early 1098: the king was exploiting vacant abbeys and bishoprics, and he was continuing to place his men on Canterbury estates that had been unencumbered in Lanfranc's days. Above all, he refused to permit Anselm to correct moral abuses by means of a primatial council — abuses "which it was wrong for me to tolerate but which I lacked episcopal freedom to correct."[265] In all these matters Anselm was endeavoring to uphold Canterbury traditions, an obligation that he continued to regard as his God-given duty. He had been firm but not unwilling to compromise — to tolerate lesser evils for the sake of a greater good. This is clear from his relatively amicable and cooperative relationship with Rufus between May 1095 and May 1097. The relationship might well have continued if Rufus had loosened his grasp on the abbeys and given Anselm his synod. But as Barlow correctly and colorfully observes, "It is plain as a pikestaff that William was determined that the primate should not hold a reform council."[266]

---

260. *VA* 93–97; *HN* 87–88.

261. Rufus had warned Anselm before he left court that a royal agent would meet him at Dover to instruct him what possessions he might carry abroad: *HN* 87.

262. *HN* 88; cf. 95 and *VA* 103.

263. *HN* 88: Eadmer states that Rufus annulled all changes and ordinances that had been made on Anselm's authority, including, presumably, the administrative separation of archiepiscopal from monastic estates; cf. AEp. 210: Anselm informs the pope that Rufus, "allowing only for the bare food and clothing of our monks, seized the whole archbishopric and converted it to his own use."

264. AEp. 210.

265. AEp. 206.

266. *Rufus*, p. 373.

The Worcester chronicler thus explains Anselm's central grievance: "Because he had not been permitted to hold a council from the time he became archbishop, or to correct the evil practices that had arisen throughout England, he crossed the sea."[267] If he could not uphold essential elements of the Canterbury tradition, he could at least make it dramatically evident, through exile, that he did not tolerate their suppression. To remain complacently in England, Anselm believed, would "establish a most vicious precedent for my successors."[268]

But Anselm had insisted on leaving England, not for a quiet exile, but to consult Urban II. What was Anselm's purpose in visiting the papal court? Most historians have heretofore concluded that he intended to obtain papal license to resign his archbishopric.[269] This conclusion is based on seemingly straightforward statements of Eadmer, and on Anselm's letter to Urban written from Lyon in early 1098, reviewing his tribulations and then begging the pope to "release my soul from the chain of such slavery and restore to it the freedom to serve God in peace."[270] Despite this evidence, Anselm probably never had any expectation of resigning his archiepiscopacy. Just as when he had asked Archbishop Maurilius so many years before to free him of the office of prior, Anselm was acting out a topos, as the following discussion will explain.

First, the conflict between Anselm, Rufus, and Count Robert at the 1097 Winchester court could have been avoided if Anselm had made clear his intention to resign, and if the king's counselors had entertained any reasonable expectation that Urban would agree to such a request. Rather than having Anselm's baggage searched, Rufus might well have funded his journey from the royal treasury and provided a guard of honor. Second, Anselm did not go directly to the papal court; instead he visited Cluny to consult at some length with its venerable Abbot Hugh, and then settled down in Lyon with his old friend Archbishop Hugh. From Lyon he wrote his letter to Urban in which he begged to resign but also stated that he was presently unable to visit the pope: "Why I cannot, you will learn from the bearer of this letter."[271] Eadmer casts a glimmer of light on Anselm's reasons for eschewing the papal court. "While we were staying in Lyon, Anselm learned from rumors that

267. Florence, 2:41.
268. AEp. 206: Anselm to Urban.
269. E.g., Southern, *Anselm*, p. 161; Barlow, *Rufus*, p. 375; Cantor, *Church, Kingship, and Lay Investiture*, pp. 114–15.
270. AEp. 206.
271. AEp. 206.

reached us that to proceed further would advance his cause very little."[272] Eadmer then provides as further reasons for staying in Lyon Anselm's poor health and the danger of ambushes on the way to Rome. Significantly, poor health and ambushes are alleged only as auxiliary reasons; the primary reason was the rumors suggesting that Anselm would gain little or nothing at the papal court. At this juncture Eadmer transcribes into his history Anselm's letter to Urban begging to resign.[273]

Anselm would surely have been wary of a pope who two years before had sent his legate secretly through Canterbury carrying the pallium to Rufus's court, and who had sent another legate the following year to threaten the Canterbury primacy by striving to reform England through the direct intervention of papal authority — and had then withdrawn him on receipt of a bribe by Rufus. Although direct evidence is lacking, Rufus and Count Robert could have sent still another envoy dashing to Rome immediately after Anselm's departure to reach a further understanding with Urban.[274] Barlow observes that the quashing of Abbot Jarento's legation in 1096 had taught Rufus "that he could bribe a pope almost as easily as he could buy lay princes."[275] The discouraging rumors circulating in Lyon suggest that Rufus may already have been in touch with the papal court. Anselm thereupon wrote his letter summarizing the wrongs he had suffered, alleging his unworthiness, and begging Urban to let him resign. The letter was not, as it purported to be, a spontaneous outpouring of emotions from a simple, saintly man to his Holy Father; rather, it was a carefully calculated effort to shame a wavering pope into giving staunch support to Anselm's cause. If we read between the lines, Anselm seems to be conveying this message: These are the scandalous problems that prevent your devoted servant from continuing to function as primate in England. My self-will (the untamed Anselm) urges me to resign. Since you will never permit me to do so, you owe me at least your undivided support in my cause against the king.

Lanfranc had written a similar letter after Christmas 1072, begging Alexander II to permit his resignation,[276] and for the similar purpose of

---

272. *HN* 91.

273. The source of the rumors was probably Anselm's close friend and host, Archbishop Hugh himself, who was serving just then as papal *vicarius* in France: Jaffé-Wattenbach, nos. 5685, 5690, 5788, 5793; Anselm wrote the letter after submitting his case to Hugh and seeking his advice: *HN* 91.

274. Cf. *HN* 98: Rufus tried through letters and bribes to stir up trouble against Anselm.

275. *Rufus*, p. 365.   276. *LEp.* 1.

prompting firm papal backing of the Canterbury primacy. Lanfranc had earlier requested that Alexander grant a papal confirmation of Canterbury's claim to primacy over York,[277] and Archdeacon Hildebrand had replied that nothing could be done unless Lanfranc presented his case personally at the papal curia.[278] Only at that point did Lanfranc plead to resign, and his arguments prefigured Anselm's in 1098: failing strength, personal unworthiness, the enduring of countless troubles and vexations from godless people, failure to achieve any useful result, and a longing to live simply and in peace.[279]

Anselm's plea for release from office, like Lanfranc's earlier plea on which it may have been modeled, was a formality without expectation of acceptance. Canon law tended strongly to the view that a bishop must remain in office as long as he is physically able: "To leave it even for a more humble life," Edward Peters observes, "was generally forbidden."[280] As Urban II told Anselm on a later occasion, "By the law of the Christian church you must always be archbishop."[281] And Archbishop Anselm himself had earlier advised Lanfrid abbot of St. Omer against resigning his prelacy, in words that were just as applicable to his own case:

> You should rejoice in your tribulation, [for] you are doubtless suffering it because of your burning zeal for God, and enduring it because of a God-given fear that you dare not flee from it. . . . God weighs not only the effort one takes to be profitable to others, but also, or perhaps somewhat more, the labor one endures in making the attempt to bring them profit, and the grief one feels at being unable to improve them as one would wish.[282]

Anselm might continue to display his reluctance, but he remained in 1097, as always before, a servant who had surrendered himself totally to God's will.[283] His letter to Urban had the effect that Anselm doubtless intended: it enabled him to go to the papal court not as a suppliant but as an invited and honored guest. The messengers who bore his letter

277. LEp. 4, 8 April – 27 May 1072; above, Chapter 5 at nn. 65 – 67.
278. LEp. 6, summer 1072.
279. Cf. Becket's similar plea to Alexander III to release him from his office: David Knowles, *Thomas Becket* (Stanford, 1971), p. 106 and n. 1.
280. "The Archbishop and the Hedgehog," in *Law, Church, and Society: Essays in Honor of Stephan Kuttner,* ed. K. Pennington and Robert Somerville (Philadelphia, 1977), p. 173.
281. HN 104.
282. AEp. 186.
283. AEp. 208: Anselm (from Lyon) to Hugh archdeacon of Canterbury: "I cannot tell you with any certainty what my future will be, or what I might do, but I commit myself completely to the divine disposition."

to Urban returned to Lyon to report that the pope bade him come quickly to Rome. Anselm obeyed and was received with joy and great honor.[284]

Eadmer weaves his entire account of Anselm's exile around a series of moral themes: Anselm's reluctance to remain in office and his desire for a simple, peaceful life; the honor and generosity with which he was everywhere received (in edifying contrast to his treatment by Rufus and his men); and the sympathy that his cause evoked in all quarters.[285] His account is to be trusted on most points, if used with discretion, but on the matter of Anselm's reluctance to remain in office it lapses into incoherence — as did Eadmer's earlier account of Anselm's visit to the dying Earl Hugh of Chester. As Eadmer tells it, Anselm wrote to Urban explaining his problems in detail and pleading to resign. Urban responded with a verbal message inviting Anselm to Rome. When Anselm arrived and again explained his problems, "in a manner that met the demands of both truth and discretion," Urban "was astonished at what he heard" — as though he had not read Anselm's letter — and "promised his total support." Eadmer does not record a word being said by either party about Anselm's resignation plea.[286] It was as though the request had never been made.

Urban's support for Anselm's cause turned out to be considerably less than total. The pope wrote to Rufus, urging and commanding him to restore Anselm's possessions, and Anselm wrote a similar letter, but nothing came of the effort. In the company of his friend and former Bec colleague, John abbot of Telese, Anselm spent early summer 1098 at the mountaintop retreat of Liberi[287] where he completed his *Cur Deus Homo* and lived the life of simple holiness that he had lived long ago before becoming abbot of Bec: "This is my resting place," he exclaimed. "Here I shall live." But all too quickly he was drawn by the invitation of Roger duke of Apulia to the siege of Capua (June 1098), after which he accompanied Pope Urban to Aversa.

Here for the first time in Eadmer's two accounts, Anselm personally asked the pope's permission to resign his pastoral cure, begging for release from the chain that pressed so heavily as to make his heart ache, and from the burden that he found intolerable because it bore no fruit.[288]

---

284. *HN* 94–96; *VA* 103, 105.
285. *VA* also, of course, places great emphasis on his holiness, wisdom, and miracles.
286. *VA* 106; cf. *HN* 96.
287. Formerly Sclavia: *VA* 106–7; *HN* 97.   288. *HN* 103.

It is as though Eadmer was providing his readers with a rerun of Anselm's earlier letter, complete with its metaphors of oppressive chains and the failure to bear fruit.[289]

Urban's response was both explosive and predictable: "Bishop! Shepherd! You have not yet suffered bloodshed, no, nor wounds, and you already seek to steal away from the care of the lord's sheep fold?" Again, as in the turbulent events surrounding his election at Rufus's bedside in March 1093, Anselm adopted a position appropriate to the reluctant prelate. Yet, as he surely must have realized, his position was legally and morally untenable. He begged release from the burden of office that pressed too heavily upon him, making a secret of his surrender to God[290] and seeming to care only for his own selfish ease. And once again he was outargued and charged with caring not for his sheep but only for his own peace of mind. Urban commanded him to retain his archiepiscopal office. When Anselm reminded him — with slight exaggeration — that Rufus had demanded that he renounce obedience to the papacy, Urban promised to avenge Anselm's wrongs "with the sword of St. Peter" at the Council of Bari the following October. For a second time — if Eadmer's sequence of events can be trusted — Anselm's petition to resign had resulted in a pledge of papal support. But once again the pledge was without definitive result. Urban presented Anselm's case at Bari, and Eadmer alleges that the pope was on the verge of excommunicating Rufus when Anselm begged him to reconsider.[291] But Eadmer is surely in error: Urban had as yet sent Rufus only the first of the traditional three warnings, and the king's answer had not yet arrived; to have excommunicated Rufus at this point would have been a flagrant violation of canonical procedures.[292] Whatever the case, Anselm was honored and admired at Bari but was given no formal canonical decision against the king.

In December 1098, William Warelwast arrived in Rome with Rufus's reply to Urban's letter: the king had given Anselm full warning that his properties would be confiscated if he left the kingdom. Finding this reply altogether unacceptable, Urban commanded that Rufus

289. AEp. 206; William of Malmesbury, drawing from Eadmer, avoids the redundancy by omitting Anselm's letter and introducing his plea to resign only at this moment: GP 97–99.
290. Cf. AEp. 156, and above, Chapter 4 at nn. 51–92, esp. 84–88.
291. HN 106–7.
292. See Southern, Anselm, p. 161: "It is probable that Anselm, or his biographer, or both, misunderstood what the pope was about to do."

restore Anselm's possessions and, on pain of excommunication, inform the pope that he had done so before the coming Roman synod scheduled for the third week after Easter 1099. William Warelwast then asked to confer with Urban privately; by distributing bribes to the pope and his counselors, the envoy obtained a postponement of the deadline to the following Michaelmas. "Seeing what had happened," Eadmer laments, "we realized that it was useless to wait in Rome for counsel or aid."[293] Anselm wanted to leave for Lyon immediately,[294] but Urban ordered him to stay on until after the Paschal synod in late April. There Anselm heard and approved the papal bans on lay investiture and the rendering of homage by clerics to laymen — the prohibitions that would so dramatically affect his own pontificate in the reign of Henry I.[295] The bishop of Lucca made an emotional public appeal for papal action on Anselm's behalf: "It has now been more than a year since he came here, but alas, what help has he found so far?" Urban assured him that the matter would receive full consideration at a future time, and the council proceeded with its agenda. At its conclusion, Anselm departed for Lyon where he remained for the next fourteen months.

When one penetrates beyond the phantom images of the topoi that Eadmer deploys and Anselm enacts — the peaceful mountaintop, the struggles to resign — there can remain no doubt that Anselm sought specific help from the papal court in his struggle for the rights of Canterbury. He sought nothing less than a formal papal judgment against Rufus, backed ultimately by the sanction of excommunication. If he opposed this sanction at Bari (and Eadmer's account is murky at this point), he did so, surely, on the grounds that it was canonically improper and poorly timed. Urban had given Rufus until April 1099 to restore Anselm's lands on pain of excommunication. When the pope postponed the date to late September, Anselm was disappointed almost to the point of despair and subsequently left the papal court as a mark of his disapproval and disillusionment.

In addition to obtaining a papal condemnation of Rufus, Anselm had a second goal in Rome. As he later wrote to Paschal II,

When I was in Rome I clearly explained to the aforesaid pope [Urban] about the Roman legateship to the kingdom of England, how the men of that kingdom

293. HN 111.   294. VA 113.
295. HN 114: The prohibitions were approved "with unanimous shouts of 'So be it! So be it!' "

declared it to have been held from antiquity to the present by the Church of Canterbury, how necessary it therefore is to have it so, and that any other arrangement would be injurious to both the Roman and the English churches. Nor did the lord pope deprive me of that legatine authority which up to our time, according to the aforesaid testimony, the Church of Canterbury has retained.[296]

Anselm's own, carefully chosen words make it likely that Urban conceded him only the sort of de facto legatine authority that Alexander II had bestowed on Lanfranc. But it was enough to protect the Canterbury primacy from threats such as Walter of Albano had presented in 1095 and Jarento of Dijon in 1096. And should Anselm return to England and resume his prelacy, the legateship, even if informal, would be a valuable weapon in his effort to convoke a reform synod.[297]

As for the possibility of excommunicating Rufus, Anselm was fully aware that such a sanction would be ineffective as long as the king's power remained otherwise unchallenged, and he dismissed unilaterally the possibility of excommunicating Rufus — at least for the time being — on the grounds of his disinclination to be both plaintiff and judge, and his conviction that the excommunication would be ridiculed and ignored in England.[298] He bided his time, leaving the future in God's hands but knowing that if and when Robert Curthose returned from Crusade, Rufus would again be vulnerable. Rufus appears to have had no intention of relinquishing Normandy to Curthose, and a resumption of the war between the two brothers would have created the opportune moment to act.[299] The dream of corule might yet be realized.

The direction of Anselm's hopes is suggested by the fact that he left Rome to settle down not in the isolated mountaintop village of Liberi but in the crossroads city of Lyon, whose archbishop was at once Anselm's confidant and Urban's vicar. Eadmer's description of Anselm's stay in Lyon evokes the topos not of the simple saint but of the honored guest. Archbishop Hugh and the people of Lyon came to regard Anselm not as a passing pilgrim but as their lord. In all episcopal activities he functioned as archbishop and Hugh as his suffragan: "Anselm officiated at the festivals, the ordinations, and the dedica-

296. AEp. 214.

297. Cf. *Charters of Norwich Cathedral Priory,* no. 260 (A.D. 1101): Anselm titles himself Archbishop of Canterbury, Primate of Great Britain and Ireland, and *Vicarius* of the Pope — exactly the term with which Urban had described Hugh of Lyon's authority in France.

298. AEp. 210.

299. C. W. Hollister, "The Strange Death of William Rufus," *Speculum* 48 (1973): 644–45.

tions of churches — and performed all episcopal functions."[300] And he did so not as God's reluctant servant but voluntarily. It was not the act of a man who sought to abandon his episcopal responsibilities and flee into anonymity.

To Rufus, Anselm's departure was clearly a relief. "I have gained my freedom," he said, "and freely I shall now do exactly as I like."[301] Rufus regarded the Canterbury tradition of corule as a challenge to his sovereignty; his own conception of due order was that of the divinely ordained monarch who ruled both church and kingdom. Robert of Meulan's role in the final break with Anselm is more difficult to discern. Robert could be sympathetic toward Anselm, as we have seen, but in the end he spoke in one voice with the king. And later, in the time of Henry I, Robert would advocate a more rigorous policy of royal control over the church than the king himself was prepared to claim.[302] To the monarchy, Robert believed, God had conferred responsibility to provide for the common good, to preserve the safety of the realm, and to protect the church.[303] When Rufus complained that Anselm was trying to rob him of the jewel of his sovereignty, the count of Meulan would surely have been sympathetic.

But royal policy in 1099 was not based simply on the upholding of an abstract concept of authority; it was aimed at the full realization of hereditary claims to Maine and the French Vexin. Rufus had planned to cross to Normandy at about the time Anselm went into exile, but bad weather delayed the royal crossing until well into November.[304] Throughout the winter of 1097–98 Rufus campaigned in the Vexin supported by his brother Count Henry, the counts and magnates of Normandy, and several lords of the French Vexin whom Rufus won over by bribery — probably through the mediation of the count of Meulan. Count Robert himself, firmly committed to Rufus's service despite his marriage to Philip I's niece, "welcomed the English into his castles and opened the way to France with them; thanks to their military strength he inflicted heavy losses on the French."[305] Rufus hurled all his resources into the ensuing campaigns, and rumors flew in Paris that he intended to dispossess the king of France himself.[306]

300. *HN* 114; *VA* 116–17.
301. *HN* 116.   302. *HN* 207–9.
303. OV 5:316; above, Chapter 5 at n. 80.
304. Barlow, *Rufus*, p. 376.   305. OV 5:214.
306. Suger, *Vie de Louis VI, le Gros*, ed. Henri Waquet (Paris, 1964), p. 11; Luchaire, *Louis VI*, p. xiv.

Rufus campaigned twice in the French Vexin — in winter 1097 – 98 and again in autumn and early winter 1098. Between these two campaigns, from February to July or August, he concentrated on Maine, where his opponents were Elias count of Maine until his capture in ambush (28 April 1098), and then Fulk count of Anjou. By August hostilities in Maine had ended with a truce altogether favorable to Rufus.[307] Fulk and Elias agreed to surrender to the king all the castles once held by William the Conqueror, and Rufus entered Le Mans triumphant. The truce also called for the freeing of all prisoners taken during the campaign. Released from his prison in Bayeux, Count Elias came to the king's court in Rouen to beg Rufus to restore his comital title and allow him to serve in Rufus's household. Rufus at first agreed, but the count of Meulan, motivated, so Orderic alleges, by a desire to secure his own position as chief royal adviser, dissuaded the king. Robert's speech, in fact, is a warning to Rufus of the dangers of admitting a former foe to one's counsels: "Your conquered enemy becomes your suppliant, and seeks perfidiously to be your intimate friend. Why does he desire this? That being admitted to your secret counsels, he may better be able, when a favorable opportunity arises, to revolt fiercely against you and to join your enemies with greater means of injuring you."[308] Robert clarified for Rufus the consequences of his generous but impulsive decision. Rufus heeded the count's advice and reversed himself.

Rufus now turned in earnest to the French Vexin. Having secured the alliance of the Vexin marcher lords, Robert had also fortified Meulan with trenches and walls.[309] The location of Meulan, and Rufus's access to the newly built castle of Gisors, opened the Normans' way into the heart of France (see Map 5; cf. Map 4).[310] Rufus had every advantage in the ensuing battle, but the lords of the French Vexin, in a desperate stand, held their castles and could not be dislodged. Rufus retired to Normandy for Christmas; by 10 April 1099, having concluded a truce, he and his entourage, including Robert, returned to England.[311] The king had been victorious in Maine but was stalemated in the Vexin. Barlow suggests that he may have suffered from Anselm's exile: his harsh treatment of the archbishop may have encouraged Ivo bishop of Chartres to release the Vexin lord Nivard of Septeuil from the oaths he

307. Barlow, *Rufus*, pp. 386 – 87.
308. OV 5:248.   309. Luchaire, *Louis VI*, p. xvi.
310. Freeman, *Rufus*, 2:184; Luchaire, *Louis VI*, pp. xvi – xvii.
311. Barlow, *Rufus*, p. 395; OV 5:218; *Regesta* 2, p. 405, no. 414a: Count Robert attests a royal charter at Westminster dated 29 May 1099.

had rendered to Rufus when he was taken captive by the king.[312] Whether or not Ivo acted with the archbishop's exile in mind, Rufus shortly afterward sent a messenger to Lyon to confer with Archbishop Hugh about Anselm.[313] The messenger made no commitment but listened carefully as Hugh of Lyon reviewed Anselm's grievances. As he departed, the messenger told Hugh to expect another royal envoy after he had reported back to Rufus, but, so far as we know, the second messenger never appeared. Anselm's next formal message from the Anglo-Norman court was a letter from King Henry I announcing Rufus's death on 2 August 1100, in a hunting accident in the New Forest, and inviting Anselm to return to England as archbishop of Canterbury.[314] With Rufus's death and Henry I's accession, the political conditions of the Anglo-Norman world were suddenly transformed.

The reign of William Rufus was pivotal in the history of the Anglo-Norman state. Although Rufus continued many of his father's policies, he also made important innovations that presaged the more secular administrative kingship of Henry I.[315] These changes were products of Rufus's exalted vision of the powers and prerogatives of kingship, and his consequent conflict with the Canterbury tradition, which was epitomized by Anselm in his metaphor of the two oxen. Anselm had begun his pontificate with a highly structured concept of the due order proper to the governance of the English realm and church. Rufus and Robert of Meulan adhered to a distinctly different concept of the king's unrivaled sovereignty over a community committed to him by God.

These political ideas and practices, which began to take shape in Rufus's reign, emerged much more clearly in the reign of Henry I. Under Rufus's successor, Anselm and Robert of Meulan dueled skillfully, using their developing concepts and methods in a much more sophisticated way than before, and justifying them by the effective marshalling of public opinion and the creation of public images. As a result of this growing sophistication, Rufus's shouts and colorful curses gave way to soft words from both sides. Henry I, with Robert of Meulan advising him, never formally withdrew his love from Anselm and never set a price on it. Although the struggle was at times ruthless, it never lost its veneer of decorum. And perhaps for that reason, the way remained open for eventual reconciliation.

312. Barlow, *Rufus*, p. 394.
313. AEp. 210.   314. AEp. 212.
315. Barlow, *Rufus,* pp. 433–37; Emma Mason, "William Rufus: Myth and Reality," *JMH* 3 (1976): 1–20, esp. 11–15; David Bates, "The Origins of the Justiciarship," *ANS* 4 (1981): 1–12.

Six

The Quest for Compromise:
The Primate, the King's Chief Adviser,
and the Pope, 1100 – 1104

Anselm's conflicts with Henry I occurred in a context distinctly unlike
that of his conflicts with Rufus. The two great differences were that the
new regime adopted a much more conciliatory attitude toward the archbishop of Canterbury and the church in England, and that the papacy
now entered the controversy directly — not simply as a potential supporter of Anselm's cause but as a third party intent on advancing its
own policy of prohibiting clerical homage and lay investiture. Anselm's
policy never changed. It remained under Henry I, as it had been under
William Rufus, a determined effort to meet his responsibilities as God's
steward by upholding the essential, interrelated components of the
Canterbury tradition. Anselm's conflict with Henry I arose from the
fact that one such component was the rendering of due canonical
obedience to the papacy. But with respect to ultimate goals, the English
Investiture Controversy was a three-sided struggle: the pope endeavored to enforce the homage and investiture decrees; the king defended
his ancestral customs; and the primate continued to champion the
traditions of Canterbury.

   Although Henry I guarded his secrets well, everything we know about
his relationship with Anselm suggests that, on Robert of Meulan's advice, he was prepared to concede all that the archbishop had requested
of Rufus and had been denied: free enjoyment of the royal favor,

freedom from acts of royal extortion or petty harassment, and, above all, freedom to summon primatial reform synods. Under these circumstances, Anselm can have had no wish to quarrel with the new regime. A relationship of trust and intimacy with the king was obviously essential to the Canterbury tradition of corule. To see the papal decrees on investiture and homage as at last providing Anselm with "a clear and simple objective for which to fight"[1] is to overlook the point that Anselm did not pick fights; he longed to work peacefully with the king in governing England. And since Henry I appears to have been willing to cooperate with Anselm along lines that the Canterbury tradition required, the papal decrees constituted a tragic impediment to Anselm's goal. Without them, he would in all probability have been spared his second exile.

Nor was Anselm inflexible in upholding the papal decrees. He agreed repeatedly to truces and lent his cautious but unmistakable support to efforts to persuade Pope Paschal II to waive the bans with respect to England. Anselm had himself ignored similar decrees issued at the Council of Clermont in 1095, which must have been reported to him by Boso of Bec, whom he had sent to the council as his personal envoy.[2] Despite Boso's mission, clerical homage and lay investiture had never been at issue under Rufus; the king continued to invest and receive homage from prelates-elect, and Anselm continued to consecrate them. The great difficulty on Anselm's return to England in 1100 was that, fourteen months beforehand, he had personally attended the Roman synod of 1099, personally heard the decrees pronounced, and personally assented to them.[3] Repeatedly in his subsequent correspondence he stresses this point: the decrees were promulgated "in my own hearing";[4] he had heard them "with my own ears."[5] As Southern has pointed out, Anselm never expressed the slightest interest in the principles underlying the papal bans.[6] He enforced them simply out of obedience to the papacy. His obedience was not, however, unthinking or uncompromising. His attitude toward the papacy embodied from beginning to end the Canterbury custom of obedience from a distance and broad primatial autonomy.

1. Southern, *Anselm*, p. 165.   2. *VB* 726.

3. *HN* 114; above, Chapter 5 at nn. 294–95.   4. AEp. 308.

5. AEp. 329. Notice that Boso, having been present at Clermont, did not ignore its decrees: in 1124, as abbot-elect of Bec, he refused to render homage to Henry I because "the pope had forbidden him to pay homage to any lay person": *VB* 728.

6. *Anselm*, p. 166.

But in 1100 the circumstances were such that Anselm could no longer, as a prelate of integrity, ignore the decrees. He could ask that they be waived, but he could not disobey them. Anselm was acting as he had to act for the sake of both his reputation and his conscience. As he himself expressed it: "They say that I forbid the king to grant investitures. . . . Tell them that they lie. I do not forbid the king to invest churches on my own authority, but because I heard the pope in a great council excommunicating laymen who grant investitures, and those who consecrate the recipients."[7]

Henry I fully shared Anselm's interests in due order and a good public reputation, and he harbored a deep commitment to his own responsibilities of stewardship. As Henry wrote to Paschal II in 1101, "So long as I live, the dignities and usages of the kingdom of England shall not, with God's help, be diminished."[8] As steward of Canterbury, Anselm could understand and, to a degree, appreciate this stance. No longer was the monarchy thwarting Canterbury traditions; now the papacy was attacking royal traditions, and Henry's response was, inevitably, to defend them with all his strength. But his style and tactics differed sharply from those of Rufus, and the difference seems to have resulted from a shift in the personal relationship between the king and his chief lay adviser. Robert of Meulan often had to persuade Rufus not to act out of impulse, to bridle his explosive temper, and to employ craft in place of force. But Henry I required no such persuasion. The count of Meulan's advice now determined the king's course of action "in all matters of policy,"[9] to the point that Henry and his great counselor seemed to think and act with a single mind.

Their principles and actions had some similarities to Anselm's. Both sides were impelled by a similar determination to uphold their God-given stewardships; both were sensitive to public opinion and the usefulness of promulgating interpretations of their behavior in ways that would enhance their public reputations. As we shall see in the next chapter, Henry took far greater pains than Rufus had done to publicize his invasion of Normandy as a selfless response to God's summons to save the Norman churches and people from destruction,[10] and Anselm

7. AEp. 327.
8. AEp. 215.
9. HN 170. Recall, for example, Robert's role in Rufus's reversal of his decision to admit Count Elias of Maine to his inner council immediately after the count's defeat. Chapter 1 at n. 35 and Chapter 5 at nn. 307–8.
10. Below, Chapter 7 at nn. 3–9.

reinterpreted his own bold initiatives in resolving the Investiture Controversy in such a way as to persuade others, then and now, that he had
done nothing whatever to transgress the proper boundary between the
pope's authority and his own.[11] The struggle between monarch and
primate, which both parties regretted but neither could avoid, became
a duel of wits and words as each side endeavored to present itself in the
best possible light while darkening the reputation of its opponent. In the
end, both succeeded in creating for themselves what we may call "public images."

From the beginning of Henry I's reign until shortly before Robert of
Meulan's death in June 1118, the count was either at the king's side or
working in Normandy and France to advance the king's interests along
with his own. Count Robert and his brother Henry earl of Warwick
were both in the royal hunting party in the New Forest on 2 August
1100, when Rufus met his death from a misaimed arrow. When the
future Henry I dashed to Winchester to seize the royal treasure and win
baronial support, his opponents were silenced by the arguments of
the earl of Warwick, described by William of Malmesbury as Prince
Henry's close friend.[12] The count of Meulan must also have been
among Prince Henry's supporters at Winchester, for Orderic states that
having seized the treasure, "thereupon Henry hastened to London
with Robert count of Meulan and the following Sunday was placed on
the throne."[13] Rufus's heavy reliance upon Robert in matters of policy
and diplomacy, and Robert's understanding of politics and the motives
of his contemporaries, suggest that the count of Meulan and his brother
had counseled Henry on the most effective means of securing the crown
before Robert Curthose could claim it. It is not difficult to understand
why Robert of Meulan would have preferred Henry to Curthose, whose
ineffective rule had earlier driven the count to Rufus's court, and whose
continued absence could have provoked a resurgence of the anarchic
baronial warfare that had occurred on the death of the Conqueror.
    Both chronicle and charter attestation evidence make it clear that
Robert of Meulan was at the center of a small group of magnates and
prelates who, from the first, constituted Henry I's innermost circle of

11. Below, Chapter 7 at nn. 100–133, especially 127–33.
12. GR 2:470. On the possible association between Robert of Meulan and Prince
Henry prior to Rufus's death, see Le Patourel, *The Norman Empire*, pp. 347–48.
13. OV 4:294.

advisers. The count of Meulan attested Henry I's surviving charters between 1100 and 1118 more frequently than any other magnate.[14] Orderic places him first among a group of four men identified by name as the king's closest advisers in 1100 — along with Hugh earl of Chester (d. 1101), Roger Bigod *Dapifer* (d. 1107), and Richard of Redvers (d. 1107).[15] Like Robert of Meulan, Roger Bigod had been a member of Rufus's court circle,[16] while Richard of Redvers and Hugh of Chester had been companions and supporters of Henry I's during his years as count of the Cotentin.[17]

But there were many magnates who preferred Curthose to Henry; as a result Henry's throne was threatened from the beginning by the rival claim of the duke and his faction. Henry's insecurity compelled him to concede a great deal to his magnates and prelates. On his coronation at Westminster, 5 August 1100, he immediately issued a charter pledging himself to uphold the laws and practices of the Confessor and the Conqueror, and to undo specific wrongs perpetrated by William Rufus, among which were his abuses of the church.[18] Henry also wrote immediately to Anselm, in exile in Lyon, recalling him to his duties as archbishop. The letter implicitly promised that the disputes between England's king and archbishop would cease: Henry committed himself "and indeed the people of the whole kingdom of England to your counsel and to the counsel of those who ought to advise me with you."[19] Indeed, Anselm, having heard of the king's death before receiving the new king's letter, was already on his way to England.[20]

As could be expected, the problems facing the new king were monumental and, according to Eadmer, could be overcome only with Anselm's advice. Messengers from the king had reported to Anselm that "the whole country was in a state of suspense awaiting his arrival, and that all the business of the kingdom was held up, delayed, awaiting his

14. *Regesta* 2, nos. 501–1200 passim: 113 attestations in eighteen years.
15. OV 5:298.
16. Hollister, "Magnates and 'Curiales,'" p. 76.
17. OV 4:220; Earl Hugh was often at Rufus's court as well: Hollister, "Magnates and 'Curiales,'" p. 76. On Robert of Meulan's preeminence among Henry's counselors, see further *GR* 2:483; Henry's clerical *familiares* included Robert Bloet bishop of Lincoln, from Rufus's inner circle; Roger, chancellor and future bishop of Salisbury, from Henry's comital entourage; and William Giffard, Rufus's chancellor whom Henry advanced to the bishopric of Winchester: *Regesta* 2, passim. For a detailed analysis see Walter Fröhlich, "Die Bischöflichen Kollegen des Hl. Erzbischofs Anselm von Canterbury, Zweiter Teil: 1100–1109," *Analecta Anselmiana* 2 (1970): 117–68.
18. *GR* 2:470; *HN* 119; Florence, 2:46; translated in *EHD* 2:432–34.
19. AEp. 212.   20. *HN* 118.

hearing how matters stood and his deciding what should be done."[21] The statement has a good deal of truth to it, for Anselm's support was crucial to the new regime. As archbishop of Canterbury, Anselm had the prerogative of crowning the king. There had even been suggestions that the archbishop of Canterbury had the right of choosing or electing the king from among rival candidates. At the accession of William Rufus, an anonymous Canterbury writer had made such an assertion with respect to Lanfranc.[22]

But Henry, intent on being consecrated at the earliest possible moment, had bypassed Anselm and arranged for the bishop of London to place the crown on his head.[23] Theoretically, Anselm could have declared the coronation invalid and crowned Curthose king of England. Henry did everything possible to placate his archbishop, pledging church reform in the coronation charter and, in his initial letter to Anselm, promising to follow his advice in all matters. Robert of Meulan, intimately acquainted with Anselm's conception of primatial authority and experienced in negotiating with him, would have been able to advise Henry on precisely how to persuade Anselm that the new regime was prepared to allow the archbishop his rightful place in the governance of the kingdom.

Anselm arrived in England on 23 September and joined Henry's court at Salisbury shortly thereafter. According to Eadmer, the whole country was in a state of rejoicing, expecting the abuses of the church to be corrected.[24] Henry himself was extremely insecure on his throne; his barons were wavering between supporting him and going over to the side of his brother, Robert Curthose, who had just arrived home in Normandy from the Holy Land.[25] The king was evidently prepared to cooperate with Anselm's plans to reform the church. But when Henry asked Anselm to do the customary homage and to receive the archbishopric from his hand, Anselm astonished the king and his court by refusing homage and investiture, in accordance with Urban's decrees of 1099.[26] With Anselm's insistence on these new and altogether unexpected conditions, the English Investiture Contest began.

21. *HN* 118–19.

22. *Acta Lanfranci*, in *Two of the Saxon Chronicles Parallel*, ed. John Earle and Charles Plummer (Oxford, 1892–99), 1:290: "Mortuo rege Willelmo trans mare, filium eius Willelmum, sicut pater constituit, Lanfrancus in regem elegit."

23. *AEp.* 212.   24. *HN* 119–20.

25. David, *Robert Curthose*, p. 123.

26. *HN* 119.

Anselm was by no means acting as a mere papal agent. To him, the primacy of Canterbury was the major issue, and all his efforts were directed toward promoting it.[27] Nor were his goals incompatible with the king's. Henry was prepared to accept a vigorous reforming archbishop, and Anselm had always been committed to the idea of a strong, peacekeeping monarchy. But Anselm could not gloss over the papal prohibitions that he had so recently heard and publicly endorsed. Equally, Henry could not submit to what would have seemed a frontal attack on his royal status — a challenge to the king's traditional authority to present churches and to receive homage from his great ecclesiastical landholders, who were also military tenants-in-chief. To forego these customs, Henry believed, would amount to forfeiting "half of his sovereignty."[28]

Nevertheless, in autumn 1100, Henry was in urgent need of Anselm's aid in retaining the English throne, and Anselm could therefore hope for concessions. Eadmer reports that Anselm addressed Henry boldly: if the king accepts and observes the decrees, "it will be well between us and bring lasting peace; but if not, I cannot see that my remaining in England would be profitable or honorable."[29] Anselm could have made a more damaging threat than exile. He could have threatened to withhold recognition from Henry on the grounds that he had been crowned improperly, and to throw his support to Henry's brother. The threat to return to exile was dangerous enough, however. While not directly challenging Henry's claim to the throne, Anselm's exile would be a public exhibition of Henry's misrule of the church that would erode his support. It would also leave Anselm free to back Curthose at some future time, meanwhile leaving the door open for further negotiations with the king.

As Anselm must have realized, the king faced quite a dilemma. Eadmer reports that both Henry's alternatives — losing investiture and

27. S. Vaughn, "St. Anselm and the English Investiture Controversy Reconsidered," *JMH* 6 (1980): 61–86.
28. *HN* 120.
29. *HN* 120. Eadmer's account seems much more plausible than Anselm's conflicting version of the episode. In AEp. 219, written in late 1101 to Paschal II, Anselm states that when he raised the issue of the papal decree on his return to England in September 1100, Henry and his magnates and bishops threatened to expel him from the kingdom and break with the Roman church. But Anselm's three previous postexile letters to Paschal (AEpp. 214, 217, 218), although mentioning the king's objections to the papal bans, say nothing about being threatened with exile. Eadmer reports that in September 1101, after Henry's conflict with Curthose had been resolved, the king did threaten

homage, or losing Anselm's support — were intolerable to him. Indeed Henry "was afraid that Anselm would approach his brother Robert, who had just then returned to Normandy from Jerusalem, and first induce him to submit himself to the Apostolic See, which he knew could easily be done, and would then make him king of England."[30] Henry had recognized this hazard in his profuse apologies to Anselm for allowing Maurice bishop of London to crown him king.[31] As Brett has pointed out, "Where the succession was in doubt, the archbishop's prerogative of crowning the new king necessarily gave him a position of great importance in deciding between candidates."[32]

In order to confirm his loyalty and allay the suspicions of Henry's supporters that he was plotting to transfer the kingdom to Robert, Anselm "allowed himself to be prevailed upon by their entreaties and agreed to do what they wished." He consented to a truce until Easter 1101, so that envoys might go to Pope Paschal and seek a dispensation allowing England to operate under its traditional customs rather than to submit to the papal decrees.[33] Although Anselm was clearly reluctant to overstep his correct archiepiscopal role by petitioning the pope to rescind papal commands, he did explain his dilemma to Paschal and ended his letter by urging the pope that, "so far as your authority under God allows, you would yield to the aforesaid petition, which the messengers will explain to you."[34] Anselm was thus making it clear that he not only had no objection to having the decrees waived but would welcome such an act. As he said afterward (according to Eadmer), the envoys were sent to the papal court "for the express purpose of having these

Anselm with exile unless he abandoned the papal decrees (HN 131; below, Chapter 6 at n. 99). By then Henry's throne was sufficiently secure to permit him to make such a threat, but it would have been foolhardy for him to have done so a year earlier. Anselm's Ep. 219, which was written after Henry's threat of September 1101, seems to misattribute the threat to September 1100 for the sake of verbal economy, and perhaps for the purpose of portraying himself as being forced toward exile rather than threatening to abandon his see for a second time.

30. HN 120.
31. AEp. 212.
32. Brett, English Church, pp. 69–71.
33. HN 120–21. Eadmer describes the mission as including representatives from both sides, but Anselm's letters suggest strongly that he sent no representative on the mission but instead communicated his views to the pope through a letter carried by the royal envoy, William Warelwast: AEpp. 218, 219, 220.
34. AEp. 217, in all probability written to accompany this mission; Anselm's three subsequent letters to Paschal — AEpp. 218, 219, and 220 — were written in connection with a second mission that Henry and Anselm dispatched to the papal court for a similar purpose in late 1101 or early 1102: below, Chapter 6 at nn. 197–202.

decrees varied."[35] In the meantime, while king and primate awaited the pope's reply, Henry restored all the lands of Canterbury, and both parties agreed to leave unchanged the present status of the English church: the king would invest no bishop or abbot, nor would Anselm perform any consecrations.[36]

Both Anselm and Henry had much to gain from the truce. If Paschal could be persuaded to exempt England from the decrees, Anselm would be free at last to undertake the reform of the English church in collaboration with a king who, apart from the issue at hand, seemed willing to cooperate in the pursuit of Anselm's goals.[37] Also, having already experienced at Bec the consequences of Curthose's well-known ineffectiveness as duke of Normandy, Anselm appears to have preferred the prudence and strength that Henry was beginning to show. Anselm held the view of most churchmen that a king should be strong, keep the peace, and protect the church. "The king should rule with a rod of equity so that the good would love him and the bad fear him."[38] Not only had Henry displayed favor toward the church, but he had also assumed the governance of England in a forceful and efficient manner calculated to ensure the peace of the realm. The situation also indicated that Anselm would have the opportunity to influence him toward both filling his proper role as a peacekeeping king and submitting to the papal decrees if Paschal II should refuse to waive them. Henry, for his part, would have hoped either to obtain the dispensation, in which case all would be well, or to delay until the throne was secure. While he was capable of acting with lightning speed at times, as his dash for the crown

---

35. *HN* 131.

36. *HN* 120. Gerard, having already received episcopal consecration as bishop of Hereford, was translated to the archbishopric of York in 1101 without the necessity of a second consecration; he assumed his full metropolitan powers on receiving the pallium from Pope Paschal in 1102: *HCY* 12–13. No source mentions his having been invested by Henry I; if he had been, it would be difficult to explain why Anselm urged Paschal to grant Gerard the pallium (*AEpp.* 214, 220) or why Paschal complied. Eadmer (*HN* 145) and William of Malmesbury (*GP* 109–110) state that William Giffard of Winchester was invested with the episcopal staff and ring by Anselm himself. Their assertion that William Giffard did not assume his episcopal duties immediately upon being "given" the bishopric by Henry I in August 1100 — as Henry of Huntingdon implies (*HA* 233) — is consistent with the fact that he continued to serve as royal chancellor until at least 12 March 1101 (*Regesta* 2, p. ix and no. 516, attested by "William Giffard, Chancellor"), and with the statement of the Winchester annalist that at Easter 1101 (21 April) William Giffard assumed the bishopric of Winchester "*assensu Anselmi*": *Annales de Wintonia*, p. 41.

37. See *HN* 140 for a further illustration of Anselm's willingness to do homage to Henry and consecrate prelates if the pope permitted it.

38. *AEpp.* 413, 427, 435, to the kings of Scotland and Ireland.

makes clear, he was also capable of delaying for great lengths of time when it suited his purposes. It is clear from the dates of Anselm's letters to Paschal that Henry delayed the mission to the papal court from late September 1100 to at least well into February 1101.[39] Henry may have been trying to arrange matters so that Paschal's reply would not arrive in England until the conflict with Curthose was settled. In the meantime the truce with Anselm would ensure the king of his primate's support regardless of Paschal's decision.

During the interval of the truce Anselm and Henry worked closely together.[40] For the sake of permitting the king to make a politically advantageous marriage, Anselm was prepared to modify his strict views against the marriages of women who had lived in nunneries and dressed as nuns without having taken religious vows. Henry's prospective bride, Matilda of Scotland, was such a person — a young woman who had lived among the nuns of Romsey and Wilton Abbeys, unprofessed but sometimes wearing the veil. She was the daughter of King Malcolm and Queen Margaret of Scotland and a descendant of the Anglo-Saxon kings. Her marriage to Henry promised not only to tighten his diplomatic bonds with Scotland but also to buttress his claim to the English throne and unite in his offspring the blood of Alfred the Great and William the Conqueror. But the project created a serious problem for Anselm, who a few years earlier had written to Osmund bishop of Salisbury ordering him to compel this same Matilda of Scotland to return to Wilton Abbey, from which she had apparently departed with the intention of marrying Count Alan of Richmond.[41] Anselm had written two letters in a similar vein to Gunhilda, daughter of King Harold Godwineson, who had also worn the religious habit at Wilton without taking vows and had subsequently departed to marry the lord

39. AEp. 214, which Anselm explicitly identifies as his first letter to Paschal after returning to England, alludes to Ranulf Flambard's escape from captivity in England on 2 February and his subsequent flight to Normandy to join Henry's enemies; since the envoys to Paschal carried either this letter or a subsequent one (probably AEp. 217), the mission cannot have departed before mid-February at the earliest. The envoys returned with Paschal's reply in August or early September: *HN* 128. Anselm himself may have contributed to the delay: in AEp. 214 he petitions Paschal to send a pallium for Gerard, elect of York, and Hugh the Chantor (pp. 12–13) reports that Anselm long delayed this petition while attempting to force Gerard to profess obedience.

40. That Anselm was often at court is suggested by his frequent attestations between September 1100 and March 1103, at the high rate of 5.2 a year: *Regesta* 2, nos. 524–647 passim; Robert of Meulan attested at the rate of 6.8 royal charters a year during his eighteen years of service to Henry I: above, Chapter 6, n. 14. Since only a small fraction of Henry's charters has survived, both these rates are extremely high.

41. AEp. 177; see *Councils and Synods* 1, pt. 2:661–67; Southern, *Anselm*, p. 183.

of Richmond.[42] Commanding Gunhilda to return to her nunnery, Anselm had explained that "both in public and in private you wore the habit pertaining to the holy life and thereby declared yourself to all who saw you to be dedicated to God, no less than if you had recited your profession."[43]

Nevertheless, Anselm's role in the arrangements for Matilda's marriage to Henry I was one of quiet, if uneasy, cooperation. The primate heard Matilda's argument that she had never professed and had worn her veil only under duress.[44] Anselm then summoned a council of bishops, abbots, and nobles at Lambeth. After they had heard testimony supporting Matilda's claims, he charged them to judge her case justly without regard to fear or favor. He then withdrew from the assemblage, and in his absence it ruled in favor of the marriage — unanimously and predictably. The council called attention to a judgment by Lanfranc that women who had fled to nunneries and taken the veil to escape the lusts of the conquering Normans might afterward leave their convents if they chose. "I do not reject your judgment," Anselm told the council. "I accept it all the more confidently because I am told it is supported by the authority of so great a father [as Lanfranc]."[45]

Anselm's voice was the only one in England that could have stopped the marriage. But rather than opposing it, as he had earlier opposed Gunhilda's marriage, he committed the decision to Henry's prelates and magnates and accepted the inevitable outcome. Overcoming his personal reservations, Anselm himself performed the marriage ceremony and exercised the primatial prerogative of consecrating the new queen of England.[46] Nobody could possibly accuse Anselm of inflexibility in this momentous affair. Indeed some people claimed that the primate "did not hew to the path of strict righteousness,"[47] and Eadmer's detailed account of the marriage project amounts to an elaborate de-

42. AEpp. 168, 169; Southern, *Anselm,* pp. 185–88 for details.

43. AEp. 168.

44. She had been forced to wear it, she said, by her Aunt Christina, sister of Queen Margaret and possibly abbess of Wilton: *HN* 121–23; Knowles, *Heads,* p. 219; Matilda further contended that her parents had not dedicated her to the religious life.

45. *HN* 124–25; on this council see Brett, *English Church,* pp. 75–76; *Councils and Synods* 1, pt. 2:661–67.

46. *HN* 121; *ASC,* A.D. 1111; Florence 2:47–48; confirmed by AEp. 242, Matilda to Anselm, and AEp. 243, Anselm to Matilda; Orderic (5:300) is clearly mistaken in saying that Gerard of Hereford consecrated her; the ceremonies took place at Westminster on 11 November 1100.

47. *HN* 121.

fense of Anselm's behavior against such accusations. Anselm's own defense seems to have taken the form of reediting the Canterbury record on behalf of his public reputation: his two letters to Gunhilda and his letter to Osmund of Salisbury commanding Matilda's return to Wilton are all absent from Lambeth ms. 59, the Canterbury collection of Anselm's correspondence prepared under his supervision.[48] Eadmer says nothing of Anselm's earlier dealings with Matilda or Gunhilda.

Henry appears to have been dealing with Anselm during these months without the aid of the chief royal adviser. Between August and December 1100, Robert of Meulan was apparently on a mission on Henry's behalf in Normandy and France. Count Robert attested neither the coronation charter (in any of its versions) nor any of Henry's known charters until the Christmas court of 1100.[49] Henry of Warwick, on the other hand, attested several royal charters during these months.[50] Since Robert of Meulan and Henry of Warwick together helped Henry I in his accession to the throne, Robert's absence from the court suggests that he was working for the king on the Continent while Henry of Warwick stayed at the king's side to lend his support and advice.

Robert had compelling reasons to cross the Channel in August. Civil strife broke out in Normandy immediately upon the news of Rufus's death. Count Elias regained Maine, and William count of Evreux and Ralph of Tosny ravaged and pillaged the Beaumont lands.[51] Robert of Meulan's activities are unrecorded, but he probably settled affairs at Beaumont and perhaps acted on Henry's behalf to secure the allegiance of certain Norman barons. He may even have attended the French court as Henry's ambassador. When Robert reappeared at Henry's court on 25 December, Louis, king-designate of France, turned up on precisely the same day, seated at Henry's Christmas banquet between the king and Anselm.[52] Luchaire believes that Louis, the heir apparent, may

48. Walter Fröhlich, "The Letters Omitted from Anselm's Collection of Letters," *ANS* 6 (1984): 58–63, 65–66; see also Fröhlich, "The Genesis of Anselm's Collection of Letters," *American Benedictine Review* 35 (1984), and above, Chapter 4 at nn. 92–128.

49. *Regesta* 2, no. 501, at Westminster, 25 December 1100.

50. Ibid., nos. 488 (the coronation charter, five versions), 491, 492, 497; Henry of Warwick's name also appears on the witness list of no. 489 (spurious).

51. OV 5:300.

52. Luchaire, *Louis VI*, nos. 8–12. Philip I still technically ruled France, but had designated Louis as king-elect sometime between 1098 and 1100. Louis had all the prerogatives of sovereignty, and Luchaire believes that he effectively extended his actions throughout the government, having his own officers and counselors separate from those of Philip (pp. xxiv, xxv).

have attended Henry's court at the behest of Philip I. Orderic adds the rather implausible story that messengers came to the English court shortly after Louis's arrival bearing a sealed letter, purportedly from King Philip, asking Henry to imprison young Louis. But, according to Orderic, the messengers had actually come from Queen Bertrade, Philip's second wife and Louis's stepmother, who sought to advance one of her own sons to the throne. After taking counsel with his barons, Orderic related, Henry refused to take part in such a perfidy, told Louis of the letter, and sent him back to France loaded with gifts.[53]

However one might interpret Orderic's tale, we know that Robert of Meulan was serving in Henry's inner council at the time of Louis's visit to the Christmas court of 1100.[54] Although we have no records of Robert's presence at the French court in 1100, he was clearly in a position to engineer an entente between Henry and the future French king. The rivalry between Louis and Bertrade presented a situation in which an understanding between Louis and Henry would be mutually advantageous. Both men faced challenges to their succession, and each could strengthen the other through recognition of his legitimacy. Robert of Meulan, as a major baron in England, Normandy, and France and the husband of the French king's niece, would have been the ideal liaison between the two courts; no one else in Henry's inner circle of advisers had interests in France or connections with the French royal family. If there is any truth in Orderic's account of the false letter, Robert would have understood French royal politics sufficiently to suspect Queen Bertrade's hand in the affair, and to advise Henry not to be drawn into the French embroilments while he still faced a serious threat to his own power.

Robert Curthose had returned to Normandy in late August or early September and had quickly regained possession of the duchy. Immediately intrigues arose in both Normandy and England. Orderic reports that the English barons "invited Curthose to invade England while the Norman barons . . . sought to unite Normandy with England by supporting Henry's cause in the duchy."[55] Thus both parties sought the reunification of Normandy and England. The result was an Anglo-

53. Ibid., pp. xxii, xxvi; OV 6:50–54; Chibnall (OV 6:50, n. 2) regards the story of Bertrade's letter as "epic invention." There is ample independent evidence that Louis visited Henry's Christmas court in 1100: Simeon of Durham, *Opera Omnia* 2:232; *Annales de Wintonia*, p. 41. And Bertrade did in fact participate in a subsequent rebellion against Louis VI on behalf of her son Philip of Mantes: Luchaire, *Louis VI*, nos. 76, 87; Suger, *Vie de Louis VI*, pp. 124–26.
54. *Regesta* 2, no. 501; OV 5:298, 310, 314; GR 2:471.
55. OV 5:308–10; 4:310–14.

Norman civil war; both contenders strove for the support of the same barons, most of whom held lands in both realms.[56] Among King Henry's supporters at this time, Orderic singles out two by name: "The venerable Archbishop Anselm and all the bishops and abbots with the consecrated clergy, as well as all the English, preserved their unshaken loyalty to their king and offered ceaseless prayers to the Lord of Hosts for his safety and the preservation of the realm. Robert of Meulan and many other loyal and provident barons followed their lord faithfully and supplied him with counsel and military support."[57]

Paschal II's correspondence with England early in Henry's reign dealt not only with the investiture issue but also with the rival claims of king and duke. The two issues were thus intertwined from the beginning. Early in 1101, as we have seen, Henry wrote to Paschal congratulating him on his election, sending him Peter's Pence, and promising the same obedience to the pope as was rendered in his father's time, provided that Paschal grant to him the same customs that his father had. Finally, he boldly stated that if Paschal did not deliberate more prudently and exercise self-restraint, he would be obliged to withdraw from his obedience.[58] Paschal first wrote to Anselm on 24 February 1101, before Henry's letter had arrived and before having heard from Anselm, whose first letter to the pope since returning from exile may have been borne by the same messengers who carried Henry's. Paschal's letter does not mention the investiture-homage issue specifically but simply cautions Anselm to order and correct the English church "following the sanctions of the Roman church."[59] Then, after urging Anselm to see that Peter's Pence was collected and sent to Rome, Paschal reported that Robert Curthose had complained to him that Henry I, in violation of an oath he had sworn to the duke, had seized the kingdom of England "by force." Taking an apparently neutral stance between the two brothers, Paschal asked Anselm to strive for peace between them and announced that he was sending two messengers (*nuntii*) to England to help negotiate such an accord and to contribute to the achieving of the above-mentioned goals — church reform and the collection of Peter's Pence. Paschal tried to soften the blow by selecting as one of the messengers "a man known to you and once educated by you, then a son, now a

56. David, *Robert Curthose*, pp. 127–28.
57. OV 5:310.
58. AEp. 215; *Regesta* 2, no. 514.
59. AEp. 213.

brother and cobishop." This was John, the former monk of Bec and abbot of Telese, now cardinal-bishop of Tusculum, who had been Anselm's host for a time in 1098 during the archbishop's exile.[60] John's companion was to be Tiberius, chamberlain of the papal household and thus inferior in rank to the cardinal-bishop. Paschal was also careful to describe the messengers as nuncios, not legates. Although his description of their duties would have seemed alarmingly sweeping, they were to be instructed by Anselm's counsel and helped by his aid. They do not appear to have been granted full legatine powers.

Nevertheless, the sending of papal messengers in whatever guise to deal with Anglo-Norman affairs was a sore point with Anselm, and he responded to the pope's intitative with total silence.[61] But in his first letter to Paschal after returning to England, which was written about February 1101 and crossed Paschal's aforementioned letter, Anselm protested vehemently against a previous visit of Guy archbishop of Vienne, whom the pope had sent to England in 1100 as papal legate over the whole of Britain. Eadmer reports that Guy went away having accomplished nothing and unrecognized as legate,[62] adding that "everyone knew that it was a thing unheard of in Britain that anyone should exercise authority over them as representing the pope except only the archbishop of Canterbury."[63] Anselm himself asserted in his letter that Urban had conceded to him the "traditional" Canterbury legateship, and that by right (for the *"utilitas ecclesiae"*) the primate of Britain should be papal legate in England.[64] Anselm was claiming his authority as primate and legate vis-à-vis Paschal, just as he had claimed his authority as the king's coregent under God vis-à-vis William Rufus and Henry I. And just as Henry opposed papal infringements on the customs of the realm, so Anselm opposed such infringements on the customs of Canterbury.

Anselm was thus continuing to strike a careful balance between the power of the pope and the power of the archbishop of Canterbury. He

---

60. Above, Chapter 5 at nn. 287–88.

61. The messengers did in fact arrive in England about August 1101, but Eadmer, like Anselm, passed over their visit in silence. See *Regesta* 2, nos. 544, 547, and 548 — all dated 3 September 1101, and attested by, among others, John of Tusculum; Tiberius attests two of the three, and both men style themselves "legatus."

62. AEp. 214; *HN* 126. See Brett, *English Church*, p. 35, for the dating of Guy's visit. Paschal had apparently sent him to England in the belief that he would be dealing with William Rufus. Guy cannot have received his legation before 22 September 1099, when the exiled Anselm visited him in Vienne: *VA* 117.

63. *HN* 126.

64. AEp. 214.

would render due obedience to the head of the church and follow papal decrees, but only to the degree permitted by "the vast and perilous extent of seas and kingdoms" separating England from the pope and his legates. Anselm remained the apostle and patriarch of that other world and would tolerate no papal agents exercising authority over him in England.

In the same letter Anselm provided an account of the investiture-homage problem. The brevity and cool, businesslike tone of this account stand in revealing contrast to the ardor with which he argued for the Canterbury legateship. He had told the king and his court about Urban II's decrees; they had refused to accept them. "I am therefore awaiting necessary advice from your eminence on this point." And Anselm thereupon turned to another subject.

His letter also touches on the dispute between Henry and Curthose. Without mentioning the duke, Anselm asked Paschal's advice about disciplining the chief ducal counselor, Ranulf Flambard bishop of Durham. As the central figure in William Rufus's financial administration, Flambard had become invaluable to the king and immensely unpopular among his subjects. In 1093 Flambard had created an uproar during Anselm's archiepiscopal coronation by instituting a lawsuit against him; not surprisingly, therefore, Anselm described him to Paschal as having been "a rent collector of the worst possible reputation."[65] One of Henry's first acts of reform and public relations was to bring Flambard to trial for embezzlement and to imprison him in the Tower of London, from which he had escaped in early February 1101 and fled to Normandy.[66] There, Anselm states, "joining the enemies of his lord the king, he is reliably reported to have made himself the lord of pirates whom he commands at sea" — a reference to his role in organizing a flotilla for the duke's oncoming invasion of England.[67] Anselm asked Paschal's counsel on the matter of deposing Flambard from his bishopric of Durham, which is "exposed to many perils amid barbarians" and "cannot long be left without a pastor."[68] The case of

65. AEp. 214; HN 41; above, Chapter 4 at nn. 170–71.
66. Hollister, "The Anglo-Norman Civil War: 1100," EHR 88 (1973): 323–24.
67. Flambard is reported to have won a number of English seamen to the duke's side by bribery and to have used some of them as pilots for Curthose's fleet: ibid., p. 325 and n. 7.
68. AEp. 214; Rufus had raised Flambard to the bishopric of Durham in 1099 during Anselm's exile; Flambard's metropolitan, Thomas archbishop of York, had supported Henry I's proceedings against him by testifying at the royal tribunal that Flambard had violated all the promises he had made at his consecration: Hollister, "Anglo-Norman Civil War," p. 325.

Ranulf Flambard vividly illustrates the interaction between primatial authority and royal policy: the threat of deposing Flambard from his bishopric gave Anselm a powerful grip on the organizer of Curthose's invasion force.[69] It also afforded an opportunity for the archbishop of Canterbury to exercise and display his primacy by judging a suffragan of the archbishop of York.

In the meantime Henry was securing allies for the coming confrontation with his brother, and Robert of Meulan was at his side. On 10 March 1101, the count of Meulan attended the king while he concluded a treaty with Robert count of Flanders at Dover.[70] Two days thereafter Henry undertook the first of a series of measures to ensure the firm backing of Anselm, whose influence on the king's undependable magnates could be crucial to the royal cause. At Rochester on 12 March, Henry granted a number of churches and tithes to Anselm's friend and vicar, Bishop Gundulf. Then followed a whole series of charters to monasteries and churches confirming grants made to them under William I and William II, and restoring properties and privileges that had been taken from them.[71] To Anselm himself the king decreed that the archbishop's men in London should enjoy the same freedom from royal customs that Lanfranc's men had enjoyed in the time of William I — a privilege that epitomized Henry's more general policy of recreating with Anselm the Conqueror's relationship with Lanfranc.[72] At Easter (21 April), the expiration date of the truce between Henry and Anselm, the envoys to the papal court had not yet returned with Paschal's answer to the request for a dispensation, and the truce was extended until the time of their arrival.[73]

By 9 June, at Henry's Whitsun court at St. Albans, rumors were circulating that Duke Robert would soon land in England, and the barons were wavering in their loyalty to the king.[74] Henry and his magnates alike chose Anselm as their mediator; in exchange for the magnates renewing their homage, the king put his hand in Anselm's and promised to govern the kingdom in all respects with just and righteous laws as long as he should live.[75] Henry then sent letters to his officials throughout England confirming the laws and rights that he had promised in his coronation charter and commanding that all free Englishmen

69. Hollister, "Anglo-Norman Civil War," pp. 323–33.
70. *Regesta* 2, no. 515: Robert attests first among Henry's lay witnesses.
71. Ibid., nos. 520–27, 528a, 529–30.
72. Ibid., no. 532.   73. *HN* 126.   74. *HN* 126.   75. *HN* 126.

solemnly swear to defend his kingdom against all men "and especially against my brother."[76] The witnesses of the one letter to have survived are Archbishop Anselm, Robert count of Meulan, Robert fitz Hamon, and Eudo *Dapifer* — in that order. Henry took the further step at his Whitsun court of formally dispossessing Ranulf Flambard of his episcopal lands,[77] and then or soon afterward he proceeded to summon an army from throughout his kingdom.

The primate responded to the royal summons by calling up the Canterbury knights and leading them personally to Pevensey, where Henry's army was encamped awaiting Curthose's invasion fleet. Anselm camped with his men in the field to demonstrate publicly his support of the royal cause. Eadmer adds that Henry at this point "could not believe or trust anyone except Anselm."[78] Although the monk of Canterbury mistakenly overlooks Robert of Meulan and a handful of other devoted royalist magnates, and ignores the bishops altogether, Henry no doubt did remain unsure of the fidelity of most of the English nobility. Anselm supported the king with both words and arms. He personally owed no less than sixty knights to the royal host, and his contingent at Pevensey probably consisted of the entire body of knights that all the Canterbury military tenants owed the archbishop — nearly 100 according to the list of knights in the *Domesday Monachorum*.[79] Again, as in 1095, Anselm had girt himself with the mantle of Lanfranc, assuming a military command in the defense of king and kingdom.[80] Henry also depended heavily at this time on Anselm's powers of persuasion, repeatedly bringing to him magnates whom the king distrusted in order that Anselm might convince them to remain loyal.

Robert of Meulan, however, required no such convincing. About this time, according to Orderic, Count Robert delivered a speech to the king and his counselors outlining the policy that Henry must follow to secure his kingdom — a speech quoted earlier in Chapter 5 in the context of Count Robert's *raison d'état*. Stating that the common utility had been committed to the king and his advisers by divine providence, Robert urged that the safety of the realm and the church of God ought to be preserved without the shedding of Christian blood so that loyal

---

76. *Regesta* 2, no. 531.   77. Ibid., no. 1124.   78. *HN* 126.
79. Hollister, "Anglo-Norman Civil War," p. 321; *Domesday Monachorum*, p. 105; above, Chapter 4 at nn. 19–22.
80. Above, Chapter 5 at nn. 200–205.

citizens of the realm could live in peace and safety. This should be done
by soothing the king's rebellious barons with soft words and magnificent promises that could later be broken.

When with God's help we have come prosperously to the end of this business,
we will propose practical measures for recovering the demesnes appropriated
by rash deserters in time of war. There is no doubt that anyone who chooses to
desert his lord for greed of gain, or insists on payment for the military service
that he ought to offer freely to his king for the defense of the realm, and attempts
to deprive him of his own demesnes, will be judged a traitor by a just and
equitable judgment, and will rightly be deprived of his inheritance and forced to
flee the country.[81]

Deceit, Robert of Meulan argued, was a legitimate means of pursuing the "common utility" and defending the realm, and the royalist
magnates concurred: "All the magnates who were with King Henry
applauded the count's speech and urged the king to follow his advice.
Being a man of remarkable sagacity, he thanked the counselors who
wished him well and readily accepted their practical suggestions, winning with promises and gifts the support of many whom he regarded
with suspicion."[82]

Some of the magnates were making extraordinary demands of Henry
to maintain their loyalty.[83] For example, William count of Mortain and
earl of Cornwall, already one of the two wealthiest magnates in the
Anglo-Norman world, was demanding that he be given the earldom of
Kent, which his uncle, Odo of Bayeux, had forfeited to Rufus in 1088.
Odo's former earldom would have more than doubled Count William's
resources, making him far wealthier than any magnate since the Nor-
man Conquest. Henry held him off with subtle and ambiguous an-
swers until the 1101 crisis had passed, and then refused him outright.[84]
The Clares, another wealthy and powerful family, were also causing
Henry great distress. Richard of Clare, a former monk of Bec, had been
appointed abbot of Ely by King Henry on the day of his consecration.
Having conceived the idea of converting the abbey into a bishopric,
Richard refused to be blessed by the bishop of Lincoln and gathered his

81. OV 5:316.
82. OV 5:316.
83. OV 5:314: "Numerous others made unreasonable demands to invent pretexts
for breaking away, threatening to leave him unless he granted their petitions."
84. GR 2:473; cf. ASC, A.D. 1104. See C. W. Hollister, "Anglo-Norman Civil War,"
p. 317, n. 5, for William of Mortain's wealth — £2100 per year in 1086. In 1086, the
earldom of Kent was the wealthiest barony in England, valued at £3050 a year: above,
Chapter 5 at nn. 17–23.

kinsmen around him. The *Liber Eliensis* reports that the Clares terror-
ized the royal curia with threats and killings, while Richard refused
to obey the mandates of the king. On the model of Lanfranc's and
Anselm's endeavors to advance the liberties and prerogatives of their
churches, although far less subtly, the Bec monk Richard of Clare was
working strenuously to promote and enrich the abbey charged to him,
adding the force of his kinsmen's military strength. Henry delayed until
after the crisis of 1101, and finally had Richard expelled from his
abbacy.[85]

Henry is reported to have made his most lavish promise to Anselm
himself. At Pevensey, apparently at Anselm's urging, the king (in Eadmer's words) "most solemnly promised to Anselm that he would leave
to him all rights of administering all Christianity in England and that he
would in perpetuity obey the decrees and commands of the Apostolic
See."[86] If we can trust Eadmer's account, Henry's promise amounted
to an unconditional surrender of clerical homage and royal investiture
unless Paschal II should be persuaded to waive the papal decrees.
Eadmer's account carries the strong implication that Anselm had taken
advantage of this critical moment in the royal fortunes to obtain this
commitment as the price of his own final and absolute endorsement of
the royal cause. Immediately following his account of Henry's promise,
Eadmer adds, "Under these circumstances [*Quibus ita se habentibus*],
Anselm assembled all the magnates," and with the whole body of the
army gathered around, he urged them in eloquent and persuasive words
to remain loyal to the king's cause. He impressed upon them "how
accursed any of them would be, in the sight of God and of every good
man, if they should in any respect betray the fealty they owed to their
prince."[87] Anselm persuaded them with such faultless logic, Eadmer
says, that their loyalty was ensured. As the *Vita Gundulfi* makes clear,
Anselm was aided in this effort by his vicar and ally, Gundulf of
Rochester.[88]

On 20 July Curthose's invasion force took the king by surprise,
landing at Portsmouth instead of Pevensey. Nevertheless, Henry's baronial support remained firmer than his enemies had hoped, and Anselm
further dampened enthusiasm for the ducal cause by making it known

---

85. *Liber Eliensis*, ed. E. O. Blake (London, 1962), pp. 224–27. Richard was
deposed at Anselm's Westminster Council of 1102, but was restored to office about 1103,
although Anselm did not give formal authorization to his restitution until 1107: Ibid.,
p. 413.

86. *HN* 127.   87. *HN* 127; cf. *GP* 105 n.   88. *VG* 59.

that he would excommunicate Curthose unless he came to terms.[89] Henry and Curthose thereupon ended their dispute with a treaty, negotiated with the help of magnates who risked dispossession if either brother won a pitched battle.[90] Even allowing for Eadmer's penchant for exaggeration, Anselm's staunch support of Henry's cause must have had considerable effect on the outcome of events, for Curthose and his men were furious and resentful over it.[91] Additional evidence suggests that Anselm may have been involved to some degree in the negotiations themselves. Part of the bargain was that Ranulf Flambard, who had been tried in a church court for simony and other high crimes at Anselm's behest and placed by papal decree under Anselm's discretion, would be forgiven and reinstated as bishop of Durham.[92] Such a provision could only have been carried out with Anselm's assent, and indeed he gave it. He issued a charter "in the stead of blessed Peter, chief of the apostles," absolving Ranulf "so far as your accusation requires."[93]

Henry, Anselm, and Robert of Meulan appear to have been working together to ensure that the invasion would be settled by treaty and to avoid open battle. Henry had kept the peace without the shedding of Christian blood, and the safety of the commonwealth was secured. Eadmer states "without fear of contradiction that . . . if Anselm's faithfulness and industry had not intervened, King Henry would at that time have lost the rule of the kingdom of England."[94] King and archbishop had worked in double harness as they had not done since the Conqueror's reign. Anselm took full advantage of the political situation in England and, with no aid from or consultation with Paschal, succeeded in gaining a full acquiescence from Henry to obey the decrees of Rome if Paschal should decide to continue enforcing them. In return Anselm used every means at his disposal to ensure that Henry stayed firmly on his throne.

C. W. Hollister has reconstructed the terms of the 1101 treaty, which has not survived. Curthose renounced his claim to England,

89. *HN* 127–28.
90. Hollister, "Anglo-Norman Civil War," pp. 328–29.
91. *HN* 131; it is possible, of course, that Eadmer has also exaggerated their fury and resentment, but his testimony seems plausible on the matter of Anselm's intervention and the ducal party's response to it.
92. Hollister, "Anglo-Norman Civil War," pp. 324, 329.
93. H. H. E. Craster, "A Contemporary Record of the Pontificate of Ranulf Flambard," *Archaeologia Aeliana* 7 (Northumberland, 1930): 48; cf. AEpp. 223, 225.
94. *HN* 128.

recognized Henry as king, and released him from an oath of homage that he had earlier rendered to the duke. Henry in return agreed to pay his brother 3000 marks a year for life and to give up the Cotentin and his other Norman possessions except the castle and town of Domfront. They agreed that if either Henry or Curthose should die without a lawful male heir, the other would inherit the entire Anglo-Norman state. Magnates who had been disseised for supporting either side in 1101 would have their lands restored. But in the future "wicked sowers of discord" would be punished. This was a loophole in the treaty that Henry I quickly began to exploit,[95] along the lines suggested by Robert of Meulan.

Anselm was one of the first to feel the results of Robert of Meulan's advice. Henry promptly went back on his promise by summoning Anselm to his court and demanding that he permit lay investiture and clerical homage. In a letter written in May or June 1101, Paschal had replied negatively to Henry's request for mitigation of the papal decrees.[96] But Paschal had also hinted broadly that if Henry relinquished investitures and clerical homage, Henry would in return receive full papal backing of his claim to the English throne against the counterclaim of Robert Curthose. "If you will give up this practice, then anything you might ask of us, which we could do with God's approval, we will grant you most willingly, and your dignity and majesty we will be most anxious to promote. . . . Then you will have a firmer hold on our friendship and intimate acquaintance and can rejoice in having the blessed apostles as guardians of your realm."[97] Paschal was fully aware of Curthose's designs on England,[98] and the bargain he offered Henry was by no means ungenerous. But it had arrived too late to be effective. "The vast and perilous extent of seas and kingdoms," to which Anselm had earlier alluded, had the effect of ruining Paschal's political timing. Henry no longer needed papal backing against Curthose and was now in a position to insist on retaining his ancestral customs. Summoning Anselm to his court — probably the court that met at Windsor on 3 September 1101 — the king told him that, despite the papal reply, he must either do homage and consecrate the royally invested bishops and abbots or leave the kingdom,[99] thus mirroring

95. Hollister, "Anglo-Norman Civil War," pp. 330–31.
96. AEp. 215: Henry to Paschal.
97. AEp. 216: Paschal to Henry.
98. AEp. 213.
99. *HN* 131.

Anselm's original terms of September 1100, but in a drastically altered political context.

The Windsor court cannot have been a pleasant occasion for Anselm. Jolted by the king's broken promise and faced with the hostility of Curthose and his faction, he was further troubled by the fact that Paschal had replied to Henry's letter but not to his own.[100] Paschal had left it to Henry to inform his primate of the papal stand on homage and investiture and had given no reply to Anselm's request to be granted legatine authority. This last difficulty was exacerbated by the arrival of Paschal's two "nuncios" — John of Tusculum and Tiberius — who by now were participating in this same Windsor court under the title of legati. That they did not act with full legatine powers is probable from their appearance on the witness lists of charters emanating from the Windsor council *after* the archbishops of Canterbury and York (always in that order) and *after* all the bishops.[101] Since Eadmer and Anselm both maintain a wintry silence on their visit, we can only conclude from the absence of independent evidence that the visit had little effect. Hugh of Flavigny mentions that Cardinal John had been sent to collect Peter's Pence; an indulgence granted to Bury St. Edmunds by an otherwise unidentified Cardinal John and confirmed by Anselm was probably a product of this mission.[102]

But Anselm himself, despite his silence, provides the most eloquent expression of Canterbury's reaction to the visit. In an archiepiscopal charter in favor of Holy Trinity, Norwich, almost certainly issued at this same Windsor council of 3 September 1101, Anselm defiantly styles himself "archbishop of Canterbury, primate of Great Britain and Ireland, and vicar of the supreme pontiff Paschal," and pointedly refers to Canterbury as "the first of all English churches."[103] I have alluded to these phrases before, because they provide the strongest assertion in any surviving charter of the grandeur of the Canterbury primacy. But now the charter can be fitted into its exact historical context. It is the battle cry of a beleaguered archbishop, pressed on all sides, yet undaunted. Anselm was unwilling at this juncture to engage in a public dispute with the papacy but was nevertheless reminding the papal nuncios

100. AEp. 218: Anselm to Paschal: "You replied to the king by letter, but you did not reply to me at all."

101. *Regesta* 2, nos. 544, 547–48.

102. Brett, *English Church*, pp. 48–49.

103. *Regesta* 2, no. 549; *The Charters of Norwich Cathedral Priory*, ed. Dodwell, no. 260; above, Chapter 5, n. 92.

that Canterbury ruled the churches of all Britain and Ireland. And he was challenging the threat to his own authority with the audacious assertion — based on no papal privilege but on Canterbury tradition alone — that it was he who rightfully bore the title "vicar of the supreme pontiff Paschal."[104] The nuncios appear to have departed England shortly thereafter, and Paschal subsequently promised Anselm that he would send no further legates during the archbishop's lifetime.[105] At no time, however, did Paschal appoint Anselm his "vicar."

Anselm responded with equal determination to Henry's demand that he either submit on the investiture and homage issues or return to exile. Anselm did neither but instead gave a reasoned defense of his position to the king and his court, based as before on his duty to obey the papal decrees, and afterward departed for Canterbury. "I will not go out of the realm as he asks me to do," Eadmer quotes Anselm as saying, "but to my own church; and doing what I find I ought to do, I will watch carefully to see who it is that would do violence to me or mine."[106] Eadmer's account of this exchange suggests that Henry had reduced his demands at least slightly. He did not ask Anselm to submit personally to royal investiture, as he had demanded a year earlier, but only to consecrate other prelates whom the king had invested and to render homage. "I am unwilling," Henry said, "to tolerate anyone in my kingdom who is not my man."[107] Since Anselm had already been invested with Canterbury by William Rufus, he need not be invested again. But homage, unlike investiture, was an act of personal submission that by custom was rendered to each successive lord. It was the bond that gave moral sanction to the lines of authority in a feudal society, and it was therefore of fundamental importance in the regime of Henry I.[108]

Despite his threat, Henry permitted Anselm to remain at Canterbury in peace for the time being, but others were less fortunate. In the period following the treaty with Curthose, Henry reneged on his promise to forgive magnates who had violated their homage oaths and supported the duke. One such magnate, William of Warenne earl of Surrey, was

104. See above, Chapter 5 at nn. 11–15; recall that Anselm's friend and host in exile, Hugh archbishop of Lyon, had received the identical title from Urban II in connection with Hugh's legatine commission in France. The one letter that Anselm had thus far received from Paschal (AEp. 213) contained not a word about a Canterbury legateship.
105. AEp. 222.
106. HN 131; cf. GP 107.
107. HN 131.
108. See Hollister, "War and Diplomacy in the Anglo-Norman World," p. 80.

disseised prior to Curthose's departure from England in autumn 1101 and returned with the duke to Normandy.[109] In 1102, Henry led a successful military campaign against one of the duke's chief supporters, Robert of Bellême earl of Shropshire, and banished and disseised him along with his brothers, Arnulf of Montgomery and Roger the Poitevin.[110] And in the same year Henry brought charges against Ivo of Grandmesnil for "waging war in England and burning the crops of his neighbors" and imposed a heavy fine on him.[111]

Ivo of Grandmesnil sought the help of Robert of Meulan, "who was the king's chief counselor," to intercede on his behalf with Henry I.[112] Ivo and Robert then entered into a contract, to which Henry I gave his formal consent, stipulating that Robert would advance Ivo 500 marks to go on a crusade. In return for the money, Robert would hold Ivo's English lands in pledge for fifteen years, and Ivo would be reconciled with Henry. At the end of that time Ivo's son would marry the daughter of Henry of Warwick and receive Ivo's inheritance. The terms of the agreement echo the earlier treaty of Robert Curthose with William Rufus to enable the duke to finance his crusade. As matters turned out, the Grandmesnil lands remained in the hands of Robert and his English heir. Ivo died abroad, his sons perished in the White Ship catastrophe in 1120, and the projected marriage never occurred. Robert of Meulan thus acquired Ivo's great holdings in Leicestershire, Warwickshire, and elsewhere. In Leicester itself, which had been divided among four lords—Ivo, the king, the bishop of Lincoln, and Simon of Senlis—Robert acquired Ivo's share together with his castellanship of Leicester castle and his right to farm the king's share of the borough.[113] He later won control of Simon of Senlis's share by marrying his daughter to Simon's son.[114] Henry I responded to Robert of Meulan's good fortune by making him earl of Leicester in April 1107.[115]

109. OV 5:320; cf. 5:308, n. 1, and *Regesta* 2, no. 621; William was reinstated in his English earldom in 1103: OV 6:12–14 and 12, n. 3.

110. OV 6:20–32; J. F. A. Mason, "Roger de Montgomery and His Sons (1067–1102)," *TRHS*, 5th ser., 13 (1963): 22–24.

111. OV 6:18; cf. 6:12.

112. OV 6:18; *Complete Peerage* 7:524.

113. OV 4:338; 6:18–20. At the end of fifteen years (1117) Henry had his back to the wall campaigning in Normandy, and Robert of Meulan was old and dying. Had Ivo's two sons survived the wreck of the White Ship in 1120, one or both might well have received portions of the Leicester earldom.

114. OV 6:20, n. 1; the bishop of Lincoln retained his share of Leicester.

115. *Regesta* 2, no. 844. Robert did not afterward use the title, preferring the more ancient dignity, "count of Meulan"; at his death, his two comital titles were divided between his two sons, Waleran count of Meulan and Robert earl of Leicester.

The soothing voice of the count of Meulan can perhaps be detected in a letter that Anselm, watching events from Canterbury, received quite unexpectedly from Henry I in about October 1101.[116] Having recently threatened Anselm with banishment, the king now addressed him "in quite friendly terms" and invited him to court, offering him unrestricted peace and announcing that the royal position had changed. On Anselm's arrival, Henry proposed another truce during which a second mission would be sent to the papal court to seek Paschal's dispensation from the homage and investiture decrees. The king had some reason to hope that this second mission might succeed where the last one had failed. The king's new envoys would be men of high ecclesiastical rank — Bishops Herbert of Thetford-Norwich and Robert of Chester, and Gerard archbishop-elect of York. Henry had the further hope that he might force Paschal to submit to his petition by threatening to cut off Peter's Pence, withdraw his recognition of the pope, and drive Anselm out of England.[117] Anselm agreed to the proposal and sent on the mission two of his most trusted monks, the Bec monk Baldwin of Tournai and Alexander of Canterbury, to bear witness to the king's threats and to report the pope's decision back to Anselm. Anselm's envoys were also under instructions to seek papal privileges for Canterbury and Bec.[118]

Henry's threat to banish his primate thus seems to have been aimed less at intimidating Anselm — obviously a hopeless prospect — than at tightening the screws on Paschal. Anselm himself now wrote three concurrent letters to be delivered to the pope by the new delegation.[119] In them he rebuked Paschal for failing to answer his previous letter and thus leaving him uncertain as to the pope's exact current position on investitures and homage. Anselm implored Paschal "to resolve the petition that the said bishops will present to you in the best and most useful manner that your wisdom may judge."[120] He made clear to the pope his own unwillingness to enforce decrees that Paschal might be prepared to mitigate: "As it does not pertain to me to loosen what you bind, so it is not up to me to bind what you loosen."[121] He made equally clear the consequences of a papal refusal to permit lay investiture in

---

116. *HN* 132.
117. Ibid. The bishops were also under instructions to attempt to win the pope over by bribery: *GP* 108.
118. Below, Chapter 6 at nn. 135–37.
119. AEpp. 218–20.
120. AEp. 218.
121. Ibid., playing on one of the papacy's favorite biblical texts.

England: "They would expel me from the kingdom rather than obey this decree, and . . . they would leave the Roman church."[122] Anselm asserted that he had already undergone endless tribulations on the papacy's behalf: "I have suffered continuously for nine years now, both in exile and in the episcopate, because I have clung inseparably to the [Apostolic] See in submission and obedience."[123] Yet not presuming to instruct the pope on papal business, he only prayed to God "that he might direct your heart to . . . the benefit of his church."[124]

Paschal responded with a letter to Henry and two to Anselm, all written in mid-April 1102.[125] The letters are couched in the friendliest of terms but are absolutely uncompromising on investitures. To Henry he offered his special friendship and support in all the king's undertakings if he would cease investing prelates, but "the investiture of churches we utterly forbid . . . to all kings and princes: indeed, to all laymen."[126] Interestingly, Paschal's letter to Henry omits any mention of clerical homage, and Southern has made the illuminating observation that the homage issue is absent from all subsequent papal letters until the close of the controversy.[127] Paschal seems to have been prepared, then or soon afterward, to accept a compromise — conceding clerical homage while continuing to forbid lay investiture. His concurrent letters to Anselm do mention clerical homage but for the last time. Paschal informed the archbishop that the Lateran Synod of Lent in 1102 had renewed the decrees solemnly forbidding clerics to render homage to laymen or to accept churches from lay hands.[128]

Anselm and Eadmer may have been coming to regard the homage ban as overly strict. Eadmer simply purges the reference to homage from his transcription of Paschal's letter to Anselm in the *Historia Novorum*.[129] Anselm himself, through one of his envoys on the mission, had questioned the practicality of a prelate's refusing homage to a

122. AEp. 219.
123. AEp. 220.
124. Ibid.
125. AEpp. 222–24.
126. AEp. 224.
127. Southern, *Anselm*, p. 171; cf. p. 173.
128. AEp. 222; cf. Uta-Renate Blumenthal, *The Early Councils of Pope Paschal II, 1100–1110* (Toronto, 1978), pp. 11, 17–18.
129. Whereas in other manuscript copies of the letter, the passage reads, "sancientes et interdicentes, ne quisquam omnio clericus *hominium faciat laico aut* de manu laici ecclesias vel ecclesiastica dona suscipiat" (my italics), Eadmer's version (p. 135) omits the italicized reference to the homage prohibition: cf. Southern, *Anselm*, p. 170, n. 1; and Blumenthal, *Early Councils of Paschal II*, pp. 17–19.

layman for a gift of nonecclesiastical property. Paschal answered by forbidding clerical homage under any circumstances whatever.[130]

Not until late in the controversy, when Henry I was struggling to conquer Normandy in 1105, did he express interest in any such compromise. Until then he would have scorned it on the grounds that the pope was merely offering to rob him of one ancestral custom instead of two. After the return of the second delegation in August or early September 1102, the conflict focused on investitures alone. But since Henry absolutely refused to relinquish the custom and Paschal absolutely refused to concede it, the two sides seemed no nearer reconciliation than before. The pressures on Anselm only increased.

Apart from the issue of investitures, Paschal had acted generously toward the royal-primatial envoys. At Anselm's and Henry's bidding,[131] he conferred the pallium on Gerard of York. He responded favorably to Robert bishop of Chester's request to move his see to the wealthy abbey of Coventry — a project that Lanfranc had earlier opposed.[132] Although unmoved by Bishop Herbert's plea to restore his episcopal jurisdiction over the abbey of Bury St. Edmunds, which had been granted full immunity by Pope Alexander II,[133] Paschal did confirm the moving of Herbert's see from Thetford to Norwich.[134] To Anselm's envoy Baldwin of Tournai, Paschal granted an important privilege for Bec in which the abbey was taken under the special protection of the apostolic see.[135]

But the pope responded most generously of all to Anselm's petitions on behalf of Canterbury. Having been made vividly aware by the envoys from both sides — and by Anselm's letters — that papal intransigence on investitures could launch the archbishop into a second exile, Paschal endeavored to placate Anselm by providing powerful support

130. AEp. 223: Paschal to Anselm in the form of a dialogue; Paschal quotes Anselm's questions, then answers them.

131. AEpp. 220–21.

132. Jaffé-Wattenbach, *Regesta Pontificum Romanorum* 1, no. 5912; cf. *GR* 2: 388–89; LEp. 27; and above, Chapter 5 at nn. 37–38.

133. V. H. Galbraith, "The East Anglian See and the Abbey of Bury St. Edmund's," *EHR* 40 (1925): 222–28; James W. Alexander, "Herbert of Norwich, 1091–1119: Studies in the History of Norman England," *Studies in Medieval and Renaissance History*, ed. William M. Bowsky, 6 (1969): 158–60; *HN*, 132–33, suggests that Herbert's case was harmed by his having been robbed en route of the money intended "to facilitate his business in Rome"; similarly, *GP* 107–8; but Alexander (pp. 156–57) doubts the story.

134. Jaffé-Wattenbach 1, no. 6594; for the date see *Councils and Synods* 1, pt. 2: 657 and n. 1.

135. Jaffé-Wattenbach, nos. 5907, 5913.

for the privileges claimed by Canterbury. Whereas the papacy had never confirmed the primacy for Lanfranc, Paschal now did so for Anselm. This particular passage strongly suggests that Anselm's messengers had also brought up the recent, painful episode of Tiberius and John of Tusculum: "The primacy we do indeed confirm to you . . . in as full and undiminished measure as it is known to have been held by your predecessors, and to you personally we grant this additional privilege: That . . . you are to be subject only to our judgment and not at any time to that of any legate."[136]

Anselm may have been hoping for a confirmation of the primacy to his successors as well as to himself, an explicit designation as the pope's "vicar" or an ex officio legateship, or a definite assertion of Canterbury's primacy over York. But Paschal's concessions were nevertheless unprecedented in recent memory. And Paschal's accompanying letter granted Anselm a third concession. The archbishop had asked through his messengers that Paschal confirm Urban's privilege that Anselm might grant at his discretion dispensations from apostolic and canon law, and Paschal agreed.[137]

Despite the uncompromising opposition to lay investiture in Paschal's letters, Henry's three episcopal envoys reported that the pope had given them verbal instructions of a radically different sort. He told them, so they said, that if Henry behaved as a good Christian prince in other respects, he would be permitted to invest prelates without incurring excommunication. Paschal did not put this concession in writing, the bishops added, for fear that other princes might hear of it and demand the same right for themselves. Anselm's envoys countered that Paschal had told them nothing of the sort, to which the bishops replied that the pope had instructed them privately.[138]

---

136. AEp. 222: "Haec ita doceas, sicut tuo scis primatui expedire. Quem profecto ita fraternitati tuae plenum et integrum confirmamus, sicut a tuis constat praedecessoribus fuisse possessum; hoc personaliter adicientes, ut, quamdiu regno illi religionem tuam divina misericordia conservaverit, nullius umquam legati, sed nostro tantum debeas subesse iudicio."

137. AEp. 223: "Paschalis: Dispensationis modus, sicut beatus Cyrillus in epistola Ephesinae synodi loquitur, nulli umquam sapientum displicuit. Novimus enim sanctos patres nostros et ipsos apostolos pro temporum articulis et qualitatibus personarum dispensationibus usos. Quam ob rem nos de religione et sapientia tua diu longeque spectata nihil penitus ambigentes, tuae deliberationi committimus, ut iuxta datum tibi divinitus intellectum, cum ecclesiae, cuius praepositus es, tanta necessitas expetit, sanctorum canonum decretorumque difficultatem opportuna et rationabili valeas providentia temperare."

138. HN 137–38.

Henry now demanded once again that Anselm either condone investitures or leave the kingdom. Anselm asked to see the letter that Henry had just received from Paschal and said that if it permitted him to do so, "I will try, as far as I can, to satisfy the king's wishes."[139] But Henry refused either to show his letter or to look at Anselm's.[140] The king and his advisers tried to keep the existence of both letters a secret, meanwhile spreading the rumor that Paschal's letter to Henry supported the royal position.[141] But Anselm's letter was "read and reread to all who cared to hear it,"[142] causing much embarrassment to Henry's episcopal envoys by casting doubt on their story. They were embarrassed still further when an anonymous supporter of Anselm's cause managed to slip out of the royal court with a copy of Paschal's letter to Henry and to make its contents known far and wide: "the more carefully it was then kept secret," Eadmer writes with a touch of glee, "the more widely it was published abroad just a few days later."[143] Gerard of York was so upset that Anselm was constrained to protest his innocence, denying that he had broken his promise to keep the letters confidential. He had neither transcribed them personally, he assured Gerard, nor caused them to be transcribed by others.[144] Anselm further assured Gerard, "I do not desire your injury or that of any of my cobishops, nor — whatever the case regarding those letters — do I think that you have been accused of telling lies."[145]

As matters now stood, Anselm was caught between two contradictory versions of the papal stand on investitures. His envoy Baldwin of Tournai adamantly denied that Paschal had given verbal instructions such as the bishops alleged. The king's spokesmen argued that the testimony of three bishops far outweighed the testimony of monks, and that the papal letters were mere ink marks on sheepskins with little lumps of lead attached. "Alas, then!" Anselm's monks retorted. "Aren't the Gospels themselves written upon sheepskins?"[146]

The bishops' story is not altogether inconsistent with the worldliness of the papal curia, as Anselm would have realized from firsthand experience during his exile under Rufus. Their explanation of Paschal's

139. *HN* 137.　　140. Ibid.; AEp. 280.
141. *GP* 108; the letters in question are AEpp. 222, Paschal to Anselm, and 224, Paschal to Henry, both written in mid-April; AEp. 223, Paschal to Anselm, does not deal directly with the investiture question.
142. *HN* 137.　　143. *HN* 137.
144. AEpp. 250, 253.
145. AEp. 253.　　146. *HN* 138.

alleged reluctance to commit his dispensation to writing is also superficially plausible. Nevertheless, their story is almost certainly false. If Paschal had intended to permit investitures in England, he would surely have communicated this message verbally to Anselm through Baldwin and Alexander. Such a message would have seemed not a betrayal of Anselm but a most welcome solution to his problems with the king. Moreover, when Paschal later received news of the bishops' story, he not only denied it vehemently but took the further step of excommunicating the three bishops.[147] The episode cannot be seen as a case of political sophisticates at the papal and royal courts negotiating over the head of a stubborn and naive archbishop.

The editors of *Councils and Synods* suggest that the bishops may simply have misconstrued a tentative papal overture to relax the homage ban in exchange for Henry's relinquishing investitures; it is unlikely, the editors believe, that the bishops were merely lying.[148] But to attribute their story to an innocent confusion of homage with investitures is to underrate the bishops' political acumen while overrating their devotion to truth. All three had risen out of the royal court.[149] Herbert of Norwich was a reformed simoniac and, in the words of his modern biographer, "a dedicated and loyal curialist."[150] Robert of Chester earned an ugly reputation by plundering Coventry Abbey and abusing its monks.[151] Gerard of York had been one of the royal agents who had dashed to the papal court for the pallium after the Council of Rockingham in 1095 and had escorted the legate Walter of Albano secretly through Canterbury en route to Rufus's court. None of the three bishops was above lying on the king's behalf.

Despite their propensities, the bishops probably did not simply improvise their story. More likely they were acting under orders from Henry I and Robert of Meulan. A year and a half later, when the king sent William Warelwast and Anselm to Rome in a final effort to persuade Paschal to permit investitures, William was provided with a secret backup plan. If he failed to sway the pope, he was to disclose the

147. AEp. 280.
148. 1, pt. 2:657, n. 3.
149. *ASC*, A.D. 1085, for Robert of Chester; OV 5:202–4 for Herbert of Norwich; *HN* 68 for Gerard of York. Alexander, "Herbert of Norwich," p. 122, expresses reservations about Orderic's statement that Herbert was a royal chaplain, but since Orderic includes him on a list of both clerics and monks in the royal curia, there seems no clear reason to reject the statement.
150. Alexander, "Herbert of Norwich," p. 156.
151. *GR* 2:388–89.

king's refusal to allow Anselm's return to England.[152] Similarly, the bishops' false testimony in 1102 bears the mark of another backup plan, probably devised by the count of Meulan before the mission departed for Rome. If the pope relented, well and good; if not, the bishops would allege that he had done so privately. In either case, the hoped-for result would be to resolve the Investiture Controversy without relinquishing a measure of the king's sovereignty. The bishops' reinterpretation of the pope's instructions would have been altogether justifiable in Robert of Meulan's mind as a lesser evil undertaken for the sake of the public utility — a *bonus dolus* which might resolve the king's quarrel with his primate while preserving his royal customs.[153] The plan had the further advantage of shielding the king from possible reprisals from the pope. Henry could now proceed to invest prelates on the basis of his bishops' report from Rome; if Paschal objected, the king could claim that his bishops had deceived him.[154]

Anselm would surely have believed the words of his devoted friends Baldwin and Alexander over those of the curial bishops. Most likely, he gave no credence whatever to the bishops' story. But his primary concern, as always, was to act correctly. As primate of Canterbury he was obliged to respect the testimony of his bishops, even if it was plainly false. As he explained in a letter to Paschal, "I could neither disbelieve your letter nor venture to despise the statement of your command put forward by the bishops."[155] Accordingly, Anselm proposed a temporary compromise, which the royal curia accepted. He would not obey Henry's command to render homage and consecrate invested prelates, but he would agree to refrain from excommunicating prelates whom the king invested, and from excommunicating the king for having invested them.[156] This was a significant new concession on Anselm's part. His previous truces with Henry had been predicated on the firm understanding that while they lasted the king would invest no prelates. Therefore, not a single bishop or abbot had received royal investiture during the two years since Anselm's return from exile. But now Anselm agreed unilaterally to relax the papal decrees. He dispatched another delegation to Rome to seek clarification, and the king began investing

152. *HN* 157. See below, Chapter 6 at nn. 232–33.
153. On the *bonus dolus*, see above, Chapter 5 at nn. 81–88.
154. See AEp. 280, Anselm to Paschal: "The king, by your authority as he thinks, is conferring bishoprics and abbacies."
155. AEp. 280.
156. *HN* 140; *GP* 109.

prelates. Henry gave the pastoral staff of the bishopric of Salisbury to his chancellor Roger and invested the royal larderer, another Roger, with the bishopric of Hereford. Anselm raised no objection, and Henry in return permitted his primate to fulfill the goal toward which he had been striving throughout his archiepiscopate: the convening of a great primatial council for the reform of the English church.[157]

The Westminster Council of late September 1102 was a notable occasion, producing legislation "on a scale which not even the most impressive of Lanfranc's councils had achieved."[158] Its canons dealt with a great variety of matters: simony and sodomy were both condemned, monastic discipline was tightened, and parish churches were protected against the inroads of unscrupulous laymen. Clergy were also required to dress and behave appropriately; for example, priests were not to wear multicolored clothing or fancy shoes, attend drinking parties, or drink to excess.[159] The most controversial canons were those enforcing clerical celibacy. Lanfranc's synod of 1076 had ordered that no priest could thenceforth marry but had permitted previously married priests to keep their wives. Anselm's council of 1102 went much farther by prohibiting clerical marriage absolutely and requiring all married clergy to abandon their wives or their vocations.[160] Demonstrating that the canons against simony and clerical misbehavior were not idle threats, the council deposed nine abbots or abbots-elect — six for simony and three for other violations of ecclesiastical discipline. Of these last three, Richard of Ely, whose Clare kinsmen had caused the king such grief, was probably deposed at Henry I's request for failing to render him full support at the time of Curthose's invasion.[161]

The council of 1102 was an occasion of further tension between Canterbury and York. Anselm's own account of the council provides an idealized image wherein the tension is altogether suppressed and the Canterbury tradition prevails: "At this council Anselm, archbishop of

157. *HN* 141.

158. Brett, *English Church*, p. 76; cf. *Councils and Synods* 1, pt. 2: 670: the canons of the council constituted "the most extensive piece of legislation in England since the Conquest." The council is discussed in detail, and all relevant sources printed in full, in ibid., pp. 668–88; for another excellent account, see Brett, *English Church*, pp. 76–79.

159. Canons 10 and 11: *Councils and Synods* 1, pt. 2:676.

160. See Brett, *English Church*, p. 77: this canon proved all but impossible to enforce. Cf. C. N. L. Brooke, "Gregorian Reform in Action: Clerical Marriage in England, 1050–1200," *Cambridge Historical Journal* 12 (1956): 1–21, 187–88.

161. *Liber Eliensis*, pp. 225–27; Brett, *English Church*, p. 78; above, Chapter 6 at nn. 84–85.

Canterbury and primate of all Britain, presided; and with him sat
the following ecclesiastical dignitaries: Gerard archbishop of York,
Maurice bishop of London, William bishop-elect of Winchester, and
others both bishops and abbots."[162] But Hugh the Chantor of York
viewed the occasion through a different lens:

> Archbishops Anselm and Gerard afterward decided to hold a council. When it
> assembled in Westminster, and the [Canterbury] monks had prepared a seat for
> their archbishop higher than any of the others, Gerard felt insulted and, openly
> calling God's wrath on the man who had done this, kicked over the seat and
> refused to sit down until his own seat was set as high as the other archbishop's —
> plainly demonstrating that he owed him no subjection.[163]

There must surely be some factual basis behind Hugh the Chantor's
report,[164] but whatever kickings, cursings, and maneuverings for precedence may have occurred at the council were edited out by Anselm.
Regardless of the heights of chairs and the claims of York, the official
account has Anselm presiding peacefully and unchallenged as primate
of all Britain, while relegating his fellow archbishop to the ranks of the
Canterbury suffragans.

Anselm's account of the council further reflects due order by naming
only three of the thirteen bishops in attendance and describing the
remaining ten simply as "others."[165] Among those unnamed others
were Roger elect of Salisbury and Roger elect of Hereford, both of
whom had been invested only days before by Henry I. Anselm was thus
willing to mitigate the papal decrees not only in refraining from excommunicating the two invested bishops-elect but in welcoming them to his
council as well. He was prepared to risk the pope's displeasure and bend
his own principle of obedience for the sake of the greater good of
assuming his rightful primatial role as the leader of a kingdomwide
assemblage working toward ecclesiastical reform.

For the moment Henry and Anselm were once more in harness
together. Anselm's Westminster council was held immediately following Henry I's Michaelmas council at Westminster. At Henry's council

162. Quoted in *HN* 141–42.
163. *HCY* 13.
164. It may be, however, that Anselm's chair was kicked over by a York canon rather
than Archbishop Gerard, who wrote to Anselm soon afterward in loving terms and
complained of the low moral character of his canons: *AEp.* 255.
165. *HN* 141; Eadmer himself provides a complete list as does Florence of Worcester
(2:51), following Eadmer: all the bishops of England attended except Osbern of Exeter,
who was ill.

the king and his magnates had rejoiced in their recent victory over Robert of Bellême and the ejection of the Montgomery family from England, and the king had invested Roger of Salisbury and Roger of Hereford.[166] Henry's magnates stayed on in Westminster to attend the primatial council at Anselm's invitation, so that the canons of the council might be ratified by both the clergy and people of England.[167] But in the months that followed, the peace between king and primate began to disintegrate as Henry pressed for the consecration of his invested prelates and the papacy resolved to have them excommunicated.[168] Anselm was again caught between two grindstones, and the number of bishoprics and abbacies lacking consecrated prelates continued to grow. With Henry insisting on investing all prelates and Anselm declining to consecrate any whom Henry had invested, it was impossible even to replace the abbots deposed at Westminster. The Investiture Controversy had thus turned one of Anselm's major conflicts with Rufus upside down. Whereas Rufus had resisted Anselm's pressure to fill ecclesiastical vacancies, now Henry I was striving to fill them and Anselm was forced into the position of preventing him from doing so.

When Roger elect of Hereford took gravely ill just after the council and pleaded that Anselm consecrate him before he died, Anselm refused, perhaps suspecting a royal trick.[169] At Roger's death, Henry nominated Reinhelm the queen's chancellor to the bishopric of Hereford and duly invested him. The English episcopate now had three unconsecrated bishops-elect: William Giffard of Winchester, Roger of Salisbury, and Reinhelm of Hereford. Henry I began putting pressure on Anselm to consecrate all three. Anselm agreed to consecrate William Giffard (whom he had himself invested) but not Roger or Reinhelm. Henry replied angrily that he would not permit Anselm to consecrate the one without the others.[170]

The king then aimed a direct challenge at the prerogatives of Canterbury by making arrangements for consecrations to be performed by his own curial bishops. To Anselm's consternation, Robert Bloet of Lincoln and John of Bath began consecrating abbots whom Henry had

---

166. Florence, 2:51.   167. HN 141.   168. AEp. 281.
169. HN 144: Eadmer, in his enthusiasm for the Canterbury cause, inadvertently provides an unflattering account of Anselm "laughing in astonishment at the man's foolishness" and refusing even to reply to his deathbed petition.
170. HN 144–45.

invested.[171] Worse still, Henry persuaded Gerard of York to consecrate the three bishops-elect in Anselm's place. This last plan collapsed, however, leaving Henry humiliated and furious. Reinhelm, rather than submitting to consecration by a prelate other than the archbishop of Canterbury, returned his ring and staff to the king and was forthwith expelled. When Gerard proceeded with the consecration of Roger of Salisbury and William Giffard, William interrupted the ceremony by announcing his refusal to accept consecration from anyone but Anselm. The attending prelates were thrown into confusion and the ceremony was left uncompleted. The irate king disseised William Giffard and expelled him from the kingdom,[172] and Roger of Salisbury remained a mere bishop-elect. Henry clearly could no longer count on the total and unanimous support of the curial bishops that Rufus had enjoyed.

Meanwhile Anselm found himself under pressure from the opposite direction — from reformers on the Continent who firmly upheld the papal position on investitures and began to reproach the primate for consorting with invested prelates. He received a letter from Hugh abbot of Cluny seemingly written for no other purpose than to recall their former friendship. Yet toward the end is a brief admonition: "Nevertheless, since the power of man is not in his own hand, give your hand to God's will, to Whom your care pertains, and Who by its light will show you more clearly the safer course for you. In Him place all your hope, seek from Him virtue and perseverance . . . enduring in all things."[173] Although writing with great caution, Hugh seems to imply that Anselm was not adhering wholeheartedly to the will of God as expressed in the papal decrees.

Anselm received a similar letter at about this time from "Cardinal John"[174] with thinly veiled implications that Anselm was not fighting wholeheartedly for the papal cause: "Therefore since you have fought 'the good fight,' see that you do not fail at the end, lest it be said of

171. *HN* 148; AEp. 261. John of Bath was an Italian physician and had been a *curialis* of William Rufus: V. H. Galbraith, "Notes on the Career of Samson Bishop of Worcester (1096–1112)," *EHR* 82 (1967): 87, n. 1.

172. *HN* 145–46; AEpp. 265, 273–76.

173. AEp. 259; during his first exile, Anselm had been warmly welcomed by Hugh at Cluny: *HN* 90–91.

174. AEp. 284; the reference in the letter to the "false bishops" limits its date range to December 1102–April 1103. Its author is probably not John of Tusculum (cf. AEp. 339, Anselm to "Iohannem episcopum Tusculanensem et Johannem cardinalem") but the learned monk John of Gaeta, papal chancellor and cardinal deacon of S. Maria in Cosmedin, the future Pope Gelasius II: Carlo Servatius, *Paschalis II. (1099–1118): Studien zu seiner Person und seiner Politik* (Stuttgart, 1979), pp. 54–55.

you, 'That man began to build, but he could not complete it.' Read
felicitously.'' Against the scriptural text that Anselm had so often
quoted to define his position vis-à-vis king and pope ("Render unto
Caesar the things that are Caesar's and unto God the things that are
God's") Cardinal John proposed another text for Anselm to consider:
"No one is able to serve two lords, God and Mammon."[175]

From his close friend and Urban II's former vicar, Hugh archbishop
of Lyon, Anselm received a letter in early 1103 intimating that exile was
preferable to cooperation with the church's enemies: "We have heard
moreover that you are excessively disturbed by the king of England and
that many things are done by him unadvisedly against God and his
church."[176] Hugh assured Anselm that if exile should become necessary he would be welcome to stay again at Lyon. Characteristically,
Anselm replied that he did not want to commit the explanation of
affairs in England to writing but relied on Hugh's messenger to transmit
it orally. The situation may have been too complex and controversial
to set down in writing or may perhaps have been compromising to
Anselm's public image. What Anselm did commit to writing was his
concern that the power of the archbishop, the primate of all Britain,
was being weakened: "Indeed the bishops themselves along with the
king so rage that even acts of consecration, which pertain only to me,
they do not fear to take upon themselves if there be one who wishes to
accept it from them."[177]

By 1103, the political context of the Investiture Contest was beginning to shift once again as Henry, secure on his throne, commenced his
challenge to Curthose's authority in Normandy. Henry's first intervention in Norman affairs was occasioned by the death without direct heirs
of William of Breteuil at Bec on 12 January 1103.[178] William of Breteuil
was an important baron of southeastern Normandy, the eldest son of
William fitz Osbern, the Conqueror's steward and companion and an
early benefactor of Bec. Henry married his natural daughter Juliana to
Eustace, William of Breteuil's illegitimate son and a leading candidate
among the rival claimants to the Breteuil barony. The other major

175. AEp. 284 is absent from Anselm's Canterbury collection, Lambeth ms. 59: see
Fröhlich, "Letters Omitted from Anselm's Collection," p. 67.
176. AEp. 260: Hugh had just returned to Lyon from Jerusalem by way of Apulia,
and therefore, presumably, Rome, the probable source of his information.
177. AEp. 261; cf. HN 145–46, 148.
178. OV 6:40 and n. 2, cf. 44.

candidate was William of Breteuil's Burgundian kinsman, Reginald of Grancey, whose claim to the Breteuil inheritance was supported by several powerful and interrelated magnates of the region: Ascelin Goel lord of Bréval, William count of Evreux, his nephew Amaury de Montfort, and Ralph of Tosny, whose family had long feuded with the Beaumonts.[179]

Orderic reports that amid the ensuing battles between Eustace's and Reginald's factions, "the king of England sent Robert count of Meulan to put down the civil disturbances in Normandy" and commanded Robert Curthose and Reginald's baronial supporters to give backing to the royal son-in-law, Eustace of Breteuil, or else be prepared to suffer the king's anger. Although this threat had some effect, Ascelin Goel continued to support Reginald of Grancey's claim. Shortly after Robert of Meulan's arrival, Goel seized a wealthy merchant of Meulan as he was returning from a conference with Count Robert at Beaumont Castle.[180] Robert, "being a cunning man," secured his merchant's release by making a treaty with all contenders in the Breteuil inheritance dispute. Robert's daughter Emma, then only a year old, was betrothed to William of Evreux's nephew, Amaury de Montfort, whose vast lordship in the Ile-de-France included Montfort-l'Amaury, Montchauvet, Houdon, and Epernon. Through his sister Bertrade, Amaury was the brother-in-law of King Philip I and uncle of the future Fulk V of Anjou. The treaty also included Eustace of Breteuil and the neighboring lords, Ralph of Tosny and Ascelin Goel, both of whom now abandoned Reginald (who departed for Burgundy) and made peace with Eustace. At this time, too, another of Henry I's natural daughters, Maud, was married to Rotrou count of Perche, near Breteuil, probably as a part of this same general settlement orchestrated by the count of Meulan.[181] Margaret, sister of Count Rotrou, had been married to Robert of Meulan's brother, Henry of Warwick, probably in the 1090s,[182] a relationship that may have aided Robert in the settlement.

179. OV 6:40 and notes: Ascelin Goel was married to William of Breteuil's natural daughter; Amaury's family seat was Montfort-l'Amaury in France, not to be confused with Montfort-sur-Risle near Bec.

180. OV 6:46: the merchant, John son of Stephen of Meulan, had probably been summoned to Beaumont to bring money to help defray Count Robert's military and diplomatic expenses.

181. OV 6:40.

182. OV 4:304 and n. 3; cf. 6:188, 200 and n. 2. Their eldest son, Robert of Neubourg, was more or less contemporary to Robert of Meulan's sons Waleran and Robert. See *Complete Peerage* 12: pt. 2, p. 360.

Robert Curthose's modern biographer, C. W. David, sees Robert of Meulan's actions as part of Henry I's program of pacifying the Norman barons, building up a party in Normandy to prepare the way for invasion.[183] Significantly, when Henry himself visited the duchy in the following year, Orderic's list of Norman magnates who welcomed him includes Robert of Meulan, Rotrou count of Perche, Eustace of Breteuil, and Ralph of Tosny.[184] But the involvement of Amaury de Montfort in the truce suggests that Count Robert was also winning influence for Henry at the courts of Anjou and France. The French king, as the nominal overlord of Normandy, would be the natural ally for Robert Curthose; if Philip could be persuaded to support Henry, the king of England could be assured that his brother would have to fight alone.

Henry had probably been preparing to invade Normandy as early as 1103, for by then the treaty with Curthose was beginning to crumble. Because of the complaints of William of Warenne, who had lost his English lands for supporting Curthose in 1101, the duke "inadvisedly" went to England without King Henry's permission. Henry purported to be exceedingly angry, both because of Curthose's unwelcome presence in the kingdom and because the duke had violated an important provision of the 1101 treaty by having recently come to terms with Robert of Bellême, whom Henry had banished from England in 1102.[185] If Wace can be trusted, Robert of Meulan met Curthose in England and, posing as his friend, terrified him with warnings about the king's anger and the danger of being seized and imprisoned by royal officials.[186] However that may be, Curthose humbly submitted to Henry and, at Queen Matilda's request, relinquished the 3000 mark annuity. Henry then confirmed the remaining provisions of the treaty of 1101 and restored the earldom of Surrey to William of Warenne.[187]

Throughout 1103 Henry levied unusually heavy taxes, evidently for the purpose of buying allies and building a war chest.[188] In summer 1104, he paid a nonviolent but intimidating visit to the duchy, where he

183. David, *Robert Curthose*, pp. 156–58.
184. OV 6:56.
185. OV 6:14–36; GR 2:472.
186. Wace, *Roman de Rou*, ed. A. J. Holden (Paris, 1970–73), 2:277–78.
187. OV 6:12–15; AEp. 296; GR 2:461.
188. A.D. 1103 is the first year in Henry's reign in which *ASC* registers a complaint about high taxes; subsequent complaints, with only a single exception, correspond to years in which Henry was campaigning in Normandy: A.D. 1104, 1105, 1110, 1116, 1117, 1118, and 1124; the one exception is A.D. 1110, when Henry imposed a heavy aid for his daughter Matilda's dowry on her betrothal to Emperor Henry V.

was received in friendship not only by the participants in Robert of Meulan's Breteuil treaty of 1103 but by other Norman landholders as well: Stephen count of Aumale, Robert fitz Hamon, Robert of Mont-fort-sur-Risle (Robert of Meulan's Norman neighbor), Ralph of Mor-temer, and the king's twelve-year-old ward, Richard earl of Chester. All these Normans, Orderic states, "held great estates from him in England, had already gone over to his side in Normandy with their vassals, and were ready and eager to fight with him against all the world."[189]

Meanwhile Henry sought alliances with princes surrounding the duchy. Sometime between 1103 and 1105, he made arrangements with counts Elias of Maine and Alan Fergaunt of Brittany, and with Geoffrey Martel, son of Fulk IV of Anjou — all of whom gave military support to Henry's 1105 campaign against Curthose. The king had earlier con-cluded a treaty with Robert count of Flanders, which included the provision that the count would undertake to dissuade the king of France from any attack on the king of England.[190] Whether through Robert of Flanders, Robert of Meulan, or other intermediaries, Henry obtained the assurance of the French monarchy that it would not oppose his designs on Normandy.[191]

While en route to Dover for the alleged purpose of conferring a second time with the count of Flanders, Henry came to Canterbury in early March 1103 to talk with Anselm.[192] Negotiating with his arch-bishop through intermediaries, Henry expressed the hope that Anselm had been sufficiently "soothed by the king's long-continued patience," and urged him no longer to oppose the customs that the Conqueror had exercised lest Henry be driven to such exasperation as to take action against the archbishop.[193] The nature of the threatened action was left unspecified, but Henry's closest advisers let it be known "to quite a number of people" that unless Anselm submitted, the king intended either to have him mutilated or to cast him out of England in disgrace

189. OV 6:56.
190. David, *Robert Curthose*, pp. 155–56; *Regesta* 2, no. 515, for date. Printed in *Diplomatic Documents*, 1, *1101–1272*, ed. P. Chaplais (London, 1964), pp. 1–4.
191. Hollister, "War and Diplomacy," p. 79 and n. 46 with references.
192. Eadmer dates Henry's meeting with Anselm at about mid-Lent and says it lasted three days; if *exactly* mid-Lent, the meeting occurred on March 8–10: see William Farrer, *An Outline Itinerary of Henry I* (Oxford, 1920), p. 19. Anselm himself was in touch with Count Robert of Flanders ("his lord and beloved in God": AEp. 248) and with Robert's wife, Countess Clemence ("his lady and dearest daughter": AEp. 249).
193. *HN* 146.

and plunder the Church of Canterbury. Undaunted, Anselm responded that his messengers had by now returned with a letter from Paschal replying to Anselm's inquiry about the verbal message allegedly given to the three bishops. Anselm had left the papal letter unopened but now offered to open and read it and abide by its instructions: "It may be found to contain something that would allow me to comply with your wishes," he told the king.[194] Henry refused to have it opened, declaring, "What business do I have with the pope about things that are mine? If anyone wishes to rob me of them, he is my enemy."[195]

If Eadmer's reconstruction of this conversation is even approximately accurate (and he was almost surely an eyewitness), it consisted entirely of courteous deceits. Although the pope's response remained unopened, Anselm must have been perfectly aware of its contents, and so very probably was Henry. Anselm would have received a thorough briefing from his messengers, who were doubtless provided — as was customary in the exchanging of letters — with a fuller account of the pope's position than the letter itself contained.[196] Eadmer attributes to Anselm the guarded but suggestive statement that the papal letter, which his messengers had brought to him, "declares the truth of the matter, so they tell me."[197] The messengers had no doubt reported the truth of the matter to Anselm the moment they returned to Canterbury. Eadmer further reports that, in the opinion of some, Henry refused to have the letter opened because, "as it gradually dawned on them, the substance of the letter had already been disclosed to him by one of the men whom Anselm had sent to Rome."[198]

The letter in question, dated at Benevento, 12 December 1102,[199] was Paschal's response to Anselm's letter reporting the confusion between the pope's written instructions and the bishops' verbal account.[200] Anselm had explained matters clearly to Paschal and had then defended his own policy of consorting with invested prelates-elect: "I gave no consent to anything being done contrary to the decrees of the Council of Rome; I am merely suffering such things, while in the meantime not branding anyone with the accusation of disobedience."

194. *HN* 147.
195. Ibid.
196. Cf. AEp. 280, Anselm's letter that evoked Paschal's unopened reply, wherein Anselm alludes to further information to be communicated to the pope "verbally by the bearers of this letter."
197. *HN* 146–47.   198. *HN* 148.
199. AEp. 281.   200. AEp. 280.

Finally, Anselm once again rehearsed the consequences that would result from continued papal intransigence:

If I should persist in doing what your letter to me commanded, he [Henry] would certainly drive me out of the kingdom. . . . Being put in a most anxious position, I beg you with all the earnestness I can that I may find within you an apostolic pity for my soul, and I imploringly invoke the entire love of the Roman church to obtain this pity. I do not fear exile, poverty, torture, or death, for being strong in God, my heart is prepared to bear all these things out of obedience to the Apostolic See. . . . I only ask for positive information, that I may know without ambiguity what I should regard as your decision.

Anselm then recapitulated the decrees of the Council of Rome that imposed excommunication on all parties participating in lay investiture and clerical homage, and concluded by urging the pope: "Either remove this excommunication with regard to England, so that I can remain here without endangering my soul, or inform me by letter that you intend to uphold it whatever it may cost me; or if, in your wisdom, you choose to make an exception of anything, tell me with the same exactness what that exception is." Anselm's letter once again makes it clear that he himself is open to any compromise the pope might deign to offer; in his bravely professed willingness to suffer exile, torture, poverty, or death for the sake of upholding the decrees, one can hardly miss the implication that he would be spared all these things if only Paschal would relent.

But Paschal held firm on investitures and tightened the noose still further by commanding the excommunication of the three "lying" bishops until they should make amends to the Roman church and acknowledge the gravity of their offense. He further ordered Anselm to make known his excommunication of all the recently invested bishops and abbots, "nor is the fact of their being deceived an adequate excuse."[201] The pope did spare Henry I, passing over in silence the fact that by investing prelates the king had himself violated the decrees of the Council of Rome. But Anselm's plight remained desperate nonetheless: Caesar had commanded him to consecrate the invested prelates, whereas God was now commanding him to excommunicate them. Anselm responded by leaving Paschal's letter unopened.

As before, Paschal recompensed Anselm by giving significant further support to the Canterbury primacy. On the very day that he wrote his as yet unopened letter, the pope wrote to Gerard of York chastising him

201. AEp. 281.

for his duplicity and commanding him to profess obedience to Anselm.[202] This letter constituted a highly significant addition to Paschal's previous privilege for Canterbury, which had acknowledged its primacy in general terms but had not specified its supremacy over York. The letter to Gerard was carried back to England by Anselm's messengers to be preserved at Canterbury, with a copy being delivered to York.[203] Eadmer viewed it as Anselm's supreme achievement, transcribing it at the end of Book IV of the *Historia Novorum* as a fitting climax to his account of Anselm's pontificate: "With that letter we will, to the glory of God, bring this work to an end."[204] It represented the fulfillment of Lanfranc's "great design" and Anselm's cherished hope: a papal recognition of Canterbury's primacy over York:

For we have heard that Thomas, your predecessor, contested this same obligation and that, when the question had been debated before Pope Alexander II, and by his direction a definite decision had been reached, Thomas, after various inquiries, made the same profession to Anselm's predecessor, Lanfranc, and his successors. Accordingly, what was decided at that time we also intend to have maintained secure and unimpaired, as God would have us do.[205]

The letter glosses over the fact that Alexander II had simply referred the case to William I's court, and that its decision in favor of Canterbury had never received papal ratification.[206] But Paschal's interpretation of the event was understandably biased toward Canterbury since his informants were Anselm's own messengers.[207] Also, having clung to a position on investitures that would clearly put Anselm in desperate straits, Paschal was inclined to be unusually generous toward Canterbury. Nor, since Gerard was one of the lying bishops, can Paschal have felt charitable toward York.

The papal letters that the messengers brought to Anselm thus promised supremacy over York but a rupture with the king. Henry ended his conference with Anselm at Canterbury with the issue unresolved and the papal letter unopened, and in the days that followed, relations between the king and primate became increasingly embittered.[208]

202. AEp. 283: dated at Benevento, 12 December 1102.
203. *HN* 215: "That letter, with the pope's seal attached, has been kept at Canterbury ever since."
204. Ibid.
205. AEp. 283.
206. Above, Chapter 5 at nn. 65–66.
207. AEp. 280: Anselm to Paschal: "In what I add to your paternity by word of mouth through the bearers of this letter, I humbly beg you not to despise my entreaties."
208. *HN* 147.

Eadmer reports that the magnates closest to the king were themselves sorrowful and sometimes reduced to tears over the troubles that were certain to come. But as before, the two sides continued to refrain from direct conflict or explosions of anger. Anselm was in fact bending his principles significantly to avoid a final break with Henry. Knowing that Paschal had commanded the excommunication of five English bishops and bishops-elect, Anselm kept his letter sealed, and he refrained from acting against the bishops on the grounds that he had not yet read it.[209] As for Henry, he left it to others to whisper of the horrors that might lie in store for Anselm while he himself played the role of the patient, reasonable monarch defending his royal customs against a pope who would rob him of them.

Only a few days after the mid-Lent confrontation at Canterbury, Henry again adopted a conciliatory tone and proposed to Anselm yet another truce and another mission to Rome. The king now begged his archbishop to seek the dispensation by going personally to Rome, where he would be joined by the king's veteran papal negotiator, William Warelwast.[210] As we know from subsequent events, this proposal was merely one component of a more elaborate secret plan, seeming to bear the stamp of Henry's chief adviser. If the pope could not be persuaded, Anselm would be courteously but firmly told that he could not return to England unless he would consent to investitures. In this way Henry could settle his problem with Anselm without suffering the opprobrium of literally driving him out of England. Indeed, as we shall see, Anselm would be coaxed to return to the church he had abandoned if only he would consent to deal with Henry as Lanfranc had dealt with Henry's father.[211] Anselm had doubts about the new proposal and asked leave to have it deferred until the coming Easter court. Henry agreed, and they parted in peace.

At Easter (29 March 1103) the unanimous advice of the magnates and prelates persuaded Anselm to adopt the king's plan. He was not seeking exile (as has been argued); indeed, the word was never mentioned, and Eadmer's testimony, corroborated by Anselm's letters, demonstrates that the primate expected to return to his archbishopric

209. *HN* 148: Eadmer, while contending that Anselm remained unaware of the letter's contents, explained that he feared that if the pope did not confirm the bishops' verbal message, excommunications might fall on men of such status that he could not break off communion with them without creating a grave scandal.

210. *HN* 147.

211. Below, Chapter 7 at nn. 37–38, 54, 56–61.

after his visit to Rome.[212] At the Easter court he once again explained that he would not advise Paschal to do anything that might be prejudicial to the liberty of the church or to the archbishop's reputation. The princes then proposed that the royal messengers present the king's case, and that Anselm need only confirm its truth. Eadmer quotes Anselm as replying, "I shall not be found, so help me God, to contradict anyone who speaks the truth."[213] Thus Anselm could go to Rome presenting an image consistent with his conception of the public example that the archbishop of Canterbury should represent. He would be neither explicitly opposing the papal decrees, nor publicly counseling the pope to do so, since it was not his place to decide papal matters; yet he would be testifying to the truth that Henry would not accept them. Anselm was thus continuing to take a prudently moderate stand between the two extreme positions, while endeavoring to behave impeccably.

On 27 April Anselm crossed to Normandy, bearing the still-unopened papal letter. On his arrival at Bec, where he was welcomed with rejoicing and reverence, he opened the letter at last. It was now too late for Anselm to publish the excommunications, and he could postpone the problem of breaking off communion with fellow bishops until his return, meanwhile pointing out personally to Pope Paschal the virtually insurmountable difficulties that his excomunications posed.

In order to maintain the peace of the English church under the leadership of Canterbury, Anselm had been walking a fine line between obedience and disobedience. To ask discreetly but repeatedly for a dispensation was "obedience" but not cooperation. To preside at a primatial council that included bishops invested by the king after the pope's ban and the primate's warning was dangerously close to disobedience. To leave unopened a crucially important papal letter obviously intended for publication in England — indeed, to take it to Normandy — was something less than direct disobedience and something less than obedience. Anselm seems to have been protecting Henry and his bishops by an adroit maneuver, which was left unmentioned in Anselm's correspondence but which Eadmer inadvertently exposed. And to go to Rome for a dispensation in the face of repeated papal refusals and even the decision of a synod confirming the bans was reluctant obedience

212. HN 157; VA 128 (after completing his business in Rome, Anselm "set out on the return journey"); cf. AEpp. 265, 294.
    213. HN 149.

at best. Nevertheless, for posterity and for the contemporary public, Anselm and Paschal had written as if Anselm's obedience was beyond question, reflecting both their views of what "ought" to be required.

By Whitsunday, 17 May 1103, Anselm had reached Chartres, where he was welcomed by Adela countess of Blois, Henry I's sister and Anselm's spiritual daughter, and by Bishop Ivo of Chartres.[214] They advised him to delay his journey into Italy to avoid the severity of what was reported to be an unusually hot Italian summer. He therefore returned to Bec and remained there until mid-August, giving spiritual instruction to the monks and corresponding in friendly terms with King Henry.[215] He then resumed his journey to Italy by way of the Valley of Maurienne[216] and probably reached Rome sometime in October.[217] The king's envoy, William Warelwast, had arrived before him and was already busy cultivating the papal curia on Henry's behalf.

Eadmer is at pains to emphasize Anselm's impartiality. When the English investiture issue came up for a formal hearing in mid-November, Anselm left it to William Warelwast to present the king's case and added not a word.[218] But by his very presence at the proceedings, Anselm was consciously if silently representing Henry's cause. Anselm had earlier expressed his intention to Henry, in a letter written while en route to Rome, to "pursue the object for which I left England."[219] That object was not simply to discover the pope's position on investitures, which Paschal had made plain to Anselm in his "unopened" letter of December 1102.[220] Rather, the hope of waiving the papal decrees for England was, as Eadmer elsewhere states, "the chief reason for Anselm's coming to Rome."[221] Although Anselm was silent at the formal hearing, he must surely have spoken privately to Paschal about the investiture issue and the related problem of the papal excommunications. As Anselm reported in his first letter to Henry after the papal hearing, "I came to Rome, and there I explained to my lord the pope the circumstances that had occasioned my coming; he replied

---

214. *HN* 151; AEpp. 286, 287.
215. *HN* 151; AEp. 294.
216. AEp. 301: the valley of the River Arc in Savoy, leading into Italy.
217. *VA* 128, n. 1.
218. *HN* 153: While William Warelwast argued, "Anselm said nothing."
219. AEp. 294.
220. AEp. 281: in permitting lay investiture anywhere, "the dignity of the Church is damaged, the force of its discipline impaired, and all Christianity trodden underfoot."
221. *HN* 152.

that he refused absolutely to dissent from the decrees of his predecessors."[222]

To Paschal, the prohibition of lay investiture was the centerpiece of the entire papal reform program, and he would not abandon the principle even for Anselm. William Warelwast concluded his argument at the papal hearing with the uncompromising statement, "The king of the English will not, even at the loss of his kingdom, allow himself to be deprived of the investiture of churches." And the pope replied in equally uncompromising terms, "I must tell you, and I speak as if in the presence of God, that not even to save his life will Pope Paschal ever permit such a right with impunity."[223] The king's position had thus, in Eadmer's words, been "adjudicated in Rome and finally decided," thereby depriving Anselm of any middle ground on which to maneuver. As in other recent exchanges on investitures, the matter of clerical homage was passed over in silence, but that was of little help to Anselm. On the issue of lay investiture itself, the king and the pope had reached a total impasse. The pope had confirmed his stand in Anselm's own presence, and there could therefore be no more truces with Henry or missions to Rome to seek mitigation. Unless Henry could yet be persuaded to yield investitures — and he had sworn that he would sooner lose England — Anselm could no longer function as archbishop without defying the Apostolic See.

On the slim chance that Henry might yet relent, Paschal offered a solution to Anselm's grave problem of having to function as primate in England without communing with the invested bishops-elect. The pope delegated to Anselm the authority to decide what amends the bishops-elect might make in order to be restored to communion.[224] But so long as Henry continued to invest prelates, Anselm's discretionary power would be useless.

After the hearing was concluded, Anselm remained in Rome for further dealings with the pope on matters which, "while secondary to the main business, were of no small importance as additional reasons for his coming to Rome."[225] As a consequence of these negotiations, and

222. AEp. 308.
223. HN 153; similarly, VA 128.
224. HN 154.
225. HN 154; cf. VA 128 and n. 3.

in order "that Anselm might not be thought to depart the papal court empty-handed,"[226] Paschal granted him the strongest written concession of the primacy that any archbishop of Canterbury was ever to receive from the papacy:

In a previous letter addressed to you from the Apostolic See, we granted you the primacy of the Church of Canterbury in as full measure as it is known to have been held by your predecessors. Now, complying with your request, that primacy and all the dignity and authority which, as is well known, attach to that holy Church of Canterbury, we confirm . . . both to you yourself and to your lawful successors as your predecessors from St. Augustine's time have undoubtedly held them by the authority of the Apostolic See.[227]

Paschal also gave Anselm a letter to deliver to Henry I, now lost but presumably stern in tone.[228] The archbishop and his companions then set out on their return journey protected by an armed escort provided by Matilda countess of Tuscany, another of Anselm's admirers.[229] William Warelwast remained in Rome for a few more days in the hope of persuading Paschal to relent. William failed to sway the pope on the matter of investitures but did convince him to write to Henry another letter more conciliatory than the letter Anselm carried.[230] If Anselm had been treating Henry too severely (which Paschal thought unlikely), then, "provided that you have abandoned investitures, we will, as you would wish, advise restraint."[231] William Warelwast, always a swift traveler, caught up with Anselm's party at Piacenza and accompanied it toward Lyon, where Anselm planned to spend Christmas with his dear friend Archbishop Hugh.[232]

226. *HN* 154.
227. AEp. 303, dated 16 November 1103. A loophole remained, in that Paschal did not explicitly define Canterbury's dignity and authority. Nevertheless, the extension of the privilege to all of Anselm's lawful successors was an extremely significant concession. In Southern's words, "This, rather than the decision of 1072, was the high-water mark in the Canterbury case": *Anselm*, p. 137; on the vital importance of the inclusions of Anselm's successors in the privilege, cf. R. W. Southern, "The Canterbury Forgeries," *EHR* 73 (1958): 215–16. An apparently concurrent papal privilege, also confirming the Canterbury primacy to Anselm and his successors, but "saving the privileges of other metropolitans" (AEp. 304), was omitted from the Canterbury collection of Anselm's correspondence, probably because it seemed both redundant and half-hearted.
228. Referred to in AEp. 315.
229. *HN* 155; cf. AEp. 325.
230. *HN* 155.
231. AEp. 305, dated 23 November 1103, after Anselm's departure.
232. *HN* 155, 157: Eadmer states that William Warelwast had lingered in Rome on the pretext of having vowed to visit the shrine of St. Nicholas of Bari; when he turned up at Piacenza, shortly afterward, Eadmer commented wryly: "We were not a little surprised at the speed with which he had traveled from St. Nicholas."

Shortly before Christmas, outside the walls of Lyon, William propelled Anselm into his second exile by disclosing in veiled but unmistakable words Henry I's backup plan of barring Anselm from England
unless he submitted on investitures. As William delicately expressed it,

I had expected that our case at Rome would turn out differently, so I refrained
until now from disclosing the message which my lord the king instructed me to
give you. But now, since I intend to return to him in haste, I don't want to
withhold his message any longer. He says that if you return to him on the
understanding that you will treat him in all respects as your predecessors are
known to have treated his, then he will joyfully approve your returning to
England and will welcome it.[233]

Anselm answered, "Is that all you have to say?" "To you," William
replied, "a word is enough." It was indeed for Anselm: "I hear what
you say, and I take your meaning." The two men parted and Anselm
entered Lyon to begin his second exile. Explaining his situation in a
letter to Paschal,[234] he said with more than a touch of irritation that he
would not bother to deliver the pope's letter to the king since it was
now superseded by the letter that William Warelwast carried.[235]

Once in Lyon, where Archbishop Hugh and his clergy greeted him
with rejoicing, Anselm sent his new papal privilege to Ernulf prior of
Canterbury "for the purpose of transcribing it and guarding it diligently."[236] He also wrote to Henry I, "his honored lord," requesting
verification of the instructions that William Warelwast had relayed and
presenting a clearly reasoned summary of his own position. For answer, Henry immediately seized all the revenues of Canterbury.[237] The
situation had reached a stalemate, and the first phase of the Investiture Controversy was over.

During the first phase Anselm had worked diligently to structure the
position of the archbishop of Canterbury in conformity with the Canterbury tradition, while Robert of Meulan had worked to bring about

233. *HN* 157.
234. AEp. 315.
235. In William's letter Paschal urged Henry to reconsider banishing his widely
revered primate, making it clear that William revealed the king's plan to Paschal, as a final
gambit to obtain the papal waiver, before disclosing it to Anselm.
236. AEpp. 306, 307.
237. AEp. 308; *HN* 159.

the due order that he conceived for the king and the kingdom. Both were concerned with the projection of public images — Anselm endeavoring to appear as a model prelate, and Robert endeavoring to counsel his king to appear as a model monarch. The results of Robert's efforts will be seen more clearly in the next phase of the Investiture Contest.

At the same time Robert of Meulan and Anselm continued to use effectively their political conceptions of *raison d'état* and *utilitas ecclesiae*. Henry I had clearly followed the methodology suggested to him by his first counselor as he faced the crisis of 1101, placating his magnates, his primate, and his brother with promises and soothing ambiguities until his kingship had been made secure. Only then did he reconsider and, reconsidering, proceed to act in the best interests of the kingdom, as he conceived them to be. With traitors in his court the kingdom was constantly endangered. To yield on homage and investitures would have been seen as a betrayal of his royal stewardship, as the renunciation of important prerogatives that had been established by William I and upheld without opposition by William II.

Anselm, too, strove through the good works of friendship and generosity for the utility and safety of his church. He gave Henry his full support up to the point that he was convinced that the bans on homage and investiture were irrevocable. At this point the logic of events forced him into a second exile. Although Paschal had ceased to press on the homage issue, his intransigence on lay investiture, and Henry I's absolute refusal to betray the responsibilities of his royal stewardship by abandoning the custom, made it impossible for Anselm to continue functioning in England as primate. He could only await the unfolding of events that might yet provide opportunities to resolve the dilemma. In the meantime his public reputation remained untarnished and his conscience at peace.

While Anselm had been working to resolve the dispute between Paschal and Henry, he had also been doing his utmost to secure from Paschal what he regarded as the traditional rights of Canterbury. On no less than three occasions, Paschal had accompanied his denial of the dispensation that Henry and Anselm requested with a concession to Anselm strengthening the Canterbury primacy. Paschal promised that no more papal legates would be sent in Anselm's lifetime; he confirmed to Anselm the right to grant dispensations from apostolic and canon law; he commanded the archbishop of York to profess obedience; and he confirmed Canterbury's privileges not only to Anselm but to all his successors. By 1103 Anselm had indeed become almost a pope of the *alter orbis*. But Henry, working closely with his chief counselor Robert of Meulan, had made the effective use of these privileges impossible; it yet remained for Anselm to secure the rights of Canterbury from the king. This he succeeded in doing in the second phase of the controversy, while Henry succeeded in retaining the most important of his royal rights and in reuniting his father's dominions.

Seven

Public Images and Political Inventiveness: The Saint, the Statesman, and the Power of Propaganda, 1104–1107

The culminating phase of the English Investiture controversy began in December 1103 when Anselm began his second exile, again as the guest of Hugh archbishop of Lyon. It was an exile that Anselm had done all in his power to avoid, short of blatant disobedience to the Apostolic See. But in the face of Paschal II's ultimatum that Henry I relinquish investitures and Henry's absolute refusal to do so, Anselm saw himself as left without a choice. Paschal had confirmed the Canterbury primacy with privileges of unparalleled force, yet Anselm was prevented from exercising that primacy by a royal-papal quarrel over an issue in which he himself had no serious interest. He had repeatedly affirmed his willingness to accept the practice of lay investiture if the papacy should allow it. Conversely, like other churchmen of his time, he was of the opinion that Henry could give up investitures "without losing an iota of those prerogatives which, with God's approval, pertain to the king's sovereignty."[1] But although Anselm would gladly have functioned as primate of Britain with or without the practice of lay investiture, he could

1. AEp. 369: Anselm to Robert of Meulan; similarly, AEp. 248: Anselm to Robert count of Flanders; cf. *HCY* 13–14: Henry I's abandonment of investitures "cost him little or nothing"; Paschal II cautioned Henry not to be misled into thinking "that we have any wish to diminish anything of your sovereignty": AEp. 216.

not do so with the king and pope at loggerheads. Although the investiture issue per se was largely irrelevant to Anselm, its resolution was essential to the achievement of his goal of exercising the Canterbury primacy.

Henry I, with his enemies subdued and his throne secure, could afford to be intransigent. He defied the pope's investiture ban, William of Malmesbury explains, "on the advice of his great men and above all that of the count of Meulan." Basing his counsel "more on ancient custom than on righteousness," Robert alleged that if Henry abandoned the usages of his predecessors with regard to investitures, "the king's majesty would be greatly diminished."[2] It is all too easy to argue from hindsight that the ceremony of royal investiture was a mere symbolic act that the king could abandon, as Anselm had observed, without compromising his real authority. Robert of Meulan would surely have grasped the point, yet he counseled that the monarch could not renounce this important traditional practice without damaging the royal majesty, which manifests itself through symbols and ceremonies. Henry and the count of Meulan were thus just as adamant on the issue of investitures as Anselm himself had been, under Rufus, on the equally symbolic issue of the pallium.

During the months and years of Anselm's second exile, despite Henry's confiscation of the Canterbury estates, the king and archbishop maintained an outwardly polite relationship. Both parties tried to enhance their public reputations by appearing reasonable and ready to forgive; both sought to advance their goals by demonstrating that they were acting righteously and in accordance with the divine will. The physical separation and ideological gap between Anselm and the royal court had the effect of intensifying the propaganda emanating from both sides, each of which endeavored to show that it was acting with reasonable and loving forbearance against a stubborn, misguided opponent. The resulting clash of public images was accompanied by the development of remarkably subtle propaganda techniques. What had begun as the setting of a good example evolved during the duel between Anselm and Robert of Meulan into the creation of idealized models of correct behavior, publicized by the sophisticated molding of public opinion.

In the eleventh century, propaganda and its uses were still imperfectly understood. Kings and their panegyrists knew the value of a

2. GR 2:493.

good public reputation, as when William the Conqueror assumed the persona of Anglo-Saxon thaumaturgic kingship in 1066,[3] and when William of Poitiers celebrated the Conqueror's victory in England as that of a triumphant emperor of ancient Rome. Ideal images had been created before through saints' lives, and through royal biographies such as the *Vita Edwardi Regis* and the works of Asser and Einhard. These "public images," created for contemporary audiences and posterity, were almost always modeled on earlier exemplars — so much so that considerable gaps often existed between the idealized portrayals, shaped by literary conventions, and the actual persons being portrayed. But at the beginning of the twelfth century the Anglo-Norman world developed a heightened awareness of the value of the public image and a new sophistication in its promulgation. From tentative experiments in the use of public images in the reign of William Rufus, Anselm and Robert of Meulan developed the technique fully in the reign of Henry I, and most notably during the years of Anselm's second exile.

These years, 1103 – 6, witnessed not only the climax and resolution of the English Investiture Controversy but also Henry I's large-scale and ultimately successful campaign to conquer Normandy and reunite his father's cross-channel dominions. The two conflicts were closely interrelated, and their outcomes, as will be demonstrated in this chapter, were interdependent. Moreover, the controversy over investitures and Henry's struggle for Normandy were both characterized by the adroit use of propaganda.

The Normans had long been portraying their military aggressions as holy wars,[4] but never as elaborately as in 1104 – 6. Orderic "quotes" Henry I as afterward defending his conquest to Pope Calixtus II on a variety of plausible and related grounds: "I did not deprive my brother of the duchy of Normandy, but laid legal claim by battle to the just inheritance of our father, which my brother and nephew did not really possess themselves because villainous bandits and blasphemous scoundrels utterly wasted it."[5] Henry then pointed out that the church was especially victimized by these conditions: "No respect was shown to priests and other servants of God, but near paganism was rampant all over Normandy." He alluded to the destruction of monasteries, the

3. Douglas, *WC*, pp. 247–59.
4. David C. Douglas, *The Norman Achievement* (Berkeley and Los Angeles, 1969), pp. 89–109.
5. OV 6:284.

scattering of monks, the plundering and burning of churches, and the pleas of Norman churchmen that he intervene out of love of God. "So I was compelled to cross to Normandy, where I . . . saw with sorrow the affliction of my ancestral inheritance but could bring no help to the needy except by force of arms."[6] Not wishing "to refuse my service to holy mother Church . . . , with the help of God, who knows the good intent of my endeavors, I triumphed over my adversaries. . . . I recovered the inheritance of my father and all his dominions and strove to uphold my father's laws in accordance with God's will for the peace of his people."[7]

Orderic is thus portraying Henry, in words ascribed to the king himself, as a champion of justice and savior of the Norman churches, compelled by God and Christian duty to conquer Normandy and rule it as a *rex pacificus*. Embodied here is a conception of kingship closely akin to that articulated — again through Orderic — by Robert of Meulan. Henry is God's chosen steward of his father's kingdom, protector of church and people and emblem of justice, divinely empowered to use military might for the higher good of ultimate peace. God and God's servants commissioned him to fulfill his sacred duty to bring the entire Anglo-Norman patrimony to a state of tranquillity and due order.

Orderic asserts that the devastation of Normandy and its churches was real[8] and provides convincing proof that at least some of the claims he attributes to Henry were based on fact. But one must remember that all propaganda, to be effective, contains elements of truth — indeed, can be completely true. What makes information propaganda is the use to which it is put, as a public justification of policy. In Henry's speech to Curthose on the eve of the battle of Tinchebrai, Orderic intends to justify the royal military campaign as the act of a *rex pacificus*, a protector of the common welfare: "I have not come here, my brother, out of cupidity for any worldly lordship, nor do I aim at depriving you of the rights of your duchy; but in response to the tearful petitions of the poor I wish to help the Church of God, which, like a pilotless ship in a stormy sea, is in peril. In truth, you occupy the land like a barren tree, and offer no fruit of justice to our Creator."[9]

6. OV 6:284–86.
7. OV 6:286.
8. OV 6:32–36, 40–44, 46–48.
9. OV 6:86.

Interestingly, this passage almost echoes Anselm's earlier protestations of unwillingness to assume the archbishopric: "Some, as I have heard, suspect me of obtaining the archbishopric . . . through covetousness. . . . I was not drawn or bound to the archbishopric over the English by the desire of anything whatsoever which a servant of God, a despiser of the world, ought to spurn; but the fear of God compelled me to suffer myself to be dragged, although grieved and afraid, from [Bec]."[10] Elsewhere, Anselm states that he had accepted the archbishopric out of "religious necessity": "Thou knowest, and Thou be my witness, that . . . I know not how I could free myself from the design of those who elected me; and that Thy fear and love and the obedience which I owe to Thee and to Thy Church, compel me, bind me, so that I may not dare obstinately to contradict their religious entreaties and the great desire they manifest to me."[11] We can see here striking parallels between Henry's claims to have conquered Normandy because duty, God, and the prelates of the church bound him, and Anselm's statement that he accepted the archbishopric for essentially the same reasons.

Orderic believed that Henry was asserting these claims with justice on his side and fully approved of the concept of the strong *rex pacificus* acting forcefully to carry out his God-ordained stewardship of his patrimony in its time of need. Moreover, several pieces of evidence indicate that this interpretation was not merely Orderic's own view of Henry's motives but reflected an "official" view promulgated by the royal court. From the beginning of his reign Henry portrayed himself as a *rex pacificus,* a protector of the church and an upholder of ancient law. These concepts are set forth in the elaborate and unprecedented coronation charter that he issued on the occasion of his royal consecration, his anointing with the holy chrism that made him a priestlike king in the tradition of his royal predecessors.[12]

Two letters of Ivo of Chartres show that pleas to conquer the duchy and "save the Norman churches" were indeed reaching Henry. One was written to Henry, and a second to Robert of Meulan on the same subject urges Robert to persuade the king to correct a specific evil in Normandy: Ranulf Flambard's usurpation of the bishopric of Lisieux. It ends with these words: "Indeed it is not instituted to kings that they

10. AEp. 160: recorded in Lambeth ms. 59.
11. AEp. 156: recorded in Lambeth ms. 59.
12. *Regesta* 2, no. 488.

might break the laws; but that they might strike law-breakers by the sword, if they cannot otherwise correct them."[13] To ask Henry to intervene in a Norman affair "by the sword" was to advocate the conquest of Normandy. Ivo also implies that it is his duty to do so as an upholder of law.

William of Malmesbury reflects a view similar to Orderic's, without the association with the church: "Therefore, warned by the extreme evils, [the Normans] requested the strength of King Henry, imploring that he might succor the laboring fatherland. That man, aiding them according to the words of Cicero — 'If law is being violated, civic grace is being violated; practice piety by other things' — sent men into Normandy so that he might lend his hand to laboring justice."[14]

These accounts reflect a point of view closely resembling Henry's own. In a letter to Anselm reporting the royal victory at Tinchebrai, Henry expressed the hope that his victory "may lead to the initiation of good works and the service of God, and to the preserving and strengthening of God's holy church in peace and tranquillity, so that she can live at liberty and not be shaken by any storms of war."[15]

This hope was translated into royal policy in the aftermath of Tinchebrai, when even Eadmer described Normandy as having been "set in order under the king's peace."[16] Orderic reports that Henry summoned a great council of Norman magnates and prelates at Lisieux less than a month after his victory and decreed "by royal authority" (regali sanctione) that peace and strict justice should be firmly established throughout the duchy and that all churches should have their lost possessions restored.[17] John LePatourel has aptly observed that these decrees "seem almost to suggest the promises of the coronation oath."[18] Henry thus appears to have displayed with some consistency the public image of the peacekeeping king who protected the church and enforced good laws, and such was the image reflected in the works of most chroniclers of his reign. The image was based on long-established traditions of good kingship, but under Henry I it was promulgated with

13. PL 162: Epp. 154, 155.
14. GR 2:462.
15. AEp. 401; cf. Orderic's above-quoted rendition of Henry's speech before the battle of Tinchebrai, in which the storm metaphor occurs in an identical context: above, Chapter 6 at nn. 80–81.
16. HN 184.
17. OV 6:92–94; cf. 6:98, 136–38.
18. Norman Empire, p. 237.

unparalleled skill and coherence. Furthermore, it bears an unmistak-able resemblance to the approach to royal policy attributed by William of Malmesbury to Robert of Meulan: "The persuader of peace, the dissuader of strife, . . . the supporter of justice; in war the insurer of victory; urging his lord the king rigorously to enforce the law; and himself not only abiding by existing laws but proposing new ones."[19]

As we have seen, Anselm was equally sensitive to the importance of an unblemished reputation. He was at pains "never under any circum-stances to incur the slightest touch of reproach,"[20] and always to inspire "the weak brethren in God's church . . . by word and exam-ple."[21] As primate of Britain, he was thus determined not only to devote his life to God and the reform of God's church but also to be perceived as a model Christian prelate. The latter intention meant edifying others, present and future, by the faultlessness of his own public conduct. To this end Anselm endeavored to shape the public record of his archiepis-copate by excluding certain data from the collection of his correspon-dence transcribed and preserved at Canterbury.[22] Like other medieval letter-writers, he usually preferred to leave matters of political detail to the words of his messengers: "As to my present position in England I leave it to the bearers of this letter to explain more fully by word of mouth."[23] To Anselm, such details were of mere passing interest and best not committed to writing for the instruction of others. They could only confuse and distort the ideal reality, blurring the image that An-selm felt duty-bound to project as a model of Christian shepherd-hood.

Anselm's conception of the model prelate was in keeping with his theological principle of "degrees of reality." Following Augustine, Anselm held that the more perfect a thing is, the more real it is. Mutable things do not truly exist; "if something is true, it can only be so by virtue of its accordance with an eternal truth," or a model existing in the mind of God.[24] Created beings can therefore be said to be "true" only insofar as they correspond to an archetypal form in the Divine Mind.[25] Adapting this vision of reality to his own archiepiscopal office,

19. GR 2:483.
20. HN 154.
21. AEp. 160; above, Chapter 1 at nn. 44–45.
22. Above, Chapter 4 at nn. 84–128.
23. AEp. 217; similarly, for example, AEpp. 164, 214, 338, 357, 388, 389, 462.
24. Hopkins, Companion to the Study of St. Anselm, pp. 18–20.
25. Ibid., p. 20.

Anselm quite naturally came to regard his conduct as "true" or "untrue" depending on how perfectly he conformed to the model of correct archiepiscopal behavior as defined by divinely guided ecclesiastical law and custom, and the Canterbury tradition.

At a much simpler level Eadmer too, as Anselm's panegyrist, was intent on picturing him as a model prelate. But Eadmer and Anselm were not always *en rapport* on the use of historical data to create an idealized portrait. Anselm once discovered Eadmer at work on his biography and ordered him to destroy it. Being an obedient Benedictine, Eadmer of course did so, but not before making a copy.[26] Thus, a comparison of Eadmer's *Vita Anselmi* and *Historia Novorum* with Anselm's correspondence can sometimes disclose important matters that neither alone would have revealed.

Anselm remained in exile in Lyon from December 1103 to April 1105, while Henry and Robert of Meulan continued to strive for the allegiances of Norman magnates and neighboring princes. These efforts at alliance building were aided by the widespread use of diplomatic bribes funded by English taxes,[27] but their success also depended on Henry's being perceived by the church and the nobility as a good and just prince who would correct the wrongs permitted by Curthose. Perceptions of Henry would not have been altogether unaffected by his treatment of Anselm, who could count a great many friends among the nobility and clergy of the duchy and its surrounding regions.

Henry received his first warning signal in the letter of Paschal II dated 23 November 1103, which William Warelwast had obtained from the pope after Anselm's departure from Rome: "Consider, my dearest son, whether it redounds to your credit or discredit that the most learned and religious of all the English bishops, Anselm bishop of Canterbury, is afraid on this account to stay at your side or live in your kingdom. Those who had up to now heard such good things of you, what will they now think of you, what will they say, when this is published abroad?"[28]

Anselm had every intention of placing the blame for his exile squarely on Henry and of publicizing the matter as widely as possible. His first

26. Southern, *Anselm*, p. 315.
27. *ASC*, A.D. 1103, 1104, 1105; Florence, 2:54.
28. AEp. 305; above, Chapter 6 at n. 231. It is curious that Eadmer substitutes "Gallicanorum" for "Anglorum" in quoting this letter (*HN* 156), thereby inflating Paschal's praise.

letter to Henry from exile, explicitly intended to be publicized, is an astute work of self-justification. In the address clause Anselm offers his prayers and faithful service to "his honored lord, Henry, king of the English."[29] The letter next provides an account of Anselm's visit to Rome, emphasizing his service to the king in presenting the royal case to Paschal. He makes the point that Paschal, in insisting on the investiture ban, was only following the decrees of his predecessors. This statement had the effect of casting the pope's position in the same terms that Henry was using by insisting that Anselm could return to England only if he would follow the customs of Lanfranc and William I. Amid protestations of love, goodwill, and readiness to serve the king faithfully and fulfill the obligations of his office toward the English people, Anselm makes it clear that he had been commanded by the pope to obey the decrees, explicitly described (and now perhaps for the first time clearly and unequivocally made public in England), and thus cannot adhere to the usages of his predecessor Lanfranc. He presents himself as a conscientious and holy man, completely at the king's mercy. The decision is Henry's as is the blame for any untoward results: "I am prepared to render the service of my office faithfully and to the best of my ability and knowledge, subject always to obedience to the rule of the church. But if it is not your pleasure that this should be so, then if any detriment to human souls should result, I think it will not be my fault."[30]

Unknown to the king, Anselm sent copies of this letter to both Gundulf of Rochester and Ernulf prior of Canterbury with meticulous instructions as to how it should be publicized. The letter to the king, protected from scrutiny by Anselm's seal, was first sent to Gundulf along with a copy that Anselm instructed Gundulf to show secretly to William Warelwast on his return to England: "And see to it that nobody besides William, excepting only our prior, is aware of that letter before it is given to the king."[31] Once William Warelwast had seen the copy, Gundulf was to deliver the original to Henry I: "And if it should please him to answer me by letter, send his reply to me by the same

29. AEp. 308.

30. AEp. 308; above, Chapter 6 at n. 211.

31. AEp. 306: Anselm to Gundulf: the purpose of confiding in William Warelwast may well have been to make certain that he would corroborate Anselm's account of the events at the papal court: "Horum omnium testis potest esse praedictus Willelmus, si vult" (AEp. 308). Malmesbury hints that Warelwast may have been more sympathetic to Anselm's cause than other royal *curiales: GR* 2:492.

messenger [that delivered Anselm's letters to Gundulf]. If he does not wish to reply in writing, tell me in your letter what his answer is. . . . After the king is acquainted with my letter, make it known to the bishops and other persons. . . . I send you a copy of the letter I am addressing to the king."[32] Anselm gave similar though less elaborate instructions to Ernulf, telling him to keep his copy of the letter to Henry I a secret until he learned what Henry's response was: "After you discover that, I think it good that the copy which I sent you should be shown publicly."[33]

But Anselm's effort to publicize the righteousness of his position was considerably deflected by the royal court's counterpropaganda campaign. The royalist propaganda continued to portray a godly king protecting his ancestral customs against a primate who unjustly sought to deprive him of them. As the exile dragged on, the royalists added the further accusation that Anselm by his intransigence was wrongfully abdicating the leadership of the English church and thereby exposing it to countless evils. The importance of Henry's retaining a faultless public image increased as his plan to conquer Normandy moved forward. In mid-1104 Robert Curthose precipitated an open break with the king by coming to terms with Robert of Bellême.[34] Shortly afterward William count of Mortain and earl of Cornwall broke with Henry and joined forces with Curthose and Robert of Bellême in Normandy; he thereby suffered the forfeiture of his English honor.[35] With the stage being set for the climactic struggle for the duchy, Henry sought to increase his revenues sharply, but without compromising his reputation as God's steward of England and savior of Normandy.

The king's normal income was radically insufficient to meet the massive expenses of buying allies and mounting a major military campaign. To Henry I, no less than to Rufus, the revenues of Canterbury constituted a significant contribution to the royal war chest.[36] But unlike Rufus, Henry acted with circumspection. Having confiscated the Canterbury lands, he assigned the collection of their revenues not to some unscrupulous royal agent but to two of Anselm's own men — thus conveying the impression that he intended them to act gently, to refrain

32. AEp. 306.
33. AEp. 307.
34. ASC, A.D. 1104; OV 6:46.
35. ASC, A.D. 1104; GR 2:473–74.
36. Henry's revenues were also enhanced by severe and extraordinary taxes in 1103, 1104, and 1105: ASC.

from harassing the monks or laying waste to their lands.[37] Eadmer hints darkly that the two collectors (unnamed) observed no such restraint, but the blame fell on them rather than on Henry.

Similarly, in his answer to Anselm's first letter from exile, Henry deftly shifted the responsibility back to the archbishop. He offered "greetings and friendship" and grieved that Anselm refused to be with him "like your predecessor Lanfranc was with my father for many years."[38] If only Anselm would consent to emulate Lanfranc, Henry would grant "all those honors and dignities and friendships that my father gave to your predecessor." The king promised to send another embassy to consult with the pope and afterward to settle matters in such a way as God would direct. In the meantime Henry regretfully consented to permit Anselm to withdraw from the benefice of Canterbury — a subtle acknowledgement that the Canterbury lands had been confiscated, but only because Anselm declined to resume their lordship. "I do this unwillingly," Henry added, "because I would wish to have no mortal man with me in my kingdom more willingly than you."[39]

Henry's self-portrait as a good and patient king confronted with an unreasonable archbishop seems to have been persuasive, not only among the English magnates and prelates, but also within the Canterbury community itself. The Canterbury monk Ordwi reported that Anselm was being attacked by false accounts on the charges of forbidding the king's ancestral right to grant investitures and permitting wicked clerks and even laymen to usurp and ravage English churches.[40] Anselm's own prior, Ernulf, pleaded with him to return, reproaching him for having abandoned his community and the Church of England for no reason except a word from William Warelwast.[41] Anselm answered these and other letters with patient and reasoned explanations of his position. He understood well enough why the Canterbury monks might regard themselves as having been abandoned. They had suffered greatly during the vacancy of 1089–93 and the exile of 1097–1100, and the issue of lay investiture meant far less to them than the immediate burden of royal exploitation and the aggressions of neighboring landholders.

37. *HN* 159.
38. AEp. 318.
39. AEp. 318.
40. AEp. 327.
41. AEp. 310: absent from Lambeth ms. 59 but transcribed in Eadmer's *Historia Novorum*, pp. 160–62.

Anselm replied that far more was at stake than the monks seemed to realize. To Ordwi he explained that he deplored and firmly opposed the exploitation of churches by laymen or avaricious clerks, and that the ban on lay investiture was a product not of his own intitiative but of Paschal's mandate.[42] To Ernulf and the Canterbury community he urged that they look beyond their present tribulations and consider the larger issues: "Do not let your present sufferings terrify or disturb you excessively."[43] He reminded them that he could not return on Henry's terms without betraying his obedience to the papacy, and that if he were to return on his own terms he would be under papal constraint to avoid all contact with wrongfully invested prelates. He could not, therefore, attend the royal court when such prelates were present and would be forced to absent himself from crown-wearing ceremonies. If the king should choose to be crowned by another prelate, Anselm's presence in the kingdom would create the impression that he was condoning the transfer of a vital Canterbury prerogative to another church.[44] This shift of emphasis from investitures to the dignity of Canterbury and the menace of York was an adept strategem to capture the attention and support of the Christ Church community. As always, Anselm was able to discern every facet of a political situation and, looking beyond the problems of the moment, to "keep his eyes fixed upon the lodestar of a single end."[45]

Queen Matilda, as one of Anselm's spiritual daughters, added her voice to the chorus pleading for his return. In a letter that blended impassioned devotion with political calculation, she begged him to soften his iron soul, to eschew no longer the ways of his archiepiscopal predecessors, and to cease challenging the customs on which the king's majesty depended. Woven around these restatements of royal doctrine are phrases expressing her enduring love toward the archbishop and her ardent longing to see him once more. Anselm is her soul, her joy, and her refuge; for him she would relinquish her royal dignity and crown, trample on her purple and satin raiment, and rush to him exhausted by grief.[46] Anselm replied to the queen's affectionate outpourings in a tone

42. AEp. 327.
43. AEp. 349.
44. AEp. 311.
45. Knowles, *Monastic Order,* p. 142; the notion that Anselm actually enjoyed his exiles is at odds with his own repeated allusions to his "grievous hardships" and "tribulations": AEpp. 217, 220, 338, 390; cf. *HN* 128.
46. AEp. 317.

of courteous restraint.[47] He clearly regarded his correspondence with Matilda as an aspect of his propaganda duel with the royal court.

Answering Henry I's letter, Anselm prepared a carefully worded, point-by-point response. He thanked the king for his expressions of kindness and goodwill and reciprocated in full measure: "Indeed, with no other king or prince on earth would I so willingly live, no other so willingly serve."[48] But the archbishop held firmly to his position: "Neither at my baptism nor at any of my ordinations did I promise to follow any law or customs of your father or Lanfranc, but only the law of God and of all the ordinations I have received." Anselm will willingly return, but only if Henry permits him to live by the law of God and the customs of his archiepiscopate, and only if everything confiscated from the Church of Canterbury is fully restored. If Henry should continue to grant investitures and hold the Canterbury lands, he would be acting in direct disobedience to God's will. "And for no man is it more necessary to obey God's law than for the king, nor does anyone disregard God's law at greater peril. For it is said, not by me but by Holy Scripture, 'mighty men shall be mightily tormented' — from which may God spare you." Anselm chides Henry for his previous ambiguities and evasions, which amount to nothing "except — if I can venture to say it — a certain pretext for delay." Henry is then warned that further delay will force Anselm to appeal his case to God — implying that the king might be faced with excommunication either by the pope, on Anselm's petition, or by Anselm himself. The letter closes with a prayer for Henry's soul: "May almighty God bend your inclinations to his will, so that after this life he may bring you into his glory."

In an apparently concurrent letter instructing Gundulf to press the king for his reply, Anselm again provided detailed instructions on how to deal with all possible royal responses.[49] If Henry chose to send Anselm a sealed letter, well and good. If not, Gundulf was to inform Anselm by letter of the king's verbal reply. If Henry chose to delay his response, Anselm would accept the delay only on condition that the Canterbury lands be restored. If Henry refused to restore the lands, Gundulf was to inform him that Anselm would thereupon regard himself as a bishop disseised without legal judgment.

47. AEpp. 346–47.
48. AEp. 319.
49. AEp. 316.

This last threat embodied a legal principle that carried considerable weight. At the time that Rufus had seized the lands of Canterbury in 1097, Anselm had himself sought exile and had been granted it by the king and his bishops and barons.[50] But Henry, against all justice, had high-handedly refused to permit Anselm's return except on the king's own terms, allowing him no opportunity to defend himself at court and bypassing the feudal custom of judgment by the king's magnates and prelates.[51] Even such persons as Ranulf Flambard and Robert of Bellême had been disseised only after a court hearing, and William of Mortain had lost his English lands through legal proceedings.[52] Anselm was thus threatening to darken Henry's reputation by branding him as a monarch who violated ecclesiastical rights and feudal customs.

If Henry replied to Anselm's threats, the letter has not survived. But the rumors of impending ecclesiastical sanctions appear to have spurred the king to action.[53] When his subjects urged him to heal the ills of the English church by recalling Anselm, Henry declared that what they were asking "was the very thing that he himself quite independently was anxious to bring about" — if only Anselm would accept the king's ancestral customs.[54] To accomplish this goal, Henry sent another legation to Rome, but without success. Since Henry and Robert of Meulan must by then have been fully aware of Paschal's unyielding stance on investitures, the purpose of the mission can only have been to delay matters still further while maneuvering to win allies in Normandy.

It was probably at this juncture, too, that Queen Matilda wrote a second letter to Anselm.[55] Amid elaborate expressions of love and undying devotion, Matilda assured her "pious and honorable father and worthy reverend lord" that the mind of the king is more composed toward him than many men estimate. The point of the letter was to announce that, at the queen's urging, Henry had restored some of the Canterbury revenues to Anselm and had promised to return the rest at some appropriate (but undisclosed) time. She implores Anselm to grant Henry in return "the sweetness of your love," eschewing the rancor of

50. *HN* 79–86; above, Chapter 5 at nn. 252–59.

51. Recall, however, Anselm's contention at Rockingham in 1095 that the primate was immune to such judgment: above, Chapter 5 at n. 162.

52. AEp. 214; OV 6:12, 20; *GR* 2:473–74.

53. On the rumor that Anselm intended to excommunicate Henry, see AEp. 310: Ernulf to Anselm.

54. *HN* 162.   55. AEp. 320.

human bitterness, "which is so unlike you," and to intercede with God for the king and queen and the welfare of their kingdom. Anselm replied lovingly but firmly that, while he was grateful for Matilda's intercession with respect to the Canterbury lands, Henry could be reconciled to God only when he had restored all the properties confiscated from the archbishopric.[56] Anselm denied harboring rancor toward anyone and declared that he had until then always interceded with God on behalf of Henry, Matilda, and their kingdom: "But as for the future," he concluded ominously, "I commit myself to the disposition of God."

The royal court reacted to Anselm's cautiously phrased threats and accusations by promulgating even more disparaging rumors about him. In his second letter to Henry from exile, Anselm had denied ever having promised to follow the customs of William I and Lanfranc but only the law of God.[57] This statement was reinterpreted at Henry's court as a boast on Anselm's part that, whereas he had always obeyed God, William I and Archbishop Lanfranc "had lived wickedly outside God's law."[58] The accusation seems to have had considerable impact on the Anglo-Norman nobility, who revered both figures and are described as being much disturbed at what was portrayed as Anselm's "intemperate behavior."[59] Anselm himself was infuriated at the suggestion that he was defaming his beloved mentor. Based on reports from inside Henry's court he attributed the accusation to the king's chief counselor. Feigning to be unaware of the counselor's identity, however, he permitted himself for once to abandon his attitude of long-suffering kindliness and to lash out at a purportedly anonymous enemy. To Queen Matilda Anselm wrote, "For as I heard, the king received my letter kindly at first, but afterward someone, I know not who, excited him against me with spiteful and deceitful intention by a wrongful interpretation. Who that person may be I do not know, but I am certain of this: that either he does not love his Lord or does not know *how* to love him."[60] The archbishop complained to Gundulf in similar terms: "I know not who it is that with evil intention, out of the malice of his

56. AEp. 321.
57. AEp. 319; above, Chapter 7 at nn. 48–49.
58. AEp. 330.
59. AEp. 329.
60. AEp. 329: for additional allusions to the topos of evil counselors see AEpp. 228 (Anselm to Henry I); 246 (Anselm to Queen Matilda); and 265 (Anselm to Henry I).

heart," misinterpreted Anselm's letter to the king. "Now surely the mind of whoever says that thing is either very wicked or very small."[61]

This battle of public images was accompanied by Henry's continued hints that he was seeking an accommodation with Anselm. In the letter to Gundulf just quoted,[62] which was written sometime in September 1104, Anselm alluded to an important message that Henry had promised to send him at Lyon in time for Anselm's answer to be considered by the king's Michaelmas court. But now Michaelmas was drawing near and Henry's message had not yet reached Anselm.[63] Henry's policy of ambiguous promises and interminable delays had by now exhausted Anselm's patience. As he stated to Gundulf in the September letter, "I will neither cause nor accept further delay before beginning to take the counsel of God and his church as to what should be done."

Anselm's haste in September 1104 was almost surely a response to Henry's notable success in expanding his power in Normandy. The king's carefully fostered image as the savior of the Norman churches was obviously vulnerable to any major ecclesiastical sanction that Anselm or Paschal might launch against him. Henry's anxiety to postpone such action had doubtlessly prompted him to restore some of the Canterbury revenues and to promise further negotiations with Anselm and Paschal.[64] Henry and Robert of Meulan probably reasoned that promises alone would deter the threat of excommunication until Normandy had been won. Anselm, however, was well aware that excommunications must be delicately timed, and that the excommunication of a well-entrenched king would be "despised and ridiculed" by his subjects.[65] As a prelate who had assumed responsibility for the defense of southeastern England against an invasion threat in 1095, and had camped with his knights in the field at the time of Curthose's invasion

61. AEp. 330: Anselm was fully aware that the architect of Henry's strategies was Robert of Meulan, whom Eadmer identifies as "the person by whose advice the king directs his actions in all matters of policy": *HN* 170; cf. AEp. 361: Paschal to Robert of Meulan: "They who know about you declare that nearly alone . . . you persuade the king to fight against the church." Robert was subsequently the only person to be identified by name in Paschal's letter excommunicating Henry I's counselors: AEp. 353.

62. AEp. 330.

63. Apparently Henry's promised messenger, the royal chaplain Everard, never arrived: AEp. 331.

64. AEp. 353, on Henry's promise to send an embassy to Paschal's 1105 Lenten Synod; the embassy apparently never arrived.

65. AEp. 210; above, Chapter 5 at nn. 297–98. Recall the effective timing of Anselm's excommunication threat against Robert Curthose in 1101: above, Chapter 6 at nn. 88–93.

of 1101,[66] Anselm was no stranger to military affairs. Nor had his exile put him out of touch with Anglo-Norman politics. Gundulf and other churchmen were keeping him closely informed of developments at Henry's court,[67] and his involvement in Norman politics is suggested by his letter to William Giffard, elect of Winchester, urging him not to betray one of his Norman castles to the king as so many others were doing.[68] In a letter to Canterbury, Anselm spoke of England's tribulations "which I know of by rumors flying in many directions."[69]

Yet Anselm's position was delicate. Like most contemporary churchmen he deplored anarchic conditions such as Curthose's rule permitted and admired the strong peacekeeping governance of Henry I.[70] Anselm's years at Bec would have left him deeply sensitive to the plight of the Norman churches on which Henry's propagandists were dwelling. But if Henry were permitted to complete his conquest while Paschal and Anselm dozed, the king would be most unlikely to concede investitures thereafter. And by September 1104, when Anselm announced his refusal to accept further delays, Henry's grip on Normandy was swiftly tightening.

Earlier in the year, after Curthose and Robert of Bellême had entered into their formal alliance, Henry had sent Robert of Meulan and other important magnates to Normandy, where they joined with the royal partisans in the duchy and harassed the duke with ravaging and burning.[71] Later that summer Henry himself crossed peacefully to Normandy where he visited his stronghold of Domfront and other fortresses under his control.[72] He was welcomed in the duchy by Robert of Meulan and a great number of other Norman landholders whom Robert had won over to his cause at the conclusion of the Breteuil succession dispute of the previous year.[73] Summoning Curthose to a conference, Henry accused him of having broken the treaty of 1101 by making peace with Robert of Bellême and other magnates without

66. Above, Chapter 6 at nn. 77–80.
67. E.g., AEpp. 330, 337. Anselm continued to attend to Canterbury affairs while at Lyon: AEpp. 331, 358–60.
68. AEp. 322; cf. ASC, A.D. 1104. William Giffard had accompanied Anselm to Rome in 1103: Florence, 2:52.
69. AEp. 357; cf. AEp. 355 to the same effect.
70. For Anselm's view on the importance of the king's peacekeeping role, see, for example, his letters to Alexander king of Scots and Murchertach king of Munster: AEpp. 413, 427.
71. ASC, A.D. 1104; HA 234; cf. OV 6:56.
72. OV 6:56.
73. Above, Chapter 6 at nn. 178–84.

consulting the king, and of granting Robert of Bellême his ancestral dominions contrary to the royal-ducal agreement to act jointly against traitors. This justification was altogether in keeping with the public image that Henry had assumed, but the royal presence in Normandy was probably intended, in concrete terms, to discourage the Bellême-Mortain alliance from impeding the growth of the king's party, which was gradually coming to include most of the major Norman lords. Henry and Robert of Meulan may have been aiming at what amounted to a bloodless coup.

Seriously alarmed, Curthose made an immediate peace with his brother and granted him lordship over the ducal *fidelis,* William count of Evreux. Orderic's account reveals that the peace was sealed by a symbolic public ceremony in which William of Evreux did homage to Henry after uttering these words: "I love the king and the duke. Indeed both are sons of my lord the king, and I desire to revere them both; but I will do homage to one, and him I will serve as my lawful lord."[74] Orderic reports that "this speech by the noble count was applauded by everyone."[75] William had epitomized the dilemma of most of the Anglo-Norman baronage owing homage to two rival lords, and the solution of renouncing homage to one in favor of the other appears at this point to have been accepted. Significantly, the count of Evreux was primarily a Norman lord with few English ties. Thus he would serve as a model not only for cross-channel barons, but also for exclusively Norman magnates.

Curthose was in a precarious position. Orderic's account implies that, besides winning the allegiance of the count of Evreux, Henry had taken over important administrative functions in the duchy. He and his nobles had established regulations "for the common safety of the province."[76] Indeed Orderic describes Curthose's meeting with Henry in the context of a royal tribunal judging the offenses of a wayward duke. With the concession of Evreux, Curthose managed to placate Henry and the two brothers parted in peace. On the king's return to England "before winter," Normandy lapsed once more into anarchy. Henry may well have been convinced by then that a second show of force would win him the entire duchy with little or no bloodshed, relegating Curthose to the role of a figurehead to be deposed eventually

74. OV 6:58.
75. Ibid.
76. Ibid.

or bought off. Henry might thus be received in Normandy as God's instrument for the bringing of peace and order to the long-tormented principality. The plan bears the imprint of Robert of Meulan, who was primarily responsible for winning over the lords of Normandy and the Vexin, and who had publicly advocated the securing of the common utility and safety of the realm without the shedding of Christian blood.[77] By autumn 1104, this policy seemed to be largely succeeding but for the resistance of Robert of Bellême and William of Mortain, and the refusal of Anselm to countenance further delay in the resolution of the Investiture Controversy.

It was very likely in response to Henry's 1104 incursion into Normandy that Anselm sent his trusted friend Baldwin of Tournai on a mission to Rome to inform the pope of the situation in the duchy and the urgent need for prompt countermeasures. In an accompanying letter to Paschal, Anselm referred to his dispute with Henry only in general terms, leaving all details to Baldwin's verbal testimony.[78] This mission's importance is suggested by Anselm's concurrent letter addressed jointly to his two closest friends among the cardinals, the papal chancellor John of Gaeta and John bishop of Tusculum, Anselm's former student at Bec, imploring them to support Baldwin's petition and defend the archiepiscopal cause.[79] A letter from Matilda countess of Tuscany urging Paschal to give Anselm's case his full and immediate backing is almost surely a response to a similar, concurrent letter from Anselm.[80] That Baldwin's mission was the consummation of Anselm's threat to appeal his case to God is suggested by the unaccustomed ardor of his letter to Paschal on that occasion: "This only I write: that because of the obedience of you and your predecessors and the liberty of the church, which I am unwilling to repudiate, I am despoiled, an exile from the bishopric and its possessions. In which matter your prudence requires neither our prayers nor our counsel."[81]

On his return to Lyon, Baldwin reported to Anselm that the mission had moved the pope to take action: Anselm's case against Henry would

---

77. On Robert's advice, Henry had succeeded in securing England in 1101 without bloodshed, for no battles ever occurred. See above, Chapter 6 at nn. 88–93.

78. AEp. 338.

79. AEp. 339.

80. AEp. 350; in 1103 Anselm and his companions had traveled from Rome to Piacenza "with an escort provided by the noble Countess Matilda": HN 155; cf. AEp. 325, Anselm to Countess Matilda, "his lady and mother in God," thanking her for the escort and reporting that he is sending her a copy of his *Orationes sive Meditationes*.

81. AEp. 338.

be heard at the pope's Lenten synod of 1105, and Paschal was informing the king of this decision.[82] Paschal's letter to Henry, prompted by
Baldwin's mission, is dated 23 December 1104.[83] Paschal wishes Henry
"health, honor, and victory" (*victoria*) — the last of which may well
refer to the Norman campaign. He invites Henry to send envoys to the
forthcoming Lenten synod, where Anselm's charges against him would
be judged. Warning Henry against heeding the advice of evil counselors,
Paschal chides him for forbidding Anselm's return to England except in
defiance of God, and for despoiling his church. The letter is polite, even
solicitous, but it contains the unmistakable threat that unless Henry
relented on investitures he would face excommunication: "Whoever
desires not the grace of Christ will feel the sword of Christ."

    In the wake of Baldwin's late-1104 visit to Rome, papal activity with
regard to England suddenly accelerated. Paschal's letter to Henry of
23 December was followed by a still stronger letter, undated, which
Paschal must have written early in 1105: "Behold, for the third time
we are forced to send you a letter of warning." Unless Henry readmitted
Anselm and ceased investing prelates, he and his counselors would be
"struck with the sword of anathema."[84] At about the same time
Paschal wrote a menacing letter to Robert of Meulan challenging the
credibility of Robert's earlier promise (in a letter now lost) to uphold the
papal interests at Henry's court as an ally of St. Peter: "Those who
know about you relate far otherwise," Paschal charged. "Alone before
the rest you persuade the king of England to fight the Roman church in
the case of investitures."[85] The letter closes with a threat of excommunication unless Robert obeyed God and his church. Paschal also fired off
a strong letter to Queen Matilda, urging her to persuade the king to
cease listening to "depraved counselors"; otherwise, Henry and his
counselors alike would be struck with anathema.[86] It seems very likely
that Anselm himself had provided Paschal with the information that
both Robert of Meulan and Queen Matilda were persons of great
influence in the royal counsels.

    The absence of Henry's envoys from the 1105 Lenten synod
prompted Paschal to act. In a letter of 26 March 1105, he informed

82. AEp. 349.
83. AEp. 348.
84. AEp. 351.
85. AEp. 361; misdated by Schmitt. The letter clearly antedates AEp. 353, 26 March
1105, in which Robert is excommunicated.
86. AEp. 352.

Anselm that, with the synod's unanimous concurrence, the doors of the church had been closed to Henry's chief adviser, Robert count of Meulan, along with his fellow counselors (unnamed) and all prelates whom the king had invested. "But sentence upon the king has been held over, because he is due to send his envoys to us at the coming Easter time" (9 April).[87] Paschal sent a concurrent letter to Gerard archbishop of York, commanding him to publicize the excommunications throughout England.[88]

The chronology of the three papal warnings to Henry and the excommunications is of exceptional interest. Paschal seems to have interpreted his relatively friendly letter to Henry I of 23 November 1103 as the first such warning.[89] The so-called second warning, dated 23 December 1104, came after a lapse of thirteen months — a period that witnessed Henry's Norman sojourn of 1104, his preparations for a major military campaign to be launched aginst Curthose in 1105, and Baldwin of Tournai's mission to Rome. The third and final warning, undated, was followed by the excommunications of the 1105 Lenten synod, announced in Paschal's letter of 26 March. Since it took some ten or twelve weeks for messages to be exchanged between England and Rome,[90] Henry could not possibly have responded to both the second and third warnings in time for Paschal's March synod. Having procrastinated through most of 1104, Paschal had launched the two final warnings and the excommunications within a period of three months. Only important new developments could have impelled Paschal suddenly to move in such haste, and these must have been related to him by Baldwin in late 1104.

Henry probably had received only Paschal's "second" letter of warning when he went to Romsey Abbey on 13 February 1105, *in transitu,* openly preparing to cross the Channel.[91] A great number of his magnates were with him, doubtless leaders of the army he was

87. AEp. 353: "in praeteriti Paschae tempore" in the Canterbury mss. should be corrected to read "in praesenti Paschae tempore": *Councils and Synods* 1, pt. 2: 660 and n. 1; on the Lenten Synod of 1105, see Blumenthal, *Early Councils of Paschal II,* pp. 23–31.

88. AEp. 354.

89. AEp. 305; Chapter 7 at nn. 27–28, and Chapter 6 at nn. 227–30. William of Malmesbury (*GR* 2:474) alludes rather vaguely to the existence ("ut aiunt") of another letter from Paschal urging Henry to conquer Normandy, but no such letter has survived, nor can it be believed that Paschal would ever have conveyed such a message except possibly in the form of ambiguous and subtle hints.

90. R. L. Poole, *Studies in Chronology,* p. 264.

91. *Regesta* 2, no. 682.

taking to Normandy.[92] Robert of Meulan, not among them, was probably already in Normandy preparing the way for the invasion. Early in April Henry landed unopposed at Barfleur in the Cotentin and then proceeded down the peninsula to Carentan, where he celebrated Easter (9 April) with Robert of Meulan once more at his side. Here Orderic attributes to Serlo bishop of Séez an Easter sermon epitomizing Henry's justification for the conquest:

All Normandy, dominated by Godless bandits, is without a true ruler, . . . a just protector. . . . Rise up boldly in the name of God, win the heritage of your fathers with the sword of justice, and rescue your ancestral land and the people of God from the hands of reprobates. . . . Your brother does not truly hold Normandy, nor does he govern the people as a duke ought, leading them along the path of righteousness. . . . Just king, in this dire distress of your native land, be angry to some purpose and, as David, prophet and king, teaches, "sin not" by taking up arms not for lust of earthly power but for the defense of your country.[93]

To heighten the image of the just *rex pacificus* and the protector of the church, Serlo engaged in a counterportrait of Curthose designed to highlight the duke's unworthiness to rule in contrast to Henry's virtues, and obviously much exaggerated:

Sunk in lethargy [Curthose] is dominated by . . . men of little worth. Sad to relate, he squanders the wealth of a great duchy on trifles and follies, while he himself often fasts until noon for lack of bread. Often he dares not rise from his bed, and cannot attend church, because he is naked and has no breeches, socks, or shoes. Indeed the jesters and harlots who constantly keep company with him steal his clothes at night while he lies snoring in drunken sleep, and guffaw as they boast that they have robbed the duke. So, when the head is sick, the whole body is afflicted; when the ruler is foolish, the whole province is in danger, and the wretched people suffer utter deprivation.[94]

This public demonstration of Henry's right to rule Normandy was probably staged deliberately on the holiest day of the Christian calendar. The king was thus inspired, so Orderic reports, "to undertake the conquest to restore peace and tranquillity to the church. The count of Meulan supported the resolution, and none of the nobles dissented from it." The ceremony was crowned by a public display of Henry's piety. The king and the count of Meulan led all the royal followers in

92. Ibid., nos. 682–87 (witness lists).
93. OV 6:60–66.
94. Ibid.

permitting Bishop Serlo to cut off their long hair,[95] which was regarded as a mark of decadence by reform churchmen of the time (including Anselm).[96] This bit of theatrics provided a vivid public display of Henry's role as God's agent in the deliverance of tormented Normandy. Nobody in the royal entourage could yet have known that Robert of Meulan had already been excommunicated by the pope, or that Anselm was about to launch a withering assault on Henry's godly image.

About mid-April Anselm received Paschal's letter of 26 March announcing the excommunication of Robert of Meulan. By then Anselm would have been well aware of Henry's 1105 campaign; among the many people who had been at the king's court at Romsey the previous February *in transitu* was Anselm's good friend and correspondent William Giffard, elect of Winchester. Eadmer reports that "on the king's arrival [in early April] almost all the principal Normans, deserting their lord the duke . . . , came rushing after the king's gold and silver and delivered towns, cities, and castles to him."[97] By about mid-April Henry and his army had burned and captured Bayeux, and shortly thereafter the inhabitants of Caen opened their gates to him.[98]

Historians have long been puzzled by Eadmer's account of Anselm's reaction to the papal letter excommunicating the royal advisers. On receiving it, Eadmer relates, "Anselm saw the uselessness of waiting longer in Lyon for any help from Rome, especially since he had already repeatedly sent messengers and letters to the pope . . . and thus far had obtained nothing from him except, from time to time, some kind of comforting promises. Further, he had for the third time written to the king of the English asking for the return of his property."[99] The papal excommunication of royal counselors was surely more than a comforting promise; it was the traditional prelude to the excommunication of the king himself. Paschal had taken a decisive step, and he had expressed his intention to take up the case of Henry himself two weeks thereafter at Easter. But with Henry's Norman campaign progressing so swiftly, it was not enough. After consulting with his old friend and host,

95. Ibid.
96. E.g., cap. 24 of Anselm's 1102 Westminster Council: *Councils and Synods* 1, pt. 2: 677–78; cf. AEp. 365.
97. *HN* 165; similarly, Florence, 2:54; *HA* 235.
98. OV 6:78; Florence, 2:53–54; *ASC*, A.D. 1105.
99. *HN* 163–64; cf. Southern, *Anselm*, p. 175: "It is . . . surprising that he should have chosen this moment to take decisive and even violent action in a sense scarcely compatible with that suggested in the papal letter."

Hugh archbishop of Lyon, Anselm left the city and headed northward with the announced purpose of personally excommunicating the king.[100]

Anselm evidently realized that with Henry's bandwagon rolling through Normandy the opportune moment for bringing him to terms was swiftly slipping away. Paschal, limited by conventions and by distance, was unable to act swiftly enough. Once Henry had completed his conquest, he could ignore the threat of papal and archiepiscopal sanctions — as Rufus had done in 1097 and Henry himself had done in 1101. Eadmer muddies the waters even further by citing Anselm's "three warnings" as a possible justification for Anselm's threat of excommunication. In Eadmer's eyes, Anselm is once more functioning as a "Pope of another world."

As a servant of the Apostolic See, Anselm was now on very slippery ground. Paschal, fully aware of Henry's misdeeds, including his confiscation of the Canterbury lands,[101] and with the unanimous assent of his synod, had deferred sentence on the king. Since the matter of Henry's excommunication was thus clearly in the hands of the pope and his curia, Anselm's threat can be viewed only as a bold usurpation of the papal prerogative.[102] Eadmer obscures this point in his muddled explanation of Anselm's departure, and nowhere in his surviving letters does Anselm so much as hint at his threat to excommunicate the king. Indeed Anselm probably hoped that the threat alone would suffice to win Henry's submission on investitures. Had he really been determined to excommunicate Henry he could have done so from Lyon. His journey provided the time and opportunity for the king to come to terms. As Anselm progressed northward, rumors of his excommunication threat spread swiftly across France, Normandy, and England.[103] Making

---

100. *HN* 164–65; *GP* 114. Note that Eadmer has tried to give Anselm some sort of justification, almost in the papal image, for his actions, with his report that Anselm had "for the third time written to the king . . . asking for the return of his lands" (*HN* 164). Anselm, the primate of the *alter orbis*, had followed the proper procedure for excommunication with three warnings.

101. AEp. 348, Paschal to Henry: "Miramur autem quod eum non solum exulem feceris, sed etiam ecclesiae suae rebus exspoliaveris."

102. Cf. *Gregorii VII Regestrum*, ed. E. Caspar, *MGH, Epistolae selectae*, 2 (Berlin, 1920–23), Book 9, Ep. 5, pp. 579–80: Gregory VII chides his legates Hugh bishop of Die (the later archbishop of Lyon) and Amatus of Oléron for excommunicating certain men who had refused to pay tithes "whereas we have, as a matter of prudence, postponed bringing persons of this sort under the ban of anathema by synodial decision." It was this same Hugh with whom Anselm had conferred immediately before leaving Lyon to excommunicate Henry I; see also ibid., Book 1, Ep. 60, p. 87, Gregory VII to Archbishop Siegfried of Mainz: "You are not to imagine that you, or indeed any of the patriarchs or primates, can take the liberty of retracting apostolic judgments."

103. *HN* 166.

effective use of public opinion, Anselm was about to sabotage Henry's carefully cultivated public image as savior of the Norman churches and halt his campaign to conquer Normandy.

On his way north, Anselm stopped over at the Cluniac priory of La Charité-sur-Loire, where he encountered messengers from Adela countess of Blois, Henry's favorite sister and one of Anselm's spiritual disciples.[104] Adela was gravely ill, so the messengers said, and needed Anselm's consolations. Arriving at Blois, Anselm "found that her sickness was greatly relieved" but nevertheless spent the next several weeks with her.[105] Along with his spiritual counsel, he disclosed his intention to excommunicate her brother. Adela had inquired specifically on this point, and now, having had it confirmed, she sent messengers to Henry. He responded by promising important concessions if Anselm would meet him at the Norman fortress of Laigle.

Anselm's excommunication threat appears to have been successful, for Henry's campaign was now breaking down. Having swept through the Cotentin and then eastward to seize Bayeux and Caen, the royal army now found itself brought to a standstill before the ducal castle of Falaise and was eventually forced to leave the fortress in Curthose's possession. Orderic explains this reverse with the cryptic statement that Henry's ally, Elias count of Maine, withdrew from the king's army "at the request of the Normans."[106] Eadmer observes more generally that Anselm's threat had "prompted many to turn against a sovereign not too well loved."[107] We know that Anselm corresponded at some point with Count Elias, "his lord and friend and beloved in God," and enjoyed a warm relationship with Elias's close friend, Hildebert of Lavardin bishop of Le Mans.[108]

Henry then went to Cinteaux around 25 May and tried to make peace with Curthose, but failed when their negotiations were interrupted by quarrels among their followers.[109] The meeting contrasted sharply with their previous encounter in 1104 when Henry all but

104. Anselm had recently interceded with the pope in Adela's behalf (AEp. 340) and had visited her en route to Rome in 1103 (AEpp. 286, 287).

105. HN 164. For other possible instances of diplomatic illness see HN 27–29 (Hugh earl of Chester), 181–82 (Anselm), and OV 4:184 (Robert Curthose).

106. OV 6:78; Henry abandoned his plan to attack Falaise "quia comes Helias a Normannis rogatus recessit."

107. HN 166.

108. AEpp. 466, 239–41. Anselm wrote his last theological treatise, De Processione Spiritus Sancti, at Hildebert's request: CB 650.

109. OV 6:80.

gained the duke's submission. Chagrined by these reverses, Henry was persuaded at last to come to terms with Anselm. After conferring with his advisers, he sent Countess Adela a message that he was willing to compromise with the primate on many points for the sake of peace.[110] On 21 July he met Anselm and Adela at the castle of Laigle in southeastern Normandy to negotiate a reconciliation.[111]

Accounts of the meeting at Laigle are sketchy and deceptive. Eadmer says simply that Henry restored his love and the Canterbury lands to Anselm, and that Baldwin of Tournai and William Warelwast were to be sent to Rome to clear up the matter of investitures "and certain other questions."[112] In a letter to Ernulf, Anselm confirmed that Henry had returned the Canterbury lands and added that the king had promised to repay all the rents he had collected while the estates were in his hands.[113] Writing to Paschal about the Laigle meeting, Anselm provided the vital information — withheld by Eadmer — that he had restored Robert of Meulan to communion.[114] On the basis of Eadmer's and Anselm's accounts, Sir Richard Southern concluded that Anselm, ignoring investitures altogether, concentrated on the single issue of the Canterbury lands and withdrew his threat of excommunication when they were restored.[115] But Anselm knew perfectly well that he could have recovered his lands at any time during his exile if he would forget the papal bans and come home.[116] He traveled to Laigle not merely to obtain what could easily have been obtained long before, but to clear his homeward path by winning Henry's concession on investitures. In doing so, Anselm was once more exceeding his proper authority, for only the pope had the right to negotiate on the subject of papal bans. Thus, Anselm's part in the negotiation was glossed over by both Eadmer and Anselm, and their equivocations have misled historians down to the present generation.[117] But Anselm's subsequent, cau-

110. HN 166.

111. HN 166 dates the meeting 22 July, but see AEp. 364 in which Anselm provides the correct date. Gilbert II, lord of Laigle, had fought against Robert of Bellême in Normandy in 1104 (OV 6:34) and, probably in the same year, had received Pevensey from Henry I on its forfeiture by William of Mortain: Sanders, Baronies, p. 136 (who misdates the forfeiture 1106; cf. ASC, A.D. 1104); he was at Henry's court in England on several occasions before Henry's victory over Curthose at Tinchebrai; Regesta 2, nos. 558, 662(?), 762, 779.

112. HN 166; VA 134–35.   113. AEp. 364.   114. AEp. 388.

115. Southern, Anselm, p. 177.

116. AEp. 318; cf. 308, 319.

117. Southern, Anselm, p. 177; Cantor, Church, Kingship, and Lay Investiture, pp. 223–25.

tiously phrased letter to Hugh archbishop of Lyon makes it clear that Henry had agreed at Laigle to relinquish lay investiture if he could retain the homage of the churchmen: "The king [Anselm tells Hugh], though he will suffer himself, so I hope, to submit to the apostolic decrees on ecclesiastical investitures, nevertheless does not yet wish, he says, to relinquish the homage of prelates."[118]

Such homage, although banned at the Roman synods of 1099 and 1102, had remained a secondary issue throughout the conflict. Indeed Paschal seems to have dropped the matter altogether in his dealings with Henry over the previous thirty months.[119] Investiture, not homage, caused the showdown at the November 1103 papal court and propelled Anselm into exile. The compromise suggested itself from the papal correspondence, and any astute participant in the controversy may have recognized it, including Anselm, Robert of Meulan, or King Henry himself. The deal may have been worked out in conference between all participants, including Adela of Blois. Although the Laigle agreement was a "compromise," it was a heavily lopsided one. The central difficulty confronting Anselm during his exile had not been to obtain Paschal's concession on homage but to win Henry's concession on investitures.[120] In essence, the "compromise" at Laigle embodied the terms that Paschal had demanded and Henry had firmly rejected at the onset of Anselm's exile in November 1103. It thus represented a notable victory for the reform papacy, won through the daring diplomatic strategy of Anselm.

Historians have supposed that Anselm had serious reservations about the agreement at Laigle.[121] Here again they have been misled by Anselm's determination to avoid the appearance of having exceeded his archiepiscopal powers. A careful reading of the evidence leaves no doubt that Anselm endorsed the investiture-homage agreement at Laigle and agreed to a truce with Henry on the realistic hope that Paschal would ratify the plan, thereby permitting Anselm's return to Canterbury. In a subsequent letter to Robert of Meulan, Anselm described the Laigle agreement as a settlement "so badly needed and so

118. AEp. 389.
119. Southern, *Anselm*, pp. 171–73.
120. That Paschal was in the process of quietly dropping the clerical homage ban from his overall reform program is suggested by the absence of any such ban in the surviving legislation of contemporary papal synods: see Uta-Renate Blumenthal, "Some Notes on Papal Politics at Guastalla, 1106," *Studia Gratiana* 19 (1976): 67–68, and *Early Councils of Paschal II*, p. 97.
121. Cantor, *Church, Kingship, and Lay Investiture*, p. 224.

clearly right."[122] On the departure of the messengers carrying the Laigle proposal to Rome, Anselm asked the Canterbury monks to pray that such concord might be effected between pope and king that he could be reconciled with both sides.[123] In his letter to Hugh of Lyon, entrusted to Baldwin of Tournai on his way to Rome, Anselm displayed his usual circumspection. He asked Hugh's advice on the matter of ecclesiastical homage yet urged him, if it seemed agreeable, to add a message suggesting to the pope how the affair ought to be settled.[124]

Analyzing this letter, one must read between the lines. Hugh and Anselm were old and intimate friends; they had recently spent fourteen months together in Lyon, and Anselm had departed to threaten Henry with excommunication only after consulting Hugh. As so often before, Anselm left all details to be communicated verbally by his messenger Baldwin. But in Hugh's reply to Anselm the curtain is for once lifted. Hugh summarized Baldwin's verbal message from Anselm in these words: "I have learned from Dom Baldwin that, because you have labored so much thus far to attain this end, and have offered up not only your goods but your very self, you have now by God's grace at last largely attained it, so that you can be animated by hope for what remains."[125] The secondary matter of ecclesiastical homage should be left to the future, since Henry had been forced to capitulate on the central issue.

But now, having won his victory, Anselm was obliged to shift ground—to reinterpret his actions in such a way that the papal prerogative would appear to have been uncompromised. Hugh of Lyon had warned Anselm of the danger of seeming to have taken apostolic authority upon himself,[126] and Anselm was keenly aware of the problem. Pope and primate must each be shown to have been acting within his proper sphere. Anselm must be seen as having had no part or interest in the investiture settlement; his concern must be limited to the rights and lands of his own archbishopric. As for his usurpation of papal and synodial authority over the case of Henry I, since the king had never actually been excommunicated, Anselm's threat could be overlooked and edited out of the historical record. No letter in Anselm's correspondence mentions the threat; we know of it only through Eadmer.

122. AEp. 369, late 1105.
123. AEp. 376, late 1105 or early 1106.
124. AEp. 389.
125. AEp. 390.
126. AEp. 390.

The outlines of Anselm's reinterpretation emerge in his letter to Paschal reporting on the Laigle conference.[127] He wrote briefly, leaving fuller explanations to the envoys. Keeping silent on the excommunication threat, he left the implication that he had gone to Normandy to make public the papal excommunication of Robert of Meulan. Through the good offices of the countess of Blois, he had conferred with the king, who agreed to restore the temporal possessions of Anselm's see and to send legates to Rome on the matters of investiture and homage:

I had not understood, moreover, that I ought to prohibit his legation or to reject my revestiture. What truly he might concede about the aforesaid matters, or what he asks, your sanctity will know through the same legate. And since the outcome of the entire case depends upon your judgment, I sent our legate at the same time, so that I may know how it is agreed between you and the king, and what your order commands me to do.[128]

Anselm was handling the matter with great delicacy, creating the impression that Paschal had the initiative and that the archbishop was a mere bystander in a controversy between king and pope. The letter continues with an oddly reasoned paragraph on the ticklish problem of Anselm's having unilaterally lifted the papal excommunication of Robert of Meulan. Eadmer overlooks this incident altogether, but Anselm, in his report to the pope, obviously could not. He based his justification on an earlier papal letter to Robert threatening God's anger if the count continued advising Henry to oppose the Roman church.[129] Since Robert had now promised Anselm that he would counsel Henry to obey the pope, Anselm had revoked the excommunication through the authority of Paschal's earlier letter of warning.[130] Anselm had been acting for the pope after all, although in this instance the archbishop had to strain his logic as seldom before to make the facts harmonize with his vision of the ideal reality.

Such was Anselm's "official" version of the Laigle meeting, and it was duly copied into the collection of his correspondence at Canterbury — Lambeth ms. 59. Anselm was determined that no conflicting accounts of the meeting should find their way into the collection, and he

127. AEp. 388.
128. AEp. 388.
129. Probably referring to AEp. 361, a letter of warning written at some point before Robert's excommunication by pope and synod in March 1105 (AEp. 353); see above, Chapter 7 at nn. 87–88.
130. AEp. 388; cf. Anselm's similar explanation to Ernulf: AEp. 369.

sent an explicit message to that effect to the Canterbury monk Thidric, the scribe who was responsible for transcribing Anselm's letters and treatises.[131] The envoys who sought Paschal's ratification of the Laigle agreement carried not only Anselm's aforementioned letters to Paschal and Hugh of Lyon but, as well, letters to the pope from Henry I, which evidently provided a different version of the meeting. Anselm had copies of these royal letters in his possession, but when Thidric asked him to send them for transcription into the correspondence collection, Anselm declined to do so: "I am not sending you the letters that you seek from the king to the pope, because I do not think it useful that they be preserved."[132]

Anselm was not trying to deceive the Apostolic See. Rather, he was showing Paschal how exceptional acts, prompted by exceptional circumstances, could be reinterpreted to reflect due order. If in the confused world of day-by-day politics Anselm had exceeded his proper authority, he had through his very disobedience rendered Paschal a great service, which could be regarded as obedience of a higher sort.

On the mundane level of reality, Henry had been forced to negotiate with his back to the wall. No doubt the threatened excommunication, if carried out, would immediately have become public knowledge throughout the Anglo-Norman world, precipitating further defections and ruining Henry's plan to conquer Normandy. Indeed even the threat of excommunication was a crippling blow, as Anselm must have realized from the beginning. Now the king's only recourse was to yield on investitures and hope that Paschal would yield on homage. Whether the consistent omission of the issue of homage from the recent papal correspondence was a conscious hint at the terms of a compromise, as Southern proposed,[133] or simply a reflection of papal priorities, it presented the king and archbishop with a basis for compromise. But a verbal agreement with Anselm alone, rather than a written agreement with Paschal, would not have seemed irrevocable to Henry, and he therefore reverted to one of his favorite tactics — delay. On his return to

---

131. AEp. 379; cf. AEp. 334, disclosing that Thidric is copying Anselm's *De Conceptu Virginali;* toward the end of Lambeth ms. 59 are the words, "Que restant modici sunt scripta manu Thidrici"; cf. Fröhlich, "Genesis of the Collections of St. Anselm's Letters," pp. 262–66, and "Letters Omitted from Anselm's Collection," pp. 62–71.

132. AEp. 379: the letters were not preserved and have since perished; cf. AEp. 357, where Anselm alludes to his sending of other letters to be preserved at Canterbury.

133. *Anselm,* pp. 171, 173.

England in August 1105, he proceeded to offer one excuse after another to postpone the promised mission to Rome, doubtless hoping that Anselm could be kept inactive and contented by the restoration of the Canterbury lands while the king rebuilt his army and alliance system. If so, Normandy might yet be won without relinquishing investitures.

But Anselm settled down at Bec, keeping a sharp eye on Henry's activities and wisely refusing to return to England until Paschal had ratified the Laigle plan.[134] Henry, in the meantime, sought to persuade Anselm to return to Canterbury at once, thereby making their reconciliation apparent to all, while still continuing to delay the mission to Rome.[135] The king seems to have mobilized his ecclesiastics in a calculated effort to lure Anselm back to Canterbury and to tarnish his public image as a dutiful archbishop. As noted earlier, from time to time various English correspondents had sent appeals pleading with Anselm to return to England and prevent the disintegration of the English church resulting from his absence. Now, on Henry's return to England in August, the propaganda campaign intensified. There was a sudden "conversion" to Anselm's cause of a number of curialist bishops — among them Gerard of York,[136] who had previously been Henry's willing instrument in the king's fruitless effort to obtain the consecrations of the recently invested bishops. As they proclaimed their loyalty to Anselm, the prelates of England vividly described the deterioration of the English churches, which they attributed to his absence.[137]

Henry probably encouraged these missives, and he himself began making a public outcry against Anselm's absence: "Even the king himself now declares that never in this country has wickedness been so brazen as it now is. Without any doubt all these things reflect upon one person, and that is you; your holiness is held responsible."[138] These letters pleaded with Anselm to return to his duty, to resume his rightful place as head of the church, and to take up once again the pastoral care of England. With Anselm reestablished at Canterbury, Henry would be

---

134. See AEp. 364: Anselm explains to Ernulf that he will not risk the possibility of Henry reneging and will therefore continue to absent himself from England until the agreement receives papal certification; similarly, AEp. 368, Anselm to Henry.

135. AEp. 364; *HN* 167.

136. Cantor, *Church, Kingship, and Lay Investiture*, pp. 243, 255–56.

137. AEpp. 363, 365, 373, 386; the first three letters, all critical of Anselm, are absent from Lambeth ms. 59; AEp. 386, the shortest of them, is included in the ms., probably to provide the context for Anselm's somewhat longer reply: AEp. 387.

138. AEp. 365.

able to point to his concord with the church, resume his role as savior
of the Norman churches, and proceed with the conquest of the duchy.
Or, alternatively, Anselm could be portrayed as derelict in his duty to
God, a less than holy man whose repeated attacks on Henry's reputation would lose their force.

But Anselm remained obdurate, and at Bec. He explained to his
English correspondents why he could not yet return,[139] and he repeatedly pressed the royal court to cease delaying the dispatch of the envoys
to Rome. At Laigle in July, Henry had promised to send them in time to
receive Paschal's answer by Christmas,[140] but by autumn they had not
yet departed. "Let it not displease you," Henry wrote Anselm, "that
I have so long held back the dispatch of those whom I resolved to send
to Rome."[141] The king added that he was now sending William Warelwast to Bec to explain the delay, and that Baldwin should thereupon
accompany William to Rome. When William failed to arrive, Anselm
wrote to Henry demanding that he set a fixed date for the sending of the
envoys: "To name an outside date," Anselm said, "I dare not delay
sending my own representative beyond next Christmas at the latest."[142]
About 29 September Henry wrote to Anselm that he was sending
William Warelwast from the Michaelmas court to Bec and thence to
Rome "unless storms and the tossing of the sea and contrary winds
have detained him."[143]

The weather must indeed have detained him, and Anselm wrote
directly to Robert of Meulan rebuking the king and his counselors for
the delays, placing the blame for the continuation of the exile squarely
on the royal court, and hinting at the renewed possibility of excommunication: "Consequently some people are thinking and saying that the
king is not very anxious to hasten my return to England, nor that the
church of God, which God has entrusted to his guardianship . . . should
be comforted by that pastor's return and presence with her. . . . For this
reason I . . . fear that the king is provoking God's anger against himself
and against those on whose advice he is acting."[144]

This not-so-veiled threat evidently had its intended effect, for Henry
at last dispatched William Warelwast to Anselm in early December

139. AEp. 387.
140. AEpp. 364, 368, 369.
141. AEp. 367.
142. AEp. 368.
143. AEp. 370; *Regesta* 2, no. 692.
144. AEp. 369, from Reims.

1105.[145] Shortly afterward, the king undertook one final effort to abort the mission. In a letter of December 1105, witnessed by Robert bishop of Lincoln and Robert of Meulan, Henry wrote to Anselm that he had heard that there were now two popes battling one another in Rome and suggested that the envoys be recalled until the situation cleared.[146] Anselm replied with a vigorous defense of Paschal's right to occupy the papal throne and informed Henry that Baldwin and William Warelwast had already left Bec for the papal court and could not be called back.[147] The matter was closed.

By now Henry was preparing in earnest for the coming spring campaign in Normandy. To that end he inflicted on England heavy taxes,[148] among which was a tax on married clergy levied on the pretext that the king was enforcing the decrees on celibacy from Anselm's 1102 Council of London. When the tax yielded too little, Henry broadened it into a tax on all churches in what Eadmer calls a campaign of extortion. Eadmer states that this policy was denounced far and wide, so that all were led to hate the king, even his partisans.[149] Anselm took the lead in these denunciations, writing two letters to Henry from Bec strongly criticizing him for levying the tax and once again, in effect, shifting responsibility for mischiefs in the English church back to the king.[150] The two letters were copied into both Lambeth ms. 59 and the *Historia Novorum*, indicating clearly that they were meant for public consumption. Eadmer included them "that they may in the future be used as precedents" against unjust taxation of the clergy.[151] Anselm began his first letter by asserting that it is his duty to correct the king for the good of his soul. According to the law of God, the correction of abuses within the church pertains not to the king but to the bishops, and ultimately to the archbishop and primate. Anselm reminded Henry that he had been restored to the archbishopric and that it was therefore his own responsibility to detect and punish such offenses.

Henry replied in vague but reassuring terms that he would explain his actions when he saw the archbishop personally, obviously intending

145. AEp. 371; cf. AEpp. 376, Anselm to Ernulf and the Canterbury monks reporting that the legates have departed, and 377 (*Regesta* 2, no. 716), which was written shortly after AEp. 371 and cannot be dated before early or mid-December; see next note.

146. AEpp. 377; *Regesta* 2, no. 716: the antipope Sylvester IV was elected on 18 November 1105, and the news can hardly have reached England before well into December.

147. AEp. 378.

148. *ASC*, A.D. 1105.   149. *HN* 171–72, 175.

150. AEpp. 391, 393.   151. *HN* 175.

to delay while continuing to collect the taxes: the king promised Anselm "an explanation that will be so satisfactory to you that . . . you will not, I feel sure, blame me for what I have done."[152] He added that whatever might be done elsewhere, Anselm could rest assured that his own lands and men had been left in peace. To a further remonstrance by Anselm, Henry replied that if he was acting improperly in even the slightest respect, then at such time as he should be able to discuss the matter with Anselm he would, "with God's guidance and yours, put the matter right."[153] Anselm's protests did, however, move the king eventually to temper the tax on the advice of Robert of Meulan.[154]

During the winter months of 1105–6, while Anselm and Henry awaited the return of the envoys bearing the pope's decision, Curthose and his party engaged in fruitless eleventh-hour negotiations with the royal court. Robert of Bellême visited Henry's court over the Christmas season, perhaps with the hope of recovering the royal love and the earldom of Shropshire in return for supporting the king in Normandy; Robert recovered neither and departed from the court "in hostile fashion."[155] Anselm himself attempted a peacemaking role, advising Robert Curthose to visit Henry and seek reconciliation. The visit probably occurred in February,[156] and Henry reported to Anselm afterward that Curthose left his court in a kindly mood.[157] Other sources, however, agree that Henry refused to relinquish any of his Norman holdings or to make peace with his brother, and that Curthose departed in anger.[158] The visit happened to coincide with Anselm's quarrel with Henry over the taxing of churches and may have constituted a gentle reminder on Anselm's part that he was not altogether hostile to Curthose's cause or altogether convinced that Henry was Normandy's divinely chosen deliverer.

The following spring the envoys at last returned, bearing Paschal's reply to Anselm endorsing the Laigle plan.[159] The pope had accepted Henry's concession and Anselm's persuasive arguments. Following Anselm's prompting, Paschal wrote as though God alone had persuaded Henry to obey the Apostolic See, through Anselm's prayers, and as though the pope had granted the concession of clerical homage to the king as an act of selfless charity "until by the grace of almighty God

152. AEp. 392.   153. AEp. 394.
154. GP 115.   155. ASC, A.D. 1105, 1106.
156. ASC, A.D. 1106.   157. AEp. 396.
158. ASC, A.D. 1106; Florence 2:54; HA 235.
159. AEp. 397, dated 23 March [1106].

the king's heart is softened by your preaching." Paschal's words in his letter to Anselm are reminiscent of Anselm's own words to Hugh of Lyon conveyed verbally by Baldwin of Tournai: "Because you have labored so much thus far to attain this end . . . you have now by God's grace at last largely attained it, so that you can be animated by hope for what remains."[160] Paschal had thus given Anselm precisely the appropriate response. So long as the king ceased investing prelates, Anselm was empowered, on Paschal's authority, to absolve those prelates who had previously received investiture from Henry and to permit them to be consecrated. And prelates who render homage to the king "are by no means to be banned on that account from the rite of consecration."

The chief impediment to the resolution of the investiture issues was thus removed, but there were further issues that still awaited resolution. One such issue involved William archbishop of Rouen, the former monk and abbot of Caen whom Lanfranc had sent to Anselm at Bec many years before for training in the religious life.[161] Archbishop William had been suspended from his office by the papacy, but at the request of Anselm's and Henry's envoys, Paschal had granted jurisdiction over the case to Anselm: "The case of the bishop of Rouen and the prohibition which, when justice so required, was pronounced against him, we have committed to you for your consideration. Whatever remission you grant him, we grant him."[162] Less than two weeks thereafter, Paschal wrote to Archbishop William ordering him to commend to Anselm's jurisdiction the case of Thorald bishop of Bayeux, who was charged with having been improperly elected.[163] Although no record has survived of Bishop Thorald's judicial hearing, he was probably deposed in 1106 and retired to Bec in 1107 to live for many years as an exemplary monk.[164] William Bonne-Ame, however, was acquitted and restored to his archiepiscopal office by an ecclesiastical tribunal in Rouen headed by Anselm.[165] In both these instances the pope had

---

160. AEp. 390: Anselm's message as summarized by Archbishop Hugh.

161. Above, Chapter 2 at n. 192.

162. AEp. 397; cf. 398. Bonne-Ame had been suspended for the second time in 1093, over a matter of his own or papal jurisdiction over Fécamp. Cf. G. H. Williams, *The Norman Anonymous of 1100 A.D.* (Cambridge, Mass., 1951), pp. 111, 112.

163. Jaffé-Wattenbach, no. 6077, dated 6 April 1106, at Salerno; cf. S. E. Gleason, *An Ecclesiastical Barony of the Middle Ages: The Bishopric of Bayeux, 1066–1204* (Cambridge, Mass., 1936), pp. 20–23.

164. OV 5:210, n. 4.

165. *HN* 177, 180; cf. David S. Spear, "The Norman Episcopacy under Henry I, King of England and Duke of Normandy (1106–1135)," unpublished Ph.D. dissertation, University of California, Santa Barbara, 1982, p. 12.

granted Anselm extraordinary if temporary power over the Norman church as a papal judge-delegate. Until his return to England in the latter part of August 1106, Anselm was exercising what amounted to de facto legatine powers in Normandy of the sort that he had been accustomed to exercise as primate of England.

Having delivered Paschal's letter to Anselm in Normandy, William Warelwast proceeded to England, probably in early May, to bear the news of the pope's decision to Henry I.[166] The king, "greatly pleased with what he had heard," immediately sent William back to Bec to ask Anselm to return to his see.[167] Henry had originally planned to cross to Normandy on 3 May to launch his 1106 campaign,[168] but he now resolved to await Anselm's return so that the campaign might be preceded and invigorated by a public reconciliation between king and archbishop in England. Anxious to rehabilitate his tarnished religious reputation by welcoming Anselm back to his see, the king had twice postponed his projected 3 May crossing,[169] and he was now determined to get on with it before more of the campaigning season slipped away.[170] But when William arrived at Bec, he found Anselm ill and unable to travel.

Eadmer reports that William doubted that it was really illness that held Anselm at Bec — "that Anselm might be hindered from going to England quite as much by his affection for Bec and the brothers there as by the illness."[171] Anselm was by now well into his seventies and may indeed have been too sick to cross the Channel, but the possibility remains that, like Adela of Blois's convenient illness of the previous year, Anselm's illness was exaggerated for reasons of diplomacy. If William Warelwast's suspicion was correct, Anselm's behavior is probably attributable less to his nostalgia for Bec than to his determination to obtain from Henry an airtight public commitment to the terms of the settlement before losing his leverage by returning to Canterbury. Anselm was by now thoroughly aware of the worth of Henry's promises and was unwilling to be deceived again as he had been in 1101 on

166. Cf. AEp. 392, Henry to Anselm, written after 23 April and before 3 May, and prior to William Warelwast's return.
167. HN 181.
168. AEp. 396, Henry to Anselm, about February 1106.
169. AEpp. 392, 394.
170. Recall that Henry had crossed in early April for his 1105 campaign: above, Chapter 7 at nn. 91–93.
171. HN 181.

the eve of Curthose's invasion of England. The archbishop had earlier explained to Ernulf his decision not to cross to England until the king's accord with the pope was "consolidated in such a way that I might without doubt have confidence that I would remain there in peace."[172] It is just possible that Anselm had now decided to use Henry's policy of delay against the king himself.

Whatever the case, William Warelwast exerted all possible influence on Anselm and his companions to set off for England, declaring that Henry longed for his return and that all England was disconsolate at his absence. William then offered his solemn promise that the king "was fully determined to meet Anselm's wishes in whatever he should thenceforth direct" and was resolved to put an end to any disagreement with the church of Rome.[173] Rejoicing at the promise, Anselm found that his health had returned, and he at once set off for Jumièges en route to England. But at Jumièges he was once again struck by illness and could proceed no further. He sent messengers to explain his delay to Henry, who replied with expressions of grief at the news of Anselm's illness, and advice that he should not afflict his body with excessive fasting:[174] "And know that if it were not that I awaited you, I would already be in Normandy. . . . I wish and order that throughout all my Norman possessions you command them like your own demesnes, and it will gladden my heart if you do so. Now await me in Normandy; for I shall go there next."[175]

With the campaigning season already far advanced, Henry could wait in England no longer. He crossed to Normandy in late July[176] to effect his reconciliation with Anselm and then resume at last his campaign of conquest. Anselm in the meantime had spent a month at Jumièges recovering his health and then had returned to Bec, "thinking that it would be more convenient and more proper to await the king's coming there than anywhere else."[177] At Bec Anselm fell ill again, more seriously than before, and rumors of his impending death drew bishops

---

172. AEp. 364, after Laigle.

173. HN 181–82.

174. AEp. 399; cf. VA 136: an anonymous churchman accuses Anselm at just this time of having had it in his power to recover his health by partaking of food and drink "if he had wanted to, and if he had swallowed his pride."

175. Cf. HN 182, where Henry's letter is summarized: Henry was not, of course, putting Anselm in command of all his Norman holdings but rather was offering to supply all of Anselm's material needs from them.

176. ASC, A.D. 1106.

177. HN 182.

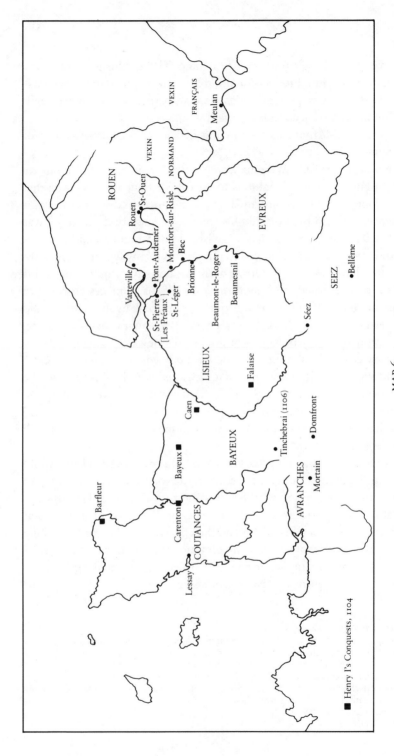

VEXIN
FRANÇAIS

VEXIN
NORMAND

Meulan

ROUEN

VEXIN
NORMAND

St-Ouen

Rouen

Vatteville

Pont-Audemer

Montfort-sur-Risle

Bec

St-Pierre
[Les Préaux]

St-Léger

Brionne

Beaumont-le-Roger

Beaumesnil

EVREUX

SEEZ

•Bellême

Séez

LISIEUX

Falaise

Caen

Tinchebrai (1106)

•Domfront

Bayeux

BAYEUX

AVRANCHES

Mortain

Barfleur

Carenton

COUTANCES

Lessay

Henry I's Conquests, 1104

MAP 6.
Henry I's Norman Campaigns, 1104 – 1106

and abbots to Bec from throughout the duchy to attend him in his last days and make arrangements for the funeral. But again Anselm recovered, in time to welcome the arrival of Henry and his entourage on 15 August.[178]

Henry thus journeyed to what could still truly be regarded as Anselm's spiritual home in Normandy, coming to Bec much as a suffragan bishop might have attended Anselm's court at Canterbury. The abbey lay well to the east of the Norman territories that Henry had occupied the previous year — the Cotentin, Bayeux, and Caen — and the ducal capital of Rouen was not far away. But Bec was by no means under ducal control in 1106. From its site on the River Risle, it was protected to the south by Robert of Meulan's castle at Brionne and to the north by the fortress of Montfort-sur-Risle, the *caput* of Henry I's ally Robert of Montfort.[179] And a few miles further downriver from Montfort-sur-Risle was Robert of Meulan's fortress at Pont-Audemer. Because of the influence of Robert of Meulan and his associates, Henry could travel into what might otherwise have been enemy territory — past the Beaumont and Montfort holdings extending almost from the Channel upriver to Bec. There the king would have been welcomed, with Bec's celebrated hospitality, by William of Beaumont, who was a kinsman of Robert of Meulan and Robert of Montfort, and Anselm's handpicked successor as abbot of Bec.

We do not know whether the Norman prelates who assembled at Bec in expectation of Anselm's death remained there during the king's visit.[180] But the conference at Bec undoubtedly provided Henry with the opportunity he had sought to ratify and publicize his accommodation with Anselm, just as it provided Anselm with the opportunity to obtain Henry's publicly proclaimed guarantees with respect to investitures, the taxing of churches, and the dignities of Canterbury. The

178. HN 182.   179. OV 6:56.

180. Their presence is strongly implied in HN 182, but in VA 136–37, Eadmer precedes his account of Henry's visit to Bec with a miracle story that is said to have occurred when "the bishops and abbots who had come together for his burial went home again" (an unnamed prelate who spoke ill of Anselm suffered the divine retribution of being thrown and dragged by his horse). The story raises certain doubts because the only homeward-bound prelate whom Eadmer names, Ralph abbot of Séez, had in fact been in self-imposed exile from his abbey since 1104 because of the harassments of Robert of Bellême, and had taken refuge under Henry I: OV 6:46; GP 127; Florence 2:53 (reporting that Abbot Ralph was present at St. Cuthbert's translation at Durham in 1104); Regesta 2, nos. 677, 845. Southern, commenting on the chronological confusions in the *Vita Anselmi*'s treatment of events in 1106–7, concludes "that this part of the *Life* was written some time after the events it describes": VA 139, n. 1; cf. n. 3.

meeting began with a solemn high mass celebrated by Anselm,[181] after which, according to the late but generally trustworthy summary of Anselm's life by Ralph of Diceto, the king and archbishop conferred "before an assembly of distinguished men, as if at law."[182] The meeting was probably the occasion on which Henry issued his charter confirming to Bec and Abbot William all the lands, churches, and tithes granted or confirmed to the abbey by William the Conqueror or William Rufus; the charter bears the attestations of three familiar royalists: William Warelwast, Robert count of Meulan, and his brother Henry earl of Warwick.[183]

No single account of the Bec convocation provides all the terms of the settlement; they must be pieced together from several sources. According to Ralph de Diceto's brief biography of Anselm, the chief item of business was Henry's formal concession on investiture and the free election of prelates: "The king promised that he would not thenceforth claim any privilege for himself or his heirs with regard to ecclesiastical investitures, and that in making elections he would demand nothing more than his mere consent, just as the judgment of the holy canons lays down."[184]

Eadmer states that Henry also restored to Anselm all the churches of England that had been let out at rent under Rufus or thereafter, free of exaction, and that the king further promised that so long as he lived he would take nothing from churches when they were without a pastor.[185] Priests who had not yet paid the disputed church tax would be released from any obligation to do so, and those who had already paid the tax were free of all taxes for three years. Finally, Eadmer reports, all that had been taken from the archbishopric of Canterbury while Anselm was in exile Henry not only promised to restore but also gave security for his doing so.[186]

181. *HN* 182.
182. Ralph de Diceto, "Abbreviationes Chronichorum," in *Opera Historica*, ed. William Stubbs (RS, London, 1876), 1:227.
183. *Regesta* 2, no. 860; the editors suggest a date range of 1100–1107; the fact that the confirmation is a general one, not limited to Bec's English lands, suggests a date of 1106–7, when Henry could plausibly have claimed authority over Normandy. During the years 1100–07, Henry is not known to have visited Bec except in mid-August 1106, and that visit provides the most likely occasion, though not the only possible one, for the issuing of the charter.
184. *Opera Historica* 1:227.
185. *HN* 183.
186. Ibid.

There was little new in these concessions, except that the king had now made them as solemn promises before a formal assemblage and could not easily reverse himself. His promises to restore the English churches that had been let out at rent and to refrain from exploiting ecclesiastical vacancies echo clauses in his coronation charter, but he appears to have resumed these practices in his effort to raise funds for his Norman campaigns.[187] His commitment to restore all revenues taken from the archbishopric had already been made at Laigle,[188] although not by oath on a solemn public occasion. Only Henry's commitment on church taxes was new. These taxes had been vitally important to Henry as he built up his war chest, but to Anselm they represented an intolerable infringement on the liberties of the English church, which he as its father was compelled to resist. The king could not be permitted to tax the churches arbitrarily in violation of custom and law lest it set an evil precedent. Henry agreed not only to abandon the practice but also to make appropriate restitutions.

Henry's settlement with Anselm involved two additional major concessions not mentioned explicitly in accounts of the negotiations at Laigle or Bec. First, the king's insistence on receiving the homage of prelates evidently did not extend to Anselm. The primate had always regarded the papal decrees to which he had assented in 1099 as more binding on himself than on those who had not attended the council.[189] As Anselm expressed it in a letter to Ernulf from exile, "It is my will that, with God's help, I should never become the man of another mortal, or promise fidelity to another person through an oath."[190] In his letter of late 1105 to Hugh of Lyon, Anselm discussed in some detail the problems that might possibly arise from the homage compromise at Laigle, but without ever suggesting that Henry was still demanding homage from Anselm.[191] And Paschal, in his letter to Anselm confirming the Laigle settlement, conceded merely that prelates-elect, "even if

187. Cf. AEp. 365, late 1105: "Ecclesiarum namque, quae tam diu manent pastoribus viduatae, possessiones diripiuntur"; HN 183.

188. AEp. 364; above, Chapter 7 at nn. 112–13.

189. On the binding nature of papal decrees on participants in the councils that promulgated them, see above, Chapter 6 at nn. 2–7. Note in particular the care of Boso of Bec in 1124.

190. AEp. 311: In the same letter Anselm states that the pope had personally forbidden him to associate with prelates whom Henry had invested, but since Ernulf and the Canterbury monks had received no such personal admonition from the pope, then if they should continue to associate with invested prelates, "I in no way rebuke you."

191. AEp. 389.

they have rendered homage to the king, are by no means to be deprived for that reason of the ceremony of consecration."[192] The papal concession in no way implies that Anselm himself should become the king's man, and nowhere in the contemporary sources is there so much as a hint that Anselm ever swore homage to Henry I. The controversy between king and primate had begun in 1100 with Henry's demand that Anselm render him homage and receive the archbishopric from his hand; it ended with Anselm doing neither.

Henry's remaining concession was in the form of a concrete endorsement of Anselm's vision of corule. Shortly after his return to England, Anselm wrote to Helgot, former prior of Caen and now abbot of St-Ouen, confirming a rumor that was circulating in Rouen: "And what you have heard, that my lord the king committed to me his kingdom and all his possessions so that my will should be done in all things that are his, is true."[193] This privilege, probably granted when Anselm and Henry were together at Bec, was repeated on the king's departure for Normandy in 1108, when Henry committed his young son and his entire kingdom to Anselm's protection.[194] Writing from Normandy in March 1109, Henry told Anselm that the management of affairs in England was "to be governed by your will and settled by your advice. Indeed, I have made this known to our justiciars."[195] The letter includes confidential information on matters of high politics, such as a stormy personal interview with King Louis VI[196] and the successful completion of negotiations with the Emperor Henry V regarding his betrothal to Henry I's daughter, Matilda. The king's readiness to confide in Anselm on such matters of state is a significant confirmation of the archbishop's new role in the Anglo-Norman governance.

The agreement at Bec thus represented the fulfillment of Anselm's most cherished hopes. During the first phase of the Investiture Contest he had secured significant papal backing for the Canterbury primacy, and now with Henry's formal concession on investitures he could return to England and exercise his primacy with the king's full support. Henry also seemed willing to accept Anselm's vision of king and archbishop pulling the plow of the church together through the fields of

192. AEp. 397.
193. AEp. 407; on Helgot, see OV 4:308 and n. 2.   194. *HN* 197.
195. AEp. 461; cf. *Regesta* 2, no. 906 (A.D. 1108–9), in which Queen Matilda establishes Holy Trinity, Aldgate, "by the advice of Archbishop Anselm and with the consent and confirmation of my lord king Henry."
196. On which see Luchaire, *Louis VI*, p. 39.

God's kingdom. Anselm could at last assume the status of coruler of the *alter orbis*. Immediately after the Bec settlement Anselm returned to England, his health restored, and landed at Dover "sound in body and mind"[197] to be greeted with delight and rejoicing by the queen and people of England.

Having made their peace with Anselm, Henry I and Robert of Meulan returned to the task of conquering Normandy. On 28 September 1106, they encountered the ducal army outside the walls of William of Mortain's castle at Tinchebrai. Orderic reports that Henry had with him four *comites* — Elias of Maine (now back in the royal fold), William of Evreux, Robert of Meulan, and William of Warenne earl of Surrey — along with other leading magnates and their followers.[198] The king sent a legation to his brother, explaining his divine commission to deliver the Norman church and people from violence, and offering half the duchy's revenues to Curthose if he would surrender his governance to Henry. Predictably, Curthose declined the offer, and the two armies met in pitched battle. Ranulf *vicomte* of Bayeux (future earl of Chester) commanded Henry's first division, Robert count of Meulan the second, and William of Warenne the third; Count Elias commanded a reserve force of Breton and Manceaux cavalry.[199] Elias of Maine won the day with a cavalry charge that sent Robert of Bellême fleeing and crushed the remainder of the ducal army. Henry took Curthose prisoner, along with William of Mortain and other ducal followers. Consigning his luckless brother to lifelong imprisonment, Henry assumed the governance of Normandy. In a great council at Lisieux the following month, Henry declared that the royal peace would thenceforth be enforced strictly, that churches would hold their possessions as they had held them when his father died, and that laymen should also hold their inheritances in peace. But whatever ducal lands Curthose had foolishly alienated, Henry would repossess.[200]

Thus, while Anselm made his vision of the primacy of Canterbury into a reality, Henry and Robert of Meulan fulfilled their own vision of a unified Anglo-Norman polity under a strong king who maintained civil order and enforced the laws. That Anselm fully shared their goal is

197. *HN* 183.
198. OV 6:84–85.
199. On the battle and its sources, see David, *Robert Curthose,* pp. 172–76, 245–48.
200. OV 6:92–94.

clear from his reply to Henry's letter announcing the royal victory at
Tinchebrai:

To Henry, by the grace of God glorious king of the English and duke of the
Normans, Archbishop Anselm sends faithful service with faithful prayers, and
may he always grow to greater and greater things and never diminish.

I rejoice and give thanks to God with all the affection that is within me . . .
for your prosperity and success. Indeed, I rejoice and give thanks from my
inmost heart because, with earthly prosperity, His grace so illuminates your
heart that you impute nothing in His benefactions or in your advancement to
yourself or to human strength, but you impute it all to His mercy; and because,
as much as is in you, you have promised the peace and liberty of His church.[201]

Henry had modestly attributed his victory not to his own energies "but
to the gift of God who so disposed it,"[202] and Anselm expressed his
hearty agreement with this pious interpretation. But Eadmer saw the
matter somewhat differently: "Not unnaturally, it was the declared
opinion of many that it was in consequence of his having made peace
with Anselm that the king gained this victory."[203]

Returning to England in spring 1107, Henry summoned a council of
all the bishops, abbots, and nobles of the realm on 1 August at Westminster Palace to ratify the agreement concluded at Laigle and promulgated
at Bec.[204] For three days he conferred with his English bishops, with
Anselm absent but nearby awaiting the outcome. Although some of the
bishops urged the king to go back on his word to Paschal and Anselm,
Henry, having summoned Anselm and the nobles to join the assemblage, declared that no one in England would ever again be invested
with an ecclesiastical office at the hands of the king or any layman.
Anselm then conceded that no one elected to any ecclesiastical preferment would be deprived of consecration because of having done homage to the king. Henry and Anselm thus jointly announced the terms
of the investiture settlement to the bishops, abbots, and nobility of
England, as they had previously been announced to the Normans at
Bec. Anselm later reported to Paschal that the king had been counseled
to keep his promises by Robert of Meulan and Richard of Redvers.[205]
The count of Meulan, unlike some of the English bishops, would have

201. AEp. 402.
202. AEp. 401.
203. HN 182–84.
204. On the Council of 1107, see Councils and Synods 1, pt. 2: 689–94.
205. AEp. 430: the aged Richard of Redvers, a member of Henry's inner council,
died a few weeks later on 8 September.

clearly seen that Henry, having formally committed himself to the concessions at Bec, would surely invite widespread reproach by repudiating them now.

As Eadmer reports, "Now that these questions had been thus settled, the king, on the advice of Anselm and the nobles of the realm, appointed fathers to nearly all the churches of England that had been so long widowed of their pastors," and he did so without requiring them to submit to royal investiture. At the same time he filled some Norman ecclesiastical vacancies, again without investiture. The filling of accumulated vacancies, combined with the breaking of the seven-year logjam of unconsecrated prelates-elect, resulted in a flood of consecrations, "so many that nobody could remember that as many had been given together before."[206] At Canterbury, on Sunday, 11 August, Anselm and his suffragans consecrated William Giffard to Winchester, Roger to Salisbury, Reinhelm to Hereford, Urban to the see of Llandaff in South Wales, and the veteran royal envoy, William Warelwast, to Exeter.[207] All rendered written professions of obedience to Canterbury, and Urban of Llandaff's profession further consolidated the Canterbury primacy in Wales.[208] Anselm also filled vacancies at the abbeys of Ramsay, Bury St. Edmunds, Battle, and Peterborough. Battle remained firmly within the Bec-Caen network with the appointment of Ralph, formerly a monk of Bec, monk and prior of Caen, and prior of Rochester.[209] And the vacancy of Peterborough was filled by Anselm's intimate associate and correspondent in exile, Ernulf prior of Canterbury.[210]

Some of these men — William of Winchester, Ralph of Battle, and Ernulf of Peterborough — were Anselm's trusted friends, and Reinhelm of Hereford had earlier brought the royal wrath upon himself by supporting Anselm in refusing consecration by Gerard of York.[211] But others — Roger of Salisbury and William Warelwast of Exeter in particular — had been staunch supporters of the king in his controversy with Anselm. When Eadmer states that Henry nominated these prelates "on the advice of Anselm and the nobles of the realm," one must conclude that Anselm was prepared to go some distance in respecting the king's wishes. There seems a degree of exaggeration in Anselm's

---

206. *ASC*, A.D. 1107.
207. *HN* 187.
208. Richter, *Canterbury Professions*, pp. 35–36, nos. 55–59.
209. Knowles, *Heads*, p. 29.
210. Ibid., p. 60; *ASC*, A.D. 1107.
211. Above, Chapter 6 at nn. 170–72.

report to Paschal that "now the king, in choosing people for preferment, does not consult his own wishes at all, but relies entirely on the advice of men of religion."[212] Roger of Salisbury was known to have had a mistress, as was Richard of Belmeis, whom Anselm consecrated as bishop of London in 1108.[213] Anselm's idea of corule, as we have seen, did not in any sense imply a distinction between church and state; rather, it envisioned cooperation and shared authority between king and primate in the governance of the English church and its Christian people. Anselm was thus prepared to allow Henry a considerable voice in the nomination of bishops. Roger of Salisbury, William Warelwast, and Richard of Belmeis were all gifted royal officials whose substantial talents would thenceforth be devoted not only to the king but to their bishoprics as well. That seems to have been enough for Anselm, who had never intended the investiture ban to deprive the king of a significant role in ecclesiastical appointments.

As Hugh the Chantor stated, Henry's concession on investitures "cost him little or nothing; a little, perhaps, of his royal dignity, but nothing of his power to enthrone anyone he pleased."[214] In making this observation, the York writer obviously intended to belittle Anselm's achievement, but Anselm had himself made a similar point when he remarked in a letter to Robert of Meulan that the king could forgo investitures without losing a scrap of his sovereignty.[215] Both statements are true; yet, in the long run, Henry's concession meant that he and his successors would no longer enjoy the virtually unrestricted control of ecclesiastical appointments that the Conqueror and Rufus had exercised. Secular-minded clerks of the royal household might still rise regularly to bishoprics, but the king could no longer count on elevating men of evil reputation, such as Ranulf Flambard, without encountering opposition.

In the process of his negotiations on investiture, Henry I had also opened some gaping holes in William the Conqueror's wall around England. "To invoke the authority of Rome in 1100," Martin Brett observes, "was no easy matter."[216] But between 1100 and 1106 legations had been moving almost constantly to and from the papal

212. AEp. 430.
213. C. N. L. Brooke, "Married Men among the English Higher Clergy, 1106–1200," *Cambridge Historical Journal* 12 (1956): 187.
214. HCY 145.
215. AEp. 369.
216. Brett, *English Church*, p. 34.

court, and they would do so increasingly in the decades and generations to come.[217] In short, the English Investiture Controversy marked the beginning of the end of the monarchy's iron grip on the English church. The result was not a diminution of royal sovereignty but a shift in royal strategy. As Sir Richard Southern has observed, although kings were quite naturally apprehensive at the reform papacy's threat to their authority over the church, "by a slow process of adjustment they discovered that they had been unnecessarily alarmed."[218] By learning the rules of a new and complicated game, they could work with the primate of Canterbury and the papal court to mutual advantage, drawing into the royal service "a larger reservoir of ecclesiastical wealth and talent than ever before."[219] In 1107 this possibility was already becoming evident as king and primate worked in double harness to bring the English church into a state of due order. A symbol of this new state of affairs is that Roger of Salisbury, whom historians regard as one of medieval England's foremost administrators, received his episcopal consecration from St. Anselm.

In the end, therefore, the political initiatives of Anselm and Robert of Meulan had led them by different paths to the same destination. Rid at last of his conflicts with the Anglo-Norman monarchy, Anselm was free to exercise the Canterbury primacy in the interest of ecclesiastical reform. Robert and Henry, although forced to submit on the investiture issue, had established firm control over the Conqueror's Anglo-Norman dominions. They found that they could, after all, live comfortably with the investiture settlement and work in cooperation with Anselm toward the shared goals of peace, reform, and effective governance. Despite their many differences, Anselm and Robert of Meulan were of one mind in their desire for a united and well-governed Anglo-Norman realm, ruled by an able, peacekeeping king who was prepared to protect the church, curb violence, and bring order to his dominions. These goals were achieved primarily through Robert of Meulan's counsel and diplomacy, and Anselm could hardly have argued with them. Similarly, Robert of Meulan had accepted the necessity of church and kingdom functioning in double harness for the welfare of the Christian community. William of Malmesbury reports that he introduced into

217. Ibid., pp. 34–62.
218. *Western Society and the Church in the Middle Ages* (Harmondsworth, 1970), p. 130.
219. Ibid.

England customs of more moderate eating and dressing: "By his example he changed the custom. Finally, this custom of eating once [a day], through his efforts," was adopted by all the baronial courts.[220] Thus Robert too endeavored to cooperate in church efforts to reform the lives of the English people, as Anselm surely would have wished, just as Anselm was cooperating with the king.

The rivalry of these two men was conducted with remarkable subtlety and political sophistication, and their reconciliation promised an era of cooperation between church and monarchy such as had not existed since Lanfranc's time. The Anglo-Norman world would not have been the same without them, nor would it ever be the same thereafter.

Observing the events of 1107 from ground level, Eadmer misleadingly attributed the king's magnanimity toward Anselm to a moral reform on the part of Robert of Meulan:

It may truthfully be said that he was in some respect a changed character, having abandoned the ways to which he was formerly addicted. Indeed, having become a lover of righteousness, he was lavish in giving some people advice, others help, and still others both advice and help, according to the requirements of the case. King Henry himself in all matters affecting the kingdom trusted his judgment and followed his advice more than that of any of his other counselors, and in doing so he came to have, he declared, a horror of following in the footsteps of his brother, the former king.[221]

---

220. *GR* 2:483; William goes on to say that some people thought Robert did so through parsimony, but William believed that it was more from fear of being thought gluttonous (gluttony was one of the seven deadly sins). Robert may well have introduced these customs at around this time, for Eadmer states that it was after 1107 that Robert changed his ways: *HN* 191–92 (see below and n. 221).

221. *HN* 191–92.

Eight

The Final Years:
St. Anselm, Robert of Meulan,
and the Art of Politics in the
Anglo-Norman State, 1107–1118

With the formal ratification of the investiture settlement in August 1107 at Westminster, the major issues between church and monarchy had been resolved to the satisfaction of both Archbishop Anselm and Robert count of Meulan. An adversary relationship that had divided them for much of the two previous decades was at an end. Anselm was by then in his mid-seventies and had less than two years of life remaining to him; Count Robert was about sixty and would devote most of his remaining eleven years, as before, to serving and counseling the king. But in doing so he was no longer vulnerable to Ivo of Chartres's earlier charge of preferring the king of the English to the King of the angels.[1] Anselm could now comfortably address the count as "his lord and friend, dearest Robert."[2]

The events of 1106–7 included triumphs not only for Henry I and Anselm but for Robert of Meulan as well. Probably in 1107 Henry

1. *PL* 162, col. 158 (Ep. 154): "Cum enim gratiam inveneris in conspectu regis Anglorum, testantur multae ecclesiasticae personae quod plus ei placere studeas quam Regi angelorum."
2. AEp. 467: "domino et amico carissimo Roberto, comiti de Mellento."

rewarded his chief adviser by making him the first earl of Leicester.[3] Robert did not style himself "earl of Leicester," preferring the more venerable title, "count of Meulan,"[4] but as the father of twin three-year-old sons, he now enjoyed the luxury of being able to bequeath a comital title to each of them. He worked out his testamentary arrangements in considerable detail, and Henry I gave them his formal endorsement in a notification probably issued in 1107. The first-born twin, Waleran, was to receive his father's continental estates along with the large English manor of Sturminster, Dorset, worth £140 a year (originally granted by the Conqueror to Roger of Beaumont); whereas the other twin, Robert, the future earl of Leicester, was to receive all the remaining lands in England.[5] If one of the twins should die, the other would inherit all; if both should die, Count Robert's daughter would succeed on condition that she marry with the king's consent. If either the continental or the English lands should be lost, the twins were to share what remained. Count Robert had thus, characteristically, prepared a comprehensive plan to ensure the hereditary rights of his sons under almost any foreseeable circumstance, and had arranged to have the settlement ratified by his friend, King Henry.

Since Robert of Meulan had inherited most of the lands designated for the "elder" of his twin sons (the Norman Beaumont patrimony and Sturminster), and had acquired most of the lands intended for the "younger," the inheritance plan approximated the normal Anglo-Norman pattern.[6] The county of Meulan was not included in Henry's endorsement because it was not in the king's gift, but it was clearly intended for the elder twin, Waleran, who was given a name unknown to earlier Beaumonts but borne by previous counts of Meulan. At Robert of Meulan's death in 1118, despite the warfare that swept across

3. OV 6:18–20 and 20 n. 1 with references; *Complete Peerage* 7:525; Sir Frank Stenton, *The First Century of English Feudalism, 1066–1166*, 2d ed. (Oxford, 1961), p. 228, n. 2; the date that Henry created the earldom is nowhere recorded, but he is likely to have done so shortly after having endorsed Count Robert's will dividing the lands that Robert held in 1107 between his twin sons: *Regesta* 2, no. 843; below, n. 5. See, in general, Levi Fox, "The Honor and Earldom of Leicester," *EHR* 54 (1939): 385–88.

4. The one possible exception is *Regesta* 2, no. 844, a notification by Henry I in favor of the church of Lincoln, addressed to Robert "Legrecestrensi comiti" and attested by Robert as earl of Leicester in a witness list that cannot be after 1107; the original has perished, and the formula of notification, *Volu ut sciatis me concessisse*, is "very unusual in form."

5. *Regesta* 2, no. 843 and p. 319; Stenton, *English Feudalism*, pp. 33–34.

6. J. C. Holt, "Politics and Property in Early Medieval England," *Past and Present* 57 (1972): 12 ff.

Normandy immediately thereafter, his inheritance plan was implemented swiftly and smoothly. At Rouen in 1119 the younger twin, then
in his mid-teens, granted property to the abbey of Bec, "for the deliverance of his father's soul," as "Robert earl of Leicester."[7] Issued
in the royal chamber, Robert's charter bore the signum and seal of
King Henry I, and its witness list was headed by "Waleran count of
Meulan."

Robert earl of Leicester inherited an English earldom that his father
had built up to vast proportions. As we have seen, Robert of Meulan's
Domesday holdings, worth about £250 a year, were of modest size
relative to those of the Conqueror's wealthiest magnates, and their
value was drastically diminished in 1088 when Count Robert ceded his
Warwickshire and Northamptonshire estates, worth about £215 a
year, to his brother Henry.[8] But by the time of his death Count Robert's
wealth had grown to such a degree as to make him one of England's
greatest landholders.[9] He acquired some lands under Rufus, including
Roger of Beaumont's estates in Dorset and Gloucestershire worth about
£80 a year,[10] but it was under Henry I that he ascended to the sum-
mit of the English aristocratic order. His acquisition in 1102 of the

7. *Regesta* 2, no. 1214.
8. Above, Chapter 3 at nn. 106–8, and n. 90.
9. OV 6:20: Robert "omnes regni proceres diuitiis et potestate precessit." In 1172,
scutage was assessed on the earldom of Leicester for 125 full knights' fees and 35 fees of
Mortain: Sanders, *Baronies*, p. 61. These figures, which probably represent actual
enfeoffment totals, are exceeded only by the scutages of estates held about 1130 by
Stephen of Richmond (about 175 fees in 1172), Stephen count of Boulogne (about 290)
and Robert earl of Gloucester (261½). The latter two magnates received much or all of
their land in the 1120s, after Robert of Meulan's death (Sanders, *Baronies*, pp. 6, 43, 126,
140, 151; *Complete Peerage* 5:683–86; *Early Yorkshire Charters*, ed. C. T. Clay 5
[1936]: 1–16; R. H. C. Davis, *King Stephen, 1135–1154* [Berkeley and Los Angeles,
1967], pp. 7–9); this fact, combined with the further fact that the later scutage figures of
the earldom of Leicester exclude the Dorset lands that Waleran received leave open the
possibility that Orderic was correct in describing Robert of Meulan as becoming the
wealthiest of all English magnates of his time.
10. Levi Fox, "The Honor and Earldom of Leicester," *EHR* 54 (1939): 385–88; see
also *CDF,* no. 325: in the reign of William II, Count Robert granted to St. Pierre's, Préaux,
the tithes and churches of Charlton Marshall (co. Dorset, *terra regis* in 1086: *DB* 1,
fol. 75) and Spettisbury (co. Dorset, held by the count of Mortain in 1086: *DB* 1,
fol. 79б). The Leicestershire manors of Wanlip, Saxelby, and Shoby, which had belonged to Earl Aubrey of Northumberland until shortly before the Domesday survey
and were in the king's hands in 1086, had passed into the earldom of Leicester by
1130: *The Leicestershire Survey*, ed. C. F. Slade (Leicester, 1956), p. 86; Slade thinks
it probable that they were granted to Robert of Meulan by William I or II soon after the
Domesday Inquest, but it may well be significant that another of Earl Aubrey's estates,
Gussage St. Michael in Dorset (*DB* 1, fol. 69; cf. *VCH, Wiltshire*, 2:135 and n. 30a) is
described explicitly in the *Liber Feodorum* (1:91) as having been granted to the count
of Meulan by Henry I.

Grandmesnil estates (£373 a year) was the chief means of his enrichment but not the only one.[11] He acquired other Leicestershire and
Northamptonshire estates from the royal demesne,[12] and Henry I
granted him a number of additional manors in Dorset, which occur in
Domesday Book as *terra regis*.[13] He received all the Leicester and
Northamptonshire properties of Aubrey earl of Northumberland (forfeited before 1086) and was lavishly enriched in Northamptonshire and
Sussex from the lands forfeited to Henry I by William count of Mortain
about 1104.[14] The absence of twelfth-century surveys for all but a few
shires makes it impossible to trace Robert of Meulan's English acquisitions in their entirety, but the Pipe Roll of 1130 records danegeld

11. Above, Chapter 6 at nn. 110–15; virtually all the Leicestershire and Northamptonshire estates attributed to Hugh of Grandmesnil in Domesday Book are in the
earl of Leicester's hands in 1130, along with four Leicestershire estates which Hugh of
Grandmesnil had held of Countess Judith in 1086 but which the earl of Leicester now held
directly of the king: *Leicestershire Survey*, pp. 86–87; "Northamptonshire Survey," in
VCH, Northampton, 1:359–60, 367–72, 384.

12. *Leicestershire Survey*, pp. 84–86; Asfordby, King's Norton, Shangton, and
Sileby, all *terra regis* in 1086, all seem to have passed, wholly or in part, to the earl of
Leicester by 1130, along with five holdings not recorded in Domesday Book. In North-
amptonshire, the earl of Leicester's holding at Pokesle (Cleyle Hundred) was probably
Domesday *terra regis*: *VCH, Northampton*, 1:374 and n. 10; since Robert earl of
Leicester had far less influence at Henry I's court than had his father, it is extremely
probable that lands not in Beaumont hands in 1086 but held by the earl of Leicester in the
Leicestershire and Northamptonshire surveys were acquired by Robert of Meulan.

13. "Dominus rex Henricus primus dedit comiti de Meulent Kingeston [Kingston
Lacy] cum pertenenciis scilicet Sapewic [Shapwick] et Kerchel Freinel [Little Critchel] et
Gessiz Dinant [Gussage St. Michael] et Bernardeste [Barnsley] et Cnolton [Knowlton] et
Upwinburne [Wimborne All Hallows]": *Liber Feodorum*, 1:91–92; cf. *DB* 1, fol. 75
(Kingston Lacy and Barnsley do not occur by name but are appurtenances of the [named]
royal estate of Wimborne Minster), and fol. 69: King William had recently taken
possession of Gussage St. Michael from Earl Aubrey.

14. *Leicestershire Survey*, p. 86; *VCH, Northampton*, 1:359–60, 368–71, 374,
377–79, 381–83. The count of Mortain did not hold Domesday lands in Leicester;
although the majority of his Domesday holdings in Northamptonshire passed to the
earldom of Leicester, others passed to the "fee of Berkhamstead," which had been
granted to Henry I's chancellor, Ranulf, and had reverted to the crown on Ranulf's death
in 1123 (Sanders, *Baronies*, p. 14); besides having acquired all of Earl Aubrey's lands in
Leicestershire and Northamptonshire, Robert of Meulan held additional estates in Dorset
and Warwickshire that Aubrey had held in the Conqueror's reign: above, nn. 10, 13;
Charters of the Honour of Mowbray, 1107–1191, ed. D. E. Greenway (London, 1972),
pp. xx–xxi, 14–15 (no. 10): Nigel of Aubigny grants Earl Aubrey's former estate at Smite
(Warwicks.) to the monks of Bec, with the consent of his lord R. count of Meulan. The
earldom of Leicester also acquired four minor holdings in Lindsey that had belonged to
Hugh fitz Baldric in 1086: *The Lincolnshire Domesday and the Lindsey Survey*, ed. C. W.
Foster and Thomas Longley (Lincoln Record Society, 19, 1924), pp. 246, 251; cf.
pp. 115–16 (*DB* 1, fol. 356). On Robert of Meulan's acquisitions in the Rape of Peven-
sey, see J. F. A. Mason, *William I and the Sussex Rapes* (The Historical Association,
Hastings and Bexhill Branch, 1966), p. 20.

exemptions for the lands of the Beaumont twins in no less than eleven shires.[15]

Robert of Meulan saw to it that his twins would possess not only vast wealth but also excellent educations. The sources are silent on the nature of Count Robert's own education, but a passing remark in the Abingdon chronicle discloses that one of his twins, Robert earl of Leicester, received his schooling at Abingdon Abbey under its learned Tuscan abbot-physician, Faritius, and Waleran is likely to have studied there as well.[16] William of Malmesbury reports that when Pope Calixtus II conferred with Henry I in 1119 near Gisors, Waleran and Robert, "young men of most noble family," engaged the cardinals in dialectical debate and discomfited them with lively reasoning.[17] If we can believe Malmesbury's account, the cardinals were surprised to encounter such "literary eminence" in the fifteen-year-old twins. It is a pity that Robert of Meulan, who so often had observed England's foremost churchman outarguing all opponents, could not have lived to see his sons turn the tables. Many years thereafter, Robert earl of Leicester would carry on the Beaumont family tradition by serving as justiciar of King Henry II; another of Henry II's great officials, Richard fitz Neal, praised Robert as being "well educated and practiced in legal affairs."[18]

Anselm's last years were saddened by the deaths of two of his dearest friends. Not long after returning to England from exile, he received a letter from Abbot Hugh of Cluny reporting the death of Anselm's comrade in controversy and host in exile, Hugh archbishop of Lyon, on 7 October 1106.[19] And on 7 March 1108, Gundulf bishop of Rochester died, depriving Anselm of an even closer and more cherished friend.[20] But Anselm remained surrounded by monk-prelates who had

15. *Pipe Roll 31 Henry I,* ed. Joseph Hunter (London, 1833, reprinted 1929), passim: Bedf. £1-0-0; Berks. 2-4-0; Cambs. 0-3-3; Dorset 1-16-9; Herts. 3-10-0; Leics. 10-2-0; Norfolk 1-2-4; Northants. 2-4-5; Oxon. 3-2-0; Warw. 3-12-0; Wilts. 6-10-0.

16. *Chronicon Monasterii de Abingdon,* 2:229; cf. Edward J. Kealey, *Medieval Medicus: A Social History of Anglo-Norman Medicine* (Baltimore, 1981), pp. 51, 65–70; Richardson and Sayles, *The Governance of Medieval England* (Edinburgh, 1963), pp. 269–73; and Ralph V. Turner, "The *Miles Literatus* in 12th- and 13th-Century England: How Rare a Phenomenon?" *AHR* 83 (1978): 928–45.

17. *GR* 2:482.

18. *Dialogus de Scaccario,* ed. Charles Johnson (Oxford, 1983), pp. 57–58; a detailed study of the Beaumont twins by Dr. David Crouch is in press.

19. *AEp.* 409.

20. *Fasti,* ed. Greenway, 2:75.

been trained in the reform ideals of Bec and its "sister" houses of St-Etienne, Caen; Lessay; and Christ Church, Canterbury.[21] Former monks of Bec who ruled English abbeys during the two closing years of Anselm's life included Ralph abbot of Battle, Richard abbot of Chester, Gilbert Crispin abbot of Westminster, and Hugh abbot of St. Augustine's, Canterbury. Moreover, Herluin abbot of Glastonbury (1100–1118) and Roger abbot of Cerne were former monks of Caen; Richard d'Aubigny abbot of St. Albans (1097–1119) had been a monk of Lessay; and Ernulf prior of Canterbury, Anselm's frequent correspondent, was advanced to the abbacy of Peterborough in 1107.[22] In some of these houses the Bec-Caen-Lessay-Canterbury influence was reinforced by successive abbots. Ralph abbot of Battle (1107–24) had succeeded Henry, a former monk of Bec and prior of Canterbury, and would himself be succeeded by Warner (1125–38), another Canterbury monk. Similarly, Richard abbot of St. Albans was the successor of the former Caen monk and nephew of Lanfranc, Paul (abbot of St. Albans, 1077–93). Abbot Richard's own successor, Geoffrey of Gorron (1119–46), was previously prior of St. Albans, thus illustrating the tendency of Bec reform influence becoming internalized to the point that a house could begin to choose its abbots from within its own reformed community.[23]

During the last two years of his life, Anselm seems to have enjoyed King Henry's unmitigated favor and confidence.[24] Having at last assumed fully his primatial role, he took his place alongside Robert of Meulan as a principal royal counselor. During the twelve-month period between the Council of Westminster (1–4 August 1107) and Henry's last Channel crossing in Anselm's lifetime (late July 1108), the primate attested no less than nine surviving royal *acta*,[25] six of which were also

21. Above, Chapter 2 at nn. 238 to end.

22. Knowles, *Heads*, passim: on Roger abbot of Cerne, see "Ex Chronico S. Michaelis in Periculo Maris," A.D. 1106, in *Recueil des historiens des Gaules et de la France* 12:772: I am indebted to C. Warren Hollister for this reference. Ernulf was translated from Peterborough to the bishopric of Rochester in 1114; his successor as prior of Canterbury, Conrad (1108/9–1126), a Canterbury monk, left his office in 1126 to become abbot of St. Benet's, Hulme. On the Bec-Caen-Canterbury influence at Battle Abbey, see Eleanor Searle, *Lordship and Community: Battle Abbey and its Banlieu, 1066–1538* (Toronto, 1974), pp. 28–29.

23. A similar pattern occurred at Caen and Lessay: *Gallia Christiana*, 11: cols. 422–25, 918–19.

24. The statements to the contrary by Hugh the Chantor (pp. 18, 33) are in conflict with all other evidence: see below, Chapter 8 at nn. 122–66, especially 154–57.

25. *Regesta* 2, nos. 825–26, 828, 831–33, 881, 885, 894.

attested by Count Robert.[26] Besides returning Canterbury's confiscated estates, King Henry also restored property that had been alienated from the archbishopric long before and had passed into royal
hands.[27] In 1108 Henry undertook a series of major administrative and
legal reforms "on the advice of Anselm and the great men of the
realm."[28] He commanded that anyone caught in the act of thievery or
robbery should be hanged; by threatening offenders with mutilation, he
brought the traditionally rapacious itinerant royal court to a state of
order and discipline, and he decreed similar penalties for false minters.[29]
Eadmer clearly approved of these measures, from which "great
good resulted immediately to the whole kingdom."[30] Henry also gave
firm backing to Anselm in insisting that priests celebrate the mass with
due reverence and proper ritual.[31] For the purpose of enforcing clerical
celibacy, Henry permitted Anselm to hold a second primatial council, in
conjunction with the king's London Whitsun court of late May 1108.[32]

Anselm's London council was devoted entirely to the problem of
clerical incontinence and the designing of administrative mechanisms
to suppress it. Priests, deacons, subdeacons, deans, archdeacons, and
canons were ordered to be celibate on pain of expulsion from their
offices and benefices.[33] The council was a noteworthy manifestation of
Anselm's two-oxen metaphor. It was held in the presence of King Henry
and his magnates, and its legislation was backed explicitly by the royal
auctoritas and *potentia*.[34] The editors of *Councils and Synods* wisely
conclude that "it is neither possible nor useful to decide whether the
assembly in which these measures were discussed was secular or ecclesiastical."[35]

A similar fusion of secular and ecclesiastical authority occurs in the
record of a lawsuit adjudicated at this same Whitsun court "in the
presence of King Henry, Archbishop Anselm, Robert count of Meulan,
and many bishops, abbots, and magnates."[36] Reinhelm bishop of

26. Ibid., nos. 828, 831–33, 881, 885.
27. Ibid., no. 756: Henry restores the vill of Slindon, Sussex, in a charter witnessed
by Queen Matilda and Anselm's former antagonists Robert bishop of Lincoln, William
Warelwast, and Robert count of Meulan.
28. *HN* 192.   29. *HN* 192–93; Florence, 2:57.
30. *HN* 193.   31. *HN* 193.
32. *HN* 193–95; *Councils and Synods* 1, pt. 2:694–704.
33. A previous council with much the same agenda may possibly have met at or been
planned for Winchester: Brett, *English Church*, pp. 79–80.
34. *HN* 193–94.
35. *Councils and Synods* 1, pt. 2:695.
36. Ibid., pp. 703–4; *Regesta* 2, no. 880.

Hereford had dug up the body of a certain Ralph fitz Ansketill, a benefactor of Gloucester Abbey, from the abbey's burial ground and carried it off to be reburied at Hereford Cathedral, claiming that Ralph had been his parishoner. Peter abbot of Gloucester was not bringing suit against Bishop Reinhelm for the return of Ralph's corpse. The court ruled in Abbot Peter's favor: all men should thenceforth have the right to choose their burial place. The judgment is described as having had the consent of all the attending bishops, yet, interestingly, it was announced by neither Anselm nor King Henry, but by Robert of Meulan.[37]

The king and the primate also worked together toward the transformation of the abbey of Ely into a new bishopric. The plan was originally advanced by Richard abbot of Ely,[38] the Clare cadet and former Bec monk whom Anselm had deposed at Henry's urging in 1102. Richard had since made his peace with the king and been restored to his abbatiate by Anselm,[39] but he died in June 1107 before he could bring his plan to fruition. The idea was discussed further at the 1108 Whitsun council, where it received the approval of Henry I, Anselm, and "the rest of the great men of the realm."[40] With the consent of Robert bishop of Lincoln, and pending papal approval, it was agreed that episcopal jurisdiction over Cambridgeshire would be transferred from the far-flung see of Lincoln to the new see of Ely, in exchange for the granting of Ely property of equivalent value to the bishop of Lincoln.[41] Henry and Anselm each petitioned Paschal II to endorse the plan, and he did so without hesitation.[42]

Anselm appears to have had reservations, however, about the person whom the king intended to appoint to the new bishopric. The church of Ely had been without a head since Abbot Richard's death the previous year, and Henry was planning to replace him with an already consecrated bishop, Hervey of Bangor, who had fled his see some years before because of the hostility of the north Welsh and had found refuge at the royal court.[43] There, having won the king's love through his useful

---

37. Cf. Brett, *English Church*, p. 98; as the result of a subsequent bargain between Bishop Reinhelm and Abbot Peter, Ralph's body remained at Hereford.

38. *Liber Eliensis*, p. 237.

39. Ibid., p. 413.   40. *HN* 195.

41. *Liber Eliensis*, p. 246; *GP* 325.

42. AEpp. 441, 457–58; *Liber Eliensis*, pp. 246–47.

43. AEp. 459; *Liber Eliensis*, p. 245, reports that the Welsh murdered Hervey's brother and would have murdered Hervey himself if they could have laid their hands on him. William of Malmesbury, however, says that Hervey left Bangor because of the scantiness of its revenues: *GR* 2:517.

services, Hervey had lobbied for an appointment to a more congenial bishopric. Shortly after the victory at Tinchebrai, King Henry had tried to translate him to the see of Lisieux, but Anselm, as Hervey's metropolitan, had refused to permit him to leave Britain for a Norman bishopric.[44] On Richard abbot of Ely's death, the king had appointed Hervey royal custodian of the Ely estates until the vacancy should be filled. At Ely, Hervey won the affection of the monks "with flattery and circumlocution" and enlisted their support in the project of changing the abbey into a monastic bishopric under his own rule.[45] Once the Whitsun council of 1108 had endorsed the change, Hervey set out for Rome as a royal envoy to obtain papal approval. He managed to persuade Paschal to approve not only the new bishopric but his own translation into it as well.[46] This last matter seems to have provoked Anselm. In his letter to Paschal recommending the project, he said not a word in Hervey's behalf.[47] But Hervey charmed Paschal no less than he had charmed Henry I and the monks of Ely, and Paschal responded with two letters to Anselm, one approving the new bishopric and the other ordering Anselm by apostolic authority to grant it to Hervey.[48] Anselm is not known to have responded. He had previously demonstrated his willingness to consecrate worldly royal favorites to English bishoprics,[49] but Hervey, with his false charm and blatant ambition, was apparently too much for Anselm to swallow. That Hervey would be succeeding a former Bec monk in the rule of Ely may well have added to Anselm's doubts.[50] As Eadmer expressed it, the bishopric of Ely that Hervey had sought "by much asking, much promising of many kinds, and the performance of many services, he finally succeeded in obtaining as soon as Anselm, that most active father, was dead."[51]

44. AEp. 404.
45. *Liber Eliensis*, p. 245.
46. Ibid., pp. 245–46.
47. AEp. 441.
48. AEpp. 458, 459; neither is preserved in Lambeth ms. 59.
49. E.g., Roger of Salisbury and Richard of London: above, Chapter 7 at nn. 210–13.
50. Anselm may also have feared that Hervey, having already been consecrated to the episcopacy (by Thomas I of York in 1092), would not profess obedience to Canterbury; no such profession by Hervey has survived. The monks of Ely were quickly disillusioned with Hervey when he won Robert bishop of Lincoln's backing by giving him the valuable Ely manor of Spaldwick (Hunts.) without consulting or even informing them: *Liber Eliensis*, p. 246; Spaldwick was worth £22 a year in 1086: *DB* 1, fol. 204.
51. *HN* 211; cf. *Regesta* 2, no. 919: Henry I formally elevates Ely to the status of a bishopric, by the authority of Pope Paschal, on 17 October 1109, in a charter witnessed by (among many others) Hervey bishop of Ely and Robert count of Meulan.

Anselm's health was already failing when he journeyed to Portsmouth in July 1108 to bless the king as he was about to cross to Normandy. There Henry conferred on Anselm viceregal authority over England during his own absence. According to Eadmer, Henry committed to Anselm's protection his son William, whom he was leaving behind, "and all the kingdom [*regnum*]. Whatever Anselm commanded should be law, what he prohibited, unlawful."[52] Eadmer's testimony is confirmed by a subsequent letter to Anselm from Henry I at Rouen, committing the people and governance of England to Anselm's will and counsel.[53] Anselm replied with gratitude "that you so diligently commended your son and daughter to my care and love, and that you committed your kingdom and its business to my will." Although asserting his unworthiness, Anselm expressed his heartfelt appreciation for the "immense benevolence and grace" that Henry had shown him, and asserted his willingness to supervise the English government: "What you committed to me, I commend to the disposition and aid of God, through whom all is disposed well."[54]

While exercising his authority over the English church and people in harness with the king, Anselm also devoted his final two years to defending the dignity of his archiepiscopate in matters great and small. At Portsmouth in July 1108, as Henry was about to leave for Normandy, he asked Anselm, "out of affection for himself," to consecrate Richard of Belmeis to the bishopric of London in the nearby cathedral of Chichester. Anselm very much preferred to perform his episcopal consecrations at the mother church of Canterbury, but Henry was anxious to have the consecration done before his departure so that Richard could leave for the west to resume his supervision of the forfeited earldom of Shropshire.[55] Anselm refused to consecrate Richard in a cathedral other than Canterbury but was willing to compromise out of affection for the king. He performed the consecration in his own chapel in the neighboring archiepiscopal manor of Pagham, having first received from Richard "the customary profession of his obedience and submission."[56]

---

52. *HN* 197; above, Chapter 7 at nn. 193–97.

53. AEp. 461.

54. AEp. 462; in answer to 461: Henry to Anselm.

55. *HN* 197; OV 6:144 and n. 4; Richard had been a chaplain of the former earl of Shropshire, Robert of Bellême: *Annales Monastici*, ed. H. R. Luard (RS, London, 1864–69), 2:43.

56. *HN* 197–98.

Even though Richard of Belmeis spent much of his time in Shropshire, he proved to be clever and aggressive in asserting the ancient
rights and claims of the see of London. Having read his Bede, he was
aware of Pope Gregory I's instructions that archbishoprics be established at London and York, and that whichever archbishop was consecrated first should have precedence over the other. Bishop Richard did
not go so far as to claim an archiepiscopal title, but he did petition Pope
Paschal to honor him with a pallium, prompting Anselm to remind the
pope that London had never been a metropolitan see, that its bishops
had therefore never received pallia, and that Richard's request was
simply a pretext "to humiliate the dignity of the primary see of
Canterbury."[57] Richard submitted for the time being, but at the first
Christmas court after Anselm's death he preempted the role of the
newly consecrated archbishop of York, Thomas II, by taking it upon
himself to crown the king, conduct him into the church, and celebrate
the Christmas office. Richard justified himself, Eadmer says, on the
ground that the bishop of London was ex officio dean of Canterbury,
and on the further ground that, on the ordinance of Gregory the Great,
he was senior to the archbishop of York because he had been consecrated before him.[58] Bishop Richard is said to have admitted privately
that it was precisely for the sake of obtaining this priority that he had
been in such a hurry to receive Anselm's consecration in July 1108.[59]

Anselm found his primatial authority further challenged by the
monks of neighboring St. Augustine's, Canterbury. It was a relatively
minor skirmish, but it caught Eadmer's full attention and prompted
Anselm to display once again his flair for logical argument in the arena
of royal and ecclesiastical politics. St. Augustine's boasted Canterbury's
first archbishop as its founder and patron saint, and there were reasonable grounds for its claim to a dignity parallel to that of the archbishop
himself and a share of his primatial authority. Until Lanfranc's elevation to the archbishopric, St. Augustine's had overshadowed Christ
Church as Canterbury's foremost religious community. St. Augustine
and a number of his archiepiscopal successors were entombed there,
together with King Ethelbert and other early Christian kings of Kent.
Abbot Aethelsige of St. Augustine's (1061–70) had received from Pope

57. AEp. 451.
58. HN 212.
59. Ibid.; Gerard archbishop of York died on 21 May 1108, and the consecration of
his successor, Thomas II, was delayed until the following year.

Alexander II the singular privilege of wearing the sandals and mitre of a primatial abbot.[60]

Lanfranc would have none of this. He regarded St. Augustine's as an ordinary abbey within the diocese of Canterbury, directly subordinate to the archbishop. Rejecting its claims to autonomy and primatial power, he adopted a policy of personally choosing its abbot, consecrating him in Canterbury Cathedral, and receiving from him a written profession of obedience.[61] When the monks of St. Augustine's protested and rebelled, Lanfranc took a hard line, deporting some of them to other monasteries, imprisoning others, and having one insubordinate monk tied naked at the portal of St. Augustine's and publicly flogged. Afterward, St. Augustine's was compelled to accept a prior and twenty-four new monks from the Christ Church community.[62]

Throughout most of Anselm's archiepiscopate St. Augustine's had no consecrated abbot. Lanfranc's controversial appointee, Abbot Guy, died in 1093, and his replacement was delayed by Rufus's policy of keeping abbeys in the royal hand and Henry I's stalemate with Anselm over investiture and consecration. With the settlement of the Investiture Controversy in 1107, and the resulting flood of consecrations, the issue of St. Augustine's reemerged. The new abbot-elect, Hugh *de Flori,* was probably chosen by Anselm. Eadmer states that he was a monk of Bec, not yet in holy orders. The still-rebellious monks of St. Augustine's would have been unlikely to have elected an abbot from outside their own community, especially one from Lanfranc's and Anselm's home abbey.[63] The monks of St. Augustine's do not appear to have objected

60. Gibson, *Lanfranc,* pp. 167–68.
61. In the twelfth century, an abbot claiming exemption from diocesan authority would demand three things in particular: exemption from the profession of obedience, the right to be consecrated in his own abbey church, and the right to choose the consecrating prelate: Marjorie Chibnall, "From Bec to Canterbury: Anselm and Monastic Privilege," *Anselm Studies* 1 (1983): 31. Cf. David Knowles, "The Growth of Exemption," *Downside Review* 50 (1932): 205–7. The first two claims were clearly at issue between Lanfranc and St. Augustine's, as was the further issue of free elections versus appointment by the archbishop: "Acta Lanfranci," in *Two of the Saxon Chronicles Parallel,* ed. J. Earle and C. Plummer, 1:290–92; Chibnall, "Bec to Canterbury," p. 35 and n. 52. Following Lanfranc's example, Samson bishop of Worcester (1096–1112) was striving to obtain professions from abbots within his own diocese: *Canterbury Professions,* p. lxxii.
62. "Acta Lanfranci," pp. 290–92.
63. *HN* 188: Eadmer's firsthand report that Hugh was a monk of Bec is to be preferred to William Thorne's very late testimony that he was a former knight and novice at St. Augustine's, handpicked by William Rufus; Thorne errs on the dates of Hugh's abbatiate: see Knowles, *Heads,* p. 36.

to Hugh, as they had objected to Lanfranc's last nominee. As a symbol of their autonomy, however, they did insist that Hugh receive his abbatial consecration at St. Augustine's rather than at the altar of Canterbury Cathedral. They may also have asserted a claim to choose a bishop other than Anselm as the consecrating prelate.[64]

Anselm, meanwhile, had Hugh ordained deacon and then priest in the archiepiscopal chapel at Canterbury and was on the verge of having him consecrated as abbot at the Canterbury altar. But the monks of St. Augustine's protested vehemently. In Eadmer's scornful words, "They made out as though their church held grants of special privileges and asserted that they would prove by clear evidence that these grants provided that their abbot should always be consecrated in their own abbey."[65] A delegation of St. Augustine's monks persuaded Henry I to direct Anselm to do so "in accordance with ancient custom," and Henry sent a group of high-ranking prelates to instruct Anselm to comply. But when Anselm received the king's message, he replied to its bearers, "there is no such custom," and added that to consecrate Hugh at St. Augustine's would imply that the primate was subordinate to the consecrated abbot "contrary to the rightful order."[66] The primate does not move from his see, Anselm continued, for the consecration of anyone except the king and queen. "If then the king wants me to show the abbot of St. Augustine's the same honor as to himself, his wish amounts to putting the abbot on a level with the king himself in the king's own kingdom." Anselm suggested that Henry think twice before disparaging the royal dignity in this way.[67]

The king's messengers then offered a second proposal. If Anselm refused to consecrate the abbot-elect in St. Augustine's abbey, let him be consecrated in the king's chapel by another bishop.[68] Anselm replied, "Why should I permit him to be consecrated by some other bishop when by God's grace I am myself able, as is my right, to ordain him at

64. This last claim is only faintly visible in Eadmer's tendentious account: *HN* 188–91; the profession of obedience was probably also at issue.

65. *HN* 188; a similar issue divided the monks of Battle from their diocesan bishop of Chichester: Anselm had angered the Battle monks by persuading his protégé Henry, abbot-elect of Battle, to receive consecration from the bishop of Chichester in Chichester Cathedral: *The Chronicle of Battle Abbey*, ed. Eleanor Searle (Oxford, 1980), p. 102.

66. The St. Augustine's and Christ Church communities had each manufactured a set of forged privileges conveying opposite views of the rightful order: Chibnall, "Bec to Canterbury," pp. 35–37: Gibson, *Lanfranc*, pp. 231–37.

67. *HN* 188–89.

68. *HN* 190, probably echoing the desire of the St. Augustine's monks to choose the consecrating prelate.

the place where it is right for me to do so?" The messenger responded that Anselm himself might consecrate the abbot in the king's chapel. "It is not for me," Anselm replied, "to celebrate mass in the king's chapel except when he is to be crowned by me. If I do so for the consecration of an abbot, the dignity of the crown will be disparaged."[69]

Having thus transposed the claims of St. Augustine's into a threat to the royal dignity, Anselm proposed a solution. Being in London at the time, and concluding that it would be inconvenient for him to return to Canterbury for the sole purpose of consecrating an abbot, Anselm agreed to consecrate him in the chapel of the bishop of Rochester's London house at Lambeth, where Anselm was then staying.[70] King Henry, "approving Anselm's reasoning," endorsed his solution. Anselm then duly consecrated Hugh as abbot of St. Augustine's at Lambeth on 27 February 1108, "having first received from him the customary profession by which he promised that, in accordance with the canons, he would in all respects be obedient to the Church of Canterbury and its archbishops."[71] Eadmer concludes spitefully that it would have been far more honorable and a greater distinction for the abbot to have received consecration in the metropolitan see of Canterbury than in a chapel of the church of Rochester.

With regard to Hugh's promise of obedience, Marjorie Chibnall recently raised the question: "Did Anselm, as archbishop and primate, claim more than had seemed just to Anselm as abbot?"[72] Anselm had formerly opposed the idea of abbots professing obedience to their diocesan bishops, not only with respect to Bec but as a general proposition. In a letter of about 1088 to his fellow abbot, Arnulf of Troarn, he had advised Arnulf not to profess in writing to Odo bishop of Bayeux on the grounds that a monk-prelate, having professed written obedience to his ecclesiastical superiors on entering monastic life, ought not to render a second profession.[73] In exacting the "customary profession" from Hugh in 1108, was Anselm guilty of inconsistency?

69. Ibid.
70. Ibid.; cf. p. 74: in 1095, "as the need was urgent," Anselm had ordained the bishops-elect of Worcester and Hereford to the priesthood at the chapel at Lambeth and had then consecrated them to the office of bishop in London Cathedral. Since the bishop of Rochester was the archiepiscopal vicar, his residence at Lambeth could be regarded as a Canterbury outpost.
71. HN 190: "accepta ab eo professione ex more, qua se ecclesiae Dorobernensi et archiepiscopis ejus canonice per omnia oboediturum promisit."
72. Chibnall, "Bec to Canterbury," p. 37.
73. AEp. 123; Chibnall, "Bec to Canterbury," pp. 27, 29–30. Anselm did not object to Arnulf's making a simple, verbal promise to obey Bishop Odo.

Chibnall absolves him of the charge, pointing out that Eadmer described Hugh as having "promised," not "professed." She concludes that this term should almost certainly be interpreted as a spoken promise, of the sort that Anselm expected all abbots to make to their superiors, rather than a written profession.

But some persuasive reasons indicate that Eadmer was indeed describing a written profession. His phrase *professione ex more* clearly refers back to the written professions that Lanfranc had extracted from two successive abbots-elect of St. Augustine's.[74] We have encountered repeated instances of Archbishop Lanfranc's initiatives becoming Archbishop Anselm's customs. If Anselm had objected in principle to professed monks rendering written professions to bishops, it would be difficult to account for the written professions that he received from the monk-bishops Samuel of Dublin and Ralph d'Escures of Rochester.[75] The word *promitto* occurs in every written profession rendered to Lanfranc and Anselm, and Eadmer employs the term in reference to the written profession rendered to Anselm by Gerard on his consecration as bishop of Hereford.[76] Gervase of Canterbury states explicitly that Hugh professed in writing,[77] and although Gervase is a late source, his testimony is consistent with Eadmer's.

If Eadmer can be trusted, one must conclude that the customs of Archbishop Lanfranc and the dignity of Canterbury were of greater importance to Anselm than adherence to his earlier view that a professed monk was not to profess a second time.[78] As primate of Canterbury, Anselm chose not to be constrained by an argument against

74. C. E. Woodruff, "Some Early Professions of Canonical Obedience to the See of Canterbury by Heads of Religious Houses," *Archaeologia Cantiana* 37 (1925): 60–61; Chibnall, "Bec to Canterbury," p. 35; Eadmer uses the term *ex more* in reference to the written professions of Bishops Samuel of Dublin and Malchus of Waterford (*HN* 74, 77); he employs the term *canonical* to describe not only Abbot Hugh's profession but also the written professions of Thomas I of York and, again, Samuel of Dublin: *HN* 10, 73–74. The phrase "canonical obedience" occurs in Anselm's standard format for written professions: *Canterbury Professions*, nos. 50a–61 passim.

75. *HN* 73; *Canterbury Professions*, nos. 51, 61.

76. *HN* 187: in 1107, as archbishop of York, Gerard promised Anselm the same submission and obedience "quam Herefordensi ecclesiae ab eo sacrandus antistes illi promiserat"; cf. *Canterbury Professions*, no. 53. The fact that no written profession by Abbot Hugh to Anselm has survived does not imply that none existed; as Richter points out, "Many of the original professions before 1146 have been lost," and copies seem to have been made rather haphazardly: ibid., p. xxv.

77. Gervase of Canterbury, *Opera Historica*, ed. William Stubbs (RS, London, 1879–80), 1:72, 163–65; Chibnall, "Bec to Canterbury," p. 38.

78. Anselm's letter to Arnulf of Troarn expressing this view (AEp. 123) is missing from Lambeth ms. 59: see Fröhlich, "Letters Omitted from Anselm's Collection of Letters," pp. 62–63.

abbatial professions that he had framed twenty years before as abbot of Bec. Although Bec would always have a unique place in Anselm's heart, he no longer had the perspective of an abbot. As he himself had told the Bec community in 1093, "I am absolved from your care and involved in greater things."[79]

Anselm asserted Canterbury's authority even more forcefully, and without opposition, in elevating Ralph d'Escures, former abbot of Séez, to the bishopric of Rochester vacated by Gundulf's death. Rochester's direct subordination to Canterbury, and its bishop's status as archiepiscopal vicar, received clear symbolic expression at each stage of Ralph d'Escures's ascent to his episcopal office. On 29 June 1108, the feast of St. Peter and St. Paul, Anselm formally presented Ralph with the bishopric of Rochester before a large gathering of clergy and laity in the Christ Church chapter house, having first publicly received Ralph's homage and fealty — "fealty which he promised he would at all times keep to Anselm and all his lawful successors and to the church of Canterbury forever; and he corroborated this by an oath taken on the four Gospels."[80] Ralph then traveled to Rochester, where he was invested with the bishopric by William, Anselm's archdeacon, and Anthony the subprior of Canterbury acting jointly in Anselm's behalf. [81] On Sunday, 9 August, Anselm received Ralph's written profession of obedience and consecrated him with great ceremony in Canterbury Cathedral, assisted by three bishops.[82]

As the circumstances of Bishop Ralph's elevation demonstrate, the symbols and rituals of subordination to Canterbury differed in accordance with the various kinds of relationships binding the subordinate churches to the primatial see. The bishop of Rochester's relationship was that of a uniquely dependent Canterbury deputy. The other bishops in the province of Canterbury rendered written professions and received their consecrations from their archbishop in his cathedral (or, on rare occasions, in other churches pertaining to Canterbury), but they did not owe him homage or fealty. In the province of York, its own metropolitan consecrated his suffragans and, following Canterbury's

79. AEp. 157.
80. HN 196.
81. HN 197: Since Ernulf had been advanced to the abbacy of Peterborough, Canterbury was temporarily without a prior.
82. HN 198: Canterbury Professions, no. 61, and p. 116 (app. 1, no. 9).

example, was beginning to extract written professions from them.[83] From the perspective of Canterbury, its primate exercised supervisory authority over the province of York through his power over its metropolitan, but in reality the issue of York's subordination to Canterbury remained bitter and unresolved. Lanfranc and Anselm succeeded in their efforts to reduce St. Augustine's, Canterbury, to the status of a diocesan abbey, but, with rare exceptions, neither of them exercised direct authority over the abbeys in other dioceses.[84] One such exception was St. Albans, which, although located in the diocese of Lincoln, had been placed under the direct authority of the archbishop of Canterbury.[85] Another exception was Bury St. Edmunds, which had both papal and royal privileges of exemption from the authority of its diocesan bishop of Norwich.[86]

Lanfranc and Anselm shared the view that an abbot who enjoyed exemption from his diocesan became directly subject to his primate.[87] Bury St. Edmunds was the one English abbey in Anselm's time that had successfully demonstrated its exempt status,[88] and it fell to Anselm to determine the means and symbols by which Canterbury would manifest its primatial authority over the wealthy East Anglian house. The long tenure of Abbot Baldwin of Bury St. Edmunds (1065–97/8) deprived Lanfranc of the opportunity either to consecrate or to extract a written profession from an abbot of Bury. Baldwin's successor, Robert I (1100–1102), a bastard son of Hugh earl of Chester and former monk of St-Evroul, proved hopelessly incompetent and of low character;[89] Anselm deposed him at the synod of 1102 without having

83. This practice was not adopted until the early twelfth century; neither William bishop of Durham nor his successor, Ranulf Flambard, professed obedience to York: Simeon of Durham, *Opera Omnia*, p. 138; cf. Brett, *English Church*, pp. 16–18, on the issue of professions to York from Scottish bishops.

84. Anselm did, however, exercise full authority over the churches located on Canterbury estates outside his diocese: *HN* 45–47; above, Chapter 5 at n. 94.

85. *HN* 37; St. Albans recovered its independent status after Anselm's death: Knowles, "Exemption," pp. 213–14.

86. Chibnall, "Bec to Canterbury," pp. 32–34; Knowles, "Exemption," pp. 208–12; Antonia Gransden, "Baldwin, Abbot of Bury St. Edmunds, 1065–1097," *ANS* 4 (1982): 69–72.

87. Chibnall, "Bec to Canterbury," p. 33; AEpp. 251, 266.

88. Most recently at Anselm's synod of 1102: *Councils and Synods* 1, pt. 2:669. Battle Abbey was claiming exempt status but without clear success as yet: Abbot Henry of Battle was consecrated in 1096 by his diocesan bishop in Chichester Cathedral, whereas the circumstances of his successor Ralph's consecration in 1107 are left unclear by the house's chronicler: *Chronicle of Battle Abbey*, pp. 102, 116–18.

89. AEpp. 266, 269, 271.

consecrated him.[90] The precise nature of the abbot of Bury's sub-ordination to Canterbury thus remained unclear until Anselm's return from his second exile.

Eadmer states in his *Historia Novorum* that Anselm visited Bury in April 1107 "to consecrate a large cross and to perform certain other episcopal offices."[91] The significance of this visitation with respect to Canterbury's authority over St. Edmunds emerges clearly from the parallel account in Eadmer's *Vita Anselmi*. Anselm visited the abbey "to confirm with his authority [*auctoritas*] the abbot who had been elected there [Robert II] and to perform certain other pontifical offices, as he was entitled to do [*pro suo jure*]."[92] But whether Anselm, as primate, was "entitled" to perform such episcopal offices at Bury is not as clear as Eadmer suggests. The Bury community had earlier claimed the privilege of choosing the bishop who would perform such functions, and its three previous abbots — Uvo (1020 – 44), Leofstan (1044 – 65), and Baldwin (1065 – 97/8) — had exercised that privilege by receiving consecration from, respectively, the bishop of London, the bishop of Winchester, and the archbishop of Canterbury.[93] But Anselm saw things quite differently. St. Edmunds, he wrote, "is in my primacy and archbishopric and the consecrations therein belong by right to the archbishop of Canterbury."[94] By adopting this position, Anselm was blazing a new trail; Lanfranc had provided him no guidance. But Anselm would doubtless have been aware that the last consecrated abbot of Bury had been blessed by an archbishop of Canterbury, albeit the despised Stigand, and that a second consecutive archiepiscopal consecration would go far toward establishing a tradition. Whereas Stigand had consecrated Baldwin at the Confessor's court at Windsor,[95] Anselm tightened the cord by performing Robert II's abbatial conse-cration at Canterbury, in mid-August 1107.[96] Anselm had thus demon-strated Canterbury's authority over Bury St. Edmunds first by perform-ing episcopal functions there (but, vide St. Augustine's, scrupulously

91. *HN* 185.
92. *VA* 139.
93. Chibnall, "Bec to Canterbury," p. 32; cf. Southern in *VA* 139, n. 3: "Since the monastery was exempt from diocesan authority, episcopal functions such as the dedica-tion of altars were performed by a bishop or — as here — an archbishop chosen by the community for the occasion."
94. *AEp.* 251; Anselm repeats this claim in *AEp.* 266.
95. Barlow, *The English Church, 1000 – 1066*, 2d ed. (London, 1979), p. 305, n. 6.
96. *HN* 188.

avoiding the function of blessing the abbot in his own abbey church), and then by arranging that he come to Canterbury to be consecrated in the primatial cathedral.

Nothing indicates that Abbot Robert or his monks objected to these procedures. Chibnall is surely correct in attributing this to their grati- tude toward Anselm, who had written them several letters of consola- tion during the troubled years following Abbot Baldwin's death in 1097/8 and had given them forceful support in their effort to rid themselves of their previous abbot, Robert I.[97] Robert II himself, who had formerly served as prior of Westminster under Anselm's devoted friend Gilbert Crispin, can probably be included among Anselm's circle of reform-minded monks.[98] Anselm could on occasion address the Bury community with the voice of primatial authority, as when he commanded (*mando atque praecipio*) that the monks accept and be obedient to Robert II.[99] But Robert was well regarded at Bury, and Anselm's command was therefore easily obeyed.[100] Eadmer says noth- ing about a profession of obedience, and his silence on a matter of such absorbing interest to him suggests that Anselm did not receive one. This conclusion is confirmed by the testimony of a Bury writer of about the mid-twelfth century who reports that on the occasion of Robert II's consecration the monks of Bury established that their abbot should render no such profession to the metropolitan or to any other bishop because none had ever been rendered before.[101] Similarly, Robert II's successor, Abbot Alebold, a Bec monk, was blessed in 1114 by Ralph archbishop of Canterbury without a written profession, "in accor- dance with the rule justly established by the monks in the presence of Archbishop Anselm when Dom Robert, Alebold's predecessor, was blessed as abbot."[102]

Such, then, was Anselm's policy toward the one fully exempt abbey of his time. He regarded himself as its unquestioned superior. In his eyes he was the only prelate empowered to exercise the episcopal functions that ordinarily devolved upon diocesan bishops and, despite earlier

97. Chibnall, "Bec to Canterbury," pp. 34–35; AEpp. 251–52, 266–67, 269, 271.
98. J. Armitage Robinson, *Gilbert Crispin, Abbot of Westminster* (Cambridge, England, 1911), pp. 29–30.
99. AEp. 408.
100. Robert II had ruled Bury unconsecrated since shortly after Robert I's deposition in 1102: Robinson, *Gilbert Crispin*, p. 29.
101. *Memorials of St. Edmund's Abbey*, ed. Thomas Arnold (RS, London, 1890–96), 1:356; Chibnall, "Bec to Canterbury," p. 34.
102. Ibid., p. 35; *Memorials of St. Edmund's*, 1:356.

practice, the only prelate authorized to bless its abbots. He did not insist on a written profession; since none had previously been rendered, he could remain true to his stewardly duty to permit no rights or customs to slip from Canterbury's possession. But as the first archbishop to consecrate an abbot of Bury in Canterbury Cathedral, he reinforced the tradition that, except in the most pressing circumstances, all primatial consecrations should occur in the mother church of Britain.

Anselm also continued to press his primatial claims in Wales and Ireland. Having restored Bishop Wilfred to his see of St. David's in 1095,[103] he manifested his supremacy over the other functioning Welsh bishopric by consecrating Urban to the see of Llandaff in 1107 and receiving his written profession.[104] By the time of Anselm's death, as Southern aptly observed, "the whole Church of Wales, which had never before been subject to Canterbury, was completely subordinated to the English primate."[105] Anselm's archiepiscopal successor, Ralph d'Escures, treading the path that Anselm had cleared, consecrated and received written professions from the bishops-elect of St. David's and the reestablished see of Bangor;[106] moreover, when Geoffrey of Monmouth was nominated to the new Welsh see of St. Asaph's in 1151, he was consecrated by and professed obedience to Archbishop Theobald.[107] The pattern that Anselm created was to continue for generations and centuries thereafter.

In Anselm's mind the Canterbury primacy was always inseparably associated with the goal of achieving due order through the process of ecclesiastical reform. The Welsh church, in subordinating itself to Canterbury, was transformed from a loosely structured body following Celtic usages into an up-to-date ecclesiastical organization on the Anglo-Norman model. It had clearly mapped dioceses, episcopal towns and cathedrals, and a growing ability to enforce canonical discipline. Anselm pursued the same goals with respect to the church in Ireland, admonishing its leaders (as had Lanfranc)[108] to institute reforms along similar lines. He wrote to his friend King Murchertach urging him to take strong measures against consanguineous marriages and casual divorces, to see that episcopal consecrations and other ecclesiastical

103. *HN* 72; above, Chapter 5 at nn. 225–26.
104. Above, Chapter 5 at nn. 226–27.
105. Southern, *Anselm*, p. 133.
106. *Canterbury Professions*, nos. 64, 67.
107. Ibid., no. 95.
108. LEp. 9, 10, 49.

functions be conducted in due canonical form, and to ensure that bishops establish fixed sees in towns of appropriate size.[109] Anselm had earlier cooperated with King Murchertach in establishing a new see at Waterford and had received a profession from its bishop.[110] More recently he had rendered the Irish king the deeply appreciated service of persuading Henry I to restore to royal favor the banished Arnulf of Montgomery — Anselm's good friend and Murchertach's son-in-law.[111] Murchertach concluded his letter of thanks to Anselm with the statement, "Know that I will be your servant in all those things which you ordered."[112]

As it turned out, Anselm's admonitions proved so effective in reforming the Irish church that it developed its own distinct diocesan hierarchy and eventually drifted out of its Canterbury orbit. The final bond was severed in 1152 when Dublin was advanced to the status of an archbishopric, but the process of separation commenced as early as 1101 when King Murchertach arranged for the convening of a great reform council at Cashel. The council legislated against simony, clerical marriage, taxation of the clergy, consanguineous marriages, and similar abuses about which Anselm had expressed concern.[113] Anselm presumably wrote his letters of admonition with the assumption that the reforms that he urged on Murchertach were to be instituted through the agency of an ecclesiastical council. Lanfranc had ended a similar letter of admonition to King Toirrdelbach of Munster (ca. 1074) with the explicit request that he summon such a council.[114]

While councils could be conducive to reform, they could also be dangerous to Canterbury. The Council of Cashel was presided over by the chief bishop of Munster, acting as papal legate — the first known

109. AEp. 435, Anselm to King Murchertach; cf. AEpp. 427, to the same king; 429, to Gilbert bishop of Limerick.

110. Above, Chapter 5 at nn. 229–31.

111. AEp. 426; Arnulf had been disseised and banished in 1102 along with his elder brother Robert of Bellême earl of Shropshire; Arnulf had married Murchertach's daughter shortly before: OV 6:30 and n. 4.

112. AEp. 426.

113. See, in general, J. A. Watt, *The Church and the Two Nations in Medieval Ireland* (Cambridge, 1970), pp. 5–19, 217–25. It was on that occasion that Murchertach granted the great center of royal authority, the Rock of Cashel, to the Irish church.

114. LEp. 10: The council that Lanfranc suggests bears an unmistakable resemblance to Canterbury primatial councils: "Order the bishops and all men of religion to assemble together, attend their holy assembly in person with your chief advisers, and strive to banish from your kingdom these evil customs and all others that are similarly condemned by canon law." Toirrdelbach may possibly have convened a reform council along these lines in 1084: Watt, *Church in Medieval Ireland*, p. 9.

legate in Irish history — and his legatine authority presaged the gradual reorientation of the Irish church from Canterbury to Rome.[115] At a second reform council held at Rathbreasail (near Cashel) in 1111, two years after Anselm's death, his friend Gilbert bishop of Limerick presided as papal legate. Gilbert's vividly expressed views on the ecclesiastical and secular hierarchies, inspired by Canterbury,[116] were clearly reflected in the legislation of his council. Ireland was to be divided into two ecclesiastical provinces, under archbishops established at Armagh and Cashel, with twelve suffragan bishops assigned to each archbishop and the primacy of Ireland to be exercised by the archbishop of Armagh. As a mirror image of Pope Gregory I's instructions to St. Augustine with regard to England, this arrangement plainly bears the mark of Canterbury, yet it also represents a grave setback to Canterbury's influence in Ireland. It was not fully implemented; a bishop of Dublin professed to Canterbury in 1121 and a bishop of Limerick did so as late as 1140,[117] but at that point the Irish professions cease.

The Canterbury primacy over Ireland, which Anselm had advanced so promisingly, proved ultimately to be a hopeless goal yet his policy toward the Irish church should by no means be dismissed as a failure. The fundamental reforms that transformed Irish Christianity in the twelfth century can be attributed to a variety of sources, but as J. A. Watt remarked, "it would surely be unwise to minimize the influence, direct or indirect, of an Anselm."[118]

Ever since the inception of Lanfranc's great design, the achievement of the Canterbury primacy had depended above all else on the subordination of York. Archbishop Gerard's death in May 1108 launched a struggle over the York profession that dominated Anselm's life during its closing months. The details of this episode, like those of previous quarrels between Canterbury and York, are difficult to reconstruct with any assurance owing to the irreconcilable differences between the accounts of Eadmer and Hugh the Chantor, neither of whom was above lying or forging on behalf of his cause. On balance, Eadmer appears

---

115. Ibid., p. 10.
116. Above, Chapter 5 at nn. 10, 230–31.
117. *Canterbury Professions*, nos. 69, 81; Patrick bishop of Limerick, who professed to Archbishop Theobold in 1140, probably did not secure possession of his see: Watt, *Church in Medieval Ireland*, p. 218.
118. Watt, *Church in Medieval Ireland*, p. 10.

somewhat more reliable than Hugh, who seems almost to have been traumatized by the outcome of the dispute, but one can never be certain. Nevertheless, from both accounts Anselm clearly devoted himself singlemindedly to upholding the Canterbury primacy over York. In this matter, as in so many others, he was modeling himself on Archbishop Lanfranc.

Lanfranc originated the idea of manifesting York's subordination by extracting a written profession of obedience from its archbishop-elect as a condition for his consecration. Archbishop Thomas I had professed in writing to Lanfranc before receiving consecration from him, and had afterward rendered a second profession to Lanfranc and all his lawful successors.[119] As Lanfranc's lawful successor, Anselm did not insist on another profession from Thomas I. It would have been both redundant and, because Anselm lacked the opportunity to withhold consecration, difficult to obtain. Anselm also lacked the leverage of withholding consecration from Thomas's successor, Gerard, who was translated from the bishopric of Hereford and had thus already been ordained to the episcopacy. Hugh the Chantor is probably correct in reporting that Anselm sought unsuccessfully to exact Gerard's archiepiscopal profession by delaying the necessary letter to Paschal II recommending that Gerard be released from Hereford and granted the pallium for York.[120] Anselm did in time send the recommendation,[121] but in the course of the next three years he also obtained unprecedented papal privileges confirming the Canterbury primacy to himself and his successors (though without explicitly defining it) and commanding Archbishop Gerard to render his profession.[122]

So matters stood when Anselm returned to England in 1106. At the Westminster Council of 1107, where the investiture settlement was ratified, he again demanded Gerard's profession. Eadmer states that the king proposed a compromise, whereby it would be mutually understood that the written profession that Anselm had earlier received from Gerard on his consecration to the bishopric of Hereford remained in full force. A second profession was unnecessary, Henry argued, because although Gerard had changed churches, "he remained in himself the same

119. *Canterbury Professions*, pp. lviii–lx and no. 34; above, Chapter 5 at nn. 51–67. Cf. Hugh the Chantor's reinterpretation of events (*HCY* 15): "Thomas had been released by Lanfranc's death from that undue, personal and extorted profession."
120. *HCY* 13.
121. Above, Chapter 6 at nn. 131–32.
122. Above, Chapter 5 at nn. 136, 200–206, and 226–30.

person and had not been absolved from his original profession."[123] Anselm consented to this understanding on condition that Gerard should now pledge to observe the same obedience as archbishop of York that he had professed as bishop. Gerard agreed and, placing his hand in Anselm's, "promised on his honor that he would as archbishop render the same submission and obedience to Anselm and his successors as he had promised him at the time of his consecration by him as bishop of Hereford."[124] Richter correctly regards this episode as a victory for Anselm.[125] He had obtained a solemn oath of obedience from the archbishop of York, which, although not in writing, was sworn in the presence of the king and queen and a great assemblage of prelates and magnates. But Anselm can have been under no illusion that York would not reopen the controversy on Gerard's death.

Gerard died within the year — on 21 May 1108, at Southwell Minster on his way to the Whitsun Council in London. His successor, Thomas II, was nominated by Henry with Anselm's approval six days thereafter, in time to participate in the council.[126] Thomas II had been a royal chaplain with highly placed ecclesiastical kinsmen. He was the son of Samson bishop of Worcester (1096-1112) and the nephew of the late Archbishop Thomas I of York. The York canons are said to have trusted him because he had been reared in their midst during his uncle's pontificate, but their trust did not impede them from subjecting him to intense pressure to refuse the profession to Anselm.[127] The York

---

123. *HN* 186–87; as bishop-elect of Hereford, Gerard had professed in writing to Anselm in 1096: *Canterbury Professions*, no. 53. Henry I's argument that personal oaths are not abrogated by changes of office is consistent with his own insistence, in his treaty of 1101 with Robert Curthose, on obtaining a formal release from the oath of homage that he had rendered to the duke before becoming king: OV 5:318.

124. *HN* 187; Florence, 2:56. A transcript of Gerard's profession as bishop of Hereford in British Library, Cotton ms. Cleopatra Ei, written at Canterbury between 1121 and 1123 and designated by Richter as ms. C (*Canterbury Professions*, p. xxvii and no. 53), carries the marginal note: "Hanc etiam professionem factus archiepiscopus Eboracensis se seruaturum promisit, et hoc Anselmo archiepiscopo coram rege et episcopis Anglie manu in manum ponendo fide interposita confirmauit"; similar phrases in Eadmer's account (*HN* 186–87) make it certain that the two are closely related. Hugh the Chantor ignores the episode entirely, saying only that Anselm had demanded that Gerard render a profession and that Gerard had "justly refused": *HCY* 15.

125. *Canterbury Professions*, p. lxx.

126. *HCY* 15; *Regesta* 2, no. 885; for Anselm's consent, see AEpp. 443 and 464.

127. *HCY* 15–17: Hugh reports that the York canons urged Thomas to emulate his predecessor: "Look at Archbishop Gerard! How honest, how manly, how excellent were his actions!" Gerard had earlier complained to Anselm that his canons were disrespectful and hostile toward him: AEp. 255.

party no doubt believed that, with Anselm advanced in years and declining in health, time was on their side.[128] Thomas II therefore delayed going to Canterbury for his consecration, knowing that if he did go, Anselm would do all in his power to force a profession from him.

In respose to the delay, Anselm ordered Thomas to come to Canterbury on Sunday, 6 September 1108, "to do what you should do and to receive your consecration. If you fail to do this, it is my duty to take charge and perform the duties that belong to the episcopal office in the archbishopric of York."[129] Anselm's threat becomes explicit in his concurrent letter to Thomas's suffragan, Ranulf Flambard bishop of Durham. Ranulf had asked Anselm's permission to act as Thomas's proxy in consecrating the monk Turgot to the Scottish bishopric of St. Andrews, because Thomas could not perform such consecrations until he himself was consecrated.[130] Anselm absolutely forbade its being done until the archbishop-elect had received consecration, "unless it is done by me, should this perchance prove necessary."[131] Anselm thus countered Thomas's opposition to Canterbury's primacy over York with a direct challenge to York's metropolitan authority over Scotland.[132]

Thomas replied to Anselm in a letter full of affectionate words and transparent excuses. He was hard pressed for money to make the journey to Canterbury; he had in fact set out on such a journey but had been unavoidably delayed at Winchester and had spent all his money there; he would indeed appear at Canterbury on 6 September "ready to receive and to do what I should" if he could "conveniently do so"; and the matter of Ranulf Flambard's seeking to consecrate Turgot to St. Andrews was mere idle gossip.[133] Thomas also asked Anselm to send him the customary letter certifying his election to the archbishopric of York. In passing he mentioned that Henry I was sending an embassy to

128. Eadmer makes precisely this allegation: HN 203. Anselm was now so weak that he could no longer travel on horseback but had to be carried lying on a litter: VA 140–41.
129. AEp. 443.   130. AEp. 442.
131. AEp. 442; cf. AEp. 443.
132. York's metropolitan authority was to be stoutly resisted by St. Andrews and other Scottish sees: Archibald A. M. Duncan, Scotland: The Making of the Kingdom (Edinburgh, 1975), pp. 258–65. Anselm may also have been foreclosing the possibility that Thomas might acquire enough suffragan bishops to consecrate him without recourse to Canterbury: a minimum of three bishops was required for a canonical episcopal ordination (AEp. 435), and in a letter of about 1109 to Earl Hacon, Anselm alludes to a recently installed bishop of the Orkneys (AEp. 449); probably Ralph Nowell: see Donald Nicholl, Thurstan, Archbishop of York (New York: 1964), p. 19.
133. AEp. 444.

Rome on royal business and that (allegedly) at Henry's suggestion, Thomas would be sending his own messengers along to ask Paschal for the pallium.

Anselm's reply betrays growing irritation. At the plea of Thomas's letter-bearer, Anselm agreed to postpone the consecration date by three weeks. Thomas was now to present himself at Canterbury without fail on Sunday, 27 September, "to do what you should do and to receive your consecration." But under no circumstances was Thomas to send messengers to Rome for the pallium. Nobody is entitled to a pallium, Anselm reminded him, until he has been consecrated. As for the letter certifying Thomas's election, Anselm would gladly provide one "when you have had a talk with me and have told me to whom I should address it."[134]

Anselm then wrote immediately to Paschal, summarizing his conflict with Thomas and justifying his demand for a written profession "in accordance with the long-established practice of my predecessors and his."[135] Anselm pleaded that Paschal not grant the pallium to Thomas until having received reliable news that Anselm had consecrated him: "Some are saying," Anselm explained, "that once you have granted him the pallium, he is confident that he can then refuse to make the profession that is due me." If that should occur, the Church of England would be split in two and Anselm "would not think of remaining in England." The primate thus stressed the depth of his commitment to the Canterbury primacy by threatening a third exile, this time to protest an assault against due order by the pope himself. The letter concludes with a warning that Henry I, having heard rumors that Emperor Henry V was investing prelates without incurring papal sanctions, was thinking of resuming the practice himself. Anselm advised Paschal to look into the matter immediately, "lest what you have so well built up be irreparably destroyed."

That Henry I was seriously considering the reintroduction of lay investiture is corroborated by no other source. Anselm may well have been overstating the danger in order to convey the hint that if Paschal abandoned Canterbury he risked losing not only Anselm's loyalty but Henry's as well. If the Canterbury primacy was at risk, so too was the investiture settlement; if Anselm chose exile, who would defend the papal cause? Paschal replied that he indeed regarded Anselm as

134. AEp. 445.
135. AEp. 451.

the representative of St. Augustine himself, the apostle of the English, and was therefore determined to permit no disparagement of Anselm or the Church of Canterbury: "Accordingly, all that you have asked of us we gladly grant."[136] Paschal concluded by denying vehemently that he was acquiescing in the investiture of churches by Henry V.

Anselm then received from Thomas elect of York another letter more candid than his earlier ones.[137] For the first time in the correspondence between Anselm and Thomas, the issue of the profession was brought into the open, no longer to be masked by the euphemism of Thomas's going to Canterbury and doing what he should. The York canons, Thomas explains, have forbidden him to profess obedience to Canterbury. If he did so, they would withdraw their obedience to him and bring a legal action against him at the papal court. Thomas was thus hemmed in on both sides and begged Anselm for advice. He offered to render any personal submission that Anselm might require but could not, without forfeiting the obedience of his chapter, profess in writing on behalf of the Church of York.

The York canons themselves wrote to Anselm confirming Thomas's predicament but in less respectful language: "You ordered and summoned him, rather roughly as we think, to come to you by a date that you fixed, to do and receive what he should. We know what he should receive from God by the imposition of your sacred hands, but we do not know what he should do. Perhaps you or your monks say, 'Make his profession.'"[138] The canons granted that their archbishop might properly show his reverence and obedience to Anselm by bowing, rising, and giving way, but to subject the Church of York to Canterbury was absolutely uncanonical and would not be tolerated. "We are not acting," they concluded, "out of rivalry, ambition, or vainglory, but in the Lord's name and in a just cause."

Anselm did not deign to reply to them.[139] He did, however, reply to Thomas, setting a new consecration date (8 November) and affirming his own absolute commitment to the duties of his stewardship: "You can be very certain that I shall exert myself in every possible way to see that the Church of Canterbury does not lose one scrap of her prestige in my time."[140]

136. AEp. 452, dated at Benevento, 12 October [1108].
137. AEp. 453.
138. AEp. 454.
139. HN 203.   140. AEp. 455.

Thomas continued to delay. His complaint about being hemmed in was probably an honest one, for he seems throughout the affair to have been devoted less to the ancient liberties of York than to the advancing of his ecclesiastical career by ascending from the royal chapel into an archbishopric. In his reply to Anselm he said nothing about the new consecration date but simply restated his dilemma.[141] Anselm then sent two bishops, Ralph of Rochester and Richard of London, to urge him still again to come to Canterbury; the bishops also relayed to Thomas Anselm's offer that if he could prove at Canterbury that he owed no profession, then Anselm would consecrate him unprofessed.[142] Thomas declined the offer, understandably reluctant to plead his case against an opponent with both a formidable intellect and viceregal authority, before a tribunal meeting at Canterbury and consisting largely of Anselm's suffragans.[143]

While Thomas equivocated, members of his cathedral chapters were in contact with both Henry I and Paschal II. Hugh the Chantor states that Henry had promised to favor the York cause and had forbidden Thomas to profess to Anselm, the reason being that "he disliked Anselm for having prohibited investitures."[144] Hugh goes on to say that the dean of York, another Hugh, visited the royal court in Normandy and obtained a letter from Henry I to be carried to Pope Paschal.[145] In this letter, so the York writer states, Henry asked the pope to send a legate *a latere* to bring the pallium to the archbishop-elect in England and "decide the cause between the two metropolitans in accordance with canon law."[146] The pope is said to have granted the request of his royal son and to have sent Cardinal Ulrich as his legate to England accompanied by Dean Hugh and another papal representative, Geoffrey prior of St-Bénigne, Dijon.[147] The party is reported to have carried papal

141. AEp. 456.
142. HN 204.
143. The king and his court had crossed to Normandy and cannot have been expected to participate in the hearing; cf. the experience of Thomas I in arguing his case against his profession in slightly less difficult circumstances: above, Chapter 5 at nn. 58–67.
144. HCY 18.
145. HCY 22.
146. HCY 22–23.
147. Dijon rather than Dunois as it is rendered in Charles Johnson's published edition of Hugh the Chantor: see *Councils and Synods* 1, pt. 2:706 and n. 4; Hugh the Chantor does not regard Geoffrey as a "legate": p. 28: "Quicquid legatus [Ulricus] dicebat Prior Dunonensis [*recte* Divionensis] attestabatur."

letters recommending the settlement of the dispute "in a way that seemed good to the pope and the Roman curia."

This York account is undoubtedly built on a substratum of historical fact, but some of its details raise grave doubts. Cardinal Ulrich did indeed carry the York pallium to England, accompanied by Prior Geoffrey and, presumably, Hugh dean of York.[148] But no contemporary source supports Hugh the Chantor's assertions that Henry I supported York over Canterbury, that he bore a grudge against Anselm, that he asked Paschal to commission Cardinal Ulrich with the authority of a legate *a latere* to decide the cause between the two metropolitans, or that Paschal granted Ulrich such powers. Neither Henry's letter to Paschal nor Paschal's letters about the settlement of the dispute have survived, and Hugh the Chantor, uncharacteristically, does not quote them. In his brief summary of Henry's letter, the king is said merely to have apologized to Paschal that Thomas could not personally travel to the papal court to receive his pallium, and to have commended the archbishop-elect as learned, chaste, and devout[149] — an opinion presumably shared by Anselm himself when he endorsed Thomas's advancement to York. Anselm did not question Thomas's moral character; the issue was Thomas's profession, and on that point, so far as one can tell from Hugh the Chantor's summary, Henry was silent.

Hugh's account is improbable on several grounds. Henry I's more or less concurrent commission to Anselm to assume the care of his son and daughter and all his kingdom does not seem to be the act of a king who bore his primate a grudge,[150] nor does it seem likely that a monarch bent on upholding his father's customs toward the church, who on other occasions forcefully opposed the entry into England of fully empowered legates,[151] would have asked Paschal to send a legate *a latere* to preside at an English tribunal.[152] As for Paschal, who had just before promised Anselm his firm support,[153] if he did indeed

148. *HN* 207; *Councils and Synods* 1, pt. 2: 705 – 7; *HCY* 23, 28; Florence, 2:60.
149. *HCY* 22.
150. AEpp. 461, 462.
151. Brett, *English Church*, pp. 40 – 41; on the one exception, John of Crema in 1125, see Hollister, "War and Diplomacy in the Anglo-Norman World," *ANS* 6 (1984): 86 and n. 104.
152. A legate *a latere* was of the highest rank, empowered to preside at councils and enforce discipline: Brett, *English Church*, p. 35.
153. AEp. 452.

grant Cardinal Ulrich such power, it was in flagrant violation of the privilege he had granted Anselm in 1102 to be, so long as he lived, "subject
only to our judgment and not at any time to that of any legate."[154]

All evidence except that of Hugh the Chantor suggests that Anselm
in his final years enjoyed the affection and high regard of Paschal and
Henry I alike. Although the papacy was turning increasingly against
primacies, as impediments to centralized papal control, the popes were,
in Barlow's words, "extremely reluctant to give a verdict against such
luminaries as Lanfranc and Anselm or to go against the express wishes
of the king."[155] Barlow and Hollister have both argued persuasively
that the outcome of the profession dispute was of no real concern to the
king, whose primary interest was in preventing the dispute itself from
threatening the peace and order of the English church.[156] With these
considerations in mind, and with a healthy measure of skepticism with
regard to Hugh the Chantor's objectivity, we can reinterpret Dean
Hugh's mission to Henry and Paschal as follows to avoid the unlikely conclusion that king and pope were engaged in a plot to betray
Anselm.

Dean Hugh visited Henry in Normandy, where the king had gone to
confront the hostile demands of Louis VI of France.[157] With more
pressing matters on his mind, Henry agreed to Hugh's plea for permission to go to Rome for the York pallium, seeing it as a convenient means
of permitting Thomas to assume full metropolitan authority as soon as
the king and his court had resolved the profession-consecration issue.
Anselm might also die before the issue was settled, thus relaxing the
pressure on Henry by opening the way for Thomas's consecration by
another bishop without professing to Canterbury. The king sent a letter
to Paschal offering routine excuses for Thomas's inability to appear in
person, and recommending him as a candidate who was morally and
intellectually suitable for his archiepiscopal office. Henry may even
have mentioned that Thomas had been nominated with Anselm's approval; such a statement would have strengthened Thomas's case at the
papal court and might also account in part for Hugh the Chantor's
failure to quote the letter.

At Rome Dean Hugh may perhaps have exaggerated Henry's support for York. In any event Paschal agreed to send the pallium despite

154. AEp. 222.   155. Barlow, *English Church*, p. 42.
156. Ibid., p. 41; Hollister, "War and Diplomacy," p. 74.
157. *HA* 237.

Anselm's request to the contrary. In doing so, however, he was by no means awarding the victory to York. He was perfectly aware that a pallium could not be granted to an unconsecrated archbishop, and the profession-consecration issue remained to be settled — in all probability at Henry's court, where Anselm's party enjoyed a distinct numerical advantage. On each of the two other occasions under the Conqueror and his sons when archbishops were unable to receive their pallia directly from the pope (Anselm in 1095, Ralph of Canterbury in 1115),[158] the pallia had been carried to England by legates and bestowed in their presence. Cardinal Ulrich too was responsible for bearing the pallium as the pope's representative, and he may have received the further charge of observing the decision of the king's court and relaying it back to Paschal.[159] He may have had the authority to hear the case if it came to that. (A legate's power was far less carefully delineated in 1109 than in later decades.) But a legatine hearing would have been at best, in Henry's mind, a measure of last resort. A much more promising solution to York's dilemma would have been for Thomas to go personally to the pope for both consecration and the pallium, as his successor Thurstan would do a decade later. But if Thomas and his canons contemplated any such strategy, Henry I prohibited it.[160]

Although the king very likely intended to resolve the dispute in his own court, probably without the formality of a judicial hearing, he much preferred to have the issue postponed for the time being. Deeply involved in his growing crisis with the new king of France, he was also occupied in concluding arrangements for the betrothal of his daughter Matilda to the emperor.[161] A further York delegation to Henry's court in Normandy seems to have had little difficulty in persuading the king to write to Anselm proposing a truce between the two archbishops. It was to last until Easter (25 April) 1109, at which time Henry, on the advice of his bishops and barons, would resolve the dispute in such a way as to bring "true concord between you and such peace as there should be between brothers."[162] Anselm had long been wary of such

158. Brett, *English Church*, pp. 237–38.
159. Such was the role of the papal legate Hubert at the Council of Winchester in 1072: *Councils and Synods* 1, pt. 2: 591–607.
160. Cf. *HCY* 36: About Christmas 1114, Thurstan, archbishop-elect of York, having similarly declined Archbishop Ralph's commands to come to Canterbury for consecration, sought out Henry I in Normandy and asked his permission to go to Rome; the king firmly denied Thurstan's request.
161. AEp. 461.
162. AEp. 470.

promises, and he was by now very likely aware of the York delegation to Rome.[163] He refused the truce, saying (according to Eadmer) that he would "sooner let his whole body be cut in pieces limb by limb."[164] But he nevertheless sent back to the king a friendly message in which he recapitulated the Canterbury position and asked once again that Henry exercise his authority to prevent the English church from being split in two. Eadmer asserts that Henry responded to Anselm's message with good cheer, promising to make it clear that he wished the English church to be unified.

Henry was doubtless behaving just as cheerfully toward the delegation from York, and the York canons may have misinterpreted the king's vague assurances as firm support. Anselm, however, was not deceived, and he continued to press for unequivocal royal backing. In a letter to Robert of Meulan, addressed in affectionate terms, Anselm urged the count to use all his influence to correct the wrong being done, threatening at last resort to himself bring Thomas under the ban of ecclesiastical censure.[165] In a final letter to Henry I, written in a tone of warmest friendship, Anselm leaves it to Baldwin of Tournai to provide recent news of the controversy but assures the king that he would sooner die than permit the dignity of Canterbury to be diminished.[166]

Leaving nothing to chance, Anselm also wrote to Thomas II's father, Samson bishop of Worcester, ordering him "like a friend and one professed to our church" to help restrain his son's intolerable presumption.[167] Anselm hinted that Thomas, who had risen to his archbishopric through Anselm's favor, now risked losing it. He asked that Samson join with the other suffragans of Canterbury in interceding with the king on Anselm's behalf. Samson promised to be true to his profession of obedience and render Anselm his devoted support.[168] He suggested further that the canons of York, few and isolated as compared with the numerous prelates and magnates supporting Canterbury, were unworthy of Anselm's anger: their "audacious presumption" would easily be overcome. Anselm should be assured, however, that Thomas II himself was well disposed toward him and, were it not for the canons of York, would subject himself devotedly to the archbishop of Canterbury and

---

163. AEp. 464; *HN* 204.
164. *HN* 205.   165. AEp. 467.
166. AEp. 462, probably April 1109, the month of Anselm's death; it is a reply to AEp. 461 in which Henry reports to Anselm his conference with Louis VI of France at Neufle in March or early April 1109: Luchaire, *Louis VI*, pp. 39–40.
167. AEp. 464.   168. AEp. 465.

his church.[169] Samson was correct in implying that Henry I, in the end, could not help but be influenced by the large numerical advantage of Canterbury suffragans and supporters over those of York.[170] It was up to Anselm, however, to rally their support, and, as his letter to Samson proves, he was doing so with much success.[171]

But Anselm's health was now declining to such a point that he could see his death swiftly approaching. In his last letter to Robert of Meulan, he had said that even if he should know that he would die tomorrow, he would lay a sentence upon the rebellious Thomas.[172] Now as he lay dying, he made good his threat in a final, dramatic effort to fulfill his stewardship of Canterbury. He had letters prepared for all the bishops of England ordering and commanding them, through the holy obedience that they owed to the Church of Canterbury and to Anselm, to treat Thomas elect of York in accordance with the instructions contained in the accompanying copy of Anselm's final letter to Thomas.[173] In his letter to Thomas, Anselm, "archbishop of Canterbury and primate of all Britain," speaking in God's name, suspended him from the priesthood to which he had been raised "at my bidding, in my diocese, as my suffragan." Thomas was forbidden to resume his priestly functions in any respect until he had professed to Canterbury. If he should persist in refusing to profess,

I forbid the bishops throughout the whole of Britain, on pain of perpetual anathema, to lay, any one of them, hands upon your head to promote you to the episcopate; or, if you should be promoted by foreign bishops, to receive you as bishop or in any Christian fellowship whatsoever. You too, Thomas, on pain of the same anathema, I forbid ever to receive consecration to the bishopric of York until you have first made the profession which your predecessors Thomas and Gerard made to the Church of Canterbury.[174]

Anselm died on 21 April 1109, in his seventy-sixth year, and was entombed in Canterbury Cathedral next to Lanfranc. He departed his

169. As events turned out, Samson did give Canterbury staunch support, motivated not only by his profession of obedience but also, Hugh the Chantor believed, by his anxiety that his son should not lose his archbishopric: HCY 28; cf. HN 208; for a somewhat different interpretation of Samson's letter, see Southern, *Anselm*, p. 140.

170. Cf. Hollister, "War and Diplomacy," p. 74: in 1114 "Henry decided for Canterbury, probably because an opposite decision [for York] would have earned him more and stronger enemies."

171. AEp. 464: Anselm planned to send the bishops of Rochester and Norwich to implore the king's support for Anselm in the name of all Canterbury's suffragan bishops.

172. AEp. 467.

173. AEp. 471; the one surviving copy is addressed to a "bishop R."; the names of no less than eight English bishops in 1109 began with R.

174. AEp. 472.

life secure in the knowledge that he had done everything in his power to see that the Canterbury primacy was upheld. As in 1105 when he had bypassed the papal curia and threatened Henry with excommunication, thereby winning Paschal's victory on investitures and his own return to Canterbury, so now in 1109 he had broken free from his double harness with Henry and acted unilaterally in a matter that Anglo-Norman custom clearly assigned to the joint jurisdiction of primate and king. Henry had planned to resolve the profession issue on his return from Normandy,[175] but Anselm, "speaking in the name of God himself," had wrested the initiative from the king and his counselors.

Anselm's final letter was a staggering blow to the hopes of the chapter of York. Hugh the Chantor went so far as to deny that Anselm had written any such letter — or even in the unlikely event that he had done so, "misled by evil counsel, it was an outrage and they ought to have concealed it."[176] Indeed from this point onward the narratives of Hugh the Chantor and Eadmer diverge significantly, not merely in their sympathies but in their facts. Eadmer reports that Cardinal Ulrich (whom he never identifies as a "legate") arrived in England a few days after Anselm's death bearing the pallium for York. Ulrich, Eadmer says, was now uncertain what to do with the pallium because he was under express papal instructions to deliver it to Anselm and afterward deal with it as Anselm should direct.[177] Hugh the Chantor's fuller account of Ulrich's visit includes not a hint of any such papal instructions, and the fact that Ulrich was accompanied northward from the papal court by Hugh dean of York renders Eadmer's version rather unlikely. Whatever the case, Cardinal Ulrich did nothing for the time being, awaiting the return of the king.

Henry I crossed to England a few weeks after Anselm's death. At the Whitsuntide court at Westminster in mid-June, after ratifying with imperial envoys the marriage arrangements between his daughter Matilda and Emperor Henry V,[178] the king turned to the York profession issue. Eadmer and Hugh the Chantor agree that the Canterbury suffragan bishops, whom Anselm had enlisted in his cause, continued to support it staunchly,[179] and Eadmer is surely correct in asserting that

175. AEp. 470.
176. HCY 23–24; that the letter is indeed Anselm's is corroborated by his earlier statement to Robert of Meulan that he would bring Thomas II under the sentence of the church unless he professed: AEp. 467.
177. HN 207.   178. ASC, A.D. 1109; HA 237.
179. HN 207–8; HCY 24–26.

their support was solidified by Anselm's deathbed letter to Thomas II. Eadmer states that Robert of Meulan was angered that any bishop would consider himself bound by the letter "without the consent and command of the king."[180] But the Canterbury suffragans — including the curialists Robert of Lincoln and Roger of Salisbury, and Thomas II's father Samson of Worcester — replied that they all accepted Anselm's letter and were determined to follow its instructions. Count Robert shook his head, expecting (so Eadmer believed) that they would all be charged with acting in contempt of the king. They were indeed acting contrary to the usages of William the Conqueror, who had forbidden excommunications without express royal consent. Count Robert was naturally taken aback at this assault on the royal dignity. But as has been said, the issue of the York profession was of no real interest to the king. When it became apparent that the bishops could not be intimidated, Henry I quickly gave way: "I side with the bishops and have no wish whatever to bring upon myself the excommunication of Father Anselm."[181]

Hugh the Chantor makes it clear that Robert of Meulan then joined the king in endeavoring to resolve the dispute by pressing Thomas II to render the profession that Anselm had demanded. Henry sent the bishops and Count Robert to the elect of York and his canons; there Robert, "beginning with flattering, coaxing, and apology," conveyed to them the royal order that Thomas make his profession to the Church of Canterbury for love of the king and the peace of the realm.[182] Hugh describes at length the desperate maneuverings of the York party to evade the profession. They asked the king to submit the dispute to a formal hearing, but he refused.[183] They sent a secret delegation to Cardinal Ulrich to beg him to judge the case, but he declined to do so except with the king's consent, explaining (so Hugh says) that Henry I had threatened to disavow his allegiance to the pope if Ulrich opposed the king's wishes.[184] Ranulf bishop of Durham, York's only suffragan, tried to win Henry over to the York side with a bribe of a thousand

180. *HN* 207.
181. *HN* 208–9.
182. *HCY* 25.
183. *HCY* 26.
184. *HCY* 27–28: Hugh asserts further, in a garbled passage, that Ulrich feared for the fate of his brother and nephews in England (otherwise unknown) and that he dared not make public the letters in support of York that he carried from the pope; Hugh remains suspiciously vague as to their contents.

silver marks and another hundred to the queen, but Hugh describes
Henry as being unmoved, "knowing well which side could bid the
higher."[185]

Samson of Worcester, true to his promise to Anselm and fearing that
his son might lose the archbishopric, urged Thomas to render his
profession, and in the end Thomas yielded to the pressures of his father,
the other Canterbury suffragans, and the royal court. "What was he to
do?" Hugh lamented. "Where to turn? He was cornered."[186] Thomas
might have chosen exile, Hugh suggests, but he lacked the strength to
endure it, being "full bodied and fatter than he should have been."[187]

Eadmer offers the improbable explanation that Thomas was persuaded to profess upon hearing Canterbury's grants of privileges read
aloud.[188] Whatever the case, Henry commanded that the profession be
committed to writing, read to the court, and then fastened with the
king's seal so that not a word might be altered. Thereupon, on Sunday,
27 June 1109, Bishop Richard of London consecrated Thomas in St.
Paul's Cathedral, assisted by five other Canterbury suffragans and
Ranulf of Durham. Eadmer hastens to explain that Bishop Richard was
acting in his ex officio capacity as dean of the Church of Canterbury.[189]
Just before the consecration the profession of obedience was handed to
Thomas, its seal was broken, and Thomas unrolled it and read it aloud.
According to Eadmer, it ran as follows:

I, Thomas, who am to be consecrated metropolitan of the Church of York,
profess subjection and canonical obedience to the holy Church of Canterbury
and to the primate of that church canonically elected and consecrated, and to
his successors canonically enthroned, saving allegiance to my lord Henry, king
of the English, and saving the obedience to be observed on my part which
Thomas my predecessor professed on his part to the holy Church of Rome.[190]

Eadmer then reports that Bishop Richard took the profession from
Thomas and delivered it to the monks of Canterbury for preservation as
a memorial to posterity.[191]

185. *HCY* 29 and n. 1.
186. *HCY* 28.
187. *HCY* 29.
188. *HN* 209.
189. *HN* 210–11; it was doubtless this special relationship that had permitted
Anselm himself to consecrate two bishops in St. Paul's Cathedral in 1095: above, Chapter 8, n. 70.
190. *HN* 210; *Canterbury Professions*, no. 62; on the format of Thomas II's
consecration, see ibid., p. 116 (app. B, no. 10).
191. *HN* 210–11.

Except for Thomas's reserving allegiance to the king and pope, which is uncharacteristic of earlier professions, Canterbury's victory, as Eadmer describes it, was complete. But Hugh the Chantor's account, the only testimony independent of Eadmer's, suggests that the profession included a much more serious qualification. Without quoting it directly, Hugh describes Thomas as having made "a strange and uncouth profession, personal but to no person — for God alone knew who would be the next archbishop of Canterbury — saving his obedience and fealty to the pope and the king of England, and saving the rights of the Church of York."[192] This last, very important reservation does not occur in Eadmer's text of the profession, nor does it appear in any of the Canterbury profession manuscripts.[193] We have earlier seen that Eadmer was quite prepared to drop unwanted phrases from quoted documents,[194] and the absence of the phrase in the Canterbury profession manuscripts might also be attributable to Eadmer's hand or to those of his fellow monks. The fact that the original of Thomas II's profession has perished is inconvenient, but not particularly suspicious in view of the low survival rate of original Canterbury professions before 1146[195] — although one might have expected the monks to make a special effort to safeguard this hard-won "memorial to posterity." Some evidence exists of subsequent Canterbury tampering with Gerard's profession as bishop of Hereford, in which the concluding words "et signo sancte crucis confirmo" are absent from earlier manuscripts and occur only in a copy dating from 1200 or later.[196]

It would of course be rash to reject Eadmer's version of the profession on Hugh the Chantor's testimony alone. Hugh buttresses his version by providing an excerpt from an address delivered by Ranulf of Durham immediately after the consecration, announcing that Thomas's profession was rendered not as a result of a formal judgment but by the king's will and command, "nor does the king wish it to prejudice the Church of York or Thomas's successors, or to be a precedent in favor of the Church of Canterbury."[197] And lest his readers suppose that Hugh had misremembered Ranulf's speech, or that Ranulf was

192. *HCY* 29: "et salvo iure Eboracensis ecclesie".
193. *Canterbury Professions*, no. 62, n., and p. xxv: the earliest of these manuscripts, Richter's ms. C, dates from about 1123.
194. AEp. 222; above, Chapter 6 at nn. 124–30, and n. 129.
195. *Canterbury Professions*, p. xxv.
196. Ibid., no. 53 and n. 3; cf. p. xxvi.
197. *HCY* 29–30.

reinterpreting the profession because of his partisanship for York, Hugh next quotes a letter of Henry I himself to all his bishops and barons, which reinforces the York version. Henry is quoted as affirming in writing that Thomas rendered his profession in accordance with the king's will and counsel, even though the York canons were prepared to prove by their privileges that he was not bound to make it: "He made it therefore in his own person only, compelled by my order, reserving beforehand his obedience to the pope and his fealty to me, expressly stipulating that the Church of York shall not lose any liberty or privileges to which it is justly entitled by this my letter or by his own act."[198] The letter concludes by ordering that if the profession issue should be adjudicated at some future time, "what has on this occasion been done by my will and command should not prejudice the Church of York or its archbishops in claiming their liberty."

Henry's letter would conclusively support Hugh's interpretation were it not that the original has perished and that all copies are derived from Hugh's own rendition of it. From the York perspective, the letter seems almost too good to be true, and we have encountered other instances of Hugh's willingness to twist facts on behalf of the good cause.[199] It is rather surprising, moreover, that Hugh himself does not mention Henry's letter again in connection with his extensive discussion of the subsequent profession-consecration struggle of 1114 – 19 between Archbishop Ralph and Thurstan of York. The York partisans clearly sought to make the most of Thomas's having professed only at the king's command, without the sort of formal judgment that might have bound his successors. But one can never be certain whether his reservation of the rights of York was suppressed by Eadmer or invented by Hugh. Anselm had triumphed from the grave, but the full extent of his triumph remains unclear. One can only say that had Anselm lived, he would have opposed such a reservation with all his powers.

After the consecration Cardinal Ulrich accompanied Archbishop Thomas back to York where, on 1 August, he presented the pallium to Thomas. The fully empowered archbishop turned at last to the long delayed consecration of Turgot as bishop of St. Andrews.[200] Hugh the Chantor makes the unverifiable and unlikely assertion that as Ulrich

198. *HCY* 30; *Regesta* 2, no. 916.
199. For a further example, see *HCY* 31, containing the highly improbable statement that Foderoc bishop of St. Andrews had professed to Thomas I of York; cf. Brett, *English Church*, pp. 16 – 17.
200. Florence, 2:60; *HCY* 31.

was about to depart for home, he ordered Thomas on the authority of the Roman church to present himself at the papal court on a specified day "to answer for having made his profession contrary to the statute of St. Gregory and the sentence of the Roman court."[201] Fortunately, Hugh assures us, Ulrich was immediately persuaded to revoke the summons, and he and Thomas parted as friends. Ulrich's summons and the papal court's sentence both appear to be figments of Hugh's fertile imagination.

At the time of Anselm's death in April 1109, Robert of Meulan, now in his sixties, had become deeply involved in the growing conflict between Henry I and Louis VI. This struggle had the effect of forcing the marcher lords of the French and Norman Vexin to choose between the two monarchs.[202] The crucial importance of Count Robert's allegiance to Henry I is suggested by Louis VI's raid on Meulan in early 1109 on his way to confer with Henry at Neufle on the Epte frontier.[203] Louis is described as ravaging and burning the possessions of the count because he "adhered to the party of the king of England." There is evidence to indicate that Louis plundered the county of Meulan a second time in 1110,[204] and that Robert retaliated about 1111 by ravaging Paris while Louis VI was holding court at Melun. Robert-Henri Bautier considers this event of "exceptional importance" to the development of the city of Paris and to the reign of King Louis VI. For Robert of Meulan "entered the *Cité*, pillaged the *Palais,* sacked the houses, cut the bridges, and prevented the king's entering the *Cité.*" He was only driven out by the townspeople, who rose up to expel him. In consequence, Louis had to rebuild the Grand-Pont of stone, with increased defenses, thereby deflecting the flow of commerce from the Grève toward the Boucherie and the Champaux. This action was necessary because Robert of Meulan controlled the crucial town of Monceau-St-Gervais in the Grève.[205] Thus Robert of Meulan's attack on Paris

201. HCY 31.
202. See, most recently, Judith Green, "Lords of the Norman Vexin," in *War and Government in the Middle Ages: Essays in Honor of J. O. Prestwich* (Woodbridge, Suffolk, 1984), pp. 47–63: although many of the Vexin lords opposed Henry I, "he did have one huge advantage in the unwavering support of Robert of Meulan" (p. 53).
203. Suger, *Louis VI,* p. 104.
204. Luchaire, *Louis VI,* no. 103.
205. Ibid., no. 111; Robert-Henri Bautier, "Paris au temps d'Abelard," in *Abelard en son temps,* ed. Jean Jolivet (Paris, 1981), pp. 41, 43, 44 (I am grateful to Andrew Lewis for this reference); for the general context, see Hollister, "War and Diplomacy," pp. 80–83.

MAP 7.
Henry I's Dominions in 1113

had resulted in the necessity of a full-scale reorientation of the Ile-de-la-Cité's trade patterns and a monumental reconstruction program for Louis IV.

Between 1111 and 1113, King Louis and King Henry engaged in open hostilities, and although Robert of Meulan's role as Henry's firm supporter was undoubtedly significant, it is not clearly discernible in the narrative sources. There are hints: for instance, Orderic ascribes to Count Robert's advice Henry's exiling of William count of Evreux in 1111 or 1112,[206] and the same writer reports that Henry granted a comprehensive charter to St-Evroul in early February 1113, "at the suggestion of Robert count of Meulan."[207] But, as far as the chroniclers disclose, Robert worked quietly in the background. It is both speculative and tempting to credit him with an important role in Henry's tremendously successful diplomacy during these years, in which Louis VI was kept so busy with rebellions in his own dominions that he was unable to extend the warfare into Normandy.[208] As we have seen, Robert of Meulan was singled out by William of Malmesbury as "the persuader of peace and the dissuader of war," and had served Henry mightily and faithfully in the long diplomatic struggle to win Normandy and contain Anselm.

In early 1113, Fulk V count of Anjou was persuaded to shift his loyalty from Louis VI to Henry I on the betrothal of his daughter to Henry's son, William. Shortly thereafter, Louis, having been hopelessly outmaneuvered, agreed to a peace on terms altogether favorable to Henry. The king of the English gained suzerainty over Maine, Brittany, and Bellême, and thus exerted his authority over the most powerful political configuration in transalpine Europe.[209] When the conflict between the two kings resumed in 1117, Robert of Meulan had retired from the court and Henry I soon found himself in a desperate struggle for survival.

Robert of Meulan had given extraordinary service to his king, and Henry, in return, had been extraordinarily generous to his chief adviser. Sir Frank Stenton has remarked on the rarity of newly created earldoms

206. OV 6:148 and n. 2.; cf. 180, and *ASC*, A.D. 1112.
207. OV 6:174.
208. Hollister, "War and Diplomacy," pp. 80–83.
209. C. W. Hollister and T. K. Keefe, "The Making of the Angevin Empire," *Journal of British Studies* 12 (1973): 8–9.

under Henry I as "one of the most remarkable features of his reign."[210] Apart from Leicester, and the earldom of Gloucester which Henry created in 1121–22 for his bastard son Robert, "the king was plainly unwilling to increase the dignity of any other baronial house" by granting it comital status or jurisdiction over a county town.[211] Robert of Meulan was closer to the king than any other counselor of his time, and this friendship clearly placed him in a position of trust such as the king would show to no other baron except, later, his own son.

Robert of Meulan also apparently engaged in administrative innovation as earl of Leicester. James Thompson has shown that Robert altered the court system of Leicester by allowing the reinstitution of the portmanmote — a court that settled disputes before a sworn tribunal of twenty-four peers — which the Normans had replaced by trial by combat. He translates a record of the crucial event:

> The burgesses, being moved by piety, then made a covenant with the earl that they should give him threepence yearly for each house in the High Street that had a gable, on condition that he should grant to them that the twenty-four jurors, who were in Leicester from ancient times, should from that time forward discuss and decide all pleas that they might have among themselves, and this was conceded to them by the earl, and in such manner were the pennies, called gavel-pennies, first levied.[212]

Robert of Meulan exercised his lordship over the merchants of Leicester by confirming their guild-merchant, in a grant closely parallel in form to writs issuing from the royal chancery: "Robert, count of Meulan, to Ralph the butler and all his barons, French and English, of all his lands in England, greeting. Know that I have granted to all my merchants of Leicester their guild-merchant with all the customs which they held in the time of King William, King William his son, and now hold in the time of King Henry. Witness: Robert son of Alcitil."[213]

Robert also granted permission to the townspeople of Leicester to gather the deadwood of the Forest of Leicester, on these conditions: they must pay the earl 7½d. for six cartloads, one penny weekly for a horseload, and one farthing weekly for a man's load. Because the collection was made near the bridges, it was called bridge-silver.[214]

When Robert of Meulan died, his son Robert earl of Leicester renewed his grants, and the writs reveal that Robert of Meulan had de-

210. Stenton, *English Feudalism*, pp. 228–29.
211. See above, Chapter 6 at nn. 110–15; and Chapter 8 at nn. 2–7, and n. 3.
212. James Thompson, *English Municipal History* (London, 1867), pp. 39–40.
213. Ibid., p. 38.   214. Ibid., p. 40.

veloped sophisticated machinery for administering his earldom, modeled after the complex administrative machinery being developed just
at that time by his king:[215] "Robert earl of Leicester, to Ralph, his
deputy, and all his barons and men, French and English, greetings.
Know that I both will and grant to my burgesses of Leicester, that they
shall hold all their customs well and in peace, both honorably and
quietly, and more honorably than they indeed held them of my
father."[216] And even more suggestively:

Robert earl of Leicester, to all his stewards, bailiffs, and foresters of the Forest
of Leicester, Greeting. I grant to my burgesses of Leicester that it shall be lawful
to them to go in the woods of the neighborhood wheresoever they will for
wood, brushwood for fences, and other necessary things, and to have free and
quiet roads through my forest . . . still better and more freely than before they
had them in the time of my father, and as the charter which they have of my
father still testifies, and none of my foresters and servants shall disturb either
their men or their wagons or their horseloads.[217]

Thus Robert earl of Leicester had inherited stewards, bailiffs, and
foresters to administer his earldom from the town of Leicester, and he
issued writs, as his father had, in almost a regal capacity, addressing his
men in terms reminiscent of the royal address. This evidence points to
a household and administrative staff like the *curia regis* in miniature.

A grant of Waleran of Meulan demonstrates that he had justices and
ministers on his lands in Sturminster. But as Sir Frank Stenton observed,
they were not among the leading *familiares* of the count of Meulan.
"Evidently they were the minor executive officers of a large organization." Their titles show that they had judicial duties, presiding in the
courts of manors or hundreds in their lord's hand. Clearly they were
responsible for collecting their lord's revenue and disbursing payments
that he might authorize. They seem to be a combination of executive,
financial, and judicial officials. Waleran's writ resembles writs of *Liberate,* which the king's chancery had begun to address to the barons of his
exchequer.[218]

Stenton has found that Robert of Meulan, probably alone among the
Anglo-Norman barons, had his own exchequer on the royal model.
Citing two charters of Robert earl of Leicester, he finds that Robert

215. C. W. Hollister and John Baldwin, "The Rise of Administrative Kingship:
Henry I and Philip Augustus," *AHR* 83 (1978): 867–91; see especially p. 872.
216. Thompson, *English Municipal History,* p. 41.
217. Ibid., p. 42.
218. Stenton, *English Feudalism,* pp. 68–69.

granted a sum of money to the abbey of St-Léger de Préaux "ad scacarium meum . . . per annum sicut pater meus ei dedit et concessit." The second charter grants a payment of 20s per year from the earl's exchequer, which his father had granted to the collegiate church of St. Mary de Castro in Leicester. "These references carry the baronial exchequer back to a time before the count of Meulan's death in 1118."[219] Stenton also uses a charter of Robert of Leicester of 1127, while in attendance on Henry at Eling, Hants., to illustrate that the barons of lords were advising them in the same way that the king's men advise him. Robert earl of Leicester, by the advice of his wife and barons, confirmed a gift to Reading Abbey by one of his men.[220] It seems probable that here, too, he was following the customs of his father. Thus Robert of Meulan had established significant and precocious administrative machinery in his domains in England.

But he also had a separate, and perhaps even superior, administrative system on the Continent. A charter of Waleran of Meulan issued in 1120 (two years after his father's death, when Waleran was about eighteen years old) shows that Waleran inherited from his father a large household of comital officials. It is issued for Bec and St-Nicaise de Meulan, and the witnesses include Walter *vicomte* of Meulan, Odo *dapifer*, Morin de Pin (tutor of Robert's sons), Humphrey *cubicularius*, Richard *pincerna*, Roger *capellanus*, Godfrey the chancellor, and others.[221]

Thus Robert of Meulan was administering his vast English and continental estates by means of a household organization — complete with exchequer, chancery-produced writs, and local justices — that mirrored the royal administrative achievements so justly praised by C. Warren Hollister.[222] It is probable that the king and his close friend and chief counselor developed these institutions together; as William of Malmesbury remarked, Robert "encouraged the king to enforce existing laws and to make new ones."[223]

Robert of Meulan's last recorded activities in the king's service related once again to the dignity of Canterbury. At the death of Arch-

219. Ibid., p. 70.
220. Ibid., p. 91.
221. Prou, *Recueil des Actes de Philippe Ier*, pp. cxcv, n. 2. Recall that Roger of Beaumont had had a household of lesser extent, which Robert of Meulan had inherited: above, Chapter 3 at nn. 75–77.
222. Hollister and Baldwin, "Rise of Administrative Kingship," pp. 867–91.
223. GR 2:483.

bishop Thomas II of York on 21 February 1114, the Canterbury-York dispute flared up once more. In mid-August Henry I appointed Thurstan, a royal chaplain and trusted royal servant, as Thomas's successor, having approved the translation of Ralph d'Escures of Rochester to the see of Canterbury the previous April. Thurstan, in the opinion of his modern biographer, had been profoundly influenced by Anselm.[224] He proved a far more capable prelate than Thomas II and a much more effective champion of York's autonomy. At once Thurstan raised the legal point that it was inconsistent that a metropolitan should profess twice — once to the pope, whom he could not refuse, and again to the archbishop of Canterbury. He further pointed out that if a dispute should arise between the king and the archbishop of Canterbury, he would be bound to obey the latter if he had professed to him. Hugh the Chantor states that Henry and the count of Meulan at first agreed with Thurstan and would not compel him to make the profession.[225] Archbishop Ralph, however, in the tradition of Lanfranc and Anselm, refused to consecrate Thurstan unless he first professed, and so matters rested for the next thirteen months.[226] As before, Henry and Count Robert were seeking to prevent the dispute from erupting, and they were content to leave it unresolved during their Norman sojourn of September 1114 – July 1115.[227]

On their return to England, before turning again to the profession quarrel, Robert of Meulan sought to uphold the royal interest over that of Canterbury in another matter. Eadmer reports that on the election of Bernard the queen's chaplain to the bishopric of St. David's (18 September 1115), there arose the familiar issue of where the bishop-elect was to be consecrated.[228] The king was in London and was once again in a hurry to have the consecration performed. Robert of Meulan asserted that the consecration of a Welsh bishop should by custom take place in the king's chapel. Archbishop Ralph, predictably, contended that Bernard should be consecrated at Canterbury. Soothing his primate, Henry told Count Robert that the issue was of only trivial significance to the royal status and that Ralph might consecrate Bernard wherever he chose. Here, as on previous occasions, Count Robert gave the appearance of being more ardently royalist that the king himself. One

---

224. Nicholl, *Thurstan*, pp. 11–14.
225. *HCY* 34.   226. *HCY* 34; *HN* 237.
227. Cf. *HN* 238, in reference to a later stage of the dispute (1116): "The king did not want to get himself in the middle except by delaying the problem."
228. *HN* 235.

cannot overlook the possibility, however, that the two old friends were playing a kind of game — Robert pressing for every inch of the royal dignity so that Henry might then magnanimously condescend to his primate's wish. Archbishop Ralph, following Anselm's precedent, agreed to consecrate Bernard immediately in the chapel of Lambeth, but in the end the consecration was performed in Westminster Abbey, because "the queen wanted to attend the ceremony."[229] It was a dangerous precedent for Canterbury. Despite his affection for the queen (and hers for her chaplain), Anselm would surely have resisted it. Although Westminster remained under the rule of the aged Gilbert Crispin (d. 1117–18), it was bound to Canterbury not by any constitutional affiliation but only by the tie of personal friendship. The primacy had clearly passed into less steady hands.

Later in the same month Henry turned again to the matter of his battling archbishops. He had previously sought the advice of Cardinal Cuno of Praeneste, who was acting as legate in France and Normandy. Cuno had suggested that if Archbishop Ralph remained obdurate, Thurstan should go directly to the pope for consecration.[230] Henry refused to permit Thurstan to do so, but at his London court of Michaelmas 1115, on the advice of Count Robert and Nigel de Aubigny, the king told Thurstan to demand consecration by Archbishop Ralph. If Ralph should "make any apparently unjust demand" before doing so, Thurstan should threaten to appeal the issue to the pope. If Hugh's account can be trusted, Henry must have been seeking to resolve the dispute by bluffing the primate into relinquishing the profession out of fear of direct papal intervention — an eventuality that was in fact as distasteful to Henry as to Ralph. But the primate was not so easily deceived. He replied that even if the pope so ordered, he would never consecrate Thurstan without receiving his profession.[231]

Although Henry was intent on avoiding formal papal intervention, the York canons took the initiative of writing directly to Paschal II and obtaining a papal order that either Ralph should consecrate Thurstan without the profession or Paschal would consecrate him personally.[232] From Henry's standpoint, the issue was rapidly getting out of hand, and he and his counselors, now fully aware that Archbishop Ralph could

229. HN 235.
230. HCY 36–37.
231. HCY 38.
232. HCY 40.

not be moved, resolved to foreclose the possibility of papal intervention by settling the dispute in favor of Canterbury. At a royal council at Salisbury in March 1116, Henry sent Thurstan a message, so Hugh states, "not by clergy, as would have been proper, but by two earls and two nobles: Robert count of Meulan, William earl of Warenne, William the king's chamberlain, and Nigel de Aubigny." Speaking in Henry's name, they ordered Thurstan, out of his love, gratitude, and fidelity to the king, to render his profession to Ralph.[233] Thurstan responded by requesting a formal judicial hearing. Henry refused, as he had in 1109, and sent Count Robert and his fellow envoys back to Thurstan with a shorter message: "You must make your profession or incur the king's hatred, nor may any of your kindred remain in all his lands."[234] Sorely pressed, Thurstan decided that his only recourse was to resign his archiepiscopal office. When the messengers returned to the king with this news, Archbishop Ralph and others at the court were incredulous. But Robert of Meulan told them, "If I know my man, he means what he said; but let him come into our presence so that many may hear it from his own mouth." Thurstan thereupon came to court and resigned his prelacy.[235]

This was Robert of Meulan's last recorded act in the service of Henry I. He was by then nearing seventy and seems to have retired from the king's court shortly after Thurstan's resignation. In the following month (April 1116) Henry crossed to Normandy to defend his duchy against assaults from France, Flanders, and Anjou, and he remained there until late 1120, more than two years after Count Robert's death. It is probable that Robert was absent from the royal entourage during even the early stages of Henry's Norman sojourn, for he attests no royal charters that can definitely be dated after February 1116.[236] Henry of Huntingdon reports that Robert in his old age suffered the humiliation of having his wife, Isabel of Vermandois, abducted by an unnamed earl and was thrown into such depression that he died shortly thereafter.[237] If this story is correct, the unnamed earl was almost surely William of

233. *HCY* 41.
234. *HCY* 42: Thurstan's brother Audouen was bishop of Evreux (1113–39).
235. *HCY* 43.
236. Robert's last datable attestations are *Regesta* 2, nos. 1124–27, all issued from Windsor, definitely or probably on 2 February 1116; ibid., no. 1131, attested by Robert, was issued from Odiham (Hants.) probably on 2 April 1116, but possibly as early as 1114.
237. *HA* 307.

Warenne earl of Surrey, who married Isabel soon after Robert's death. It is intriguing to note that Robert of Meulan and William of Warenne were the two comital messengers whom Henry chose to negotiate with Thurstan during the closing days of Robert's public career.

Upon retiring from court, Robert probably entered monastic life, as his father had before him, at the Beaumonts' ancestral monastery of St-Pierre de Préaux under its learned abbot and former student of Anselm Richard de Fourneaux.[238] He died on 9 June 1118, at about the age of seventy-two, and was entombed in the chapter house of Préaux next to the tombs of his father Roger and other Beaumont kinsmen.[239] Henry of Huntingdon reports that a crowd of priests and an archbishop were gathered at Robert's deathbed, reflecting the importance and prestige of the count of Meulan. They asked him, on pain of being denied the last rites, to return to their rightful owners the lands that he had stolen. Robert is said to have replied, "If I divide the lands that I have gathered, what can I leave my sons?" When told that his own inherited lands were enough, Robert is quoted as responding, "I give all to my sons; they will act mercifully for my salvation when I am dead."[240] We have already seen how Robert's twin sons acquired their inheritances upon his death, and how Robert earl of Leicester immediately granted a charter to Bec "for the deliverance of his father's soul."[241] At about the same time the other young twin, Waleran count of Meulan, granted a benefaction to Préaux "for my father's soul";[242] although Waleran's gift was by no means lavish, the matter of Count Robert's salvation was clearly not neglected by his sons.

Despite the disapproving account of his final days in Henry of Huntingdon's "De contemptu mundi," Robert of Meulan had by no means been ungenerous toward the church. He was an important benefactor of both his family monastery at Préaux[243] and the abbey of

---

238. *La Normandie Bénédictine*, p. 198; Porée, *Bec* 1:273 and n. 2; OV 4:304–6 and 306 n. 4; Le Prévost, *Eure* 2:495–96, 548–49. *HA* 307: an archbishop was present at his deathbed; cf. *HN* 248–50, 254–55, and *GP* 129–31: Archbishop Ralph of Canterbury was in Normandy in mid-1118, as were Archbishop Geoffrey of Rouen and quite possibly Archbishop Thurstan of York. See David Crouch, *The Beaumont Twins* (Cambridge, 1986), p. 143, for a similar case.

239. OV 4:302; 6:188; Count Robert's grandfather, Humphrey de Vieilles, was also entombed at Préaux, and when Henry earl of Warwick died in 1119, he too was entombed there: *Complete Peerage* 7:521–23; 12, pt. 2:360.

240. *HA* 307.

241. Above, Chapter 8 at nn. 2–7.   242. *CDF,* no. 331.

243. *CDF,* nos. 318, 321, 325, 326, and 329; Houth, "Robert Prud'homme," pp. 825–26, nos. 3, 6, 8, 9.

Bec. In 1112 he had granted Bec his manor of Chisenbury on Avon (Wilts.),[244] and sometime between 1106 and 1118 he granted the community customary rights in the town of Bec.[245] He was also a benefactor of Jumièges, St-Nicaise de Meulan, and the cathedral chapter of Evreux. He founded the church of St. Mary de Castro in Leicester; the hospital of Brackley, Northamptonshire; and the priory of St-Etienne, Grandmont (Eure).[246] Henry of Huntingdon makes reference to the lands that Robert had stolen, and Orderic hints that Robert had obtained Ivo of Grandmesnil's estates through trickery,[247] deflecting them from Ivo's heirs to his own. But Ivo's sons (Ivo and Hugh) were later included in Orderic's list of the victims of the White Ship tragedy of 1120 "who were crossing the sea at the king's command to receive the estates of their fathers in England."[248] Robert of Meulan's son, Robert earl of Leicester, had already assumed his comital title before the White Ship sailed,[249] but Orderic's words indicate that some kind of compensation was intended for Ivo's sons, and the subsequent marriage in about 1154 of Robert earl of Leicester's son and heir, Robert *Blanchesmains,* to Petronilla of Grandmesnil seems likely to have been intended to resolve a lingering Grandmesnil interest in the earldom.[250]

Robert of Meulan's retirement and death left Henry to face two major unresolved crises without the guidance of his great adviser, and the outcomes of these crises suggest that Robert's counsel and diplomacy were sorely missed. Thurstan of York withdrew his resignation from his see and subsequently infuriated King Henry and Archbishop Ralph by receiving consecration directly from the pope. Thurstan also obtained a decisive papal privilege freeing him and his successors from

244. *Regesta* 2, no. 1004: for the souls of William I and Matilda, for the welfare of Henry I and his wife Matilda and their children, for the souls of his own parents, for his own salvation and that of his wife Isabel and their children, and for the welfare of his brother Henry and his wife Margaret and their children. It is noteworthy that Robert omitted William Rufus from this extensive list (cf. Barlow, *Rufus,* p. 431, n. 86), but Rufus's soul was remembered in Robert's grant to Préaux of 1106–18: CDF, no. 329.

245. Seventeenth-century paraphrase in "Chronicon Becci": Bibliothèque Nationale, ms. Lat. 12884, fol. 165: "Robertus comes Mellenti, jus consuetudinis in oppido Becci concessit monachis beccensibus propter suum dominium in eodem oppido Briosne cujus erat comes subjecto. Et hac donatio ab eodem rege Henrico confirmata fuit."

246. Houth, "Robert Prud'homme," pp. 824–29, nos. 2, 10, 14–16, 19.

247. OV 6:18.

248. OV 6:304.

249. Above, Chapter 8 at nn. 1–8.

250. *Complete Peerage* 7:530ff. Petronilla was from the Norman-Sicilian branch of the Grandmesnil family.

the profession to Canterbury.[251] The king eventually forgave Thurstan, but Ralph d'Escures never appears to have done so, since Thurstan's initiative left Canterbury's claim over York in ruins. Moreover, while Thurstan and Ralph battled on behalf of their churches, Henry was struggling for his very survival in Normandy against Louis VI of France, Fulk V of Anjou, Baldwin VII of Flanders, and many of his own Norman barons, all fighting in support of William Clito's claim to the duchy.

Throughout the decade between Henry's victory at Tinchebrai and Robert of Meulan's retirement from court, the peace of Normandy had remained unbroken. Even in the period 1111–13, when Henry and Louis were at war, the fighting all occurred beyond the Norman frontiers.[252] But in 1118–19 Henry was so beset with external and internal enemies that his authority over Normandy seemed at times to be nearing collapse. Orderic calls attention to the deaths of three important persons in 1118: William count of Evreux, whose death in April resulted in a furious struggle for the succession to his strategic frontier county; Queen Matilda, whose death in May deprived Henry not only of a wife but of a valuable political ally; and Robert of Meulan, whose death on 5 June marked the unrecoverable loss of Henry's most astute advisor. "After these people had died," Orderic comments, "great trials commenced for the Normans."[253] In Suger's words, "the king of England, after such long and marvelous successes and such peacefully enjoyed prosperity, fell so to speak from the highest point on the wheel of fortune and saw himself subjected to the changing vicissitudes and misfortunes of events."[254] Henry managed to survive the onslaught, profiting from Baldwin VII's death from a battle wound, winning over Anjou by a marriage alliance, and routing Louis VI at the battle of Brémule (20 August 1119).[255] But the campaigns of 1118–19 proved to be the most dangerous challenge of his reign.

Some of the most cherished hopes of both Anselm and Robert of Meulan were dashed in the decades after their deaths. Robert's son

251. Nicholl, *Thurstan*, pp. 41–74, provides a full account, corrected in some respects by Mary Cheney, "Some Observations on a Papal Privilege of 1120 for the Archbishop of York," *JEH* 31 (1980): 429–39; and Hollister, "War and Diplomacy," pp. 73–76.

252. Hollister, "War and Diplomacy," pp. 80–83.

253. OV 6:188.   254. Suger, *Louis VI*, 188.

255. Hollister and Keefe, "Making of the Angevin Empire," pp. 9–10.

Waleran betrayed his Beaumont principles by rebelling against Henry I in 1123–24; he was captured, imprisoned, and then released and restored five years later, doubtless owing his survival to the king's affection toward his father.[256] Similarly, Anselm's nephew and namesake, Anselm of St. Saba, may have chilled his uncle's grave by turning up at Henry I's court in 1116 as a fully empowered papal legate[257] before settling down as abbot of Bury St. Edmunds (1121–48). More importantly, Anselm's heroic struggle on behalf of the Canterbury primacy over York was lost when his less able successor, Ralph d'Escures, confronted the astute and determined Thurstan of York. Robert of Meulan's dream of a united and tranquil Anglo-Norman state was badly disturbed by the ineptitude of King Stephen and shattered by the catastrophes of John's reign. Neither Anselm nor Henry I were fortunate in their successors, whom they neither chose nor foresaw.

But although Lanfranc's great design did not survive the decades following Anselm's death, the blame can hardly be ascribed to Anselm. He held back single-handedly a swelling tide of papal opposition to primatial power and reinforced Lanfranc's plan with papal privileges such as Lanfranc himself had never succeeded in obtaining. Nor should Robert of Meulan be any the less respected because the trans-Channel state that he served so well — from his youth on the field of Hastings to his retirement in 1116 — ultimately split apart. The greatest earthly objects of Anselm's and Robert's devotion, the Church of Canterbury and the English monarchy, survived the loss of the primacy battle and the loss of Normandy and endure still. Although the name of Robert of Meulan has been long forgotten in the royal council chambers of today, he clearly deserves a place among the great counselors of the English realm.

Anselm, on the other hand, will never be forgotten at Canterbury. In July 1979, Archbishop Michael Ramsey began his address to the Third International Anselm Conference, at Canterbury, with these perceptive words:

We commemorate today the greatest of the Archbishops of Canterbury, Anselm of Bec. He served God as a monk, as a man of contemplation who led many and still leads many in the way of prayer, as a loving pastor, as a profound thinker, and as a courageous statesman. To excel in two or three of these roles is not indeed rare in the history of Christianity. But we see Anselm using all five talents

256. OV 6:332–50, 354–56; Hollister, "War and Diplomacy," pp. 84–86.
257. Brett, *English Church*, pp. 36–38.

to the full, and it is remembered not only that all these talents were his but that these aspects had an inner unity and were all of one piece.[258]

In Anselm and Robert's generation Europe was undergoing significant intellectual, psychological, devotional, political, and economic changes. One notices a growing sophistication and a powerful impulse toward reason and system that found expression in such diverse areas as administration, diplomacy, law, theology, and religious practice. Neither Anselm nor Robert would have wished to be remembered as administrators, but they were great statesmen and pioneering diplomats who fought for their goals with an unprecedented degree of intellectual analysis and sophistication. Anselm, William of Malmesbury observes, "understood human nature, as we can see from his writings." Quoting this passage, Marjorie Chibnall adds that "the theologian who wrote of the fall of man was well qualified to understand individual fallen men."[259] Robert and Anselm were both prominent among the early systematizers. Although both were fiercely devoted to the traditional idea of stewardship — the divinely commissioned duty of the king and primate to safeguard every scrap of their lands and dignities — they carried out their stewardly duties in new and sometimes daring ways. They looked upon the institutions they served with a degree of logical analysis unknown in the medieval world before their time. Anselm learned much from Lanfranc yet seemed to possess a clearer vision of due order and the means necessary to achieve it than had his mentor and predecessor. Whereas Lanfranc was, in the wise words of David Knowles, "a supremely able administrator and organizer of the plans and needs of the moment," Anselm was "a creative genius who could keep his eyes fixed upon the lodestar of a single end."[260] Robert of Meulan, who derived his devotion to the king of the English from his father, went far beyond him in articulating a theory of royal authority presaging what would later be termed *raison d'état*.

Anselm and Robert thus contributed importantly to some of the central trends of their own and subsequent generations. But they were more than simply trailblazers into a more sophisticated future. They were individuals in their own right, extraordinarily gifted men with

258. *Anselm Studies* 1:1.
259. *GP* 122. Chibnall, "Bec to Canterbury," p. 38.
260. Knowles, *Monastic Order*, p. 142.

styles and personalities very much their own. They could lose their tempers. For instance, Robert had joined Rufus in responding to Anselm's arguments in 1097 by crying out, "Oh! Oh! Words, words! All he is saying is only words!"[261] Anselm, too, had once lashed out from exile at Henry's allegedly unidentifiable counselor: "Now surely the mind of whoever says that thing is either very wicked or very small."[262] But such outbursts are remarkably rare, and Anselm depersonalized his thrust by pretending not to know its victim's identity. In glaring contrast to the later controversy between Becket and Henry II, the resolution of which was seriously impeded by harsh public displays of personal antagonism, the diplomatic maneuverings of Anselm, Robert, and Henry I demonstrate that the politics of early twelfth-century England could at times be far more subtle and intelligently pursued than those of later twelfth-century England. The English Investiture Controversy was marked by bold initiatives and the pains of exile, but that its reconciliation could have been thwarted by the refusal of a kiss of peace, or that the dispute could have ended with a murder in the cathedral, is simply unimaginable.

The conflicts between Robert of Meulan and Anselm were characterized not by unforgivable insults or shouts of rage but, from beginning to end, by soft words. To Anselm it was always a matter of responding to hatred with love, while at the same time upholding his principles unflinchingly. In the end he achieved reconciliation with his greatest antagonists, Henry I and Robert of Meulan, and by 1109 he had enlisted in Canterbury's cause the entire community of his suffragan bishops, who had defied him back in 1097 with the words, "We owe allegiance to the king and from that allegiance we shall not depart."[263] As for Robert of Meulan, even Hugh the Chantor, observing him in 1109 toward the close of his career, could describe him as asking the York delegation "with flattery, coaxing, and apology" that Thomas II render his profession to Canterbury.[264] Robert was acting very much in character, as he had done long before at Bec when he asked the monks

261. HN 86; above, Chapter 5 at n. 257.
262. AEp. 330; above, Chapter 7 at n. 61.
263. HN 83; above, Chapter 5 at nn. 254–55; on the gradual shift of episcopal support from the king to the primate during the course of Anselm's pontificate, see Walter Fröhlich, "Anselm and the Bishops of the Province of Canterbury," in *Les mutations socio-culturelles au tournant des XIᵉ–XIIᵉ siècles: Etudes Anselmiennes (IV Session)* (Paris, 1984), pp. 125–45.
264. HCY 25; above, Chapter 8 at nn. 181–82.

in "affectionate language, as was his custom,"[265] to recognize his authority over the abbey. When the monks responded with violent words, Abbot Anselm sat down between the two parties, checked their quarreling, and quietly reasoned with the count.

Although Robert left in a towering rage and landed for a time in prison, he had learned a valuable lesson. He had discovered in Anselm the two qualities that Jesus had urged on his disciples when he sent them out into the world: the innocence of the dove and the wisdom of the serpent. Robert himself can hardly be regarded as innocent, but he could be disarmingly reasonable and soft spoken. Both men displayed in full measure the wisdom of the serpent, in the service of *regnum* and *sacerdotium,* throughout their interlaced careers.

265. *DLB* 602.

Appendix A

William I's Confirmation Charter to Bec

Grants confirmed

William I   Freedom from tolls.

Queen Matilda   Brixton Deverill (Wilts.): Entire manor (Domesday: Bec).

Hugh of Gournay   Property in London.
Fordham (Essex): Church and tithes of the manor, 1 villain.
Ardleigh (Essex): Tithes of the manor and 1 villain.
Liston (Essex): ½ tithes of the manor; ½ church; 1 villain.

Baldwin fitz Gilbert   Bridford (= Christow, Devon): Entire manor.

Henry of Ferrers   Woodham Ferrers (Essex): Tithes of the manor, 1 villain.
Stebbing (Essex): Tithes of the manor, 1 villain.
Standen (Wilts.): Tithes of the manor, 1 villain.

Ernulf of Hesdin   Ruislip (Msx.): Entire manor.
(Marjorie Morgan, *The English Lands of the Abbey of Bec*, [Oxford, 1946], p. 147, dates grant 1090, citing Porée, *Bec*, 2:574).

Milo Crispin   Concedes benefactions of his men:

 Hugh fitz Milo   Swyncombe (Oxf.): Entire manor.
Mapledurham (Oxf.): Tithes of the manor.
Berewell (Oxf.): Tithes of the manor (not identified).
"Duncherche" (= Witcherche? Oxf.): Tithes of the manor.

Gothampton (Oxf.): Tithes of the manor.
North Stoke (Oxf.): Tithes of the manor.
Nuncham Murren (Oxf.): Tithes of the manor.
Calgrove (Oxf.): Tithes of the manor.
Haseley (Oxf.): Tithes of the manor.
Aston Rowent (Oxf.): Tithes of the manor.
Alderly (Glos.): Tithes of the manor.
Clapcot (Berks.): Tithes of the manor.
Quainton (Bucks.): Tithes of the manor.
Shabbingdon (Bucks.): Tithes of the manor.
Kingston ("Bucks." = Kingston Blount, Oxf.?): Tithes of the manor.
Wycombe (Oxf.?): Tithes of the manor (Domesday: Robert d'Oyly).

Richard fitz Reinfrid (d. ca. 1115 – 16)
Appleton (Berks.): Tithes of the manor (Domesday: Richard under Milo Crispin).
Ickford (Bucks.): Tithes of the manor (Domesday: Richard under Milo Crispin).
Alkerton (Oxf.): Tithes of the manor (Domesday: Richard under Milo Crispin).

Hugh (fitz Milo?)
Adwell (Oxf.): Tithes of the manor (Domesday: William).
Chesterton (Oxf.): Tithes of the manor (Domesday: William).
Henton (Oxf.): Tithes of the manor (Domesday: William).

Richard fitz Gilbert
Tooting (Surrey): Entire manor.
Streatham (Surrey): Entire manor (see Morgan, p. 149).
Haverychesham (3 virgates) (Surrey): Entire manor.
Bleckingley (Surrey): ⅔ tithe and 1 villain.
Chivington in Bleckingley (Surrey): ⅔ tithe.
Woodamsterne (Surrey): ⅔ tithe.
Chipstead (Surrey): ⅔ tithe.
Thorncroft (Surrey): ⅔ tithe.
Wolton Leigh (Surrey): ⅔ tithe.
Tunbridge (Surrey): ⅔ tithe.
Standon (Hereford): ⅔ tithe and 1 villain.

Men of Girold   Wimundestuna (Suffolk): Tithe of the manor (Domesday: Girold under Richard).

Toffridus   Wratting (Suffolk): Tithe of the manor (Domesday: Geoffrey fitz Hamo).
Oilardus   Gindesfell (= Undresfelda, mod. Witherfield, Suffolk): Tithe of the manor (Domesday: Wilardus).

Willelmus   Dalham (Suffolk): Tithe of the manor (Domesday: Willelmus peccaturm).

Guanerus   "Cogenda" (Exeter?): ⅔ tithe (Domesday: Garnerus
under Richard fitz Gilbert in Essex).

Not in Charter

Queen Matilda also gave Quarley (Hants.) to Bec, but ca. 1080 the gift had
not become effective (Morgan, p. 149).

Ralph de Tosny gave East Wretham 1085–86 (Morgan p. 145). Not in
Domesday.

Walter Giffard gave Blakenham (Suffolk) ca. 1075 (Morgan, p. 148).

Richard of Clare gave Little Sampford (Essex) ⅔ demesne tithe Tempus William I (Morgan, p. 147).

Garnerius and his men   Tithes in Chawreth (Essex) (Morgan, p. 147).

Hugh of Gournay   ⅔ demesne tithe and 1 villain in Liston, Fordham, and
Ardleigh, Tempus William I (Morgan, p. 147, citing Salter, *EHR* 40 [1925],
74–76; and Domesday 2:56–7).

Gerard of Gournay   Lessingham (Norfolk), ca. 1090 (Domesday: Terra
Regis) (Morgan, p. 148).

Richard fitz Gilbert   Betchworth, Talworth (Surrey) (Morgan, p. 150, citing Domesday 1:35 and Windsor White Book).

Emmelina, wife of Ernulf of Hesden   Combe (Hants.), entire manor, before 1100 (Morgan, p. 149, citing Windsor White Book, f. 147).

Hugh of Grandmesnil   Monxton (Hants.), entire manor, ca. Tempus William II (Morgan, p. 149, citing Porée, *Bec,* 2:573–74, and *VCH* Hants.,
4:310–11).

William fitz Baldwin   Cowick (Exeter), entire manor, between 1090 and
1096 (Morgan, p. 11; David Knowles and R. N. Hadcock, *Medieval Religious Houses, England and Wales,* 2d ed. [London, 1971], p. 63; cf. Sanders,
Baronies, p. 69).

From *EHR* 40 (1925), 74–76; ed. H. Salter.

Appendix B

Genealogies of the Beaumont and Clare Families

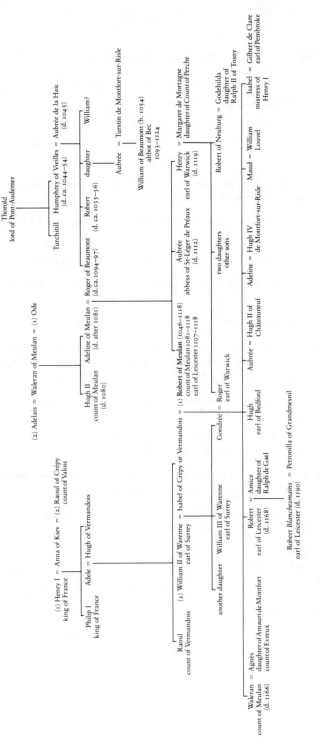

The Beaumont Family

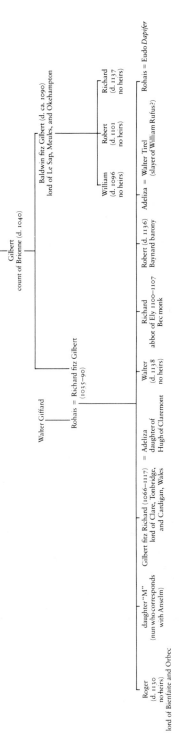

Richard I
duke of Normandy
942–96

Godfrey of Brionne and Eu
(d. ca. 1015)

Gilbert
count of Brionne (d. 1040)

Walter Giffard

Rohais = Richard fitz Gilbert
(1035–90)

Baldwin fitz Gilbert (d. ca. 1090)
lord of Le Sap, Meules, and Okehampton

Roger
(d. 1130
no heirs)
lord of Bienfaite and Orbec

daughter "M"
(nun who corresponds
with Anselm)

Gilbert fitz Richard (1066–1117)
lord of Clare, Tonbridge,
and Cardigan, Wales

= Adeliza
daughter of
Hugh of Claremont

Walter
(d. 1138
no heirs)

Richard
abbot of Ely 1100–1107
Bec monk

Robert (d. 1136)
Baynard barony

William
(d. 1096
no heirs)

Adeliza = Walter Tirel
(slayer of William Rufus?)

Robert
(d. 1101
no heirs)

Richard
(d. 1137
no heirs)

Rohais = Eudo Dapifer

The Clare Family

Index

Medieval figures are alphabetized by first name; first names are subsequently alphabetized by the next proper name given in a person's title or description.

Designer: Betty Gee
Compositor: Skillful Means Press
Text: 10/13 Sabon
Display: Sabon
Printer: Edwards Brothers, Inc.
Binder: Edwards Brothers, Inc.